THE IRISH IN IRELAND

THE IRISH IN IRELAND

Constantine FitzGibbon

DAVID & CHARLES
NEWTON ABBOT   LONDON
W · W · NORTON & CO · INC
NEW YORK

For
FANNY
with love

British Library Cataloguing in Publication Data

FitzGibbon, Constantine
  The Irish in Ireland.
  1. Ireland—History
  I. Title
  941.5   DA910

  ISBN 0-7153-8129-6 (Great Britain)
  ISBN 0-393-01745-1 (United States)

© Constantine FitzGibbon 1983

Unless otherwise acknowledged, all photographs are by George Mott

Typeset by ABM Typographics Limited, Hull
and printed in Great Britain
by Butler & Tanner Limited, Frome & London
for David & Charles (Publishers) Limited
Brunel House   Newton Abbot   Devon

First American edition 1983
W · W · Norton & Company
New York · London

CONTENTS

	Introduction	7
1	Before the Celts	13
2	The Celts	30
3	The Celts in History	45
4	St. Patrick	51
5	Celtic Ireland's Golden Age	66
6	The Vikings	84
7	The Coming of the Normans	97
8	The Conquest that Failed	115
9	Henry VIII's Reformation	124
10	The Irish under the Tudor Kings	135
11	Ireland before Queen Elizabeth	148
12	The First Tudor Invasions	159
13	Conquest	169
14	'Thorough'	182
15	The Wars without Roses	197
16	Ascendancy	211
17	The Cultural Eclipse	227
18	Grattan's Parliament	248
19	Daniel O'Connell	265
20	Famine	276
21	Parnell	292
22	Without End . . .	305
	Further Reading	317
	Acknowledgements	319
	Index	321

The reference numbers found in the text relate to the notes at the end of the chapter. A modern map of Ireland will be found on page 313.

Private faces in public places
Are wiser and nicer
Than public faces in private places.
W. H. Auden, *The Orators*

INTRODUCTION

This book is about the Irish, about their own ways of doing and of being, of perception and belief, about what distinguishes Irish men and women and even children from their fellow humans, about 'Irishry', a word beloved by W. B. Yeats and which he is said to have learned from the late Prof. Arnold Toynbee. First, therefore, an attempt must be made to define who the Irish are.

It is believed that Dean Swift was the first man to speak of 'the Irish nation', or at least to commit those words to paper, in the early eighteenth century. He was undoubtedly referring to the people who inhabited Ireland, of whom he was one even though his father may have been his powerful, English patron, Sir William Temple or even Sir William's father, Sir John, an Englishman who had held high office in Dublin in 1667, which is where and when Swift was born. To the day he died, however, in 1745, Jonathan Swift, probably the greatest of all Irish prose writers – at least in the English language – denied violently that he was an Irishman, a son of 'this land of slaves', and indeed even insisted that he be buried in what he incorrectly considered 'English' soil, in the Welsh town of Holyhead. Similarly the great Duke of Wellington firmly denied his Irish ancestry and birth and is reported to have remarked that to have been born in a stable does not make one a horse. His great-grandfather, however, born Richard Colley, had inherited the large estate of Dangan, Co. Meath, in 1728 from his cousin, Garrett Wesley, whose name he took; the future Duke of Wellington later reverted to the older spelling of Wellesley. A Miss Elizabeth Wellesley, also of Dangan, had in the late sixteenth century married a distant English cousin. Her great-grandson was John Wesley, the founder of Methodism.

Richard Colley, now Wesley, became, in 1746, Baron Mornington and his son was created an earl, and fathered the Iron Duke. The second Earl, the future Duke's brother, became in due course one of the best lords lieutenant ever to govern Ireland. The Duke of Wellington himself had sat, when young, in the old Irish parliament carrying the name of the Hon. Arthur Wesley. In fact his Irish roots went far deeper than the epigram attributed to him would indicate. Edmund Burke (1729–1797) was an Irishman beyond any doubt, of ancient Norman ancestry, with a Roman Catholic mother and a Roman Catholic wife, yet is known as an English political philosopher and is indeed generally regarded as the creator of English conservatism. Bishop Berkeley (1685–1753), one of the very greatest philosophers ever to write in English, was born and spent a large part of his life in Ireland. Neither he nor Burke ever denied that they were Irishmen: it probably seemed to them both supremely unimportant. Nobody would have expected either of them to identify himself with the remote Irish-speaking population of rural Celtic Ireland: Jefferson or Adams, when speaking of America, was not referring to Navajos or Seminoles. But the parallel is remote. For by the eighteenth century, the Celtic conquerors of approximately 300 B.C. had for over two thousand years been absorbing waves of new conquerors – Vikings, Normans, Elizabethan English, Scots, Cromwellians and Williamites. Swift was prescient in speaking of an 'Irish nation'. The Williamites had not then been absorbed, if indeed all of them ever were, and visitors then still distinguished between those Irish living under English control and 'the savages' who lived hungry lives among the ruins of a once great Celtic society in the west. But then in Swift's time the very concept of 'nationality' was new. It has remained ill-defined, and nowhere more so than in Ireland. What is the nationality today of a Belfast Orange terrorist?

The ancestor, a very remote ancestor, of 'nationality' is 'citizenship'. The citizen of, say, Athens, was a denizen of the city, later of the city state. But the inverse did not apply. Slaves and women did not have the rights of citizens. The Romans gave the word a new meaning. Though Tarsus is a long way from Rome, St. Paul could say with truth and pride, though in what language we do not know: 'Civis Romanus sum.' This meant in effect that he paid his taxes and received, in return, the protection of the legions and of the other administrative forces which derived their ultimate authority from Rome. It did not mean that he was a Roman, nor even that he spoke Latin. Indeed in Rome itself there was no linguistic patriotism. Professor Bedell Stanford has told this writer that when Julius Caesar cried 'Et tu, Brute!' he probably did so in Greek, the language of the educated, even as French was the language of Frederick the Great and his Prussian court. The Roman Empire was thus in no way racist. Carthage was destroyed because the Carthaginians were dangerous, not because they were inferior. Cleopatra was wooed by Julius Caesar and later by Antony, not for her retroussé nose, but because she was Egypt and Egypt to the Romans meant corn. Gaul, Spain, Numidia, Illyria, Syria, Britain, Greece were not countries ruled from Rome, but were geographical terms in which lived Roman citizens enjoying Roman protection, Roman law and perhaps above all Roman administration, and any of the provinces could produce a Roman emperor: most did, including probably black Africa. (That the Romans never came to Ireland is a fact of supreme importance in discussing the development of the Irish, and one that will be dealt with at length later on.)

The British Empire, of which Ireland was the first colony, was modelled in many ways on that of Rome. It, too, brought the peace of good laws and the pleasures of competent administration (roads, water and so on) to many hitherto turbulent and troubled parts of the world. It failed and disintegrated with remarkable speed because it forgot one Roman essential. Few of its many million citizens who were not themselves British-born ever boasted of their British citizenship, for they were not the equals of their conquerors. When Kipling wrote the famous line: 'You're a better man than I am, Gunga Din', it was, to his readers, a brilliant paradox. By British definition Mr. Smuts or Lord Snooks was automatically a better man than Gunga Din, who could never even sit in the Westminster Parliament, let alone aspire to the Imperial Throne for himself or any of his descendants. It is impossible to imagine any Roman poet, even so proud a patriot as Virgil, writing: 'You're a better man than I am, Callisthenes', with Kiplingesque effect.

Before returning to this question of 'the Irish nation' but without departing from Irish matters, this is a convenient point at which to attempt an explanation of English racism. When the Normans conquered England in 1066 they created a class system of extraordinary rigidity, the remnants of which linger on in the matter of accent. For two centuries or so the Norman–Angevin ruling class spoke a different language to that of their Anglo-Saxon and British subjects. Although they had only been residents in France for a little over a century, they had in three generations or so completely forgotten their Scandinavian language or languages under the influence of the superior culture of the French. They were to do the same with almost equal speed in Ireland. But were someone to have told King John's barons that they were *Englishmen* he would have received an extremely dusty answer. King John might be King of England as well as being Duke of Normandy but the Anglo-Saxon aristocracy had been eliminated and almost the only 'Englishmen' were Anglo-Saxon peasants. Class and language were one and the same. When at last the Normans began to speak English, they retained a pride in 'Norman blood', and indeed often claimed it without justification. This form of pride endured almost to our own time. And when the Elizabethans and Cromwellians conquered Ireland, they adapted this linguistic racism to the new situation. Unlike the tenth century Norsemen in France, the sixteenth and seventeenth century English did not meet a functioning superior Celtic society but one in a state of chaos and confusion made infinitely worse by the long internal wars. Beyond the Pale and outside the few cities of Viking creation lived the 'mere Irish'. For the English, the Irish were 'savages' and the language they spoke was a badge of inferiority, a justification of servitude on the one hand, of contempt and fear on the other. What is more surprising is that educated Irishmen came to accept this. By the early nineteenth century so great a patriot as Daniel O'Connell, himself a fluent Irish speaker, never used his native tongue in public and urged the people he led to forget it as quickly as possible. Despite the attempts of Eamon de Valera and others to revive its use, it is a moribund language. It is hard to find a monoglot Irish family today save among the very poor in the very wildest parts of the west. And it is certain that television will very rapidly make it a dead language studied by scholars and perhaps used for a few state occasions.

Which brings us to another definition of 'the nation' as the meaning of that word has developed since Swift's time.

For students of pre- and proto-history, philology and archaeology are the two main sources of data. A pre-literate society can vanish utterly, leaving nothing but a few broken pots, a weapon or two and some place names. The popularisation of Darwin's survival-of-the-fittest in the last century, combined with the temporary technological superiority of Europeans over the rest of the world, not only gave an aura of respectability to imperialism but brought about the nadir of racism in King Leopold's Belgian Congo, the Ku Klux Klan and Hitler's Germany. Linguistics were enrolled, quite wrongly, as a proof of race. This reached its extremity in the theory of German National Socialism, whereby everyone who spoke German, except the Jews, belonged to a non-existent German race and therefore should be a German national.

The Jews had, tragically, styled themselves 'the chosen people', though for them this had originally meant belief in Jehovah and in the Law as given to Moses and elaborated by the prophets throughout the centuries. Any convert to Judah became a Jew and usually took a Jewish name, while one who ceased to believe ceased to be a Jew. There was no question of 'blood' in this concept of race. Conversion to Judaism was particularly prevalent in Roman Gaul.[1]

The French attitude to the relationship between language and nation is more subtle, closer to the Jewish, and long predated that of the Germans. It is generally accepted that the creator of modern France was Cardinal Richelieu (1585–1642). He not only founded the *Académie Française* but as one of its first tasks ordered the compiling of a French dictionary which was to define, absolutely and for ever, the correct meaning of a unified country's language. The Roman heritage lived on in the classicism of the literature over which the Academy presided. French culture became the hallmark of France, racism almost irrelevant. When the French acquired an empire overseas, once the inhabitants of those lands had accepted French culture they became legally Frenchmen, with representation in the French Chamber of Deputies. Nobody has ever disputed that colonials, such as Dumas or Camus, or even foreigners, such as Rousseau, were French writers. A Frenchman of Irish descent and with an Irish name, Marshall MacMahon, was proposed as French head of state. An Italian, Mazarin, could succeed Richelieu as the effective ruler of France, and of course a Corsican became her Emperor. This acceptance of foreigners into the French national culture was true, with variations, of the other closer heirs of Rome, of Spain, Portugal, Italy. The Roman papacy succeeded directly to the moral authority of the Roman imperium: at the time of writing the Pope is a Pole. There has, however, never been an Irish pope.

The English nation began to assume its modern form under the Tudors and its definition is largely geographic, its principal boundaries the Channel and the oceans. However, the Romans had scarcely penetrated its extremities, Cornwall, Highland Scotland and much of Wales, and though the Cornish language became finally extinct in the late eighteenth century, Scotland and Wales have maintained, in some measure, their linguistic and therefore their national identity to this day. Despite innumerable wars, the English never succeeded in total conquest and absorption of the Scots and Welsh. Only dynastic marriages forced the two nations to accept, with some reluctance that is even now not entirely gone, political union with England, using the revised Roman and pre-Roman name of Britain. In effect the English did not penetrate, save in the coldest political terms, far beyond the old Roman *limes*, though they did absorb a multitude of Scots, Welsh and Irish into England and into the colonies. Indeed within the last century they have accepted two Scots and one Welshman as prime ministers. But it is of significance that with the Reformation both Scotland and Wales showed a growing reluctance to accept Canterbury and the English or British monarch as a spiritual and administrative substitute for Rome and the Pope, preferring their own version of Protestant Christianity.

The literary-cultural framework into which the English tried and failed to incorporate Ireland and the Celtic peoples of their own island was far looser than that which had evolved in France. English classicism was largely a foreign importation of brief duration. This meant that all books and plays written in English can be and have been incorporated into English literature regardless of whether their authors are in spirit as Scots as Burns, as Welsh as Dylan Thomas or as Irish as Synge. This matter of so-called 'Anglo-Irish' writing is one to which we shall return, principally in order to demolish that pseudo-concept.

From the above it will be seen that there is no generally accepted European definition of what does or does not constitute a nation of any more revealing subtlety than that of a group of people living under a single administration. If we are to attempt to understand the Irishness of the Irish we must dig back, among the names and the broken beakers and the old rusty weapons to find, if we can, the roots of Irish society. And this will bring us, almost but not quite directly, to the pre-Roman Celts, whose society prevailed in Ireland for well over a thousand years and whose modes made the most fundamental impression on the Irish without ever creating an 'Irish nation'. First, however, there is need for a largely speculative chapter about pre-Celtic Ireland.

NOTE

1 As Léon Poliakov has remarked in his *Histoire de l'Antisémitisme*, Vol. 1 (1955), a Parisian banker named Monsieur Lévy is as likely to be descended from Vercingétorix as is his *concierge*.

I

BEFORE THE CELTS

There is no need to begin at the beginning: that is a matter for the geologists, the macrophysicists and the teleologians. In modern, human times Ireland before the last Ice Age did not exist save as a westerly part of the Euro-Asian land mass. If anything human or hominid lived there then, it has left no traces so far discovered. There are no Lascaux caves, no Neanderthal bones. And then the ice came, glaciers that are said to have been a thousand feet deep, stretching as far south as what is now, roughly, central Ireland, grinding down – as they came and went – the old, jagged mountain ranges to produce the rounded, almost feminine, necklace of high or higher hills that well nigh encircles the great central plain and lakes made shallow by the debris washed down with the rough, and melting, ice. By about 8,000 B.C. the island, as we know it, existed much as it does today. The melting ice-cap had created the Irish Sea, which was then deeper than it is today. Another two thousand years or so were to pass before the English Channel separated Britain from the Continent. As the climate grew more temperate, there was a massive movement of animals northwards, to live off the new tundra that was soon replaced by northern forests and, of course, also to live off one another. And with or shortly after them came man.

The seas rose and fell as the ice melted. The landbridge between what is now County Antrim and what is now Scotland did not, apparently, exist when the larger island was still joined to the Continent and also warm enough for warm-blooded snakes. As we shall see, what St. Patrick expelled from Ireland were not *real* snakes in the zoological sense, since there were none, or at least the archaeologists have found no skeletal remains. Some animals may have swum the narrows where the Giant's Causeway now lies, but apart from human importations the Irish fauna generally predates that of Britain. This is also true of the flora, though in both cases the resemblance is close.

From pre-glacial times there are few carboniferous relics, a little coal and perhaps oil in the Continental shelf and beyond. The great peat bogs are post-glacial, dead tundra and other trees and vegetation that have rotted on hilltops or been washed down by a myriad of streams into the lower, central plain. These great bogs, often thirty or more feet deep and easily dug, have long provided much of Ireland's fuel. They have also sealed and preserved wooden and other artifacts, but few of them are very old.

A human skeleton has been found, beside the ashes of his fire, in a cave in County Waterford, and the half-life carbon test has dated him at approximately 2,500 B.C. He was certainly far from being the first Irishman. A drop of the sealevel has exposed ancient beaches, particularly in the area of Larne in County Antrim but also as far south as Dalkey Island, near Dublin, to reveal huge piles of sea-shells together with some other debris which are attributed to palaeolithic man of a considerably earlier date. Very recently, even earlier relics, believed to be human, have been found in Sligo and Offaly and have been dated as early as 8,000 B.C. These most primitive people left few traces, and what we assume about them is derived either from deduction or by analogy with the most primitive isolated communities such as linger in New Guinea. They lived so long ago that even traces of their passage in the most ancient myths and legend are highly suspect and even improbable.

They pursued the animals, northwards and westwards, as the wild animals followed the receding ice. They were to have a few domestic animals, the sheep, the cow, later the horse (for eating rather than for traction or portage), eventually the wheel. They were probably tribal, their relationships ritualistic, very conscious of death but unaware of paternity and therefore worshipping (for lack of a better word) the feminine as the source of life and early nourishment. Birth, copulation and death, beneath the winking stars and the unblinking planets. What did it all mean, this rising of the moon and setting of the sun? Numerate long before ever they were literate, their endless search for food was helped by their ability to calculate the seasons. They can have had no concept of magic, since everything (or nothing) was magical. Yet perhaps they could influence, perhaps even appease, the powers of the universe.

We do not know why, nor even how, they evolved into the societies of the Boyne valley and elsewhere that built such huge tombs as New Grange, Dowth and Knowth. Were they indeed tombs, as is generally assumed? Had they heard garbled stories of the first pyramids that the unknown Egyptians were even then building, far away? The pyramids did, it is true, serve as burial places for the once omnipotent Pharaoh, his treasures, his women, his slaves. Our own nineteenth century saw them as elaborate, futile preparations for 'the resurrection of the body', of Pharaoh's body equipped for what he must need in his future life. This implies a silliness on the part of the Egyptians that is better ascribed to the Victorians. The pharaonic tomb and the pyramid above it were sealed *against* resurrection, not for it. Together they comprised a philosophical statement in stone, gold, mummified flesh, sealed containers of food and drinks, even service solidified into dead slaves. This was the present to be preserved for ever, simultaneously a denial and an assertion of the existential world of change. As well as being a statement, they were an enormously elaborate work of art. The Egyptians immortalised their divine rulers much as Degas penned *for ever* his divine *Baigneuses* emerging from their baths in a moment that happened, to us, a century ago.

Perhaps those communities who built New Grange and the other great mounds that the archaeologists have dubbed 'passage graves' were not primarily concerned with the occasional cremation of dead bodies that took place deep within them? New Grange was built some five to eight thousand years ago. It must have been the work of a very considerable, more or less static, community. Here is an abridged description of this enormous mound, as written by two archaeologists (Michael Herity and George Eogan in their *Ireland in Pre-history*):

> The New Grange tumulus, a pear-shaped heap mainly of water-rolled pebbles, has a diameter of roughly 80m and was built to a height of about 15m. The edge of the mound is revetted by a kerb of oblong boulders, averaging 3m by 1m. Most of these bear designs; three, the entrance stone and numbers 52 and 67, are exceptionally well ornamented. The monumental tumulus, which required the labours of at least several hundred workers to pile up its 200,000 tons, contains at least three times the material of Gavrinis and Le Petit Mont, the largest tumuli of this class in Brittany. The ornamented kerb encircling it displays the standard art motifs of the Irish *ateliers* in the open air, but the display is overshadowed by the tumulus above. The tomb underneath has a passage 19m long entering a cruciform chamber 6.50m wide and 6m high. An angular, hexagonal vault roofs the chamber, springing from the endstone of the smaller left-hand recess and the lintel of the larger right-hand one. It is built of corbelled blocks each weighing up to a ton and bedded on large pebbles which have been crushed by the weight of the roof and the tumulus above. This vault, an insular translation of the Atlantic drywalled beehive (tholas) roof of L'Ile Longue in

Brittany and Romeral in Spain, integrates the central chambers and the three side-recesses into a single unit.

The ornamentation of this chamber is not of the same exceptional standard as its imaginative architecture, its skilled building, and the artistry of its entrance stone, its clearest feature being the embellishment of the horizontals of lintels and corbels above eye level. An accomplished triple spiral is hidden away inside the end-recess and the lightly incised designs – including an abstracted human face – on the roofstone of the right recess would have been more striking if placed in an architecturally more prominent position.

That this chamber was a burial-place is clear from fragments of cremated human bone found in the recesses in recent excavations. With them were a few ornaments which had been heat-cracked on the funeral-pyre. In each of the three recesses are stone basins – there are two, one on top of the other, in the right-hand recess, laboriously hollowed out from large granite boulders, which are best explained as the repositories in which each new cremation was placed during the burial ceremony.

The creative energies of an artistic genius in the New Grange community were reserved for the ring of kerbstones which girdled the tumulus at its completion. His masterpiece was the entrance stone, set on a slight incurve of the kerb against the backdrop of the doorway, the fanlight above, and the receding walls of the façade. Five spirals, a group of three and group of two, with a vertical groove separating them, form the central motifs of a design which is completed with lozenges and with nested arcs undulating to the edge of the stone and then dispersing. The spiral motif is also engraved on Stone K52 at the north-west side of the tumulus. The division into two parts which is a marked feature of the entrance stone is executed with even more formality here. To one side of the central groove a net-pattern of lozenges is grouped below a pair of opposed spirals. On the right of the groove a series of three shields filled with rows of cupmarks nests within an arrangement of grouped arcs. The shields and grouped arcs are both Breton in character, their arrangement and the lozenge and spiral of the other half of the stone insular. Kerbstone K67, nearby, has a shallower design, an insular face made by combining an S-shaped pair of spirals with a pair of lozenges. To one side of this is a net-pattern of lozenge and triangle. Both these kerbstones have the appearance of being experiments through which the confident artistry of the entrance stone was developed.

At New Grange, then, an adventurous and imaginative architect, adapting a Breton plan, designed and built a transeptal tomb into which he incorporated an Irish version of the Atlantic beehive roof, constructed of rough ice-boulders rather than neat building stones, and an approach passage the equal in length of any yet built in Atlantic Europe. He aligned this passage to face the rising of the midwinter sun, and later had to incorporate the fanlight over the doorway to compensate for the slope on which the tomb was built in order to allow the rising sun to play on the centre of the chamber floor on midwinter's

Most of Ireland was glacier-covered until about 8,000 B.C. Areas such as the Burren in Co. Clare remain much as the retreating glaciers left them – rocky and largely sterile. The majority of the country became thickly wooded, as in this picture of primeval forest, until cleared by early farmers. Some trees, such as the oak and may, being holy in Druidic eyes, remained largely untouched until, in the eighteenth century, the British felled them. Nelson's wooden walls of England were in large measure Irish timber. Now the countryside is in general bare and rolling

The age of New Grange – a great burial or fertility mound in the Boyne valley – is a matter of dispute. It is probably between 5,000 and 8,000 years old, roughly contemporary with the pyramids of Egypt. There is little carved decorative work, this stone outside the only entrance perhaps displaying the finest. The wave- and lozenge motif remained popular with the Celts, as it was with the contemporary Cretans and Greeks day. The religious fervour of the people of the Boyne moved them to crown this tomb with a massive tumulus more imposing than any yet erected in Europe. The artist of New Grange came too late on the scene to influence in any significant way the ornamentation of chamber and passage. He did, however, evolve a new, insular idiom in which the spiral became a dominant motif, and he realised his potential in the conception and execution of the entrance stone, a marvellous primitive abstract. The circular peristalith of thirty-five pillars set standing free 10m to 15m outside the edge of the tumulus was a later addition built by the Beaker people of the Early Bronze Age.

The archaeologists take it for granted that New Grange and its like were graves. But the facts of cremation (relics of only three bodies have been found) seem to have been absurdly insignificant in comparison with the vastness of the edifice. And they omit that New Grange was apparently covered with polished quartz, brilliantly reflective of sunshine. Nor do they comment on the fact that the spiral motif, as they call it, is also the wave motif of the earliest – and perhaps near contemporary – Cretan art, and New Grange is only a few miles further from the mysterious ocean than is Cnossos. The brilliance of the sun, the turbulence of the waves and a building that resembles a womb beneath a big and rounded belly, were New Grange and the other 'passage graves' perhaps a vast fertility symbol in a world when fertility was still female, yet affected by sun and sea? Unlike the pyramids of Egypt, these Atlantic 'passage graves' were not sealed, or if there were a doorstone it must have been easily moved since the construction was so laid out that the rays of the winter solstice should penetrate the lintel as far as the central chamber. Did this first ray that presaged the coming of summer serve to fertilise, or re-fertilise, the human ashes in their very temporary, almost makeshift, stone basins? It is all lost, all unknown, but these enormous constructions remain.

And then, later, they built their great stone circles, as they did around New Grange which must therefore still have been a sacred place, none in Ireland as big as Stonehenge in England, but many built without doubt for some astronomic or astrologic purpose. So advanced by now was their numeracy that many of these huge circles, ovals or egg-shaped arrangements of big stones are mathematically almost perfect. There must have been many more, built of wood, that have not survived, perhaps particularly in Ireland where boulders are comparatively rare but great trees were abundant. Why were they built? Like vast sundials, they were often more accurate chronometers than many a modern watch, but they certainly were not built to 'tell the time' unless it were to tell all time, the divine time. An aura of human sacrifice hangs about them. At sunrise on mid-summer's day did a shadow fall upon a victim spreadeagled on a sacrificial stone and did the stone axe or the bronze spear fall? We do not know, and we certainly know not why, since we have no inkling of their old beliefs.

Only one curious fact is known, which may be relevant or mere coincidence. These great stone monuments left by Stone and Bronze Age man are all pre-Celtic. The Celts, and particularly that administrative class called Druids, had nothing whatever to do with them save perhaps to wonder, as do we, what purpose they may once have served. (By comparison with Stone Age man the Celts are our contemporaries.) Yet those stone circles, to use a single word in describing a great variety of stone and wood creations, existed only in those areas of Europe that were later to be conquered or dominated by the Celtic-speaking people. Furthermore, the sophisticated, metal age Celts only infiltrated permanently those parts of western, central and eastern Europe where Stone Age man has left his mark.

Before dealing with Celtic modes and with their arrival in their last area of dominance, Ireland, let us then speculate concerning the nature of their conquest.

No tribe is originally nomadic by choice, though it may become so by custom. Originally a tribe will go to the immense trouble of moving from a familiar to a strange territory because it lacks natural resources, in particular food. It will have killed the wild game or driven it away or, if it has become pastoral, its flocks and herds will have eaten the grasses even more quickly than the earliest farmers will have exhausted the fertility of its soil. Its numbers may have increased and those of its domestic animals. So, in a thinly populated area it will simply move on to fresh fields and pastures new. It will be looking for virgin land, of which there was plenty in Europe as the ice retreated northwards, up to about six or seven thousand years ago. But slowly this grew less and less. A tribe had therefore two choices, and usually chose both simultaneously. The first was a more productive use of natural resources by means of new technological and administrative skills. This the original Celtic tribes were doing, some four thousand years ago, in the area that is now, very roughly, southern Germany about Lake Constance and the upper reaches of the Rhine and Danube valleys. The second, and far less satisfactory, was to dispossess their neighbours (thus setting up a more or less limited chain reaction as those neighbours dispossessed *theirs*) and occupying non-virgin land which could be better exploited by its new and more advanced inhabitants. In this century, in Europe, we have seen the equivalent of such a *Völkerwanderung* in the expulsion of the Poles by Russians from the old eastern Polish territories, and the expulsion of Germans by Poles from the area east of the so-called Oder–Neisse line. In ancient times, as today, this led to hostility or even permanent warfare between the expellers and the expelled. It is a brutal, wasteful and painful way of dealing with a population expansion and a desire for natural resources hitherto exploited by others. Technical and administrative skill on the part of the conquerors may be replaced by overwhelming numerical superiority. This, however, usually has a peculiar outcome, in that the nature of the conqueror's society, if it be the more primitive, will be subordinated and eventually destroyed by that of the more sophisticated conquered people, so that their roles become quite quickly reversed, as happened, for example, to the Franks in Gaul. Since a society is a living entity to which its individual members have strong feelings of loyalty and even patriotic devotion, this is also an unhappy and painful process. It is rare, but in either case it is the weak that go to the wall. Genocide is the only means by which an inferior society can ensure for itself a permanent supremacy, and genocide is an extremely complex and difficult crime to commit.

There is another form of conquest which is probably not as old as tribal migration into hostile territory but which is hardly much younger. As agriculture began to supplement and then to replace hunting and pasturage as the main source of food, nomadic life became increasingly difficult, for hunting was at a discount and an excess of strong, able-bodied men became available for other employment. We see what is perhaps an echo of resultant internal strife in the biblical story of Cain and Abel. Cain was a shepherd, that is to say a semi-nomad. His tribal 'brother', Abel, tilled the soil, which meant that he was himself rooted to the ground at least until one harvest was gathered in and soon enough until an increased tribal population had exhausted the land's fertility. The tribe, speaking through its godhead, preferred Abel's food gathering to Cain's methods. In what is perhaps the first recorded act of reactionary or conservative violence, Cain slew his brother. The tribe, however, speaking through its God, would not accept a return to older ways and Cain was expelled. He was not killed and indeed the 'mark of Cain' made him unkillable or more probably implied that his death at the hands of 'foreigners' would be avenged by the tribe as a whole. With an apparent shrug of his shoulders and a sarcastic remark to the effect that how his tribal brethren chose to live was no concern of his, he set off for foreign parts. This freebooter found a foreign wife and his descendants did extremely well for themselves, inventing cities, a more satisfactory method of pasturage (tents, or movable dwellings, for shepherds), musical instruments, and finally ushered in both the Bronze and the Iron ages. Cain committed what are surely two of the very grossest offences against the tribal taboos: he murdered one of his fellows and he gave an impertinent answer to his God who spoke, presumably, through the mouths of the tribal elders. Yet his glory far exceeds that of Abel and the other stick-in-the-muds. He is the spiritual ancestor, at least, of the great discoverers and perhaps of all original thinkers. Do the astronauts of our time also bear the mark of Cain?

For present purposes Cain symbolises those men who went, sword in hand, to foreign parts in search of plunder and women and power. They provided a spearhead when the tribe turned aggressive: similar men became a shield to guard the tribe against its neighbours' aggression. From them there came a warrior caste very close, but usually subservient, to the temporal and spiritual leadership. In combination they became an army, far more mobile and far more dangerous than the tribe as a whole.

Such conquests have frequently occurred in historical times. Equipped with horses, armour, steel and gunpowder, Cortez and a handful of Spaniards not only overthrew Montezuma and his huge ferocious armies but enforced Spanish administration, Spanish religion and ultimately the Spanish language upon the people of Mexico. With reservations (in both senses of the word) the English and the French did much the same in North America though, to a far greater degree than the Spaniards and the Portuguese, they soon brought their own women with them. The process did not stop. The descendants of the original settlers, who had overwhelmed the numerically superior Amerindians by the usual means, settled down to farm and plant and become, in their turn, tribes of Abels. Cain, however, was immortal. He hit out for the west, a nomad engaged upon his endless quest for pelts, for gold, for women. Behind him came the latter-day equivalent of the more painful *Völkerwanderung*, the redundant, the religiously dispossessed, or the immigrants, all in search of virgin land, many in the almost mythical convoys of covered waggons.

To this writer it would seem highly probable that it was such a conquest, rather than a *Völkerwanderung*, that originally brought Celtic Ireland into being. Such conquests appear to be utterly destructive, save for those enormous megalithic creations too big to pull down, and perhaps for a few legends, and sometimes physiognomy. The Celts were in general tall, blond or red-haired and, according to the Greeks, garrulous. Of Ireland's Stone Age inhabitants we have no records or pictures, and we know virtually nothing about their language. Some have suggested that they were small and dark and that their language was akin to that of the Basques. No good arguments have been advanced for or against this hypothesis. Yet this was the stock on to which Celtic manners, mores and administration were grafted. Of all these we know a great deal. Save as a geographical concept, the Celts created the first Ireland that exists for us and, so strong was their imprint, much of their Ireland has survived until today.

Before we turn to Celtic Ireland, let us digress briefly on what else they may have inherited from the oldest Ireland beside blood and tumuli and stone circles. Who had crossed the seas before them? To paraphrase St. Thomas Aquinas: the seas have always been a watery highway, uniting the peoples, unlike the great mountain ranges that divide them.

❈ ❈ ❈

That foreigners came to pre-Celtic Ireland may be taken for granted, but who they were and when they came is a matter of dispute. Indeed the chronology of all pre-history is extremely vague and perhaps pointless. The anthropologists prefer to speak of periods based upon the tools people used, the pottery they made, their methods of burying the dead, and in more modern European times the variants of the basic Indo-Germanic root words that became languages and the folklore that they handed down. Vegetation, since it can be carbon-dated, will sometimes help to date a co-eval stone or pottery artifact provided we are satisfied that the wood or peat and the stone or metal are co-eval, but this is seldom certain, while the margin of error increases with age. Nor, it seems, is this margin quite as constant as once was thought and may be on occasion in excess of 10% and seldom less than 5%, as comparison between the carbon half-life and the rings of very ancient American redwoods has shown. From other, historical evidence we know that if we are 'dating', say, the Parthenon (and even accept the most improbable thesis that all the stones on the Acropolis date from the time of

Pericles) we may find our carbon test wrong by at least 250 years. When dating something much older – say a very early bronze implement – the potential error is very much greater, perhaps as much as a thousand years. All we can do, by comparison and means, is to state that before an approximate date we know of no bronze implements in one area and that at a much earlier and even vaguer date there were probably no bronze instruments in existence anywhere at all. This, in turn, will give us an even looser indication of when the Bronze Age 'began'.

Because, obviously, even in so small and relatively homogeneous an area as Europe (a geographical concept for what was probably closer to a linguistic unit) bronze implements were not invented like, say, the telephone nor the smelting of metals 'discovered' like penicillin. Again, and what is equally obvious, people did not suddenly stop using stone axes and begin to use more efficient metal ones. The ages of the archaeologists merge the one into the other, and technical innovations spread from their point of origin outwards, like the ripples of a stone cast into water but without the regularity of ripples. This is even more true of techniques. Money was becoming a regular means of exchange in most of the eastern Mediterranean countries over two and a half thousand years ago: during the Irish famine of the last century it scarcely existed or was understood in the province of Connaught.

Similarly, folklore and philology may give a moderately firm indication of what happened in pre- or proto-history, but will almost never say when the events or series of events occurred. Therefore all dates concerning such matters as the arrival of the Celts or the celticisation of the aboriginal Irish are extremely suspect and must be treated as such. They are usually little more than a consensus, and by its very nature a consensus is only an average between errors. It is simply more convenient to say that the Celts reached Ireland about 500 B.C. than to write than the Celts were probably arriving in Ireland between about 1,000 and about 200 B.C., for undoubtedly people who may be described, rightly or wrongly, as Celts reached or influenced Ireland at an earlier date and many partly romanised Britons came centuries later.

If we would speculate about other, early foreign intrusions into the Irish scene, there are four approaches to the subject; the first, which should be the most revealing, is the evidence supplied by the Irish myths and legends. The second is a probability thesis: who can have come to Ireland, and why? The third is the appearance of Irish artefacts elsewhere, and the fourth the legends and histories of other peoples. Since we are here dealing with pre-Celtic times, these last are almost as fragmentary as the first.

Scholars have tried to treat Homer as if he were a historian and have proved the impossibility of such an undertaking. Homer was a poet and the *Iliad* is a poem based upon legends of one or more Trojan wars, a compilation designed to interest the listener and please his ear. There was a Trojan war and there were almost certainly Greek princelings named Agamemnon, Achilles and so on: there may even have been a princess called Helen, or more probably a sacred feminity symbol, maybe a Cycladic statue of the mother goddess Rhea that was stolen when Mycenae was sacked. Homer casts light on the customs of his time, on how men at arms fought and wherein lay their concept of honour and how they felt about their gods. The same is even more true of that collection of fantastic traveller's tales that he spun together to form the *Odyssey*, from which we learn something about the ships and the sailors of his age. But in the account of Odysseus's long, at times pathetic, attempts to reach his home in Ithaca the listener hears of some very weird characters and visits some very strange and foreign places, yet in all this sailing around the Aegean and the Adriatic Odysseus never sights another ship, and we learn nothing about the very active trade and the probable naval struggle that must have been taking place in those post-Minoan waters.

This is even more true of the Irish legends of a considerably later date. They were compiled in the form known to us, though seldom with a narrative skill approaching Homer's, in the early centuries A.D., though the two main series, that of the Cuchulain saga and that of Finn, are inspired by earlier events but probably not much earlier, say two or three hundred years. They concern inter-tribal rivalry and war within what is basically a homogeneous Celtic society in which one code of conduct prevails and, probably, one language is spoken. Yet embedded, as it were, in Irish folklore are other, much older tales and two of these concern foreigners, aliens, from a truly mythical past, semi-human and semi-supernatural.

The first and less interesting of these are the Formorians, malevolent and destructive giants, at war with the Celtic or more likely the pre-Celtic Irish. They have to be repeatedly beaten off, but the ugly great things keep coming back with mischievous or murderous intent, sometimes by sea, sometimes by air. Their wish was to destroy the people, or even to tow the whole island away to some dreadful place and there freeze it or drown it. Fortunately they seem to be rather stupid and despite their great size and strange powers are regularly foiled in their foul and pointless endeavours. Upon what may they be based? They do not come as warrior hosts or even in great numbers. Were they perhaps the very first Celtic freebooters, seen through pre-Celtic eyes, driven out at first but forever coming back, the same men in new bodies? Or were they part of the mythology that the Celts brought with them? These evil figures from some remote past seem to haunt Europe, usually men of enormous stature, giants and Titans, determined to interfere but doomed to permanent defeat at the hands of the Greek gods or even of Jack with his own magical beanstalk. Do they represent anything in history? We know of no race that ever inhabited what is now Europe or neighbouring lands that was big and dangerous to the Indo-Germanic speaking peoples. In their recurrence they seem a creation of psychological fantasy, the endlessly recreated father figure of Freudian psychiatry who in certain circumstances can be hostile and dangerous but who, in the very nature of life, can never hope to win the last battle with his beanstalk son. In a society of rapid change, the more conservative father will be in conflict with the more innovative son. Celtic society appears to have been remarkably static and contented. Perhaps the Formorians were, indeed, those older Celts imposing a new or at least a modified social structure upon the pre-Celtic peoples?

* * *

The other foreign element is far more attractive and intriguing. I have deliberately avoided referring to the pre-Celtic Irish as *fir bolg*, a Celtic term meaning 'men of the bag', a derogatory description which has retained its tone even in the English language. Perhaps it was first used by the Celts to describe their predecessors, those Stone Age men who, in vast numbers and for many generations, must have been employed in huge numbers as carriers, since they lacked both the horse and, while New Grange was building, perhaps even the wheel. To feed this army of builders, farming on a large scale must have been practised in and about the Boyne valley, again by hand. Such labourers were probably but not necessarily slaves. Their governors may have resembled the Brahmin, their very distant linguistic cousins in northwest India whose social and theocratic arrangements in some ways resemble those of the Celts too.

The basic Celtic social unit was the extended family or *tuatha* in which its members took great pride of ancestry, and which has been translated as nation, tribe, clan or sept. The word 'sept' is usually reserved for the Irish type of this social unit, and will be so used here. The most essential element of Celtic conquest must have been the celticisation of the pre-Celtic sept, or whatever form of society may have prevailed, where this was necessary. The men who fled from this process or were expelled, would have taken to the primaeval forests and the bogs. To this day a 'bog man', a 'bog trotter', a man 'from the back of the bog' are terms of patronising insult in Ireland. Those who had changed with the times would regard the 'bog men' as more primitive persons, as bees without a hive, as savages. Such persons, of course, may always have existed even when men in society were building New Grange and the rest. This would seem, however, unlikely, since man is essentially a social creature and always has been. Nevertheless it is quite comprehensible that the more civilised Irishman, whether Celtic or pre-Celtic, should come to identify the men of the bog with the *fir bolg*, a more primitive and therefore older type of humanity than himself.

Now to judge by the inextricably confused chronology of the legends, one of the earliest groups from overseas to arrive in Ireland were the *tuatha de Danaan*. They were as magical, if a comparative be possible more magical, than the Formorians. They were capable of the most extraordinary sorts of powerful metamorphosis, turning themselves at will into beasts or eagles or even waves of the sea. Either in such disguise or in other ways they could disappear for long periods of time, even for several human generations, some taking a beloved human to their fairyland, but could return as human beings once again with or without this beloved. For they could and did mate with ordinary mortals and produce offspring which, if they remained in Ireland, retained some or all of the Danaan magic. The Danaans were a sept and the Irish legends claimed that this sept came from Greece. According to Euripides the Danaans were the pre-Helladic inhabitants of Greece, coming from the present eastern shores of the Mediterranean, north of Egypt. Euripides, who died in 406 B.C., was thus dealing with what was for him the most remote and mythical antiquity. A pre-Olympian god of justice, whose basic name was Dan, was the tribal 'ancestor'. One of his princely descendants who remained in Asia fell foul of King Nebuchadnezzar, who decided in about 580 B.C. he would be best fed to the lions at Babylon, his new city. At perhaps an earlier date a semi-mortal Danaan, a young woman named Danae, was possessed by Zeus: for this escapade the top Greek god chose to disguise himself as a shower of gold. He, who for similar purposes could be a bull or a swan, had no need to buy young women. Papa Zeus was no sugar daddy. Some, but far from all, of the gold available to him *may* have come from Ireland. Since golden ornaments of that period bore no hallmarks, we cannot identify any as having come from any particular source let alone sept, either before or after the Celtic eruption. We are back among myths.

The *tuatha de Danaan* were, when in human form, persons of very great physical beauty and what they built, or made with their hands, were also objects of great beauty though these vanished with their creators. Since Ventris deciphered some Cretan inscriptions and records, we know that the people of Minos were writing, and presumably speaking, an early form of Greek about 2,000 B.C. and earlier. Minos's homeland needed no defensive walls, for his navies dominated the eastern Mediterranean. If they could ride out the awful storms of the Aegean, then they were quite capable of passing the Pillars of Hercules, hugging the Spanish coast and crossing what is nowadays called the Celtic Sea to Ireland. So, probably, could the Mycenaean merchants and after the fall of that great city, about a thousand years before the birth of Christ, so could Odysseus. That is to say, at any time, though probably long after New Grange was built, 'Greek' ships could have reached Ireland. Had they come as conquerors, they would have left more substantial remains. Had they come as traders, probably in search of Irish gold which then was plentiful and easily panned in the streams that flow through the Wicklow hills, their stay would have been short, long enough to build wooden houses more elegant than any known hitherto in Ireland, long enough perhaps to teach the early Irish how to beat and twist their gold into those beautiful ornamental discs and torcs, perhaps in honour of Apollo and Selene and Poseidon, long enough even to teach a few Irish masons how to carve their own sacred wave motifs upon a few important stones. Then these Greeks or proto-Greeks would sail away, to rejoin their own septs, leaving perhaps a few half-Greek children among the Irish septs, persons to be venerated, and Irish mythopoesis would transform the departed seamen into sea eagles, butterflies, waves of the sea, their destination a fairyland. When, years or generations later, a new boatload of men from what the Irish must have regarded as members of the same sept sailed up the Lee or the Shannon or the Boyne, it must have been obvious to the Irish that the *tuatha de Danaan* had chosen once again to assume human form. The Irish would lead them back to their old, magical settlements. It is an easy transference to assume that in fact they had never gone away at all, that they had simply rendered themselves and their homes (now splendid palaces in the Irish imagination) invisible, that provided no one interfered with their trails and wells and the site of their homes, they would be beneficent strangers, very occasionally visible to propitiate mysterious gods and help the harvest grow – in a word, fairies bearing gifts.

If, from what Yeats called 'the entangled stories of the past' one may guess that the Formorians came from the dark night of the Irish soul, why should not one also speculate that the *tuatha de Danaan* sailed to Ireland long ago from the sunny, warm south? It is, for this writer, hard to think that from the evidence of their nomenclature's stem, their voyage may have been around the north of Scotland, their place of origin what is now called Denmark. Yet even so the ancient voices will not be silenced. The legendary Book of Invasions tells us that the Danaans did indeed come from Scandinavia, by air, landing in the middle of what is now Connaught. Norway, however, and Scotland too were only stages of a journey that had started in Athens and Achaea. How many miles to Babylon? Can I get there by candle-light? Yes, and back again.

2

THE CELTS

Very early in his magnificent opus on the visual arts André Malraux remarks that while there is most certainly 'decadent' art, there is no such thing as 'primitive' art. Styles, of course, clash and influence one another, sometimes for what we consider the better, more often for what we regard as the worse, but an autochthonous style seems to spring from the soul of a people, fully equipped, for its own purposes, like Pallas Athene from the brow of Zeus. As an archaeologist and a sinologist, as well as being an aesthete and himself a superb artist of words, Malraux knew that the most ancient work of Chinese art is in no way more 'primitive' than the most supreme creation by the great artists who also and later embellished that magnificent and enormous land. Similarly the most magnificent pharaonic statues are in no way an 'improvement' on, let alone a 'progression' from, certain small pre-dynastic Egyption sculptures save in size, and even here the Sphinx still smiles on the enigma.

Decadent art, on the other hand, is constantly visible and easily identified by the very simple test that it is unsatisfactory. (Individual works of mediocrity, usually though not invariably produced by mediocre artists, are not here considered: our subject is the acclaimed style of a particular period in a specific area.) Decadence, again according to Malraux, is often preceded by what he calls 'aristocratic' art, that is to say the artist is creating works to please an aristocracy, a power élite, which by its very nature must desire a repetition of that which it knows (even if all it knows is what it thinks is novelty). We see this in the successful attempts of the Greek Hellenists to please their Roman masters by the production of inferior and elaborate copies of Greek classical art. We see it in the drawing-rooms of certain western millionaires of today who will only accept the highly priced incomprehensible: the price tag will fool some of the people all of the time. We see the 'aristocrat' principle in the equally boring rigidity of Soviet 'proletarian art' or 'socialist realism': state censorship, or even more powerful religious iconoclasm, will fool all of the people some of the time.

A formalised 'aristocratic' style in the arts can endure for a long time, to be precise for as long as the society which it serves. It will, however, become ever more fragile as copy succeeds copy and the original inspiration disappears into an ever more remote past. This of course is visible not only in the arts but in many other aspects of an ageing, and finally a moribund, society, as weapons become obsolete or mere ornaments, religious rituals are recited in dead languages, the administration ceases to function adequately, the system in whole or in part cannot adjust to changing circumstances and so on.

Certain great philosophers of history, such as Vico, Spengler and Toynbee, have sought a rather crude, anthropomorphic analogy. A society (or a civilisation or a culture) is born, passes through a primitive childhood, reaches full maturity, decays and dies. Oswald Spengler, at least, produced a great, subjective literary work of art in his *Decline of the West*. It is, however, based upon a fallacy. A society, whether it be as small as a tribe or as large as the Roman Empire, must consist of the mutual relationships between human beings and of their relationship to the environment, human and material, but it in no way resembles a human being any more than *Lycidas* resembles the ink that once flowed from Milton's pen. The men of the tribes which followed the retreating icecap northwards across Europe, ten thousand and less years ago, were no more primitive than the men running to catch a commuters' train this morning, while the social arrangements within that tribe were almost certainly at least as well suited to the tribal needs as are the social systems now prevalent in London or Prague to those of the commuter. The nineteenth century English liked to compare the period of Queen Elizabeth I to the glorious springtime of their country's early manhood: Shakespeare and his contemporaries, on the contrary, saw themselves as living in an age of doubt, dissension, economic decline and impending doom. We may think of the Augustan age as the very pinnacle of Rome's grandeur, a view that was certainly not shared by Ciceronian republicans who saw tyranny imposed upon a populace exhausted and demoralised by generations of greedy civil war, nor even, perhaps, so viewed by Augustus himself. No society, anywhere, has ever enjoyed the sunny evening of tranquillity, its work well done, seated before some metaphorical cottage door. Should a society die, its death is almost always violent: perhaps a geological accident such as the Santorin explosion or eruption that flattened Cnossos or the slower but remorseless advance of the Gobi and the Sahara sand over once great cities; or murder, in apparent full and happy maturity, as happened to the people of the Inca; or ingurgitation, a warm blooded creature swallowed whole by a boa constrictor, as appears to have been the fate of the Etruscans and the Maoris. But perhaps more often than any ending, whether with a bang or with a whimper, there is a slow erosion, caused as often or not by conquest or symbiosis or both. Thence can arise a social style that is both new and as old as its components. When St. Benedict, fifteen hundred years ago, decided to build the Abbey of Monte Cassino upon the foundations of a temple to Apollo, he knew precisely what he was doing, and his deliberate act has no parallel in the physical life of man. When, a thousand or so years earlier, the Celts claimed Ireland they certainly had no plan. They were not a new, young people, but the representatives of a very mature and self-assured society which had flourished for many centuries in central Europe, which had sent conquerors or colonists as far south as southern Spain, Rome and Delphi, as far east as the area around where Ankara now stands, as far north as Scandinavia and now as far west as the very uttermost ends of the known world. They did not create Ireland, but they imprinted upon the Irish a style which in some measure has endured. Though the Celtic nature of the Irish has often been grossly exaggerated and as frequently misunderstood, that imprint was certainly stronger than any which has followed. For a thousand years, apart from the conquered aborigines whom they absorbed probably as slaves, they had the island almost entirely to themselves, unmolested. In the history of Europe a millenium of freedom from external aggression is an almost unparalleled period for a people to develop as they choose. During that long period the Celtic style changed little, but its roots struck deep, and that first Celtic imprint is even now quite easy to discern.

Until ossification and decadence set in, any social organism is so arranged as best to function for the mutual benefit of its component members. The larger the unit, the greater must be its administrative complexity, administration being here used in a pluralistic sense. There are four main fields of human activity that require different and varying forms of administration, the administrators being *ipso facto* the governing élite. The first is the collection, creation and distribution of goods often including slaves within the society, first of all food, then tools, then luxury goods and finally services. The second is the relationship of the society with other, neighbouring societies, which depending on circumstances, such as physical proximity, shared ideas of conduct and even the personalities of the governors will vary from mutual hospitality and friendship to open war. The third is the relationship of the collective will to the individual's desires. Unless the former predominates, usually in the collective unconscious, over the latter, anarchy will ensue and the society disintegrate. The collective will is reinforced in many ways, and among the most important is a conscious awareness of a shared past, often a very remote past, handed down in folk tales, poems and history and given actuality by custom and law. The fourth is the relationship of the individual, both *qua* individual and as a member of his social unit, with those forces over which he can exercise very little if any control save perhaps that of propitiation. This also is a job for specialists. Thus we may say, in shorthand, that the governing élite consists of the temporal leader or 'king', the warrior-diplomat, the poet-legislator and the priest: none of these in remote time or place corresponds precisely to our concept of such professionals and all overlap in their functions and are of varying relative importance, but no society has ever existed or endured without them. It is improbable that any human society ever will.

The Bronze Age central European Celts formed a large congeries of societies, unlike their contemporaries, the Hittites, the Egyptians and the Mycenaean Greeks; they have left no trace of any effective supra-tribal, centralised administration, though the evolution of a single artistic style, known to the archaeologists as La Tène in what is probably its earliest form, reveals at least the existence of traditional modes of vision, and evidence from place names and such indicates that the tribes shared a language some three thousand years ago, presumably with strong or stronger variations of dialect as the tribes began to move outwards. (These dialects or languages are usually divided into two main groups of which the older is believed to be Q-Celtic, the younger P-Celtic, the labial consonant merely replacing the guttural. The pronunication that prevailed in Scotland and Ireland was the older of the two, in Britain and Wales the younger: the Irish or Scots *ken*, or in rough translation 'head', is the same word as the British and Welsh *pen*, both to be encountered in well-nigh innumerable place names.)

The Celts, then, had no empire, but remained tribal even when they ceased to be nomadic. And it is from their early Stone Age, nomadic, pastoral forebears that they inherited much of their organisation and many of their values. If we are to understand the Irish, we must, as best we can, follow the Celts far back into their pre-Irish past. Above all, certain key words in the Celtic hierarchical structure must be disentangled from their more modern, often grossly misleading meanings. We must, however, remember that the Celts, and similar tribes, existed socially for a very long time indeed. When a post-nomadic Celtic society first came into existence, we do not know. It is known that a terrible 'time of troubles' disrupted all Aryan-speaking society when iron first came into use, about 1,000 B.C. or a little later. A highly sophisticated society based around the valleys of the Tigris and the Euphrates collapsed, though never totally, under the impact of a new technology. Greater adaptability, perhaps combined with a higher birth rate, led to migration and wars. New power centres, such as Rome, in due course appeared. But what concerns us is that the once pastoral and nomadic Celts began to send forces outwards from their settlements in south Germany.

The nomadic tribe, clan or sept was essentially the extended family unit. It consisted, therefore, of men (and usually women) who were born free and equal, though very frequently owning or acquiring slaves or servile septs. Its leader, or king, had to be strong, brave, skilful, virile and if possible handsome, for he incorporated the collective conscious of the tribe. It was as such, not as an individual, that he ruled. Among the O'Neills, he was The O'Neill, among the O'Donovans, he was The O'Donovan. Nomads own no land, nor do they build houses save of the most temporary sort and taxation takes the form of extra work, usually farming, to support the administration. Save for personal possessions, which at one time might include a chariot that was buried with its owner, the chieftain owned little more than did any other member of the family. He did not own his wife. Matrimony in our sense existed, but loosely. Divorce was simple and in many cases bigamy was practised. As late as 1634 the viceroy Strafford (the only man known to us ever effectively to have ruled all Ireland) met the greatest opposition in his determination to make bigamy illegal. The chieftain was, in theory, subject to the same druidical laws as the rest of his sept. In practice, of course, he had more sexual freedom, though no *droit de seigneur*. Indeed, as the male ideal incorporate of his sept, it is unlikely that many young women would have resisted his advances, nor would they have been expected to do so. His desire for her was an honour, while for the sept as a whole it was clearly desirable the *ri* or 'king' should father as many fine children as possible who, through the system of fosterage, would strengthen the dominant class and also cement social unity through the hierarchy.

The pre-Celtic Irish built stone circles (long after New Grange and other such mounds, but not infrequently surrounding them). Some, like this one at Drombeg, Co. Cork, are quite small. (None is as big as Stonehenge in England)

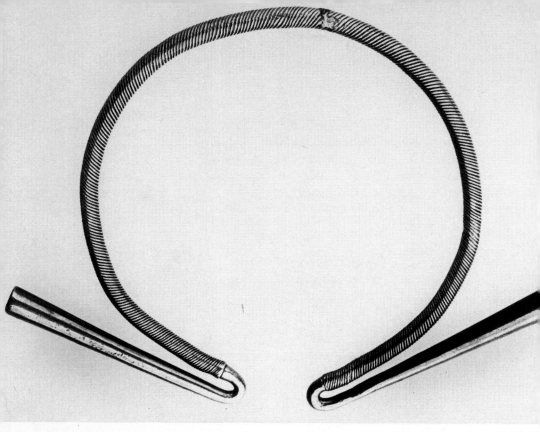

(above) An early Celtic gold torc. A torc would be worn by a woman, either as a necklace or a head-dress. Many were exported; others were stolen by Vikings. There was much gold in ancient Ireland – most of it was probably panned in the streams of Wicklow (*National Museum of Ireland*).

(right) Brooches made of gold, enamel and sometimes precious stones were perhaps the finest smaller artistic objects of Celtic times. On the reverse of this one is a little ogham writing – a simple form of inscription usually limited to names and more frequently associated with standing stones (*National Museum of Ireland*)

The sept consisted of a greater or lesser number of families which were in themselves miniature versions of the sept itself, paying taxes and owing obedience to the *ri*, collectively owning slaves or servile septs, and in time of war, known as hostings, duty-bound to provide warriors for the *ri*'s host. Frequently several septs would appoint a higher authority, with his own court but usually with little permanent real authority other than that provided by an occasional conclave. From these there developed eventually the so-called provinces of Ulster, Leinster, Munster, Connaught and, at one time, Meath. For generations one sept would be dominant over the others in its own province. Very rarely the provinces might go to war with one another, but any concept of a province as a nation would be grossly misleading, for frontiers as such scarcely existed. And though there was, in theory, a high king of all Ireland, in fact he never existed. For some centuries the sept of O'Neill, descendants of 'Niall of the Nine Hostages', claimed this high kingship with their capital at Tara, in Meath, but their writ did not run in, say, Kerry or Waterford or Donegal, for communications save by sea or river scarcely existed. And all this was based on the family, but their families were very different from what we understand by that word.

Love, in our sense of that word, had not of course been invented, and even when the troubadours made it popular in the eleventh and twelfth centuries it was invariably adulterous love. Sexual infatuation, however, was well known: defeating all reason, the irrational lust of one man for one woman, or vice versa, lies at the root of all the tragic sagas that are not primarily concerned with stealing other people's cows. For a chieftain to ignore the real interests of his people in order, to use an ancient Celtic expression, that he might follow a woman's rump hardly evoked respect. Also an infatuation could give the woman involved far too much power. In legend and in history, from Maebh to Lady Macbeth, from Gormflath to Mary Queen of Scots, the intrusion of women's passions into high politics has almost invariably been the precursor of disaster in the Celtic world. It would be extremely rash to suggest that sexual passion runs higher among Celts than among other Europeans, but the prevalence of puritanism in the very different modern churches of Scotland, Wales and Ireland would indicate a need for external control that is lacking in the basic social code. If it be not controlled by a restrictive morality based on religion, far better that the strange force be diffused, not merely or even principally for hedonistic reasons, but lest by concentration it result in folly which, among the masters, will inevitably effect far more people than the men and women involved, and, with almost equal inevitability, will endanger the stability of their society.

The last great popular leader of the Irish, Daniel O'Connell, was alleged by his enemies to have countless bastards: a generation later Parnell was hated by many, not because of his adultery (though the priests held it against him) but because he appeared to have allowed his heart to rule his head and to have placed his people second to his paramour. To this day, if chastity is so highly prized among Irish-women it is perhaps because it is so rare. Among Irishmen it is scarcely prized at all. Until very recent times it was felt that such paragons belonged in the priesthood, the monastery or the nunnery.

For in ancient days, the extended family system was enormously strengthened by the system of fosterage. Children were not brought up by their parents but by their cousins or uncles or aunts. (A faint echo of this can be detected in the appointment of god-parents.) This not only cemented the sept as the unit of society but made legitimacy far less relevant than in a purely patriarchal society. From pastoral times all real property, such as cows and sheep and slaves and usually horses, belonged to all the sept. With nothing of value to pass on to one's children save perhaps courage and beauty and brains, the very idea of primogeniture of succession became not merely meaningless but positively incomprehensible. When a new leader is needed, the best man within a certain kinship of the old, usually to a second or third cousinage, has usually already been selected, and the more children the old leader had the wider the candidacy from which his successor, the *Tanaiste*, could be made. There seldom seems to have been any doubt as to who the best *Tanaiste* was, nor any need for electioneering, for the Irish to this day watch their neighbours (in olden days their relations) most attentively, and the heir was usually accepted well before the old chieftain's death. Until the arrival of feudalism, struggles for the succession appear to have been so rare as to be noteworthy enough for occasional mention in the sagas. To this writer it would seem an almost ideal way to govern a small, homogeneous and basically classless though hierarchic society, for as will be seen the power of the *ri* was far from absolute.

Within the family or sept there were, of course, no slaves. There were however, as stated earlier, both slave and servile septs. This is a concept hard to express in meaningful terms of today, and in Celtic times it undoubtedly varied both in permanence and in quality. Thus at one time the O'Kennedys were a sept, probably of professional soldiers, servile to the O'Brien sept, roughly in the area where Limerick city now stands. The O'Kennedys, however, maintained their identity as a sept, and therefore preserved their own governing élite. Since the idea of property, as we know it, was alien to the Celts, it would be quite wrong to say that the O'Briens 'owned' the O'Kennedys. It would seem more likely that the servile sept, having been defeated in a tribal war and lost its leaders, was administered by a 'foreign' governing group either directly or through its own people. In effect this would probably mean that the servile sept was told in peacetime where it might graze its cows and sheep and, in time of war, was ordered to put its warriors (their *fianna* or host) at the disposal of their masters. Or it may have suffered the humiliation of tribal emasculation in being permitted no *fianna* of its own at all. Certainly the members of the servile sept extended family group were not, in our conventional sense, serfs or slaves, and not infrequently regained or gained 'free' status. Servility, however, was a humiliating condition, a sort of communal brand, which is occasionally used as an insult to this day. This emphasises once again the physical individuality and the historical continuity of the Celtic sept.

That continuity was in large measure entrusted to the poets, again an inadequate word, since they must be divided into two completely distinct categories, the *filidh* (whom we shall call the poets, since they were not only scholars but also creative) and the bards, who were in essence interpretative artists who learned, recited and sang the poets' words, often to the accompaniment of a harp or lute. The poet was the voice of undisputed authority, the bard its mouthpiece to reach the ears of the people. The words, however, were not those of the living poet (though a few might be his addition) but the saga of the sept into which was incorporated not only much genealogy leading back to the supreme and semi-divine prime ancestor but also 'good stories' acquired from almost any source and arranged with small regard for chronology or even probability. In order to qualify as a *file*, the poet had to learn, precisely, at least seven stories of varying length. There were ten grades: the highest, or *ollamh*, had to know at least three hundred and fifty. At the height of their power, in the fifth century A.D., the *ollamh* had the status of a small chieftain, with twenty-four attendants. As in the case with very learned men elsewhere, their tendency to arrogance aroused hostility among other members of the governing élite, so that thenceforth their power diminished. It must be repeated that while usually based on some sort of history, what they knew were not histories but stories. The greatest Welsh saga, the *Mabinogion*, contains large sections lifted directly from the slightly earlier Irish epics or more probably imported by those Irish who invaded Wales in the immediate post-Roman period. Similarly, much that is in the Irish sagas must have been acquired from the pre-Celtic inhabitants or imported from the continent of Europe. From internal evidence the scholars calculate that they became standarised sometime about the third century A.D. Local variants and additions, such as the genealogies already mentioned and tribal self-praise and perhaps something of tribal current affairs, were permitted, but otherwise it was the poet's duty to pass them on, and for the bards to broadcast those that were most popular, precisely as the poet first had heard them. Their importance for Celtic Ireland cannot be exaggerated. The stories of Cuchulain, Finn, Queen Maebh cut across the boundaries of sept, ignored the absence of any central administration and gave to the whole people a jealously guarded storehouse of language, tradition and custom.[1] It would hardly be an exaggeration that they fulfilled for the septs of Ireland a role that the Old Testament played for the scattered tribe of Judah, and the part of the *filidh* was not altogether dissimilar to that of the Prophets for their poems incorporated the so-called Brehon laws. As will be seen in a later chapter, this distant similarity was to endure in the *diaspora* of those two great peoples.

The poet, then, was a courtier and a most powerful one. Among his duties were the glorification of the sept in the person of its chieftain and the vilification of his foes. The Celts were well aware of the magic that lies dormant in words and that can be evoked by the magical power of the poet. To be cursed by an expert is at any time an unpleasant experience. In ancient Irish times it could lead to the death of the accursed. Perhaps a faint parallel can be found in the contemporary power of propaganda. A well-orchestrated propaganda barrage can persuade a class, even a nation, that it is so contemptible, puny and even immoral that it will lose the will to resist its enemies. Such was the technique applied by the poet to the hostile chieftain who incorporated the enemy sept. A great poet then was, in the most practical sense, a powerful and a dangerous man. The early Irish monks inherited, among much else, both the powers and the methods of the poets. The Norsemen (Vikings and Normans) and the original English did not. This is one of the basic reasons why the Irish have never really been conquered.

The bard, though he too might compose poems and songs, was not an awesome figure. He might be a sedentary member of the sept, but he appears more often to have been the forerunner of the strolling player. Save for the Dyke of the Black Pig between what is now, roughly, Ulster and the rest of Ireland and indicative of semi-permanent hostility, the four other 'kingdoms', as already stated, were geographical concepts rather than real political or administrative units, quite without borders and almost without roads. Most of Ireland was then forest or bog. Woodland tracks and ridge walks would connect the clearings, natural or man-made, where the septs would graze their herds or engage in rudimentary cultivation of their small, square fields. Hospitality was one of the customary virtues, and strangers with tales brought from far away were very welcome, none more so, we may be sure, than the bard tramping the woodland track with his head full of stories and songs, news and gossip from beyond the mountains. From *Samhain* to *Beltain*, from the autumn festival to that of early summer, the cold wet months of winter, this was the season for ballads and stories, seated around the turf fire in the blowy, smoky wooden hut. Then when the sun broke through and the grass began to grow and there was once again work to be done out of doors, perhaps the bard would rise and twitch his saffron cloak, sling his harp and move on, leaving songs and memories behind him. He long outlived the purely Celtic society whence he sprang. Blind Raftery, perhaps the last, died in 1835 and his songs and poems were collected and edited by Douglas Hyde – who many years later was to be first President of the Irish Free State – and published in 1903.[2]

Of the Celts as warriors we know a great deal and from sources that generally confirm one another. During its millenium of near-isolation or at least freedom from large scale invasion, Ireland's wars were inter-tribal affairs, almost always fought according to the rules and customs by what would nowadays be called professional armies. These courtly struggles were either fought for booty, usually in the form of cows, or to avenge a personal insult. These skirmishes – for they were little more – between septs, occasionally in temporary alliances, were not exterminatory though they probably on occasion produced that status of servility earlier mentioned. Meanwhile in the middle of this period of quiet in Ireland, a major Celtic war was fought in what is now France. And the Roman legions were not only commanded by one of the most skilled generals known to history but by a general who, for political reasons, had to send home a long despatch or description of each campaign. Being a first rate general, he attached great importance to military intelligence, and much of what he learned about the Celtic enemy found its way into his despatches. The nature of his war was very different from those of Cuchulain or Finn, for he realised that in order to protect Provence from Celtic attack he must defeat and occupy all Gaul. This was no tribal war, but a head-on collision between two societies. Although the Gauls, too, had a brilliant general in Vercingétorix he could not rally the tribes (whose fighting men far outnumbered the Roman legionaries) in time to prevent their destruction in detail. It was Roman administration that really won the war, for this enabled Caesar to evolve a strategy while his enemies usually had none, the tactics of the Gauls being those suitable to tribal skirmishes, not to a major war. These tactics, however, confirm what we can glean from the Irish sagas and are supported by archaeological evidence.

Each sept or tribe had its own army or *fianna*, the chieftain being the supreme commander and leader in battle. The warriors enjoyed a somewhat privileged status, their needs being provided by the sept as a whole, nor were they expected to work save perhaps when some crisis, such as a bumper harvest, called for immediate extra manpower. A varying proportion of these experts with sword, shield and javelin were mercenaries: later, when such mercenaries were imported from the Hebrides into Ireland they were known as 'galloglasses', a particular ferocious warrior of mixed Viking and Celtic descent, but there is nothing derogatory about the word. A war tax was paid by all, with exceptions among the Druids (of whom more later) and other administrators: and in a major war almost the entire male population – and sometimes the women too – were expected to fight. The leaders and officers of the host formed part of the chieftain's court, and besides providing him with a bodyguard when needed, were also on occasion used in what we would call a diplomatic role. Chariots were rare apparently and were not used as fighting vehicles, but for ceremonial purposes. The warriors frequently fought naked and probably oiled their bodies so that there was nothing for the enemy to grasp.

In attack the most popular tactic was the ambush. In defence use was, of course, made of territory, but the Celts did not build walls. They were still, psychologically, nomads and relied on speed both in attack and in retreat. It may be merely coincidence that the Irish were using the same tactics against the British in 1920 and that the ambush-and-vanish tactic is basic to the Irish Army of today. Or it may not: how a people reacts to a killing situation may emanate from the collective unconscious.

Sometimes a tribal dispute would develop slowly enough for diplomacy to be invoked, but sometimes such diplomacy would fail. A battle would then be arranged by the opposing Druids, a type of trial by combat which seems to have been as formalised as a medieval tournament. Though it is believed that on occasion the Druids would forbid a war. Since they were the voice of divinity, their orders were usually obeyed. (The Druids, whose role varied from place to place and time to time, were always the spiritual and very often the temporal advisers of the *ri*, as well as being custodians of the sept's beliefs and education. Thus in some ways the form of government was theocratic, again not unlike Brahmin rule in parts of pre-British India.) If there were to be war, the opposing hosts would be drawn up, facing one another. The two kings, perhaps in chariots, would ride up and down, each accompanied by his *file* and an administrative Druid. The *ri* might not speak before his Druid, but first the long ritual of mutual insults was tried. If neither leader was shamed into retreat or even death, single combat, almost certainly on foot, was the next step: we may perhaps envisage something not unlike the fight between Hector and Achilles, the two hosts doubtless cheering on their champions. After this, anything might happen. One *ri* might be killed or disabled, and the Druids might agree that the battle had been won or lost. Or the warriors might hurl themselves upon one another in a bloody mêlée. Then the killing would probably be great, another saga born. Whatever the outcome, be it victory or a draw, the battle would only be of short duration, since there was no organised method of supply. Rout must have been the normal ending. Or both armies might withdraw, to fight again. Or diplomacy would be renewed, the Druids deciding on the outcome and pronouncing on the spoils of war. No doubt the women of both sides usually watched from some convenient hilltop, and helped the wounded, and keened the dead. While for the victors there followed the great feast with ample wine, imported of course, perhaps by latter-day Danaans.

The role of what are here called 'the Druids' is perhaps what is most striking, since the same men seem both to have served, advised and even pre-empted their chieftain while also acting as umpires and even perhaps linesmen at this, the real sport of kings. So it might be as well to end this chapter here and to devote the next to Celtic religion and to summarising what we know about the nature and function of these Druids, remembering always that we are not dealing with a generation but with some thirty or forty generations. During such a time even the most static society must change, and the nature and activities of the men who run it must change even more. But we are here most concerned with the period, roughly, between Caesar's Gallic War (58–52 B.C.), the great Ulster saga of Cuchulain, probably based on events that took place in the first century A.D., and the Fenian saga's historic basis which is dated as having its root in events further south about one hundred and fifty or two hundred years later.

NOTES

1 These sagas, quasi-myths and legends have been recounted so often in English over the past two and a half centuries since 'Ossian' – each generation finding in them what it would – that there is no definite English version. Quite apart from the poetry which is of their essence, the Irish in which they were composed is a matter of constant scholarly examination. And the audiences to which they were recited or sung are more remote from ourselves than are those who first listened to Homer, for the Homeric tradition has never died in western literature: the ancient Irish sagas are preserved in academic formaldehyde. Even in those pockets of the Gaeltacht where Irish is still a living language, these old stories are perhaps as meaningful as is the *Iliad* to the inhabitants of remote corners of modern Greece.

2 Antoine O'Reachtabra was born in the County Mayo in 1784 and blinded by smallpox in his early years. As a travelling fiddler he spent most of his life in and around the County Galway. He was a poet without formal education. He chose as his subjects for his poems and ballads contemporary events, such as Daniel O'Connell's victory in the famous Clare election of 1828, a drowning tragedy and the hanging of a Whiteboy leader. He also wrote a metrical history of Ireland and some most attractive love lyrics.

3
THE CELTS IN HISTORY

The migrant Celtic-speaking peoples first appear unmistakably in European history in the middle of the first millenium B.C., though evidence of their cultural identity in their south German and Swiss homeland predates this by another thousand years, when they were trading with the Mycenaeans, among others. (For the best brief and readable history of this group of tribes the reader is referred to *The Celts* by T. G. E. Powell.) They moved first into what we now call Bohemia, the Balkans, northern Italy and France. In Italy they clashed with the Etruscans, whom they overcame to create what the Romans were to call Cisalpine Gaul. They gave tribal names to what are now the cities of Milan and Bologna, among many others, and in about 390 B.C. they sacked Rome itself. They only ceased to be a menace when the Romans defeated them at the Battle of Telamon in 225 B.C. and finally subdued them thirty years later. By then the second Carthaginian War had been won, Rome was the greatest Mediterranean power, and the creation of the Roman Empire under way.

In the Balkans Alexander the Great had had to fight Celtic migrant tribes, described as coming from the Adriatic, in Bulgaria. Two generations later there was a tribal invasion of Greece itself, in which the warriors were accompanied by their families. Raiders captured Delphi in 279 B.C., but were repulsed. Kinsmen, however, went on to create Galatia in what is now Turkey. In France, or Transalpine Gaul, they occupied or controlled the whole area save for the Greek province based on Marseilles. It was the threat they constituted to Provence that caused Julius Caesar finally to compel their submission. The Romans failed to subdue the trans-Rhenish Celts (the names Allemanni and Teutones both refer to Celtic-speaking tribes) and the Belgae, who straddled the lower Rhine, migrated in large numbers to southern England in about 150 B.C. These spoke the later and more sophisticated P-Celtic. How and whence the Q-Celtic speakers had earlier come to Ireland is unknown, but their remains indicate that they and their culture were well established by 300 B.C. and possibly earlier. It is this author's belief that this was no tribal migration, as with the later move of the Belgae into Britain, but conquest by dominant warriors who imposed their language and their modes on the earlier inhabitants. Whether there had been an invasion between the time of the New Grange people and the arrival of the Celts is unknown. It seems improbable that there was not. Certainly the Basques were great sailors and near at hand. Legend speaks of Milesians, who came from Spain. These may have been Basques or Celtiberians. In any event, such invaders left little trace. Skull measurements, so popular in the last century, are no longer regarded as particularly indicative. Both the ancient Irish and the Celts appear to have been a mixture of the brachycephalic (round skulled) and dolichacephalic (long skulls). It does seem that in general the Celts were tall and blond or red-headed, the older Irish smaller, swarthier and black haired. The two contrasting types are still very apparent today, despite much subsequent immigration and intermarriage.

Nor were the Q-Celts followed in any great numbers by the more sophisticated, house-building P-speaking Gaels, though contact existed with these once they were established in Wales and the Strathclyde area, which must have been moderately close contact but usually hostile. There were probably numerous fugitives when the Roman general Agricola conquered and incorporated the Welsh and lowland Scots (as we would now call them) into the British province. In emulation, perhaps, of Julius Caesar's pursuit of the Belgae into Britain, Agricola prepared to invade Ireland in A.D. 82, moving troops and amassing military stores, particularly in Anglesey, but abandoned the idea either on his own initiative or perhaps on orders from Rome. This would indicate that there was no mass migration from Britain, nor did the Irish ever cause the Romans in Britain enough trouble to necessitate a major campaign. Besides, the Romans hated going to sea: an occasional pirate or even a raid was not enough to warrant an attempt to capture and colonise Ireland. Thus apart from a few Roman coins and wares brought by merchants, the Romans of the Empire left no trace in Ireland nor affected Irish culture. It was left to another Rome to conquer, in another way, Ireland and to make the first great imprint on the Celtic Irish soul.

It would be wrong to say that the Irish had a religion, in any way resembling what we mean by that word, before their conversion to Christianity. It would be wrong to say that they 'believed' in magic save in the way that we 'believe' in weather. Magic, good or bad, was always with them, inescapable. Certain aspects of this magic, certain forces, might be given names, and these the Romans in the Celtic-speaking lands that they controlled attempted to identify with the gods of their pantheon. In Ireland, however, there was no imported Mount Olympus. For the Irish the magic was very old, very powerful, omnipresent. It still is, and not merely among country people who revere holy wells or certain trees and are cautious about fairies and such, but in far deeper and more widespread ways that at times can come close to fatalism, at other times to suicidal, sense-less violence. In modern times it is to be detected in Bishop Berkeley's philosophy and the paradox that was Oscar Wilde, as in much of Yeats' poetry and prose. Foreigners find it hard to understand, so attractive to some, so infuriating to others. An anonymous Irish poem, here translated by Frank O'Connor, perhaps sums up what cannot easily be explained in English prose:

> 'Have you seen Hugh,
> The Connacht king in the field?'
> 'All that we saw
> Was his shadow under his shield.'

In so far as these intimations of the supernatural could be formed into a coherent proto-religion, this was done by the Celts in Ireland – or more probably by their precursors – according to the calendar. The year was based upon the lunar month (with the twelve extra days forming 'the twelve days of Christmas') and the pre-Celtic stone circles are concerned astronomically with the rising and setting of the moon in the first place, only incidentally with the solar year. The extreme age of this calendar is shown not only in the Stonehenge-type circles, but also in the fact that it refers to a pastoral, as opposed to an agricultural, way of life. It is probable that there were originally three seasons, the opening dates of which coincide only by deliberate, later adaptation to those of the great Christian festivals.

Samhain became for the Christians Hallowe'en, that is to say All Souls' and All Saints' day or to be more precise the night between them. It marked the end of one year and the beginning of the next, for it was then that the herds were gathered in from the hillsides and the whole *tuath* assembled for a great feast, the majority of the sheep or cattle being killed off, enough kept for breeding in the spring and probably to make the mid-winter feast. The first day of spring, in Ireland, is still 1 February and is Saint Brigid's day. Here there is not even a substitution of names. Brigid, at the other end of the Aryanspeakers' spectrum, is Brhati in Sanskrit, 'the exalted one', the essence of life-giving femininity. Winter, in fact, does not of course end on 1 February, but it is about then that the ewes begin to lactate. As the 'goddess' of fertility, Brigid was the most important of all the named and incorporated powers and can without doubt be connected to Rhea, the Helladic and pre-Helladic mother goddess of those most remote times when paternity was not understood and the essence of magical divinity was Robert Graves's 'white goddess', the mother of Zeus and of all that lives. The third great festival was *Beltain*, our May Day, when the cattle and sheep were driven forth to graze and the *tuatha* scattered. A fourth ancient festival was that of *Lug*, on 1 August. This most important divine force seems to have been a comparatively late comer, for he was responsible for the ripening of crops. He was, indeed, the lord of every skill, probably including the building of houses, for derivatives of his name occur in early place-names from areas the length and breadth of Europe.

There was a plethora of other divine forces, anthropomorphic or zoomorphic, that cut across tribal boundaries and varied in importance both in time and in place. The mystery of the woman whom age transforms from beautiful maiden to hideous hag recurs. She is frequently connected with battles and slaughter. As Badh, she appeared to the Ulster hero Cuchulain, wearing a blood-red cloak with red eyebrows, mounted in a chariot, a figure of horror. Later she becomes a carrion crow, who terrifies and weakens warriors and gloats over bloodshed and death. The gentle, loving, life-giving Brigit was not the only aspect of the feminine to strike roots in the Irish unconscious.[1]

When Rome was sacked, and later Delphi, the Romans and the Greeks were both informed by their Celtic conquerors that their general's name was Brennus. Over a century separates these events. It is quite possible that there were two warriors with the same name. It is more likely that a tribe which gave its name to Brno in Bohemia came over the Brenner pass, defeated the Etruscans and settled in Cisalpine Gaul. Coming from the Adriatic, they may have fought Alexander the Great in what is now Bulgaria while other warriors found the Roman senators rigid in their seats, mysterious and frightening, until some soldier pulled one of their beards. Later still this fierce sept, or group of septs, may have attacked Greece. But so homogeneous and ferocious a group would hardly then have vanished from history. To this writer it would seem far more probable that some form of a word with the stem 'Bren' was a 'god' of war. Did not the ancient Jews, after Moses had melted all their gods into a single divinity, on occasion refer to Jahveh as 'the lord of hosts'? Perhaps Brennus was never a man but only the principle of war and of conquest. Whether man, or god or abstract principle, Brennus does not appear to have reached Irish shores, though many of his like did so.

It is probable that each of the *tuatha*, besides being in itself 'divine' with its magical identity incorporated in its chieftain or kinglet, had its own 'gods' of fertility, war and so on, which may or may not have formed part of a greater non-being. In his intriguing book *Ten Thousand Saints*, Hubert Butler advances the hypothesis that every Celtic name derived from the tribe's most remote known ancestor, himself automatically divine, that divinity later being expressed in a tribal name and, with the arrival of Christianity, the founder's divinity becoming sainthood. With the much later introduction of surnames and the break-up of the ancient septs a man's surname becomes an integral part of his own magical identity, while the bestowal of Christian names, on his child, is a deliberate invocation of saintly patronage.

If the beliefs of the ancient Irish are in no way to be equated with a religion, so the role of the Druid was not at all that of a rabbi or Christian priest, though in general closer to the first than to the second. Since the Druid's whole justification, like that of the *filidh* and the Brehon 'lawyer', was based on an enormous knowledge of tribal history, passed down verbally and with the greatest possible exactitude, it was really in their functions alone that these powerful courtiers and king-makers differed the one from the other. In Ireland some, if not all, of these men could write and some knew Latin and probably Greek. We know this from their Ogham inscriptions of memorial names, in which notches in stone corners (or more often in wood which has not survived) are based upon the Greek alphabet. That they did not write the sagas and genealogies can only have been a rigid form of professional protection. To have druidical power, a man had to have a long and arduous training. The absolute purity of druidical knowledge could only be maintained by such exclusivity, for the written word can be tampered with in a multitude of ways for a multitude of purposes. There, too, was the Irish language preserved with almost no change for a very long time. The druidical student had to be word perfect in the many poems and sagas that he learned. It is of course possible, and even probable, that there were druidical writings which have perished. If so, they were kept secret. But it is hard to believe that the Druid Divitiacus, friend of Cicero and Caesar, was illiterate.

The early Irish monks were the successors of the Druids, even in some of their methods of training. They, too, were drawn from the governing warrior group or, in modern parlance, class, but rather less so than their predecessors, the Brahmins of Ireland. Only later, when they were victims of intensive propaganda, were the Druids portrayed as vulgar magicians or conjurors. In effect their real powers passed first to the monks, and with the decay and final abolition of monasticism in Ireland, to the rejuvenated priesthood of the Counter-reformation. Just as the Irish had had little contact with the Romano-Grecian world of antiquity, so they had no Renaissance in the Italian or French or English sense, for there was nothing of classical antiquity to be reborn. Only a certain spiritual continuity links the modern mixture of people called the Irish with their remote forebears. 'The land of saints and scholars' is a description of Ireland now used only as sarcasm. Yet it has within it a grain of truth, if only that since druidical times such is what many Irishmen would have liked their country to be, and a few have tried to make it so. It is not their fault that they have always failed. The Druids would have given short shrift to the gunman or the gombeen man.

NOTE

1 According to some, Brigid had an alternative name, Dana or Danu and presided over a sort of Celtic pantheon named, after her, Danans. The great god, the 'good' god, Dagda, was her son or her father or perhaps both. This Dagda was enormous, very strong, carried a huge club. He is the man of Cerne and brews a very strong beer. T. G. E. Powell mentions Dana or Danu and her pantheon once only in his study of the Celtic 'other' world. Since there was no Celtic-speaking centre of administrative power, this writer can see no reason why or how they should have conceived of a divine pantheon ruled by a goddess.

4
ST. PATRICK

So long as a Christian Ireland exists its apostle and its first patron saint will be St. Patrick. He was undoubtedly an historical figure of European importance, and his story was written in the late eighth and early ninth centuries. Since he had then been dead for over two hundred years (that is to say for a period longer than what is usually accepted between the Crucifixion and the writing of the Gospels) and since the scribes at Armagh, Cashel and elsewhere who were ordered to write down the stories were themselves Christian monks, *The Book of Armagh* can hardly be called a biography. Yet the druidical insistence on precise repetition had been passed on to the monks and there is enough evidence from other sources to have permitted scholars to compile a fairly accurate life of the saint.

St. Patrick was born, probably in Britain, most likely in North Wales or what is now Lancashire or Cumbria, in about the year 385. Britain was in a state of chaos. Maximus had withdrawn the three legions that garrisoned their part of the island two years before, and almost immediately the wild Irish from Scotland and the Welsh began to raid and plunder what is now England. In 390 a legion was sent to restore order, which it seems to have done in some measure before it was finally withdrawn by a usurper, in 407, with the purpose of making himself emperor. Immediately the raiders were back, and, lacking any armed forces themsleves according to deliberate Roman policy, the Romano-British called upon the northern European barbarians, who had prototypical navies, for help. Soon enough the Anglo-Saxons (though there were few Angles among them) and the Jutes arrived. That these ferocious pagans did not go away is well known, but they did clear the wilder Celts from most of what was now England. Some of the romanised British undoubtedly went with the Romans, others fled to Brittany, which had hitherto been Armorica, a remote but romanised province, but the majority were absorbed into becoming the English.

It was in these chaotic conditions that at an early age, though we do not know when, the boy Patrick was kidnapped and taken across the seas, probably to what is now the County Antrim where he was made to tend sheep. Of his origins we know nothing. It may be purely coincidental, or even a captor's joke, that links his name with the patricians of Romano-Britain.[1] It is unlikely that pirates would normally bother with a boy of less than about ten years of age, since his value would be too slight. We know that he had no education, since this fact was held against him in later life, so let us assume that he was transported to Ireland in about 395 and that he was a shepherd for twelve years, for he left Ireland in 407, when he was about twenty-two. He thus arrived in England at the time when the last Roman legion, having restored a semblance of order, was about to depart for ever. Having lived through a generation of terror undoubtedly many Romano-Britons who were not tied to the land (the administrative class) would have foreseen the new horrors to come and, if possible, have gone with them. It was, incidentally, among this class of Romano-Britons that Christianity was by then most widespread. Would the future saint have joined them?

This is the purest supposition, but we know that St. Patrick spent very little time in England, if indeed he went there at all, and was taken by friendly sailors to France, where he was once again taken prisoner by the pagan Franks: in any event by 410 he was in Tours, the city of the great and fierce St. Martin, where he could and presumably did learn much from the great man's disciples, though what he learned would seem to have been of a religious rather than of a purely cultural nature.

Had he come of peasant stock, why should his lack of education been later held against him as it explicitly was? And who, as he walked across France, in those days when the still semi-pagan Franks were plundering and murdering the largely Christianised Gauls, would have understood the remote Q-Celtic of County Antrim or even the P-Celtic of Wales? Yet he travelled the country, from one Christian centre to another, first to Milan, where he may have met or at least seen St. Ambrose. It is pure speculation to guess that his original family had been Latin-speaking Romano-Britons of patrician origin and the Christian religion, and that among the lovely hills and glens of Antrim, while herding his sheep, the boy had remembered a past where Latin was spoken and the God of Christ worshipped. Such childish memories are the foundations upon which a paradise can be built. Perhaps it was this that he wished to create when, in 432, a man nearing fifty, he returned, voluntarily this time, to Ireland.

The administrative structure of the Christian Church in the time of St. Patrick was very different from what it later became, though it was already in a state of 'becoming'. Owing in part to the so-called Donation of Constantine (much later shown to be an eighth century forgery), the Bishop of Rome was appointed the spiritual and temporal head of the Church in the old Western Empire. Constantine the Great had become a Christian in 312, though he was not baptised until 335. Meanwhile he had moved the capital of the whole Empire from Rome to Byzantium (Constantinople) in 326. With the supreme administrative apparatus, the intellectual and spiritual authority also moved to the East. Jerusalem, which would, in addition now to Constantinople, have been the obvious centre of Christendom, was unsuitable partly because of the intransigence of the Jews, partly because of the Judaeo-Roman wars. There were already two eastern episcopacies of prime importance, that of Antioch, the city of St. Paul, and that of Alexandria, the intellectual capital of the late Graeco-Roman world. In the West, Rome was the fourth but the least important in St. Patrick's time. (Antioch and Alexandria did not fall to the Persians and the Arabs until early in the seventh century.) The great theological disputes had already taken place, in the East, and though the final break between the Roman and the Orthodox churches did not take place until 1054, there was already a marked divergence. It has been said that the Eastern Church was primarily concerned with theology, that is to say with the nature of God, while the primary interest of the Western Church lay in anthropology, by which is meant the spiritual nature and needs of man and his relationship with the divine. In any event the two churches were beginning to evolve in differing directions by 407 and certain theological disagreements were unresolved. In St. Patrick's time the Patriarch of Asia still had his seat in Antioch, while Alexandria was the centre of theology.

The Bishop of Rome had other problems. Not only were the provinces being overrun by pagans, but various heresies were rife. The Goths had recently overrun most of Italy and in 408 first besieged Rome itself. In 410, after a slave revolt within the city, under their king Alaric they captured Rome, the first foreigners to do so since Brennus. They were Christians of a sort, though those who settled in northern Italy had only recently received the faith from the Eastern Church and tended towards the Arian heresy. The great rival of Christianity, particularly among the Roman soldiers, had been the originally Persian religion of Mithras. Although

Mithraism had vanished, or was vanishing along with the last Roman legions, it had infected the approved Christianity of Rome in the form of the Manichaean heresy, rampant in North Africa, Spain and above all in the south of France, where it lingered on in Provence, as an element of the Albigensian heresy, until finally suppressed by the northern French with the utmost brutality in the fourteenth century. There were other heresies active in the disintegrating Western Empire, quite apart from the influx of Arian or totally pagan Germanic and Hunnish tribes. Frankish tribes were pouring across the Rhine from Germany, in the late fourth and early fifth centuries, and it was not until near the end of this that the first Frankish 'king', one Clodorich, became a Christian in 496.

Throughout that horrible fifth century in western Europe, the Bishop of Rome who was beginning to call himself the Pope (in the Eastern Church all Christian priests are popes, *papas*, fathers to their parishioners) had therefore very little power save in one respect: he had inherited the old Roman administration and, of course, the roads which had made that administration possible were in existence up to the limits or *limes* of the old Empire. *Grosso modo*, the imperial system was given a new clerical life. As late as the time of Richelieu the French dioceses corresponded almost exactly with the old proconsulates and the bishop replaced the pro-consul in spiritual and often in temporal matters too. It is true that the prince-bishop was a commoner type of ruler later in Germany, but the concept was one that was totally acceptable in the rest of Europe, an adaptation *in petto* of the Roman god–emperor. One of the root causes of Henry VIII of England's breach with Rome was that he claimed to be an emperor and therefore head of the Church in his empire and in no way, spiritual or temporal, answerable to anyone in Rome or anywhere else. At the time of writing, 1982, Mr. Ian Paisley, self-appointed head of his church, is making an almost identical claim in Northern Ireland. He would strengthen his hand, at least among scholars, if he were to promote himself bishop.

For this matter of bishops is one that has played a major part in the history of Christian administration, and nowhere more so than in Ireland. The bishop was and is above all an administrator. In the Western Church, which will for convenience henceforth be referred to as the Roman Church, these successors to the pro-consuls were under the direct control of the pope, who was almost always elected by the patricians of Rome. Even when the great nation states arose, and their rulers claimed autonomy, they only went all the way by courting almost certain excommunication. In the French Gallican Church, for example, the king or head of state when France has been an empire or a republic, has appointed the French bishops, but only after the choice has received the approval of Rome. Ireland had known no pro-consuls and had no Roman roads. And when St. Patrick attempted to introduce the Roman system, he failed, as will be seen. The earliest Christian Irish looked beyond Rome for a model and exemplar. What they found was the monasticism which had been introduced into France from Egypt and, to a lesser extent, from Africa.

St Paul, unlike Christ, had insisted on abstinence, on chastity, on poverty, in a word on asceticism. This implied withdrawal from the world, and led logically to the life of the hermit. In approximately the year 270 St Anthony (the model but certainly not the first hermit) sold his property at Heracleopolis, in Middle Egypt, and went to live in the desert. For some fifteen years he saw only other cenobites, who lived as he did, attending mass with the inhabitants of a nearby village. Desiring still greater solitude he went further, to a place named Pispir. After some twenty-five years of such solitude, during which his way of life must nevertheless have been bruited about, he suddenly found that a veritable horde of would-be ascetics had arrived at Pispir, to emulate his way of life. St. Anthony obliged them and gave them an occasional lecture on how they should live. Thus was the first Christian monastic settlement established.

Some three hundred miles up the Nile from Pispir a certain ascetic named Palaemon established a similar settlement, presumably while St. Anthony, who is reputed to have lived to the age of 105, was still alive. Among Palaemon's followers was Pachomius, the son of pagan parents and at one time a soldier and probably an officer in the army of Constantine, where no doubt he had learned of Christianity, though he was baptised at one of the small churches in the Thebaid named Chenoboskion, near Palaemon's settlement. Before his death in 348 Pachomius had founded at least four monastic settlements and, what is here more relevant, had laid down a rule for their administration. It was written in Coptic, translated into Greek and, in 404, by St. Jerome into Latin.

These basic regulations for the monastic life and for the administration of monasteries have an almost military ring to them. For example, all the monks were to be dressed alike, i.e. were put into uniform, and previous spiritual rank in the outside world meant nothing: that is to say, a priest who became a monk was in no way superior nor could expect any difference in treatment than any other monk who had taken the vows of chastity, obedience and so on. Each monastery had its commanding officer or abbot and he was appointed by the supreme monastic officer of the group of monasteries, the archimandrite, who appointed the abbots and could discipline or transfer them or their subject monks. Each superior or abbot had a second-in-command who assumed total responsibility if his direct superior were for some reason unable to discharge his duties. Accounts were rendered annually to the chief steward of the brotherhood. At an annual meeting of all the monks, but presumably at no other time, complaints could be made by the ordinary monks to the archimandrite, and the rules could even be changed. The archimandrite appointed his successor on his deathbed or earlier. The tasks assigned to each monk, the hours of prayer and so on were rigidly laid down. One feels that not for nothing had Pachomius learned of Christianity while a soldier. Even the proper number of souls for each group of monasteries, some six to seven thousand, seems to have corresponded to the Constantinian legion. It is obvious from its great and immediate popularity that the system was highly efficient, and fulfilled well the purpose for which it was designed. It endured until the Muslims overran the area in the mid-seventh century.

John Cassian, who had been with the Egyptian monks at the very end of the fourth century, brought back their monastic theories which rapidly spread throughout southeast Gaul after certain superficial adaptations to suit the climate. Early in the new century, for he died in 429, St. Honoratus, a member of a noble family, founded such a monastery on the then bleak island of Lérins, off the coast near what is now Cannes. St. Honoratus was an exceptionally strict abbot on his snake- and scorpion-infested island, and although there was no written book of rules, he adhered to the Egyptian traditions.

St. Patrick had heard, probably in Milan, of the strictly ruled monastic settlement on Lérins. It had been his intention to go on to the holy city of Rome, but the Gothic armies may have made this impossible. Instead he went to Lérins. It was there, under the rule of Honoratus, that he learned much, but not enough. Somehow he appears to have received a letter from Ireland. 'We beseech thee, holy youth, to come hitherto and walk once more among us.' In a book ascribed to St. Jerome he is reported to have described Lérins as a veritable paradise. Yet he knew that he had a great mission to fulfil and he decided that he must evangelise Ireland. For this purpose, Honoratus would have told him, he must be more than a mere devout monk, but must have ecclesiastical orders and a commission from the authorities of the Church. He must, in fact, become a bishop if he would ordain Irish priests.

Again he tried to walk to Rome and beg for such a commission from the Holy See. He got, however, no further than Auxerre. What he had learned at Lérins was enough to allow the ruling bishop, St. Amator, to ordain him for the diaconate, a deacon in those days being the least educated priest in the hierarchy. He remained in Auxerre for some years, studying under St. Germanus who succeeded Amator as bishop in 418. He studied hard and acquired the profound knowledge of holy writ needed for his mission. However, it was not he who was sent to Ireland but the obviously more powerful and experienced Palladius, in the year 431.

The background is curious and elusive. In 429 St. Germanus (St. Patrick's superior at Auxerre) and St. Lupus of Troyes had been sent under the aegis of Palladius as representatives of the Holy See and of the Gallic Church to Britain, to quell yet another outburst of heresy. This time the Pelagian one. This seems to have been a comparatively easy mission, for a year later the two saints were back in Gaul, but it was now decided that a missionary be sent to Ireland. Why? Perhaps the few Christians in Ireland had been tainted with the Pelagian heresy, or perhaps Pelagian heretics had fled there from Britain. Nobody had ever bothered about the Irish before. It may be assumed that Germanus asked Patrick about these remote people, since there can have been few if any other clerics in Gaul who knew the remote place at all. In any event it was decided, on the return of Germanus from Britain in 430, that a mission, headed by a bishop, be sent to Ireland. Patrick ardently desired the appointment, and a council was called at Auxerre, without apparently consulting the Pope. Patrick had a close friend in whom he had confided some secret sin committed in his early teens, more than twenty years before. Now the Gallic churchmen prided themselves not merely on their priestly qualifications but also on their worldly sophistication. Patrick's simple, country ways and his lack of general education, what has been quaintly called his 'rusticity', counted heavily against him in such an assembly. The betrayal by his friend of the boyhood secret sin was seized upon as sufficient reason not to appoint him bishop. The council recommended the far better known and more powerful priest, Palladius, the man who had himself first recommended the Germanus mission to Britain. Pope Celestine, who in distant Rome had certainly never even heard of Patrick, could only agree, and Palladius was appointed first bishop and missionary to the Irish. It almost broke Patrick's heart, and as he is reported to have said it well nigh destroyed his faith in his mission if not in his God. Palladius set off for Ireland in 431. Whether he arrived there or not, and if so what experiences he had, we do not know. We do know that within a year he was dead, and left no legend behind him. St. Patrick was annointed bishop and sent to Ireland in his place. That was in the year A.D. 432.

He walked the wild and wooded country for twenty-nine years. It is often said that he converted 'the Irish'. He certainly did not convert all the Irish, but he laid such foundations for Christianity that those who came after him and those he trained had little difficulty in continuing his mission. One wonders if occasionally, as he made his way through almost trackless forest beneath the endless rain, he ever remembered the sunny certainties of the disciplined life he had known on Lérins. Certainly he spoke in high praise of the monastic system. He did not, however, found any monasteries, or at the most one, for while he appointed many bishops he consecrated but a single abbot.

The Ireland to which St. Patrick returned had changed little since his departure. Indeed the fifth century's turbulence and migrations scarcely touched the remote island in the Atlantic. Since it had formed no part of the Roman Empire, the total and atrocious collapse of the Western Empire scarcely affected it. In the extreme north the Irish increased their offensive against the Picts and, calling themselves now Scots, became the dominant people there. With the final withdrawal of the legions, northern Wales became easier prey for raiders, but lacking any central political authority the Irish failed to create any form of colony there, though Anglesey became once again a druidical centre. For the first, and up to the present day the last, time the Irish could have become the dominant political force in their part of the world. They lacked the administration, and perhaps the will, to play the imperialist role. They were enjoying a period of public tranquillity, and as always happens everywhere were unaware of their good fortune.

In Ireland itself the five provinces (the Irish word equivalent to province means a fifth) had become the four green fields that have endured, Ulster, Munster, Leinster and Connaught. The island was politically dominated, though certainly not ruled, from two centres, or meeting places, Tara, of the Ui Neills, in the north and Cashel, of the Eoghanast dynasties, in the south, with a vague and fluctuating border between the two. The great fights of the past were now part of the sagas. Only smaller cattle-raids and personal vendettas disturbed an essentially peaceful country, where Brehon law and druidical culture were accepted as permanent.[2] An almost uniform language and art prevailed.

It is now, almost for the first and certainly for the last time, that we can see the artistic creation of the Irish with a minimum of foreign influence and adulteration. What we find is a period of what Malraux called 'aristocratic' art – at least so far as the visual arts are concerned, an ossification of forms to please an established taste, in a word a period of decadence. Indeed until the infusion of Christianity, and with it the echoes of a dead world, had really permeated the Irish vision, in the seventh century, there was little if any originality even in their famous metal and enamel work.

Work in gold and silver had always been remarkably skilled among the Celts, and this skill was imported into Ireland as part of the La Tène culture. Among the most remarkable objects made by the Celts were their torcs and their very elaborate brooches. Not many of the torcs were in fact twisted metal but the word *torqui* was applied by the Romans to all these neck rings. From the earliest times they were beautiful and costly objects, usually of gold, less often of silver, while a few bronze torcs have been found. The terminals of the torc were often most elaborately cast, to represent the heads of real or mythical animals or abstract forms. They appear to have originated in ancient Persia and their purpose is not fully understood. Many have been found in women's graves, and it was long thought that they were ornaments worn either as collars or as diadems. A more recent theory is that they were status symbols and that the bronze ones, for instance, were worn by soldiers to indicate that they were freemen.

The purpose of the elaborate safety pins and ordinary pins is obvious and utilitarian, since men and women wore cloaks over kilts, only servingmen and charioteers wearing a form of breeches. The beauty and complexity of these brooches, made of precious metal and further decorated with coral and enamel, clearly reflect the wealth of the owner. Bracelets and rings were also worn for purely decorative purposes.

None of these forms, or indeed any other form of metal work, originated in Ireland, but the Irish craftsmen were very highly skilled and since there was much gold in Ireland some of the most beautiful objects were of Irish origin, though the highest artistic period of Celtic metal work seems to have corresponded with the great expansions of the first millenium B.C. and thus before or during the Celtic invasion. That so much of this exquisite metal work had been found in Ireland is explicable in that it was looted neither by Romans nor by fifth century barbarians. This was left to the Vikings, and it has been suggested that today there is more ancient Irish jewellery and ornamental gold or silver in Scandinavia than in Ireland. By the time of St. Patrick, in any case, little was being made and even less shows any originality, being copies of earlier work. It may well be that the gold supply was becoming exhausted.

Nor was other decorative work, such as is to be found on Irish scabbards and spearheads, of greater originality. The normal motifs were curvilinear ornamentation of S-shaped or scroll forms, highly stylised palmettes, tight spirals and basketry hatching. These motifs reappear later in repoussé metal work, and must be described as Celtic rather than Irish. There is little metal work, indeed, to which this does not apply. The fundamentally abstract nature of early Celtic art is vividly seen in the coinage (none of which was minted in Ireland) and specifically in the *stater* of Philip of Macedon, a silver coin that in pre-Roman times assumed an international currency value comparable to that of the Maria Theresa dollar in Abyssinia or, at one time, the British gold sovereign throughout the world. Some Celts minted their own *stater*, but the further removed they became from Macedonia, the less did the head on the one side resemble Philip's head nor the horses on the obverse his animals. Indeed it is only by seeing a whole series, as it were, of these coins that one can detect in the *stater* of Brittany its Macedonian origin. And this was not because the highly skilled smiths could not have copied the original exactly, but because they preferred the symbolic verging on and eventually becoming the abstract. Seldom did the pre-Christian Celts make many attempts at representational art, or even distortions of the original. We know this from their metal and stone work that has survived. We see the love of the fantastical in their poetry and sagas. No painting has survived, but it is safe to assume that it was in no way realistic. For the Celt reality lay elsewhere than in realism. The Irish language, extraordinarily rich in abstractions, contains no words for 'yes' or 'no'.

St. Patrick and his companions (for we know that, like St. Martin, he travelled in the company of other clerics) are unlikely to have shown much interest in Irish art, though he could hardly have failed to compare its dead abstraction with what he had seen in his travels and perhaps even on beautiful, austere Lérins.

'Rusticity' could hardly have been a handicap in utterly rural Ireland, where there was then no city or town at all. The long business of clearing forests for pasturage was proceeding and the population was no longer nomadic but each *tuath* lived on its own communal land, controlled by the patriarch. The houses were scattered raths with turf walls and wooden roofs, or crannogs, lake dwellings built on wooden piles, providing protection for both man and, in winter, beasts against the prevalence of wolves and robbers. These dwellings were not built close together, for mutual protection, but the chieftain's rath would have outbuildings in which to house his 'courtiers' and slaves, the number of both depending of course on his wealth, that is to say the amount of land and heads of cattle or sheep that his sept owned.

The fields that were cultivated were square or roughly oblong and light cross-ploughing (that is to say ploughing each field both ways) was normal. Such cross-ploughing had been imported by the Celts from drier climates and was not suited to the wet climate of Britain, even less so to that of Ireland. The Belgae in Britain had long ago changed to long furrow ploughing with a much heavier plough that could turn the heavy soil. The more conservative Irish continued to use the light plough, often stone or wood, to scratch the surface. As late as the end of the eighteenth century Arthur Young, the famous agronomist, on his visit to Ireland, noted that the Irish were still 'ploughing by the tail', that is to say by tying one of these light ploughs to a horse's tail, an impossibility with a heavier implement. Corn plots were often cultivated by hand alone.

Not only were there no towns, there were also no ports in St. Patrick's time. Where Dublin now stands, there was but a marsh and ships docked at mere anchorages. The importation of the relatively large quantity of wine that was drunk by the rich must have been as difficult as its transportation through the roadless forests. River and coastal craft were the only commercial vehicles, such roads as existed being mere tracks liable to become mud-baths when the rain fell. There were no bridges nor, it would seem, any but natural fords. There were, of course, no shops or inns. St. Patrick's 'rusticity' must have been a positive advantage as he tramped from sept to sept, preaching the new religion in their own language to men who must have longed for almost any form of novelty which they rewarded with an abundant, soon to become a traditional, hospitality. The tradition has endured.

His work must be clearly distinguished from that of modern missionaries. Unlike the Spanish priests in Central and South America, he was not brought to his mission by armed men, nor did he have the armed forces, and a powerful Christian administration, to rely upon or at least to render him the support of their mere existence. The brave missionaries who went to Africa in the last century had the backing not only of their various national armed forces – seldom invoked – but of the mercantile class and of a far higher standard of technology and administrative skills than that possessed by the natives. St. Patrick had little of the former and, coming from a Europe in chaos, only the theory of civil administration. The European missionaries who attempted to convert Asia, though with great mercantile and on occasion naval or military backing, often found themselves confronted by a highly suspicious native population, highly suspicious that is of the merchants who followed or accompanied the missionaries, a population, moreover, with what it usually regarded as a perfectly adequate religion of its own. Here, and here alone, St. Patrick had an advantage that few missionaries have ever enjoyed. He represented, apart from the Holy See's reliance on the spurious Donation of Constantine, no temporal power and no mercantile class: and he came to a country which had highly educated spiritual leaders but no religion in an established sense.[3] Even the druidical magical, traditional substitute had become, it would seem, desiccated and decadent: it is not impossible that some of the more sophisticated Druids regarded their own alleged supernatural powers as charlatanism. St. Patrick met them with a pure, young, unsullied faith and with nothing more. To quote T. S. Eliot: 'In the juvescence of the year came Christ the tiger.'

Very properly, he approached the leaders of the people, from the high kings to the local tribal chieftains. They would not have appreciated an approach by this stranger to their subordinates: in any case by then Christianity had long since ceased to be a religion of slaves, if, indeed, it ever was save in the eyes of its enemies and certain of its own propagandists. (St. Paul's epistles are not addressed to slaves, anywhere.)

It was among the lesser chieftains and their peoples that St. Patrick was most successful. The more important kings, such as

Loiguire, the High King based on Tara, and Enda Cennsalech, King of Leinster, refused conversion. In defiance of the Ard Ri's order, St. Patrick lit the first Paschal fire in Ireland at Slane, almost if not quite visible from Tara itself. Fiachu, son of Niall, killed two foreign members of St. Patrick's household and Loiguire had to be persuaded that he agree not to kill the Saint himself. But important members of all these families did accept Christianity. Indeed Loiguire's son, whom St. Patrick consecrated bishop, was described by him as his ideal, 'a man of good birth without defect or blemish, and of moderate wealth'. And it was from such men, the chieftains of the septs, that he derived his immediate support. To refer back for a moment to the suppositions made earlier in this chapter about St. Patrick's heritage, his definition of the type of convert he desired hardly sounds like the ideas a peasant would advance.

So great was his success that three bishops were sent from Gaul in the year 439 to assist him and it seems that in his lifetime he built, or ordered built, over fifty churches, at least two of which were entrusted to 'holy women'. It may be assumed that such a building would not have been possible unless the *tuath* on whose land it stood had agreed and, almost certainly, accepted the faith. Indeed we have examples of the chieftain donating land to the church for the purpose of building, and this he could not do personally but only as the representative of the sept he headed. It has been estimated that there were then about 150 *tuatha* in all Ireland. The pre-Patrician Christians were concentrated roughly in the southeast, and these St. Patrick does not seem to have bothered about. We know of three centres of Christianity in his time, Armagh, Slane (on the Boyne, near Tara) and Sletty (in what is now the County Carlow). Sletty may have served these earlier Christians; Slane, where St. Patrick appointed St. Earc bishop, does not appear to have flourished as an ecclesiastical centre, but Armagh rapidly became and has remained the administrative capital of the Roman Church in all Ireland and, after the Reformation, of the Church of Ireland too. Cashel, perhaps now the most beautiful ruin in all Ireland, was the most important centre in the south. It is at Armagh that the primates have their cathedrals, and the first primate was explicitly St. Patrick, appointed by the authorities on the Continent who also sent him assistance in the form of priests and even of supplies, including gold. He probably used Armagh as his main base, for his activities were principally in Ulster, Leinster and Connaught, though he also visited western Munster.

The *Catalogue of the Saints of Ireland* states that St. Patrick created no less than 350 bishops. (Another early source says 450.) These figures sound ridiculous. He would probably have built one church or, more often, shrine for each *tuath* that was converted but as will be seen he may have made each of these a bishopric. According to the *Catalogue* the bishops were Romans, Franks, Britons and Irishmen.

The appointment of a large number of bishops is significant in that it shows St. Patrick's determination to carry out his mission in the spirit, and on the model, of Rome rather than of the Eastern Church as transmitted to him at Lérins. This, however, was not yet possible in Ireland, and within a century almost all these bishoprics had disappeared and with them the Patrician ecclesiastical structure.

The churches were small, we believe, and probably built of wood and wattle, for none has survived. Both then and later, Mass was usually celebrated outside the shrine. Like the winter homes of the people, the church was built inside a rath which also contained the priest's house and a house or houses to lodge visitors, with a cook-house and dining hall.[4] Since the bishop requires a town to de-nominate his diocese and since it seems probable that every priest was a bishop, these early churches were designated towns by St. Patrick, though in most cases no such town ever came into existence. But people gathered around some of the churches and St. Patrick does not appear to have been displeased by such quasi-monasticism. From the very beginning St. Patrick and his Church accepted the absolute authority of the Holy See in Rome.

The Irish priests, who must rapidly have outnumbered the foreigners, were drawn from the more highly educated stratum of society, that is to say the Druids, and their peers. The first man of Leinster to be consecrated bishop was the poet Fiacre, the first Bishop of Sletty. Many druidical practices of little importance passed into Christian clerical usage, such as the ear-to-ear tonsure as opposed to the Roman style of pate, the calculation of the date of Easter and the celebration of ancient festivals with new names.

In no way did the Patrician Church interfere with the civil administration. Only such obviously pagan festivals as the Tara *feis*, when the high king was 'married' to the land, were abandoned, though this was revived once, in 560, by Diarmait MacCerbaill, who would appear to have been something of an apostate to judge by the echoes of his conflicts with the priests and monks which ended with his defeat in battle. At what date the Druids introduced Christian teaching into their schools is not known. It must have been early, and in the opinion of this writer some of the earliest monasteries had been druidical schools before they became schools for monks. But this belongs in the next, post-Patrician chapter.

NOTES

1 It is the opinion of this writer that Patrick was probably indeed of Romano-British patrician stock; that he was referred to by his captors as 'the patrician boy'; and that he had been baptised but was perhaps younger than ten years old. In Ireland, the name is not recorded before his time. Space on these pirate ships was very limited, nor were plebeian or even slave boys in short supply or worth transporting. The offspring, though young, of a patrician family, on the other hand (the 'noble' rank of patrician had been created by Constantine the Great less than a century before), might have seemed valuable loot, perhaps against a ransom that was never in fact paid. Since the British, like the Gauls and the Celtiberians, spoke a vulgar Latin that dispensed with suffixes, his captors might well have simply called him 'Patrick'. If this hypothesis is accepted, his origin was in effect what is nowadays called 'upper class'. His whole career tends to support this.

2 The reader is referred to *Early Christian Ireland* by Maire and Liam de Poer.

3 St. Patrick, if my assumption is correct and he was a patrician, would inherit the social status of the Druids and be acceptable to the Irish chieftains. The Irish clergy have usually, in their turn, been so received.

4 According to the Rev. John Ryan, S.J., on whose authoritative *Irish Monasticism*, I have drawn for much of the factual information in this and the next chapter, St. Patrick himself laid down the proper dimensions. 'The normal settlement was thus a *less* or enclosure, 140 feet in diameter, surrounded by a high wall of earth. Within this enclosure were three buildings – a "large house" where the clerics dwelt, a church or oratory where Mass was celebrated, and a kitchen which probably served also as a refectory.' The actual church was thus as small as are most Greek churches today, and if the congregation were of any size, the majority must have stood and prayed out of doors, as they do in Greece where, as in Lérins, the climate is better suited to religious service so celebrated.

   Throughout this portion of this book my interpretation of ancient documents and other material is based on Fr. Ryan's book rather than on the earlier, long regarded as authoritative, *Life of St. Patrick* by Prof. John Bury.

5

CELTIC IRELAND'S GOLDEN AGE

The better part of four centuries from St. Patrick's mission to the first Viking raid on Lambey Island, north of Dublin, in 795, were in many respects Celtic Ireland's golden age. Here the Irish were once again out of step with almost all the rest of Europe, where chaos usually reigned. While little altered in Ireland, save for the re-organisation of Christian administration, a few European dates are significant.

Alaric the Goth had, as stated in the previous chapter, captured Rome in 410 and within a few years his people had conquered all Italy, though they failed to create a Gothic kingdom of any duration. They did, however, quite soon abandon the Arian heresy and usually recognised the spiritual and sometimes the temporal authority of the papacy, though this was in large measure dependent on the quality of the individual popes. But they were far from being the last invaders.

At about the time of St. Patrick's birth the Huns had begun to migrate westwards from the area north of the Caspian. Rapidly they pushed aside and drove forward the Ostrogoths. In 405 Huns and Ostrogoths, in alliance, were in Italy and were defeated near Florence. By then they had occupied most of the Balkans. Pannonia, now Hungary, and Illyria, now roughly Yugoslavia, disappeared from the map for ever. In 447 Attila reached Thermopylae, Gallipoli and the very walls of Constantinople itself, but was bought off with a heavy annual payment from the Emperor. In 451 he crossed the Rhine and occupied, if that be the word for those ferocious nomads, most of northern and eastern France, being finally thrown back by Franks and Gauls in the terrible slaughter known as the Battle of the Catalaunian Plains, which probably took place near Méry-sur-Seine, some fifty miles east of Paris. In 452 he was ravaging northeast Italy, but was persuaded by Pope Leo I to withdraw.

The Lombards, coming from the north of Germany or probably

from Scandinavia, defeated the Vandals in Germany during the mid-fifth century and continued south. These 'long beards' were of sufficient force for the Emperor Justinian to make an alliance with them against the Ostrogoths: against these, led by the semi-Christian Totila, they fought a ferocious Battle of the Apennines in 553. In 568 they created the Lombard state, which consisted of most of northern Italy from which they raided the rest of the peninsula for some two hundred years. By now they were Christians of a sort, but strongly tinged with the Arian heresy, condemned but for a long time tolerated by the popes. Their savagery, nonetheless, seems to have outdone that of Attila's Huns. There were other foreign 'armies' loose in Italy, early in this period that of Belisarios, who after having defeated the Vandals in North Africa was sent to reconquer Italy for the Emperor in Byzantium, and the Gepides, yet another Germanic or Slavic tribe. There were more . . .

The Vandals, Alans and other destructive peoples had moved across France into Celtiberian Spain. In 428 the Vandals moved on to Africa and the Romans gave Spain to the Visigoths, where a king was appointed. His subordination to any Roman authority was purely nominal, and he spent most of his time in southern France, while in Spain the chaos increased. A King Reccared (who ruled 586–601) introduced Christianity as the state religion, but it soon degenerated into quasi-paganism. It made no difference, for a terrible wind had arisen in the East and swept the last feeble remnants of Byzantine rule from North Africa. With them the Muslims brought fatalism and the goat, and these rapidly turned what had been a granary into a desert. In 711 the first Berber, one Tariq, was brought to Spain by Visigoth rebels against King Roderick. By 714 the Moors, who were in reality a coalition of Arabs, Syrians and Berbers to whom must be soon added black Africans and Visigoths who turned Mohammedan, had swept away the remnants of Roman and Visigothic rule. Only the Basques retained their independence and their Christian faith in the lands where they still live, straddling the Pyrenees. In 718 they crossed the Pyrenees and occupied Aquitania and it was not until 732 that the Moorish advance through France was stopped by the Frankish King, Charles the Hammer, in the very fateful Battle of Poitiers. Fifty years later another Frankish Charles, Charlemagne or Karl der Grosse according to taste, swept the last of the Saracens from France. He might have conquered Spain, but at the Battle of Roncevaux his nephew, Roland, lost most of Spain to Christianity for some five hundred years.

Charlemagne now turned on the land of his ancestors, conquered and by force converted the Germans (or to be more exact those peoples who were living in what is now called Germany) to Christianity. In the year 800, on Christmas Day, the Pope was happy to crown him Western Roman Emperor.

The worst of the turmoil was over. Apart from the eastern frontier of Christendom in Europe, which remains uncertain to this day, the Europe we know could be plainly discerned. The Turkish scourge lay in the future. The Vikings were the last savages to feast off the miserable scraps of the Western Roman Empire. And of all these fearful hordes, they alone had any direct effect on Ireland. But that effect was to be very great indeed, so great as to modify the Irish character and to a large extent the Irish way of life.

During those four centuries Ireland's history is a happy one. As George Eliot remarked: ' . . . the happiest nations have no history'. She was, I think, referring to political history, and apart from extending their way of life into Scotland, the Irish really had none. The same two dynasties reigned lightly, though Tara was apparently abandoned while Cashel became also a great religious centre. The semi-pastoral, semi-agricultural way of life went on. The little courts of the chieftains continued to function and there were undoubtedly minor frictions – though no major wars, for had there been we would know of them – between the *tuatha*. Yet in the deepest sense all was changing, for Ireland was now a Christian country. And there was a spiritual change of another and very personal sort that affected Irish Christianity. St. Patrick had brought episcopal rule to Ireland. By the time the Vikings arrived, the religion of the Irish was in essence and in its florescence monastic. What did this change mean both then and later and how did it come about? All this happened while the rest of Europe was collapsing in screams and blood and flames.

St. Patrick was, so far as the evidence goes, completely loyal to the clerical authorities who had sent him to Ireland and who continued to support him throughout his mission. The Irish Church never deviated from its acceptance of ultimate authority resting with the Roman papacy. Once Antioch and Alexandria had gone to the Muslims there was in any case no other ultimate terrestrial authority than Rome. Hence St. Patrick's annointment of a very large number of bishops in Ireland, though most of these bishoprics rapidly disappeared from a country where the old, pre-Christian organisation of society had very little place for such a superimposed hierarchy.

The high cross at Ahenny, Co. Carlow. These high crosses, of which there are a great many in Ireland, are the earliest known pieces of representative sculpture designed to explain the Scriptures to the illiterate. They were usually built by monks and had the advantage of being too big for the Vikings to steal

Ruins of a twelfth century, early Romanesque church, probably built on the site of an ancient pre-Christian holy place at Toureen Peehaun, Co. Tipperary. Even today the fairies and angels seem close at hand

Mellifont, Co. Louth. The first great Cistercian abbey, built about 1,200 A.D., and the mother house of the Cistercians in all Ireland. Many of the masons, and even some of the stone, came from France

It is not hard to imagine the scene in the Irish chieftain's house, around the turf fire, when St. Patrick with his accompanying priests, some Irish, some foreign, had been dined and wined by the chieftain and his court, among whom the Druid or Druids would have been prominent and where the wives and daughters of the sept's own leading family would also have been present. The lives of the three great saints of the previous century would have been recounted – St. Martin of Tours (who had established a small monastery near his city), St. Ambrose (who had done the same at Milan, a place which St. Patrick may well have visited before going on to Lérins) and St. Augustine, who had a religious household near Hippo. St. Patrick is quoted as commenting on the number of women, not only the daughters of kings but also slave girls, who wished to embrace a life of chastity and religious obedience. A church would be established, on ground consecrated by the Saint and by no one else in his life-time, in collaboration with either one of the priests in St. Patrick's entourage or a local man – or, as we have seen, in a few cases a woman. (Women were not chattels in Celtic society, unless they were slaves.) Then the church was usually officially designated a city and the priest, it would seem, annointed bishop. The adherents of the religious life would frequently cluster in its neighbourhood, the women in one place, the men in another, but as yet there were neither closed monasteries nor convents. The *dun* or home of the chieftain was not suitable to be a church, while the sept's assembly place, usually a hilltop, was also usually eschewed, probably because of its many non-Christian associations. There is no evidence that St. Patrick created any monasteries or convents at all. When the title abbot occurs, and this is rare, it was apparently linked to that of bishop and his duties were probably to administer the small flock of the converted that had assembled near his shrine. We may take it that a proportion of the new Irish priests were converted Druids, since spiritual matters were their concern, while in other cases the local chieftain may have simply added the title of priest or bishop to his other honours.

It is only to be assumed that some Druids must have resented the claims of Christianity, but St. Patrick and his followers seem to have been very tactful. There is, after all, nothing in the Gospels that denies the existence of holy wells, the sanctity of mistletoe and may trees or even the existence of fairies. The sacred grove, or *nemeton*, of the Druids easily became the sanctuary, or *nemed*, of the converts: why not? If the endurance of such superstitions made the acceptance of Christ's message simpler, provided that they did not involve the worship of other divinities or of graven images, then why not let them be? It is significant how the one really powerful deity of the ancient Celts, the mother goddess, was made to serve the purposes of Christianity, though this development was not to take place until after the death of St. Patrick.

St. Brigid, who was born in what is now the County Louth, towards the middle of the fifth century, was of noble Christian parents. (That is, at least on her father's side. Her mother may have been originally a slave. One or both of them must have been among the earliest Irish converts, not impossibly at the hands of St. Patrick himself.) She was named after (or later took the name of?) the great goddess of fertility. She founded the large religious house of Kildare, where she died about 525. It is said that she converted a man on his deathbed by explaining the Redemption to him with a cross which she had plaited from rushes that covered the floor, as was then usual in well-kept households. The plaiting of rushes had had a magical overtone in pre-Christian Europe, to be found in the making of corn dollies in East Anglia today. It is certainly an elaborate and lengthy way to make a cross with which to convert a man whose very hours are numbered. St. Brigid, who was the very real and efficient administrator of a large religious foundation for women, is accepted as the second of Ireland's three patron saints. (St. Patrick was the first, and St. Brigid's contemporary and junior, St. Columcille, the third.) It is not coincidence that her birthday, and therefore the saint's day of the countless Irishwomen who have borne her name, is 1 February, the first day of spring in the pre- and post-Christian Irish calendar and since time immemorial the day of her predecessor, the pagan goddess Brigid.

An anecdote recounted to me by a most reliable friend, less than thirty years ago, is here relevant to this intermixture of the pagan and the Christian. My friend was lunching alone in an expensive Dublin restaurant. At a neighbouring table four obviously prosperous businessmen in middle age were discussing their golf club. It seems that in the middle of the fairway there stood a large may tree, a constant irritant to the golfers. The club secretary, however, had explained that none of his men would cut it down. The businessmen were grumbling about such ridiculous superstitions, until one of them asked: 'Would you take an axe to it? Or you? Or you?' Each admitted, reluctantly, that he would not. After all, you cannot be too careful, now, can you?

This little episode epitomises, for me, what is frequently the Irish attitude to matters far more important than may trees inconveniently sited on golf links. Superstition verges on mysticism which in turn is one ingredient of religiosity. Indeed it is not always possible to distinguish between them. An Irishman may lead a quite shameless and scandalous life, may make blasphemous jokes, yet go to church every Sunday; and this is as true of Protestants, who lack the surcease provided by the confessional, as it is of Roman Catholics. An Irish woman who worked for me for many years, and was in every respect an extremely devout and virtuous Christian, was actively, acutely unhappy if she missed Mass on a Sunday or any other holiday of obligation. Then she reached the age at which church attendance ceased to be compulsory. She remained equally devout, equally virtuous, but never went to church again. Any person who would regard this as hypocrisy has completely missed the point.

That most Irishmen will genuinely welcome, and be interested in, foreigners is true. It is also true that when the same foreigners return in uniform to exact authority, many Irishmen will shoot them. Finally, when the foreign soldiers have been expelled and return as civilians or tourists, they will once again receive a genuine welcome. Many a British politician would not have seen his career ruined in Ireland had he grasped this simple fact.

* * *

The Christian Church in Ireland assumed its basic, monastic character, which was to last for a very long time, in the post-Patrician era, and its creators were what is known as the second generation of saints, of whom St. Columcille (521–597) is perhaps the best known and St. Columban (543–615) the most influential, in that he founded a great many monasteries in Ireland, Britain, France and Burgundy, and above all, perhaps, St. Columcille's Iona. This followed a rule which, in its austerity, was based on that of St. Pachomius. If the original impetus towards the life of the cenobite or hermit, which, as we have seen, formed the background to the institution of the monastery, originated in Egypt and the countries to its north, that influence, if it was ever direct, vanished with Mohammedanism. It had, however, already made a very real appeal to the Irish who throughout the ages seem to have produced both an extreme sociability and, among many, a marked desire to be alone. The evident, often eccentric, individuality of Irish men and women has been noted. So too has a periodic tendency to gregariousness that, for better or for worse, can with great rapidity produce a crowd or even a mob. The pastoral, agricultural people who knew no towns were either alone with their flocks and their fields, or within the crowded *rath* except when attending the assembly of the whole *tuatha* for the recurrent ceremonials. Foreign visitors in the last few centuries have repeatedly commented on the fact that dances and other such social occasions are, in their opinion, 'over-crowded'. Yet the man or woman or married couple that leads almost no social life at all, be his residence in the very centre of Dublin, is not regarded as peculiar. The degree of austerity varied from one monastic order to another. A monk could ask to be trans-ferred to a more austere monastery, and this was frequently done, though the obverse was seldom if ever permitted. For some monks even the most austere monastic settlement was too social, and one would seek refuge by running away and becoming a hermit. Such an action, if wilful, was in defiance of the monastic rule, and the hermit when discovered was brought back. The location of the early foundations was deliberately remote, however, and the earliest that remains to us (because it was built of stone, there being no trees available) was on the Skellig rock, off the Kerry coast. It is a very harsh climb today to the scattering of dry-stone beehive cells: when the weather was at all rough, the handful of monks on Skellig can have had no contact with the rest of humanity whatsoever.

The speed with which a mob can collect in Dublin or Belfast is quite amazing and at times very frightening. To take a banal example from one's own day, an urban Irish pub is, at the appropriate times of day, so crowded and convivial as to be almost intolerable to strangers: or it is virtually empty and sad. The Irish did not invent towns, and though nowadays most of them live in one, Irish literature shows how basically non-urban the Irishmen is. James Joyce's Leopold Bloom is, really, a displaced person, and this not because he is a Jew (although it is why Joyce made him one), for the same is true of Stephen Dedalus, the lone high-flyer with no Icarus.

In view of St. Patrick's immense success, the Church he founded in Ireland was short-lived and the bishops, having laid hands on an appropriate number of converts, mostly vanished or died, not to be replaced. Some, however, became abbots. A bishop, in those days, was of no great spiritual significance. He was above all an ad-ministrator for whom there was little place in the age-old, well functioning society of Ireland. The already limited spiritual power of the kinglets and kings offered no scope for the pro-consular diocese, while the extended family unit did not then require any further administration than what it already had. It is probable that many, if not most, of the Druids accepted some elements of Christianity and these quite simply became priests, retaining their spiritual authority. The early life of St. Finnbar, later first Bishop of Cork, is almost certainly a parable of such a conversion. At beautiful Gougane Barra there is a holy well which is the source of the river Lee that debouches into the sea at Cork. Finnbar 'slew' the Druid of the holy well and, as a Christian priest, took over its responsibility. It would seem likely that he was the Druid, before conversion, that it was a metaphorical, spiritual slaying. He lived a long and adventurous life. (It included a visit to Rome where Pope Gregory the Great declined to annoint him bishop. On his return to Cork, however, a miracle occurred: the roof of the little church opened, and Christ himself annointed him bishop.) He then returned to a solitary hermitage on a little peninsula beside the holy well at Gougane Barra. Here he was joined by a handful of other men, and a miniature monastery, which never grew, was created. Whatever episcopal duties may have been entailed in his miraculous elevation to bishop were, presumably, forgotten. In his story, which I have written elsewhere and which is far more complicated, one can see the whole history of the earliest Irish churchman, Druid to priest to bishop to hermit to abbot. Indeed the episcopacy (for there was then no such town as Cork save about the shrine) may have been a mere formal addition to this story which gave him spiritual authority over the entire length of the river Lee. Rivers played a greater part in the druidical than in the Christian scheme. Pope Gregory may have decided that Finnbar's Christianity was far from complete. And a bishopric, in Rome, was then of great and growing importance.

The importance of bishoprics, and with it the question of celibacy of clergy, must here be discussed. The reader must excuse what may appear to be a digression, but religion has almost always played so important a part in the formation of Irish character and the course of Irish history that it cannot be passed over any more lightly than the question of celibacy of clergy, with which it is not unconnected.

It must be repeated that this, the Patrician and post-Patrician period of Irish conversion to Christianity, took place before the first great ecclesiastical schism between East and West, but that the seeds of that schism had been sown and firmly rooted by the theological divergencies of the early synods. When Stalin asked his famous question: 'How many divisions has the Pope?' he was not being as fatuous as his enemies have alleged. Having been trained for the priesthood at Tiflis, in Georgia, it may be assumed Stalin knew some ecclesiastical history. Within early Christianity, dogmatic power was not unconnected with administrative – that is to say in the final analysis military – power. In the very earliest days of the Church, both lay in Rome. When Constantine moved the seat of Empire, both lay in the Greek sphere of belief. Under the impact of paganism or Islam in West and East, the centre of authority oscil-lated, until in 1054 the final break took place, but it had been in preparation for a long, long time. At the time of St. Patrick, and even more so of the second generation of saints (the sixth and early seventh centuries), the basic break had occurred but not been acknowledged by either side, perhaps because communications were more difficult then than they ever were before or since.

A bishop, an *episcopus*, was a priest appointed overseer, in spiritual and often in civil societies a supervisor. His position in the hierarchy was very much the same in the Roman (and its successor) churches as it is in the various churches that are generally described as Orthodox. So were his functions. A priest can only be ordained by a bishop, for example, which is why the head of a mission, such as St. Patrick, must be a bishop, and which may be one reason why he created so many in Ireland. But he was not the only bishop to come to Ireland, being reinforced, as we have seen. For while a bishop will normally have a diocese in which he is the supreme cleric and, in rank, the theoretical equivalent of the Pope in the Roman Church, there are bishops who do not. Among these, there were the *chorepiscopi*, who were 'country bishops' with powers delegated by the diocesan bishops to act in remote rural areas recently converted from paganism. This class of bishopric had by then been greatly curtailed in the East, in the year 343, and by the end of the first millenium was almost extinct everywhere save in Ireland, where it lasted until 1152 when a synod, presided over by the papal legate, declared that after the deaths of the present *chorepiscopi* no more would be created to replace them. This would indicate, probably, that communication in Ireland had at last so improved that a single bishop could in fact control his diocese. Another type of non-diocesan bishop was the missionary without a definite see. St. Patrick, it will be recalled, had a see, namely Ireland, but many of the early missionaries from Ireland originally had none. These were known as *episcopi regionarii* or *gentium* with regions or peoples vaguely undefined. The Irish Church was to provide many such bishops, and has indeed been called a 'missionary' Church, a title in which it has always taken great pride and a role which it has continued to exercise until the present day. However, of the many Irish priests who have served, and are now serving, as missionaries in Africa and Asia, very few if any are *episcopi regionarii*: modern maps have made them largely redundant.

Now, we do know that in the Roman Church the bishops were usually, though not invariably, appointed from among the clergy. We also know that in the Eastern Church they were and are, by decree, unmarried, and this was undoubtedly the case in the early Roman Church too. On the other hand the celibacy of the clergy as a whole is a very different story, for in the Orthodox Church at an early date it became compulsory for parish priests to be married men, while in the Roman, gradually and at a much later day, the celibacy of priests became, and is now universally, mandatory. The result of this has been that, unlike in the Church of Rome, Orthodox bishops cannot be appointed from the ranks of the parish clergy but only from the monasteries in most of which a vow of chastity forms part of the rules and usually though not invariably the monk has taken priestly vows as well. In both churches, perhaps especially in medieval Ireland, the dual rank of abbot–bishop was not uncommon, and, in both, the great centres of learning were the monasteries (and nowhere more so than in Ireland). In the Eastern Church, therefore, the parish priest could have few aspirations to any higher position, and correspondingly little incentive to study or prepare himself for any greater duties than his purely parochial ones: the Irish priest, on the other hand, in centuries far later than St. Patrick's, lacked any such clerical or psychological restrictions. In very similar circumstances, one thousand and more years after St. Patrick, the Greek and the Irish priesthood were in similar situations, outlaws or semi-outlaws beneath a pagan or anti-Roman government. But whereas in Greece the priest became and remained what he has always been, a man of the people, the Irish priest became the spiritual and at times the temporal leader of his flock, the best-educated or perhaps the only educated man with whom his parishioners could talk freely. This was to be a matter of supreme importance for the centuries between Henry VIII and Edward VII.

The reasons for this divergence are to be directly traced to St. Paul's I Corinthians, VII. The gospels are here of little help. In St. Matthew X, 12, Christ spoke with some sympathy of asceticism, and never preached against the ascetic Essenes, as He did against the Pharisees and Sadduccees, but according to the gospels He was not particularly favourable to asceticism, while celibacy is not mentioned. St. Paul, in the chapter of Corinthians I referred to above, is, for him, curiously ambiguous. Being himself unmarried, he seems to regard celibacy as no hardship and indeed advantageous in that it will concentrate the mind, but positively disadvantageous since it may lead weaker brethren into sin. The Eastern fathers of the Church, assuming not unreasonably that the weaker will outnumber the stronger brethren even in the priesthood, made a single marriage compulsory, but adultery or bigamy, or presumably the sin of Sodom, a very grave crime. In the West a different interpretation slowly prevailed. As early as about 220, the right of a second marriage was being denied to priests, while a hundred years later married men might be admitted to the priesthood, but priests might not marry: the tendency increased and Leo the Great (ob. 461) and Gregory the Great (ob. 604) extended celibacy to the entire priesthood. It was a rule often flagrantly broken. In Italy clerical marriages, with or without a church service, remained common. For more than a century (942–1054) the See of Rouen was held by three successive married bishops (two openly so and all with children). In Ireland that son of St. Patrick's greatest enemy High King Loiguire, St. Fiacre, who had himself turned his bishopric into a powerful abbacy, with himself as abbot, was succeeded in that position by his legitimate son and grandson. When the Reformation swept Europe, most Protestant sects, and all important ones, immediately dropped the theory of a celibate clergy. Indeed, it was still largely a theory, for Henry VIII's contemporary, King Charles V of Spain, petitioned from Pope Paul III dispensation for married priests in all his vast dominions both in Europe and overseas. It was only against strong opposition that the Council of Trent, in 1545, made sacerdotal celibacy practically, if not formally, an article of faith. But the wisdom, or even the papal authority, for such insistence on clerical celibacy has remained open to question until the present time.

The rapid transfer of Irish Christianity from an episcopal to a monastic and missionary basis is explicable. The nature of the country and the difficulties of administration have already been mentioned. So have the monastic propensities of St. Patrick himself, to which must be added that the British and Welsh churches had close ties with Alexandria in the fifth and sixth centuries, and that many of the early church leaders were educated in Wales or Britain. (St. Enda, educated at Candida Casa in northern Britain, returned early in the sixth century to found what may have been the first Irish monastery to be built, as it were, from scratch: this was on the Aran Islands, where a rule of the greatest severity prevailed.) The influence of that British monastic establishment, of St. David's at Mynyas in Wales, and of the ever-busy St. Gildas of Britain who kept a very close eye on Irish, as he did on British, religious affairs cannot be overestimated. Then, too, the Celtic way of life, the extended family unit with its patriarch, could be and was adopted without great difficulty to the democratic monastery ruled by its despotic abbot. Finally, as has been remarked, it seems probable that many of the Druids became priests and their schools were taken over as monastic training centres. We can see this transition in the earliest Irish copies of the scriptures, with the pagan sagas written in the margin of the bible, and we know that some at least of their methods of tuition, such as memorisation, were identical. Of the very earliest monastic foundations throughout Ireland, most have long disappeared, but some, such as Clonmacnois and Glendalough, have remained. It is this writer's belief that those two, and undoubtedly many more, existed as training schools long before the boy Patrick herded sheep in the County Antrim.

Finally, the Irish Christians almost immediately began their missionary work. Among the most famous of these was St. Columcille, who died in 599. On his father's side this great nobleman was descended from Niall of the Nine Hostages, and was within the blood relationship to have been himself a high king. He preferred to be a missionary monk. In 546 he built a monastery at Derry. Ten years later he founded another great and famous monastery at Durrow. He is also credited with the great monasteries on Tory Island, at Drumcliffe and Swords. But his real home was on the island of Iona, between Ireland and Scotland, which is still one of the most holy, as it is one of the most beautiful and peaceful, places in all the British Isles. It was to this monastery that he retired to die.

In fact St. Patrick's mission was doubly successful. He created a Church which naturally tended towards his own favoured monasticism, and his Church preserved its missionary nature, first in the conversion of the pagan Picts in Scotland and then among the barbarians of central Europe. The visitor to Wuerzburg Cathedral will there see the enormous flag of St. Killian. It is but one among many mementoes of the Irish missionaries who helped largely to Christianise, or re-Christianise, northern and central Europe.

❋　❋　❋

The introduction of Christianity into Ireland had no immediate effect on the somewhat decadent art of the Irish. The early monasteries were places of austerity, but some of them soon became extremely rich as chieftain after chieftain celebrated his conversion by a donation of land which the monks worked. The profits went to the abbacy, of course, not in taxes. And the seventh century saw what might be called almost the beginning of a renaissance of Irish art, brought about in part by the demands of the Church (which will be discussed in a moment), in part by much greater contact with foreigners, for which the missionaries were largely responsible, but above all by the great widening of the spirit and hence of the senses that missionary monasticism brought to the cramped and all too familiar world in which the Irish lived. It was spring time.

This is not a history of Irish art, and the student is referred, in the first place, to Maire de Poer's *Early Irish Art* and, for a far more detailed study in depth, to the work of Dr. Françoise Henry, in several volumes, now all quite adequately translated.

To deal with pre-Christian art first of all, the traditional forms of jewellery continued to be made, though the torc appears to have long become obsolete. In other forms of jewellery the Irish smiths, having passed through a period of decadence, appear to have enjoyed a revival. Though we know not what may have been made before or since and lost, the so-called 'Tara' brooch (which was found on the seashore near Drogheda and which the experts date at c. 700) is probably the most beautiful of all Irish brooches and has, indeed, no superior in skill and artistry anywhere. More important, probably, is the superb silver chalice from Ardagh, in the County Limerick, made at about the same time. For it represents a whole new series of artefacts both of metal and undoubtedly of cloth (lost, alas!) that were becoming needed for clerical use and for the embellishment of churches and monasteries as they became less austere. The enormous accumulation of precious, portable objects was to lead directly to the looting of the monasteries by the Vikings in the ninth century. Meanwhile the general Celtic motifs scarcely changed, the spiral and wave in a multitude of combinations remaining basic.

The Church introduced two new forms of the plastic arts. The first was not strictly an innovation, for carved stones had, as we have seen, existed in Ireland since New Grange days, but of stone sculpture there was very little, and there is no reason to imagine that there was much in wood which has perished. Now every church needed its Cross, and from these there soon evolved the great carved stone High Crosses, invariably outside churches, which are almost unique to Ireland, and which are generally regarded as perhaps the greatest Irish contribution to the arts. These were often large enough to portray biblical themes which in turn required a measure of realism in the portrayal of human and, in smaller number, of animal figures. True realism, always distasteful to the Celts, was not attempted, but the figures could not and did not become symbolic and thus abstractions. There were undoubtedly wooden crosses, which have gone, but the great stone High Crosses, mostly built during the Viking period or even later, remain, weather-beaten but enormously impressive, at the site of almost every one of all save the very earliest, vanished monasteries. There were also carved gravestones of great, and intrinsically Irish, beauty, and here the ancient, abstract interlocking forms do recur. But the great Irish sculptors do not appear to have attempted portraiture, nor is there any hint in legend that any of the figures carved upon the High Crosses was intended to represent any especial abbot or saint. Like the Greeks of Pericles' day the Irish sculptors carved for the greater glory of God and the insertion of the purely human would have been a blasphemy.

That they painted, if only abstract patterns, is certain. None, unfortunately, remains or is even described.

The second great novelty that came with Christianity was the illuminated manuscript (which surely proves that they did paint). The motifs, in particular of the great capital letters, are intensely complex and derive directly from their earlier and contemporary metal work. Since druidical learning had been secret, verbal, hermetic, the arrival of written gospels and psalters, and the means to copy these, gave the Irish scribes and illuminative artists a whole new field in which to work. As with the High Crosses, this proved an art in which they excelled. Only a few have survived, such as the Book of Durrow and the Book of Kells, but from 'first drafts' carved on bone or on wood discarded and preserved in bogs, we know the intense application given to this work, even if the work itself did not place these meticulous pages beyond dispute. The detailed and minute work occupied many monks entirely. These illuminated manuscripts were the greatest creation of the Irish golden age and are perhaps early Ireland's most remarkable artistic gift to mankind. But the art was short-lived. The Viking raids and the destruction of the monasteries destroyed it, for the artists were probably physically exterminated, with most of their work.

Of their music we know almost nothing, save that they did sing and dance. They had few musical instruments, of which the harp was certainly not one for many years to come. They seem to have possessed a violin-type instrument of a very primitive nature and something that developed into bagpipes in addition to a pipe and of course drums. Some Irish folk tunes may be very old, others may have come from Britain, Gaul and thus ultimately from the Mediterranean, before or with Christianity, but since they had no form of musical notation, the experts hesitate to speak with any sort of authority on this subject.

It may be worth noting that the golden period between the arrival of St. Patrick and that of the Vikings followed in time directly on the temporary iconoclasm of the Greek Church and the total iconoclasm of Islam. Some have thought to find traces of Byzantine art in Ireland, but if they exist they are very faint indeed. Music, in particular church music, may have been influenced in some measure by the Persians, who occupied Alexandria for a while before the Arabs. The Coptic Church, almost totally isolated by Islam shortly after Ireland became Christian, was also an essentially cenobitic and monastic church. Some have seen a certain resemblance between the two. It is curious to think that perhaps the psalms were once sung to the same music in Ireland as in Abyssinia, but such speculation, if pleasurable, is fruitless.

Whatever the cultural influences of the other Christian churches may have been, the Irish Church never failed to accept in its entirety the ecclesiastical authority of Rome, from the time of St. Patrick on. Nor did any heresy ever succeed in Ireland. In writing to Gregory the Great at the end of the sixth century, St. Columban stated with the uttermost clarity that the Irish Church clearly acknowledged the primacy of the Roman pontiff. He boasted that no heretic or Jew or schismatic had ever been found upon the island. When the Council of Whitby was called, two generations later, to settle certain matters of comparatively minor importance, such as the date of Easter and the nature of the tonsure, the two sides represented, roughly, the Celtic churches of which of course the Irish Church, with Armagh as primacy, was the most important, and the younger but larger Anglo-Saxon Church, with its primacy at Canterbury since 603. Gregory the Great gave St. Augustine, its first primate, authority over the older Celtic churches in Britain, and he set about stamping out such relics of druidism (as the shape of the tonsure) which culminated at Whitby. The position of Armagh was weakened by the complete victory of Canterbury at this synod, though it was a victory without any overt hostility. The relationship between such English monasteries as Lindisfarne with Iona and the Irish monasteries remained extremely close, with much coming and going of monks. Yet a precedent had been established. Canterbury was physically far nearer to Rome than was Armagh. There was no definite hierarchy, but in centuries to come the primacy of Canterbury was not always reluctant to interfere in Irish affairs. No one could have foreseen it at the time, nor in the England of the Heptarchy nor of the Danelaw nor of the earliest years of the Norman conquest, but at Whitby, in the year 664, the English had won their first victory over the Irish.

6
THE VIKINGS

The coast of Norway is much indented by fjords, behind which rise mountain ranges that are steep, covered with pine forest throughout the year to which is added snow in wintertime, and generally impassable until modern times. In ancient days the villages huddled beside the fjord, and the villagers cultivated what little land could be hacked from the primaeval forests. What communication existed between them was by water. This was true to only a lesser extent of Sweden and of the multitude of islands that constitute Denmark. To the Scandinavians of the seventh century a boat was as familiar an object as was a horse to an early settler or an Amerindian in the American west. Since there were no ports and few harbours, the boat that was in daily use was of shallow draught, so that it could be driven ashore and pulled on to dry land in times of storm. It was also designed for speed. A single, square sheet, augmented by a single row of rowers, enabled it to achieve considerable speed, and its narrowness of beam gave these longships great manoeuvrability as well.

It has been said that early in the Christian era there was a population explosion in Scandinavia. There are of course no statistics available and, to the writer, a 'population explosion' is a very problematical phrase. A rapid increase in the population of any given society can usually be traced to one or more of three main causes: a fall in the death rate, and particularly of infantile mortality; a climatic or agro-technological change, leading to a rapid increase in the food supply and thus to the population that any given territory can support; or the removal, by conquest or other means, of a hereditary and predatory enemy. None of these seems applicable to Scandinavia, save perhaps that the ice-cap may have retreated a little, leaving slightly more land fit for cultivation. This would scarcely account for the sudden appearance, in the seventh century, of the Vikings.

Far more probable is the fact that they must have heard of the rich loot that their Germanic neighbours, far to the south, and other

migrants from Asia were picking up with the collapse of the Western
Roman Empire. The Danes, in particular, must have known much
about the overrunning of Roman Britain, since not only did the
Saxons pass by them, but the Jutes themselves played a very considerable part in it all. Even this urge to emulate the Franks, Lombards and the others does not account for the special nature of the
Viking raids and settlements. The answer, as to many such problems,
is probably a technological one. Some time about the year 600 the
Norwegians invented the modern keel, which they attached to their
long boats. These needed no longer slip from fjord to fjord, nor hug
the coastline as almost all Atlantic shipping had done hitherto, but
became, in the exact meaning of the word, seaworthy. (At about
this time St. Brendan in the sixth century probably sailed to America
and back in a leather coracle[1] that is unlikely to have had a keel, and
when the Norsemen reached Iceland in the ninth century they
found a small Irish colony recently established there: but these were
undoubtedly flukes.) Indeed the English word 'keel' is of old Norse
origin, as is the word 'starboard'. The longboat was steered by
an oar that was attached to the righthand gunwale. When tying up,
therefore, the other side of the boat was run along the quai or port
side.

Another, social factor is probably involved. The Germanic tribes
of the *Völkerwanderung*, and in particular the Franks, had found the
need for a more centralised control than that of a static people.
Kings arose, merging various tribes and culminating in the claim to
total sovereignty by the Merovingians. From this came the elaborate
arrangements of feudalism, a hierarchical society, which Charlemagne
tried and failed to extend to all Europe, though the Holy Roman
Empire was not finally pronounced dead until Napoleon took this
step in 1806.

Now the Nordic peoples had a quasi-democratic system of
government, not dissimilar to that of the early Celtic Irish. The
clans were each headed by their jarl or earl who combined heredity
with election in his title. In case of war one earl would predominate,
much as happened in Ireland, but it seems that some of the most
powerful tribal leaders aimed at a Frankish-type kingship, in
particular a certain Harold Fairhair, and with the better means of
transportation provided by the new keeled longships, set about
attempting to impose his new role on the rest of his compatriots. The
Norse sagas indicate that something of the sort did occur. (Almost
the first act of the Norwegians in Iceland was to create a parliament

or *thing*, which is now the most ancient political institution of its sort in the world.) But this hardly accounts for the earliest Vikings raiders, since these returned, with their loot, in the autumn. The prevailing winds in those days were probably rather different from what they are today. A northeasterly, in the spring, would bring them from Norway to northern England and around the tip of Scotland, a southwesterly, prevalent in the autumn, would carry them home again. Lacking these winds, they would furl their sail and row.

If I am referring to the Vikings as Norwegians, this is because it was primarily from Norway that the raiders descended on Ireland, though later the Danes joined in. Indeed, without any sort of agreement, the three Scandinavian peoples roughly divided the world between them. The Danes had England, the western Baltic, and Frisia. The Swedes sailed up the Russian rivers and then, after transporting their longships overland, down the Volga. Indeed they created Russia, its name being derived from their tendency to red hair, and their first capital city was Nijni-Novgorod (now called Gorki) where they instituted the great fair to which merchants from as far east as China came. Later they founded Kiev and made that their capital, the Black Sea their lake. They even made two attempts to attack Constantinople, but were repulsed by the mysterious and terrifying 'Greek fire', a form of petrol bomb or flame-thrower. The Norwegians went far beyond Ireland and France, along the Portuguese coast and into the Mediterranean at least as far as Genoa. Ventures against Africa failed, for they met their match in the Muslim corsairs. At the other end of their spectrum they established bases in southern Greenland and visited what is now Canada and perhaps the northern United States, but there they found no loot.

If the Finns did not take part in these Viking activities, it is because they reached what is now Finland, from their Asiatic point of origin, in the seventh or early eighth century and were fully occupied in expelling the Lapps and occasionally murdering a few Swedes. The Finns in any case have never been a seafaring nation.

The chronicles of the Viking incursions in the west are fairly well documented, at least from the year 787, when they sacked the great abbey at Lindisfarne, off the Lothian coast. Before that date they had probably made incursions in the extreme northern islands of Scotland, where in due course they were to settle, but Lindisfarne is the first major raid. Each longship carried approximately forty to

The pre-Romanesque Dunbrody Abbey, Co. Wexford. It can be seen how small the 'churches' were – the congregation worshipped outside them

Dean Odo's door, Clonmacnois, Co. Offaly, a very rare example of Irish gothic carving, c.1460. Clonmacnois, though certainly pre-Christian in origin, became one of Ireland's most important religious foundations and remains one of the most beautiful. Monks from here served Charlemagne in the late eighth century sixty warriors, their painted shields sometimes hanging from the gunwales. For weapons they had swords, axes, spears, and when fighting they wore helmets often horned and sometimes breastplates of iron. They were free men, at first in search of loot, and they were extremely dangerous. Even a single boatload of these men could rapidly and easily overwhelm the monks of Lindisfarne, killing such monks as may have tried to prevent them, ripping anything of apparent value from the churches and other monastic buildings (since the monks apparently valued their books and manuscripts they took these too, but as the illiterate Norsemen saw no purpose in them, they tossed them in the sea) and when they had loaded up with as many precious objects as their boats could carry, they headed for home, leaving the wooden buildings aflame behind them. It may be assumed that they had gorged themselves with the monks' food, drunk what wine there was on the island, and if there were any women in Lindisfarne in those days, it is not hard to guess what happened to them. Back in their own village these strong young men would be welcomed as heroes, with tall tales to tell and many precious, glittering objects to prove them.

In 794 they were back, in greater strength, off the coast of Northumbria and sailed up the Tyne to the double monastery of Jarrow, where the great Bede, known as the Venerable and 'the father of English history', had lived, and died, some sixty years before. Not only a historian, he was among the greatest theologians of his day and an early scientist. What must have been among the finest libraries in Europe made excellent fires for the Norsemen to cook on, and Bede's great fame would have taken concrete form in church ornaments of peerless beauty and incalculable value. Perhaps it was here that the Vikings first heard of another great monastery, the last home of St. Columcille, on an island between England and Scotland, for in 795 it was Iona's turn.

It was a longer journey home, and they decided to spend the winter ashore. They chose Lambay Island, off the Irish coast and to the north of Dublin, where they wintered safely, occasionally raiding the mainland for food and women and anything of value that they might come upon. The next year they raided Iona again and then returned to Norway. It was at this time that the *Book of Kells* was taken from Iona, where it had probably been made, to what was regarded as a safer monastery, namely Kells. The destruction of Iona, among the very holiest of places in the world of the Scots and the Irish, must have seemed as incredible as it was

atrocious. But the horrors had hardly begun. The richest Irish
monasteries, as the Vikings soon learned, were inland. The arteries
of Ireland were the rivers. What were obstacles to armies were
highways to Viking longships, and with their shallow draught they
could penetrate far upstream. Almost no place in Ireland was safe
in the ninth century.

The Vikings never ceased to be isolated in small groups of pirates,
but they also and quite rapidly became veritable navies. Similarly
islands such as Lambay soon ceased to be mere wintering quarters.
As permanent bases they became too small. Though *terra firma*
lacked the total security which the Vikings enjoyed at sea, they
found that they had little to fear from their Irish victims, and
they established small fortified strongpoints near the mouths of the
rivers up which their ships raided the still rich interior. Thus did the
very first town in Ireland come into being: Vickingsalo (Wicklow),
Veiksfjord (Wexford), Allymrick (Limerick) and above all one of
the few to keep its Irish name, Dubhlinn (which means the Black
Pool) where had been a monastic establishment west of the pool
formed by the confluence of the river Poddle (now underground)
and the Liffey near its mouth, thus giving the Norse settlement
protection by water and marsh on three sides. The original stronghold was set up in 840, from which the Viking town rapidly expanded
westwards and northwards towards the Liffey in the second half of
the ninth century.[2] At this same time they established ship-forts on
Lough Neagh and at Annagassan on the site of a monastery founded
by St. Colman, now a fishing village at the joint estuaries of the
rivers Dee and Clyde, in what is now the County Louth.

By now fairly substantial colonies of Norsemen were making the
crossing accompanied sometimes by their women. In the 830s a
certain 'King' Turgeis had been rowed up the Boyne and sacked
Tara. Perhaps after an overland march – for the Vikings were
becoming less timid of land operations – but more probably after
circumnavigating Ireland and sailing up the Shannon, he had
looted Clonmacnois. His 'wife' is said to have uttered 'heathen
oracles', whatever these may be, seated upon the Clonmacnois high
altar, or alternatively to have danced upon the high altar at Armagh,
in which case Turgeis presumably brought the lady from the Vikings'
Lough Neagh stronghold. They were in fact all over Ireland, save
only the poorest, most mountainous and least habited areas. Loot
included young women, the men being usually massacred.

By 853 a certain Olaf the White had proclaimed himself or been elected King of Dublin by the local *thing* and in 866 and again in 870 led large scale raids from Ireland to Scotland. It was his Christian widow, Queen Aud, who sailed from the Western Isles of Scotland to colonise Iceland. Some twenty years earlier a handful of Vikings had landed there, to find that they had been preceded by a few Irish, known as Culdees, but it was Queen Aud's colonists who really created Iceland. To transport women and livestock, including cattle, in a longboat across many leagues of sea would have been well nigh impossible, so one longboat towed another with them aboard. Meanwhile the situation had become complicated in the mid-ninth century by the arrival in Ireland of Danish Vikings, from Denmark or more probably from England, who fought the Norse, often in alliance with the Irish. To judge by the Irish sagas, written down a few centuries later, this was a long period of war between the Irish and the Vikings, but that is a poetic simplification.

For the old Irish system had in great measure broken down, undermined first of all by the advent of Christianity and then by the power of the abbots, which frequently exceeded that of the old Irish chieftains. A measure of hostility had existed between the *tuatha* long before the arrival of the Vikings, and greater power structures had arisen. The Vikings only accelerated a state of almost permanent civil war, nor were they the first to loot the abbeys. Irish hosts had preceded them. The monks not infrequently fought back, and there were also pitched battles of abbey against abbey. The anonymous authors of *Viking*, published by a semi-official body called the Curriculum Development Unit, Dublin, 1978, state that between 795 and 810 there were only 26 raids or other acts of organised violence by the Vikings, while the Irish annals record 87 such attacks by groups of Irishmen on their compatriots. Such simple mathematics are, however, misleading. Apart from these very earliest Viking raids, the attackers, and often the defenders, were of mixed Norse and Irish origin, while Irish chieftains frequently called in Viking forces as allies. As the Viking strongpoints became towns, their inhabitants became inextricably mixed. For quite a long time, until the Battle of Clontarf in 1014, the Norsemen usually held political power, such as it was, but with intermarriage, the accept-ance of Christianity and finally of the Irish language, the smaller population of invaders was incorporated into the larger population of Irish men and women. This intermixture of Celt and Nordic was particularly true of the towns, which were subject to attack by Norse, Irish or mixed bands of marauders, who did not stop to question a man's origins before putting him to the sword and then enslaving his women and children.

The Vikings, however, were somewhat less successful in the northern parts of Ireland than in the south. It will be recalled that the Ui Neill (or O'Neill for the convenience of readers) had established an almost titular right to the northern high kingship, based on Tara, which was probably used more for assemblies than as a dwelling place. In 867 – that is to say some thirty years after Turgeis had desecrated the Christian altars – a high king of this time, Aed Finnliath, counter-attacked. First he defeated the Norsemen in a naval battle on Lough Foyle. He then marched southward, with a relic of the True Cross, and defeated them again on land near where Drogheda now stands. Thenceforth the northern part of the island remained relatively untroubled by the Norsemen, as it was in some degree to remain after the arrival of the Normans. Indeed no foreign army permanently penetrated the fastnesses of the extreme north and northwest for a further thousand or so years, and Christian Celtic civilisation lingered on there until the surrender of Hugh O'Neill in 1603 and the Flight of the Earls four years later. O'Neill only lost his war with the English in battles fought in the south. This very rough geographical distinction has left its mark upon the Irish, detectable to the present time.

The chaos of the tenth century in the south culminated in the great Battle of Clontarf, which used to be narrated as a victory of the Irish over the invaders, though the emphasis is rather different in the Icelandic saga. The Irish chieftain, Brian Boru, was something of an upstart from the County Clare. After a long series of campaigns, by his father and then by himself, during the course of which he proclaimed himself Ard Ri and even 'Imperator Scottorum' in total disregard of all Irish law and tradition, he met his final resistance from the Dubliners, who he defeated in a battle where he lost his life. In this, the greatest battle so far fought on Irish soil, the armies on both sides contained Irishmen and Norsemen. The distinction, already eroded, between them had lapsed: after Clontarf it became virtually meaningless. Men might claim the title of Ard Ri for the better part of another two centuries, but none had any real power over the whole island which was now inhabited, quite simply, by tribes of Irishmen, usually at war with one another. The old Celtic system lingered on, in theory, but the *tuath* resembled increasingly the Frankish tribe, with an hereditary kingship or even an hereditary abbacy. And because the Vikings had become a very international people, the Irish were never again to know the almost total isolation from the rest of Europe that they had enjoyed when the Celts alone ruled the island.

During these centuries of armed chaos, it is not surprising that Irish art declined. Viking motifs, which were not very different from the semi- or totally abstract motifs of the Celts, influenced the smiths, but their work was on the whole coarser and less elegant than that of their predecessors. The illumination of manuscripts also became far less elaborate and writing more utilitarian. Building was still almost entirely in wood and has perished, save for a few monastic buildings, usually now stone ruins. A ninth century Irish monk wrote a poem which was found at St. Gall, in Switzerland, and which has been translated as:

> Fierce and wild is the wind tonight,
> The sea's rough tresses are tossed to white.
> On such a night men may sleep at ease.
> Ferocious Norsemen will sail on sweet seas.

Perhaps the poet-monk took this poem with him, when he fled his burned and desecrated monastery.

Only the great High Crosses, most of which were carved during this period, have remained, since they were too big for marauders to steal. And it was now that the other edifice, unique to Ireland, save for a few the Irish made in Scotland, was built, the round towers that still dot the countryside almost wherever a monastery exists or once existed.

These pencil-shaped buildings, from about seventy to about one hundred and twenty feet in height, were first built in the early ninth century and one of the finest and last, at Ardmore, County Waterford, towards the end of the twelfth. About eighty of these survive. Undoubtedly they were originally *campaniles* for where the top remains there are always four openings from which a monk could ring a bell in all directions, summoning the monks to their religious duties or their meals. As the unknown poet wrote:

> Sweet little bell
> Rung on a windswept night.

The stonework becomes progessively finer and smoother, nor are they decorated. At an early date they also became used for defensive purposes, since the entry is usually some twelve feet or so above ground level, reached by a ladder that could then be pulled up. A series of floors would have led to the belfries, and within the towers could be stored the reliquaries and chalices and other precious objects. From the windows the monks who sought shelter in them could drop stones or pour boiling liquids on their attackers. Their efficiency as works of military engineering, however, is not particularly impressive, since they would have provided little protection against fire, heavy catapults or battering rams. As campaniles they add a touch of beauty to the Irish countryside that is both surprising and serene. The theory, said to have been advanced by some Englishman in the eighteenth century, that they were built in order to bewilder the English in centuries then to come, also strikes a cheerful note in the usually glum chronicle of Anglo-Irish relations.

Before leaving the now Irish Vikings with the towns that they had built and where their spiritual heritage still surpasses that to be found in the more Celtic countryside, it would be well, briefly, to examine their story in the countries with which Ireland was most closely connected.

In the Highlands of Scotland the Irish influence continued and continues to be dominant, the Picts having been conquered and absorbed. In the Scots islands, and particularly the most northerly ones, the Viking element was very great. Here, and in the Highlands, were bred those extraordinarily fine fighting men known, in Ireland, as galloglasses, and frequently imported into Ireland as mercenaries. In the Lowlands, as in Wales, the P-Celts were influenced though not yet conquered by the English. England itself was almost entirely colonised by the Danes who occupied large parts of the country and who might have conquered it all had they not been defeated in a series of battles by Alfred the Great, who became King of Wessex in 871, and who put the seal on his land victories by building a navy which cut the Danish lifelines. Like the Norsemen in Ireland, the Danes in England became an important ingredient of the English people. The logical sequence: raider, strongpoints, conquest and colony came nearer to working in England than in Ireland. Meanwhile the English were far too busy defending themselves – for after Alfred's time there were renewed Danish assaults – to concern themselves with bothering the Irish.

France was another story. Throughout the ninth century, once Charlemagne's strong hand was still, the Norsemen ravaged the country far and wide. Paris was twice besieged, and only saved by the miraculous intervention of St. Germain. The rivers, in particular the Loire and the Seine, were Norse rivers, Le Havre one of their principal cities. Under their repeated blows the country disintegrated while the Norsemen became increasingly a single force under one commander. Finally, in 911, the French King (whose authority by then was little greater than that of the Ard Ri in Ireland) offered Duke Rollo dominion of what is now Normandy in exchange for an oath of allegiance. Rather surprisingly, since most of Normandy was already under his control, Rollo accepted. He did his best to keep his now Christian subjects within their boundaries and became indeed the very model of a great feudal lord, obedient to his king and keeping order in his territory, where French rapidly became the natural language of the Normans. It was to be several centuries before the rest of France could emulate the excellent administration and tranquillity that Duke Rollo imposed by force of arms upon his province. He and his successors seem in general to have kept their pact with the King of France most scrupulously. Those descendants of the Vikings who had inherited the itch tó travel and to fight were diverted to England and to Italy.

Only a century and a half after Duke Rollo had legally taken over Normandy, Duke William began planning an independent kingdom for himself in England, where neither a Danish nor an Anglo-Saxon dynasty could achieve permanency. After he had defeated and killed Harold in 1066, he methodically subdued the rest of the country. This completed, Wales and the Scottish Lowlands covered by new Norman castles, William the Conqueror, a mere twenty years after the Battle of Hastings, carried out one of the most remarkable pieces of administration ever known. In some two years his servants compiled Domesday Book, a virtually complete and almost invariably correct survey of the entire kingdom.

Among his most important noblemen and warriors were a certain Walter FitzOther who, in Domesday Book, held lands from the King in the Home Counties, was Castellan of Windsor and Keeper of the Forest. His second son, Gerald FitzWalther, was appointed by Henry I to be Constable of Pembroke Castle, and thus the ancestor of all the Irish Geraldines. He married Nesta, daughter of Gruffyd of Tudor Mawr, Prince of Wales. Their son, Maurice FitzGerald, later Lord of Maynooth and Baron Naas, was thus of royal Celtic blood on his mother's side and was with the first Normans to land in Ireland, with the son of Gilbert de Clare, Earl of Pembroke. That son, Richard FitzGilbert, is known to history – incorrectly, as it happens, for this was his father's nickname – as Strongbow.

* * *

The Battle of Clontarf may have ended Danish and Norman domination in large parts of Ireland, particularly Leinster, but it did not bring peace to the country. In form at least the old Celtic system prevailed, particularly in remote areas of the north and west, but the four kingdoms were as fictional (save in geographical terms) as were the high kingships. The democratic basis of the *tuatha* was becoming obsolete, and power passed into the hands of great chieftains who were frequently if not usually at war with one another. Many of the abbacies were little different from such tribes, and the position of abbot was passed, in the now feudal fashion, from father to oldest son. There was neither civil nor religious administration on any but the most local scale. A debased form of druidism, centred about holy wells, groves of oak and the rest, was enjoying if not exactly a revival at least a fairly vigorous life. Ireland, in fact, was reverting to paganism, not to the more or less orderly paganism that had preceded St. Patrick but to a voodoo-like mishmash of Christianity and magic.

Yet the longboats came no more. Brendan Kennelly has translated an anonymous, undated poem:

> Only a fool would fail
> To praise God in his might
> When the tiny mindless birds
> Praise Him in their flight.

Instead, came the Normans.

NOTES
1 The medieval book about him, *Navigationis Brendani*, was the equivalent of a perpetual best-seller for centuries.
2 It says something – what, precisely, shall be left to the reader to decide – for the city fathers and those bureaucrats who were appointed to Hibernicise English place names fifty years ago. They ordered that the capital of the Free State, now the Republic, should be officially called *Baile ath Cliath*, 'the Ford of the Hurdles'. There was such a ford, that enabled persons coming from the north to approach the Liffey. Apart from being on the other side of the unfordable river, it is several miles to the north of ancient Dublin. The American Founding Fathers might as well have re-named Manhatten, Brooklyn Heights.

7

THE COMING
OF THE NORMANS

Life in the Irish countryside seems to have changed little from
ancient times until about the year 1300. Thereafter there came, in
historically rapid succession, the Scots invasion associated with the
name of Bruce, the recurrent plague called the Black Death (though
there may have been more than one variety of plague), the perpetual
tribal wars that affected almost the entire country, and the periodic
Anglo-Irish skirmishes and campaigns that merged into the Tudor
wars of conquest. In 1300, however, the old *tuatha* system was alive
if moribund in most of the Irish countryside. Moribund, that is to
say, as an accepted organisation of society rather than as a way of
life. The farmers and their families continued to live in their round
houses, arable land was planted with the usual three-crop rotation,
dues – usually in the form of labour – paid to the tribal chieftains.
(These were in general low by comparison with those of English
villeins, an estimated fifteen days per annum as opposed to one
hundred in the larger island. Hence an illegal influx, in part also
political, of Anglo-Saxon villeins from England after the Norman
Conquest.[1] Villages were deliberately founded in Ireland by great
landowners such as the monasteries, on the Breteuil model of
quasi-self-administration, to attract such peasants, who brought with
them more advanced methods of cultivation, among them the
ox-drawn plough.) There thus came into existence an increasing
amount of casual labour. This weakened the *tuatha* system and also
produced a complementary effect. The old rural structure, at least
in large parts of Ireland, decayed at the very roots of authority.
Then septs became merged into ever larger units, which did not
usually correspond with the old 'kingships'. A single family, say the
O'Tooles or the O'Byrnes south of Dublin, would acquire great
territorial power, but without any form of fixed frontier or accepted
leadership. Such territories might even be run by great families
from distant parts of Ireland: thus there was O'Connor territory in

the southeast, O'Neill in the southwest, after a generation or two
quite cut off from the O'Connors of the Lower Shannon or the
O'Neills of Ulster. The land still 'belonged' to no one, but its tribute
often did. And where such tribute was in effect paid to a distant
chieftain, he was the Irish prototype of the 'absentee landlord', to
become so notorious in Norman and English times. The usual
absence of territorial borders and of any trace of centralised administration (save when imposed from without), combined with the
incursions of Norman, Welsh, Scottish and finally English invaders,
meant that for much of the time most of Ireland was living in a war
zone, or at least in what was likely to become one at any moment,
owing to some squabble between territorial magnates (or among
members of their families) quite incomprehensible to the farmers
across whose farmlands they would brawl and loot, killing the
livestock and frequently burning the standing crops.

For these little wars, a special class of man arose, who frequently
crop up in the annals as 'kerns or idlemen'. Usually attached to
some chieftain, they were what might be called 'military material'
and were frequently engaged by other chieftains. Far more formidable
than these were those professional soldiers called galloglasses,
mercenaries imported by the greatest magnates from the Highlands
and Islands of Scotland and extremely difficult or expensive to be
rid of once installed, sometimes forming septs of their own.

Apart from enemies, the Irish farmers met few strangers. The
tin-smith (the oldest itinerant profession known to man, and from
whom the tinkers of today may claim some very vague descent)
would come by and mend pots and pans. Merchants, on their way
from one chieftain to another with, primarily, wine and other foreign
luxuries, would pass but seldom stop. There were the bards already
referred to. After 1224 Dominican friars, and after 1232 Franciscans,
both Irish-speakers, might be met with. Augustinians and Carmelites
came in smaller numbers a little earlier.

How Christian were the Irish countrymen to whom they brought
the Gospel? Before touching on life in the towns the Vikings had
created, it would be as well to examine this question of Irish
Christianity during the comparatively placid eleventh and twelfth
centuries. For the past thousand years, more perhaps than with most
other European peoples with the possible exception of the Poles, the
relationship of the Irish with God through their priests has had a very
great influence on their relationship with one another and with
foreigners: certainly for the second half of that period religion and

politics have often been inextricably intertwined.

Early in our millenium Christianity in Ireland was in poor shape. The post-Patrician monastic system had not only been physically smashed by the Vikings, though these were quite quickly converted if they remained in Ireland; such stone monasteries as resisted the flames – in many cases indubitably old druidical training colleges – were increasingly secularised. They had grown rich and, by tradition, were run by the successors (*combarba*) of their founders. As feudal influences reached Ireland, the role of *combarba* had become in many cases hereditary. The new Irish–Viking ports might be run from a monastery, as was Dublin's in large measure from St. Mary's, but the number of citizens as opposed to countrymen was very small. An estimate for the year 1100 gives the population of Dublin and its suburbs as a little over fifteen hundred of whom approximately half were of Viking, Welsh and Wessex origin: at a guess this number should be doubled to include the other Viking ports and towns, with similar ethnic origin. If the population of all Ireland was then in the region of one million, the 'old Irish' – that is to say the Irish-speaking descendants of Gaelic and of pre-Celtic-speaking peoples – must have been well over 90%. The *combarba* and their missionary monks must have had their work cut out for them. In fact it is most improbable that Christianity was much more than a façade in the neighbourhood of the monasteries, while to the west of the Shannon and the Bann it would seem improbable that many people had ever pretended to be Christians at all.

Ireland was far from unique in this back-sliding towards paganism. As has been said, Christian administration travelled along the arteries, administrative as well as physical, of the old Western Empire. But when Charlemagne had himself crowned as Roman Emperor by the Pope, and more or less simultaneously converted the Germans, he was, and almost certainly on purpose, giving divine authority to his new feudal system of government by this fusion of the secular with the clerical. In the couple of centuries since his time the map of western Europe had changed vastly. The last and final schism with Byzantium was open and undisguised: Spain was in Muslim hands, France in a state of chaos, Provence in one of open heresy, anti-popes proliferated (in 1046 there were three); assorted Germans, Lombards, Normans marched and counter-marched the length and breadth of Italy. It was only in the eleventh century that the present system, whereby the pope is elected by the College of Cardinals, was introduced. Before then, he had been appointed by the Holy Roman Emperor, almost always a German. Gregory VII, a Tuscan, was only the third pope to be elected and not so appointed, in 1073, when he was some forty years old. The emperor, on the other hand, remained elected, though his *Imperium* was not beyond dispute until he had been crowned by the pope.

What had been intended nearly three hundred years before as a fusion of powers had degenerated into a dangerous fission of authority. That of the spirit (though not necessarily of the pope) has never been greater than when Hildebrand became Gregory and few more pugnacious men have ever worn the triple tiara. He was a brilliant lawyer and theologian, and he immediately called a council where he sought and obtained the backing of the leading churchmen, against the Emperor Henry IV, a German who had been ordaining bishops and thus infringing what the papacy regarded as papal authority. When Henry IV refused to back down, Pope Gregory excommunicated him and therefore placed an interdict on all his vast territories, where no one might be baptised, married or buried with the rites of the Church. The Pope's ambition has been construed as enormous, as no less than the abolition of the state and its replacement by the Church. He knew, of course, of the triumphs of Islam, and had he had his way the government of Christendom might have resembled that of the highly successful early Muslim rulers. Whether it would have lasted any longer than did Islam as a political unit is doubtful, and Voltaire would probably still have been able to make his joke: neither Holy, nor Roman, nor an Empire. As it was, Gregory VII's bid for total theocracy was skilfully and immediately undercut by Henry IV's surrender.

The story of Henry IV's atonement at Canossa in Italy is one of the great incidents of the Middle Ages. In 1077, legend has it, the Emperor waited, bare-headed and barefoot, for three days in the snow, before the Pope would receive him, hear his confession, and lift the sentence of excommunication. That he was in Canossa for three days is probably true, that he spent them in the snow less so. And even this is less likely to have been a deliberate insult to the western world's greatest monarch than a respite in which Gregory VII could decide what to do next, for he had greatly overplayed his hand.

What he had doubtless hoped for was that the Imperial electors would, by force or some other means, dispose of Henry IV and substitute a more pliable, obedient emperor in his place. Since the Pope would thenceforth be appointing the bishops (who often had great secular powers too), the strings of authority would gradually all end in his or his successors' hands. But this could hardly happen overnight, and under the curse of the interdict the people were becoming restive. Yet no more could the Supreme Christian Pontiff refuse forgiveness to a penitent sinner. Henry IV must have known this, too. The more abject his repentance, the more total his ultimate victory. He gave way on every point, was pardoned, and nothing was changed, save that for a long time there was hostility, in varying degrees, between emperor and pope, and Europe never became a theocracy.

How does all this affect Ireland? The answer is: via England. William the Conqueror brought with him to England another Tuscan, Lanfranc, who replaced the Anglo-Saxon Archbishop of Canterbury. Lanfranc was not only a compatriot of Pope Gregory's but also very much a follower. He was not having any nonsense from the Archbishop of York, who laid claim to clerical authority in the North of England, a claim which Lanfranc rapidly scotched. More important, he 'bestowed' England on King William and crowned him in the name of the Pope. This he could do in view of the Donation of Constantine, which we know (and Lanfranc and William almost certainly knew) to be a forgery. However, when Constantine split the Empire there must have been some arrangements made between Rome and Constantinople. One, which appears in the forged Donation but which was probably not in itself a forgery, gave Rome (that is to say the Pope) ultimate jurisdiction over all islands. The islands referred to were probably those of the Aegean and the Adriatic, possibly of the Mediterranean as a whole and Roman Britain. Thus, in the Pope's name, Lanfranc could legitimise William's conquest. In pursuit of Gregorian policy, Lanfranc was soon quarrelling with the Conqueror about lay and clerical jurisdiction. Nor, so far as we know, did the question of Ireland arise until the following century.

Dates now become important. In 1154 an Englishman named Breakspeare became Pope (the only Englishman ever to sit on St. Peter's throne) and in 1155 King Henry II of England sent a delegation to Rome with the request that, in view of the Donation of Constantine, he be authorised to conquer Ireland for the Pope. This was a good fifteen years before Strongbow's invasion, and Henry II's request was turned down by the Pope. A papal bull was then forged, with the opening word by which such bulls are known, *Laudabiliter*. At least it is assumed it was a forgery, if it ever existed at all, for no trace or authentification of it has been found in the archives of the Vatican or anywhere else, and later history makes its existence highly improbable. (The idea, advanced by certain Irish nationalists in the last century, that there is an obvious, sinister connection between Breakspeare's nationality and the Norman invasion of Ireland is obvious rubbish: 'nationality' in the twelfth century had a very different meaning from that of the nineteenth.)

In 1213, Pope Innocent III, a man of power in the Gregorian tradition, forced King John of England to admit that he held Ireland *and England* as fiefs of the Holy See, once again relying on the Donation of Constantine. This, needless to say, did not please King John. But it makes a further nonsense of the theory that Adrian IV had urged Henry II to invade Ireland and straighten out the Church there (though it certainly needed it). The Norman invasion had no Roman inspiration, nor did it need any. And if Canterbury was meddling in Irish church affairs, this had been going ever since the Gregorian reforms, although Canterbury had no jurisdiction, save perhaps of prestige, over Armagh.

For Lanfranc had been succeeded by his pupil, friend and fellow-Tuscan, later canonised by Alexander (VI) Borgia as St. Anselm. A believer in Gregorian reform, he soon tangled with the Conqueror's unattractive successor, William II. This red-headed sodomite not only seized archi-episcopal church lands, but also flirted with an anti-pope and refused to nominate Anselm to the vacant see. On what he thought was his deathbed, Rufus, as an act of repentance, did nominate Anselm, but that prelate refused to accept until the King had restored church lands and acknowledged the real pope. This occurred in 1093. The King recovered and immediately regretted his acknowledgement of Pope Urban, nor would he permit Anselm to go to Rome to receive the *pallium*. A compromise was reached, but it did not last. In 1097, when at last Anselm was permitted by his king to go to Rome, William Rufus immediately seized the revenues of the archi-episcopal lands. The new king, Henry I, who succeeded Rufus in 1100, was no more accommodating and resurrected the matter of Anselm's investiture. Anselm, from exile, threatened to excommunicate King Henry. A compromise was again reached, and in 1107 Anselm returned to Canterbury. He died two years later. Thus of his seventeen year archi-episcopacy he had spent a mere seven in England.

It might be thought that Anselm's English problems were enough for any man, but he intervened at least twice in Irish affairs. True,

Dublin, Waterford and later Limerick had occasionally been sending priests to Canterbury for consecration as bishops, but in 1093 (a particularly difficult year for him) St. Anselm wrote to the King of Munster, Murtagh O'Brien, whom he addressed curiously as 'King of Ireland', listing the numerous abuses prevalent within the Church there. This he repeated, from exile, ten years later. Murtagh had as good a claim as anyone of being Ard Ri, and in 1101 he made an unprecedented gesture towards the Church: he 'gave' it the Rock of Cashel, which contained churches, a monastery of probably pre-Christian origin, and fortifications against Vikings. It was not, of course, his to give. Rather more usefully, he set about reforming the Irish Church and in 1110 he was present at a great national synod, clearly of Gregorian inspiration, near Cashel. Here it was decided that Ireland should be divided into archbishoprics with twenty-four bishoprics, well defined on the British model.

Among those present was a young man named Malachy, later also canonised, who carried on the work of reform until his death in 1148, first 'rooting out barbarous rites' and in particular remnants of Brehon law such as bigamy, and rising to be at last Archbishop of Armagh. His most important contribution, perhaps, to the Church in Ireland is still visible. He twice went to Rome, on both occasions visiting St. Bernard at Clairvaux, the father of the Cistercian order. From him he introduced a new form of monasticism into Ireland. He imported it in every sense, both the means to build, and teach Irishmen to build, the fine stone monasteries, and arranging that young Irishmen be properly trained in the Rule in order to inhabit them and to instruct others. We have here a very firm date. In 1142 St. Bernard sent to St. Malachy some Irish monks whom he had trained, together with an architect and presumably skilled stone masons. Malachy had obtained the necessary, secluded land from a devout chieftain, and in that same year work began on Mellifont Abbey, in the Boyne valley. In fifteen years the abbey church was finished. No such building had been hitherto constructed in Ireland. The great church was two hundred feet long and it was consecrated, with a congregation containing many kinglets and church dignitaries, in 1157. Among those present was Dervorgilla O'Rourke, who donated 10 oz. of gold. Around the great abbey clustered the cells of the monks together with all the other buildings then required for an absolutely modern monastery.

Mellifont – to our ears the very name mingles the sweetness of honey and the plashing of cool waters – was the first, but very far from the last. Throughout the remainder of the twelfth century and all the thirteenth, what was left of the old Irish monasticism was rebuilt in stone, and much that was new as well. Now it is all, or almost all, in ruins. For this writer, just as Mellifont was the first, so in the elegance and simplicity of its very early Gothic it has remained the most beautiful, perhaps even in its aura of peace and silent meditation the most Christian, of them all.

❋ ❋ ❋

It will be recalled that the towns of Ireland had all begun their lives, in the ninth century, as Viking strongpoints near river mouths. Of them the most important soon became Dublin, principally for its geographical location, near the centre of the east coast and what was to become the convergence of the rudimentary Irish system of roads. It was not built as a port any more than were Cork or Limerick. Indeed the Liffey degenerated into little more than marshland opposite the hilltop where stood pre-Norman Dublin with its population, according to Otway Ruthven (op. cit.) of about two thousand or less. This hilltop is where Christ Church and Dublin Castle now stand, but it had expanded westwards and the city walls came to a point west of St. Audoen's and the market. As was usual in medieval towns, many lived outside the walls, only withdrawing behind them when danger threatened. Outside, to the east, was the *thing* mound which was where College Green now is: here the Vikings' 'parliament' met. Not until Norman times did the town expand northwards to the Liffey, to Wood Quay, so named because its basis was scrapped and broken Viking longboats. At the time of writing the city fathers of ath Cliath are busy bulldozing the old Norman walls in order to construct office blocks for their fellow civil servants. Since they have refused adequate time to the archaeological experts before constructing the pastel-coloured mini-skyscrapers which they fancy, by the time these words are printed the finest Viking remains in Europe will have been cemented out of existence.

Dublin, then, was not a port. Cross-channel shipping usually discharged its passengers at Dalkey, some ten miles to the south, or, less conveniently, at Howth on the far side of the Liffey. Nor was it essentially an Irish town. Indeed on more than one occasion the Viking residents attempted, without success, to expel the Irish while apparently welcoming Welsh and English. Yet even while Tara and Cashel were still in theory the assembly places of theoretical high kings, Dublin was becoming, as it has remained, the capital city. Here all medieval trades were practised and, once the Normans had made the *thing* irrelevant, the guilds were very powerful. It was primarily a workingman's town, and every weaver or wheelwright, every cobbler or cutler, had to serve his time as an unpaid apprentice, then show his skill as a journeyman, before being accepted into the guild. It was normal for a boy to adopt his father's (or foster-father's) trade, while certain streets were reserved for particular merchandise. Street names such as Fishamble and Winetavern even today reveal what once these were. The people lived in mud and wattle cottages, with thatched roofs. The life of such dwellings was short, and when one collapsed another was built on its remains. Layers of these dwellings have been found. In most cases they consisted of but a single room, with an open fire in the middle for cooking and for warmth, and a hole in the ceiling through which a proportion of the smoke escaped. Sometimes a rug-like curtain would give an element of privacy to one corner. And charred remains of cottages prove the obvious: fire was a constant hazard.

It seems that a lot of livestock was kept, in particular pigs (small by our standards, perhaps the size of a collie dog), pet dogs, again small mongrels, and cats. There were hens, too. All seem to have been most useful scavengers, for there was no form of sanitation or drainage apart from a gutter down the centre of the narrow streets of logs and rough wooden planks, along which goods were carried by pack-mules, the width being in general too small for carts. In such insanitary conditions, mortality must have been very high. Indeed it is said that in 1349 the Black Death, which exterminated about half the population of Europe, killed *everyone* in Dublin. On the other hand they usually seem to have eaten well, for to judge by the large number of bones that escaped the dogs they consumed a great deal of meat. Corn they would have got from the country, ground it into flour and baked this into coarse bread on their open fires. Up in the Castle they had finer fare no doubt, and apparently a great deal of wine.

Beer, a thick and sour sort of beer, was the drink of the poor. They also had whiskey. *Usque baugh*, the water of life, had indeed been invented by the Irish shortly before the arrival of the first Vikings, who translated it into dog Latin as 'akavit' or *aqua vitae*. No doubt it tasted exactly like the poteen of today, both good and bad depending on the length of time it was allowed to age in the cask. (The distilling of a potable alcoholic beverage seems to have been the only purely Irish invention that spread around the globe. It predated the making of brandy in Cognac by many centuries.)

The principal garment of both sexes was the heavy cloak, often with an ornamental frieze. Decorative and useful brooches were made, though the exquisite work of earlier smiths was no longer to be found. Such teaching as existed outside the new monasteries was religious and elementary, the work of priests. The populace was illiterate.

Some of the now settled Vikings, having abandoned loot as their source of wealth, had taken to trade, and though Dublin was not a port, it was an important trading centre, serviceable by lighter, both with inland Ireland and with Britain, where Bristol was the principal port for Irish goods. Indeed the Dublin–Bristol link was closer than that between Dublin and Cork. Some seagoing ships would transport Irish goods further afield, at least as far as Bordeaux, and would doubtless come back laden largely with wine.

Pre- and post-Norman Dublin can have differed little from the other Irish towns.which had started as Viking strongpoints and had not yet become seaports, save for one relative difference. Dublin's Celtic–Irish population formed a smaller segment. Only Wexford, which was virtually Welsh at the time in question, was less 'Irish' than was Dublin. And throughout the centuries, Ireland's capital has perhaps remained the least 'Irish' place in Ireland. This is but one paradox among many.

* * *

There was no Norman conquest of Ireland, for the very simple reason that there was no Ireland to be conquered. After Hastings had been won and lost, with Harold conveniently dead, Duke William simply took over the old administration based on the shires and hundreds, and installed his own men in key positions of Church and state. Once the papacy had legitimised his kingship, he only needed Domesday Book to extend his authority and make it total, and an Anglo-Saxon attempt to restore the old order became a rebellion, quite easily crushed. Many of the old governing class fled abroad, some to become the Sultan's janissaries. The feudal system generated its own momentum and stability. England was conquered, and could even survive the terrible civil war between Stephen and Matilda.

That was ended with the recognition of Matilda's son, Henry II, as King of England as well as Duke of Normandy and Anjou, in 1153. He had, by marriage, also acquired the French provinces of Poitou, Guienne and Gascony. Despite these vast possessions, the young king – he was twenty-one in 1154 – was, as we have seen, asking for papal authorisation to conquer Ireland, ostensibly to purify the Church which was in a state of decay. If he obtained that authorisation, he did not use it. For fifteen years he watched the post-Patrician monastic system in its death throes, and apart from the monasteries, Christianity in Ireland meant very little. Local attempts at reform were built on sand.

But if such was to be the Norman excuse for the invasion in years and centuries to come, the reality was far less dignified. The Irish tribal system, undermined in one way by Christianity since this had banned Brehon law, in another by the Viking towns for which there was no place in the *tuatha* system, had in some ways received its mortal blow long before at the hands of Brian Boru, who had become High King by conquest and not through election by his peers. In the ensuing struggles for an essentially worthless throne, the septs fought a long series of wars. It is scarcely an exaggeration to state that whenever any one man succeeded, or seemed near to succeeding, in his ambition to emulate Boru, enough of his peers would form a temporary alliance to thwart him. Now, as so often in Irish legend and history, a woman appeared on the scene, with disastrous result. She was Dervorgilla, who had attended the original consecration of Mellifont Abbey, the wife of the O'Rourke chieftain, then an ally of an O'Connor chieftain, and she was 'abducted' by another chieftain named Dermot MacMurrough, who had become King of Leinster by murdering the previous king, Don MacLochlainn, a protégé of the O'Connors. That murder had taken place in 1152. In a confusion of wars and shifting alliances MacMurrough remained the dominant figure. Spasmodic fighting went on, but in 1166 one Rory O'Connor, in alliance with the Dubliners and certain tribes or warrior bands, seized the high kingship and forced MacMurrough to do him obeisance. He was still in theory King of Leinster, but not for long. O'Rourke had not forgotten the insult to his honour – few Irishmen ever do – and attacked MacMurrough, who fled to Wales.

A year later he returned with Norman–Welsh mercenaries and regained his kingship of Leinster. The Welsh knights went home, but almost at once MacMurrough was defeated by his old enemies. In 1168 he landed again, with a larger Welsh–Norman force, and this time he managed to establish himself in Wexford. At some point he had promised his daughter, Eva, in marriage to Strongbow. He had gone further, and in total defiance of all Irish law had promised to make Strongbow his heir. Meanwhile he pretended to accept O'Connor as his High King, while in correspondence with his

Welsh friends, who were collecting an army. On or about 1 May 1169 this army landed at Bannow Bay, in the south of what is now County Wexford. They built fortifications of earth, which even today look formidable enough to discourage tanks. More important, they had about a hundred armoured cavalrymen, hitherto unknown in Ireland, and a strong force of archers, also a novelty to the Irish. MacMurrough and his forces joined them, and together they captured Wexford town before marching on. However, the Welsh–Normans quarrelled among themselves, and most of them went home, leaving MacMurrough with a fair amount of territory but little hope of holding it. He asked Henry II for help, but was refused it by the King, who suggested – it seems – that he again ask his Welsh friends to come to his assistance.

Strongbow now set about collecting a formidable army in Wales. He appears to have accepted Henry II's suggestion to MacMurrough, which may have been sarcastic, as permission for this expedition, but if so that tough and foul tempered monarch (within a few months, in December 1170, he was, perhaps inadvertently or while drunk, to order the murder of Thomas à Becket) had wiser thoughts. He knew too much about armed Norman bands to wish to see a Norman army, not under his direct control, beyond the Irish Sea. At the last moment he cancelled the expedition. He was too late, whether or not Strongbow received the message at Haverfordwest.

Strongbow's force landed in August 1170 and was joined by MacMurrough, whose daughter, Eva, Strongbow immediately married. What was now a Norman army with Irish auxiliaries under MacMurrough advanced on Dublin, which it captured but in which it was immediately besieged by O'Connor on land and by his ally Gottfred, King of Man, by sea. In May of 1171 MacMurrough died and Strongbow claimed all his titles, though not the high kingship. O'Connor offered him only the towns of Dublin, Wexford and Waterford.

At this point O'Connor, who was also having trouble with the O'Briens in Munster, made a grave tactical error. He divided his besieging army into three parts, one of which raided through south Leinster, one of which moved north of Dublin and destroyed the standing crops which might have served to feed Strongbow's men, while the third remained outside Dublin. This third Strongbow attacked and destroyed. His cavalry terrified the Irish and his archers caused many casualties. The siege was lifted and O'Connor's other armies melted away.

Military technology, in the form of armour, horses and the longbow, gave Strongbow's small force an immense advantage over the Irish hosts. So, too, did military discipline and a knowledge of contemporary battlefield tactics, in both of which the Irish were deficient. It was unlikely that any Irish chieftain would be able, in the foreseeable future, to put in the field an army fit to withstand the Normans. All Ireland lay open to them, and wherever they might choose to go they were as likely to pick up temporary friends as to encounter temporary enemies.

Strongbow's troubles lay to his rear. So angry was Henry II that he had already ordered all English and Welshmen to return immediately to Britain, under threat of sequestering all their possessions both there and in the French provinces.

King Henry went further. He entered into agreement with certain Irish chieftains in the west and south, including Dermot MacCarthy, 'king' of Cork, and Durend, 'king' of Limerick, both of whom swore fealty to the King of England. Strongbow, who appears never to have contemplated any serious disloyalty, had already offered his king Dublin, Waterford and other strong points, which Henry II had accepted, restoring Strongbow's lands in Wales, England and France. Nevertheless he prepared with great speed what was then an enormous army for his own conquest of Ireland, including five hundred knights and several thousand archers together with the elaborate apparatus needed for siege warfare.

On 16 October 1171 he landed at Crook near Waterford, which town Strongbow immediately surrendered to him, at the same time doing him obeisance as King of Leinster. Then, taking a roundabout route and accepting submissions as he went, including it seems O'Connor's, the King marched to Dublin. According to Giraldus Cambrensis, however, the men of Ulster did not surrender. Dublin he 'gave' to Bristol, whatever that may mean. He had thus, in less than a month, subdued (permanently he doubtless hoped) three of Ireland's four green fields at almost no cost. He spent Christmas in Dublin.

The evil murder of Becket did not prevent him from ordering an immediate and total reorganisation of the Church in Ireland. All the bishops and other church dignitaries were summoned to a great synod at Cashel, where they swore an act of fealty to Henry who was represented by the abbot of Buildwas, a Cistercian house to which St. Mary's, Dublin, was subject. It is significant of the monastic nature of the Irish Church at that time that this prebend should have represented the King rather than the Archbishop of Dublin, St. Laurence O'Toole, who was also present and who had already sworn a personal act of loyalty to King Henry. (The Primate could not leave Armagh because, it is said, of old age. However he later gave his approval to all that the Synod of Cashel had enacted.)

It was a great deal. An entire new constitution was drafted. The sins of the Irish people and their clergy were roundly condemned. The new Church was to be modelled on that of England, and the whole country was divided into bishoprics, each bishop again swearing loyalty to the King. Parishes were created everywhere, groups beneath rural deans (though how this was done rapidly without maps it is hard to see), and arrangements laid down for the paying of parish priests, out of monastic funds in some cases where the parishes were monastic land, but generally by the collection of tithes. And that was that, though it was many years before the tithes could be collected.

Meanwhile Henry's engineers were building castles strategically located with the intention of controlling all Ireland. And, on the model of Mellifont, great stone monasteries began to appear everywhere. Had Henry remained in Ireland even for a very few years, he might well have completed his conquest. But in late March of 1172 he received most disquieting news. The papal legate in England was threatening an interdict unless Henry returned immediately to make reparation for Becket's murder. And his eldest son, later Henry III, was actively and obviously planning a rebellion.

So he sailed from Wexford, in April 1172, never to return. He had laid what must have appeared to him firm foundations, both lay and clerical, for his new realm in Ireland. But he trusted no man, least of all Strongbow, to act as viceroy and build on those foundations. Instead he appointed half a dozen Norman noblemen to positions of power in Ireland, and especially in Dublin, all great offices but none of them predominant. For Henry II misconstrued the old Roman maxims, and in his own absence proposed to divide and rule. The man he had left in charge continued to build castles and found monasteries, but the administrative apparatus he had designed never came to life. (It must, however, be said that there was no racial hostility within the Church. When in 1275 Mellifont attempted to limit acceptance as monks to Irish-speakers only, it was firmly refused permission so to do by the Church authorities.) However the pyramid of feudal power, based on hundreds and shires, the parish with its priest and its lord of the manor, the county with its sheriff, the great noblemen with their duty to provide military support to the Crown, all of this was utterly alien to Irish society and save in the extreme eastern part of the country was not to be successfully clamped upon the Irish for another five centuries. Indeed King Henry had never attempted to create shires, but had appointed a sheriff over several *tuatha*. In the usual Norman style he tried to use local institutions, but he failed.

On the contrary, it was the Normans who became hibernicised. In the northwest the de Burgos became Burkes. In the south the Geraldines became a great Irish clan, intermarrying or at war with the MacCarthys, O'Connors, and so on, while an attempt in 1276 to enforce English, as opposed to Brehon, law on all the Irish was a complete failure.

For several centuries the almost perpetual struggle for power continued, only now there were several Norman cards added to the unruled and unruly pack. And the ultimate prize was no longer the high kingship, but control of Dublin and the land. The power of the bishops rapidly withered away, that of the great abbots became as peculiar as that of their predecessors, and tithes were rarely collected for non-existent priests in forgotten parishes.

By the late fifteenth century the abbot of Mellifont was reporting to his superior at Citeaux or Clairvaux that his order was in ruins in Ireland. Apart from his own house and that of St. Mary's, Dublin, none kept the Rule, nor was the Cistercian habit still worn. He asked that he be excused from even visiting the other monasteries. When last he had attempted to do so, the monks had manned their battlements and belfries and had repelled his own monks with javelins, stones and arrows.

Ireland in the Middle Ages is a tortuous tale of perpetual guerrilla warfare and of a decline into barbarous paganism. Furthermore the situation, bad enough in the first century after the Norman invasion, did then have certain ameliorating aspects. Most of the monasteries were then built, and no doubt decorated with considerable beauty, while the level of scholarship or at least of scholasticism within them was high. Certain traditions, in war and peace, continued to be observed: for instance hostages were not usually murdered or blinded, nor standing crops regularly burned. Some beautiful poems were written, many old ones put down in writing. Friars appeared to spread the Gospel, Augustinians and Carmelites, followed by Dominicans (not yet the activists of the Roman inquisition) and then Franciscans (not yet its spies). They went some way to replace the almost non-existent priesthood, particularly in the west and north. Slowly the forests were being forced back and roads built. Dublin grew, and the Liffey was confined within artificial banks. To the Irish of the time, untroubled at least by invaders, the thirteenth century must have seemed a period of comparative calm and even of progress. If it had not been for what were now pestilential chieftains with their ambitions and marauding armies of mercenaries, had there been any sort of government to preserve the peace, the thirteenth century might well have gone down to history as a sort of golden age. Even so, Ireland did produce wealth in this century, even though most of this was syphoned off by Norman potentates to England and France. In any case, a far worse century was to follow.

* * *

It will be recalled that what was by then called Scotland had, long before, been first occupied by men from Ireland, who had defeated and absorbed the Picts. Brian Boru might still style himself 'Imperator Scottorum', meaning emperor of both countries, but even by his time they were two distinct societies, though the Highland Scots spoke the same language as the Irish, while the Lowland Scots spoke the P-Celtic of the Welsh and Strathclyde British. The border between them was not the sea, for Antrim was only a few miles from Galloway. Indeed King John had given large tracts of Antrim to Alan of Galloway and to Duncan of Carrick early in the thirteenth century, while the Bruce dynasty had connections in the Derry area. But Ireland and Scotland had remained two lands nevertheless, since Ireland had its first parliament in 1264 and Pope Innocent III had permitted King John in 1213 to style himself King of Ireland provided, as stated earlier in this chapter, it be clearly understood that he held both Ireland *and* England as fiefs of the Holy See according to the clause of the Donation of Constantine concerning islands. Scotland, meanwhile, had been a kingdom on its own since Viking times.

The first record we have of the importation of galloglasses, those mercenaries of mixed Scottish and Viking descent already mentioned, is in 1302, which does not mean that they had not been imported into Ireland, piecemeal, at a considerably earlier date. In the Anglo-Scottish war, after Robert the Bruce had defeated the English at Bannockburn in 1314, he decided to exploit this victory by invading King Edward's kingdom of Ireland. In 1315 his brother Edward Bruce landed at Larne with a ferocious army, which rampaged through Ireland. In May 1316 Edward Bruce had himself crowned 'King of Ireland' at Faughart, near Dundalk, but his was an unstable, brutal character. At Christmas Robert Bruce had to bring over another Scots army. There was much fighting and the Anglo-Normans lost control of all Ireland west of the Shannon and the Bann and north of what is now the Ulster border. But the Scots repeatedly raided even up to the walls of Dublin. Then at last, in 1318, Edward Bruce was killed in battle. His brother had long gone home, and since there was nothing much left to loot in Ireland, his hated Scots followed him. Some lingered on in what is now the County Down, leaving a ruined, ravaged country behind them. The annals say: 'For in this Bruce's time, for three years and a half, falsehood and famine and homicide filled the country, and undoubtedly men ate each other in Ireland.'

After the Scottish horror, the community of interest between what must now be called the Norman–Irish and the rest of the native population became obvious to all. And when, in 1341, King Edward III of England attempted to introduce English officials with the idea of making Ireland solvent once again, the measure was met with universal detestation. A *modus vivendi* had been reached whereby the Normans controlled the lowlands, while the Irish had land over 600 feet above sea level. None of them wished to be run by English officials.

Then a far worse horror struck Ireland. In 1348 rats carried the Black Death to Dublin. In the first and worst epidemic (there were several milder recurrences before the century's end) it is estimated that half the population of Ireland, which has been reckoned at a million and half before the epidemic struck, died. Casualties were of course worst in the horribly unhygienic towns and indeed it has been reported that in Dublin *everyone* died. This cannot be true, but what is true is that the majority of the English and Welsh lived in the towns and suffered far the heaviest casualties. Of the country people, the richer lowlands, with their harvest of grain and hence the rats in the granaries, suffered more than the people of the highlands who tended to be pastoral and therefore less bothered by rats.

There followed a reoccupation by the aboriginal Irish and the Irish–Normans of most of the country. By the time Edward III died, in 1377, the English-administered territory was very small, about a dozen miles of coastline on either side of Dublin and a hinterland of little more than thirty miles depth at the most. This was named the Pale and varied in size, but was never much smaller than this.

Had the Irish possessed any tradition, or even folk memory, of self-government, had they indeed possessed anything like our concept of nationality, it would have been extremely simple for them to expel the English. But they had neither, and produced no leader of talent who might have inspired them as Bruce had inspired his Scots.

Indeed, as already mentioned, we read in the late fourteenth century of men hanging about the 'courts' of kinglets, and referred to as 'kerns and idlemen'. The kerns were presumably former soldiers now turned vagabonds who, if they were not too far gone in despondency, might have been formed into some sort of fighting force, again of dubious reliability. As for the idlemen, who exist everywhere but somehow seem to be more conspicuous in Ireland as they lean against corners and pick at their teeth, there is really nothing than can be done with them at any time or in any capacity. They seldom even bother to make their own poteen.

NOTE
1 *History of Medieval Ireland* by H. J. Otway-Ruthven. I have drawn on this scholarly work more than on *History of Medieval Ireland from 1086–1513* by Edmund Curtis, though both works are of course scholarly and thorough.

8

THE CONQUEST THAT FAILED

In 1210 King John visited Ireland and attempted to establish a rational form of government: the administration that his father, Henry II, had left behind him was grossly inadequate. The head of the Dublin administration was usually the justiciar and when he was a powerful nobleman, preferably of royal stock, a Duke of Clarence or a Duke of York – for the Irish will more readily accept government by great men than by efficient nonentities – comparative tranquillity ensued, particularly in Leinster and eastern Munster. But King John could not stay in Ireland long enough to create an adequate mechanism with which to rule Ireland. Indeed his barons in England were showing signs of dangerous turbulence, and he had to return after only a few months to his larger kingdom, there to surrender part of his powers in Magna Carta, the conditions of which were sometimes claimed as applicable to the Irish nobility, sometimes not.

Nearly two centuries were to pass before another English king, Richard II, also asserting his right to the kingdom of Ireland, was to cross the Irish Sea. To any who would study the political history of this period, the details of inter-tribal warfare are both intensely confusing and to most readers, I fear, exceedingly boring as the petty tribes of Celtic or Norman–Irish, increasingly interwined, fought one another in an almost unending series of futile wars while the English government, with at least equal futility, attempted and failed to exact its supremacy over the whole island. What is of more interest than political or military events is to be found in the fact that Ireland was left, relatively, alone and almost untroubled for some three centuries – but never quite abandoned – while the English fought the French for a hundred years and, having been defeated in France, proceeded to fight one another in the Wars of the Roses for the best part of another. Meanwhile what happened in Ireland was of more social, and sociological, importance than political.

Indeed throughout this period there was nothing that could be called an English 'policy' towards Ireland save of the most basic, commonplace sort. The Irish were to pay, through taxation in its multiple forms, more than enough to support the Anglo-Norman occupation and for the administration of this. Here the English failed, for numerous reasons. One was the absence of an administrative apparatus inherited from any more or less indigenous system, as in Anglo-Saxon Britain, or re-imposed, as in France, from an earlier and more tranquil system, that of Gaul. Ireland almost never paid for its own administration at anything above the *tuatha* level. In the absence of any real monetary system, save to a certain extent in the trading ports, how could it? The Irish tribes could pay their immediate tribal rulers in labour, free or slave, or in kind. Only in the most indirect, cumbersome and protracted manner could they pay Dublin, let alone London, in this fashion. In England itself the old feudal levy was breaking down and, after the Black Death, when labour became a comparatively scarce and valuable commodity, the old governing class by its competition for labourers rapidly brought the old villein system to an end. An Ireland that had never known such a class system, and that was never sufficiently conquered to have one imposed upon it, lacked the fundamental basis upon which feudal land tenure rested. The English administration of Ireland was almost never self-supporting, let alone financially productive, and at almost all times had to be supported by the London exchequer, the alternative being to abandon larger and larger parts of Ireland to self- or non-administration. This is what usually happened. Numerous attempts to re-impose English rule by the sending of inadequate expeditionary forces to Ireland only aggravated the situation. The money to pay the troops was almost never forthcoming from the authorities. At least once the English soldiers were paid in the form of dried peas. Though the habit of billeting them on the Irish made them very unpopular, on one occasion such an expeditionary force deserted *en masse*.

Secondly, the Norman governing class disappeared. The great families of the original conquerors frequently had lands in England, Wales or Norman-controlled France. They often provided the earliest class of 'absentee landlord', exporting goods produced in Ireland to be sold or enjoyed in England. When the English government made its most strenuous efforts to prevent this essentially private form of tax-gathering by punitive measures prohibiting the passage of men, horses and provisions from Ireland, in 1369, many of the landlords simply sold or even abandoned their Irish territories to the Irish. A Statute of Absentees, passed in 1380, merely served to accelerate the process. Other settlers, such as the Geraldines, had never been, or spoken, English at all. These Norman–Irish gradually became part of the Irish scene, speaking Irish, adopting Irish modes, creating around themselves little courts like those of Irish chieftains, complete with poets and Brehon lawyers. Later arrivals, such as the Butlers, became in their turn great Irish families. The symbolism of the Ard Ri was replaced by the equally symbolic figure of the King of Ireland (who, since the days of King John, had always been the King of England), and repeated efforts were made to use the great Irish families of Norman descent to govern the decreasing area of Ireland that accepted any type of English rule at all. A final attempt at this type of racial authority took place in 1366, when an Irish parliament met at Kilkenny.

The importance of the Statutes of Kilkenny has been in one way exaggerated. They were essentially a codification of much law and practice that had sprung up in the previous two centuries, and were principally directed against the hibernification of the Normans, now referred to as 'the English'. The population was divided into three, so called 'the loyal English', almost all of whom lived in or near Dublin and the east coast, 'the rebel English' who lived more or less like Irishmen, and 'the Irish enemy' who constituted far and away the greater part of the population. Since there was no form of Irish 'nation' with whom peace could be made or against whom war declared, as with Scotland, little if any attempt was made at this time to deal with them. The phrase 'loyal English' speaks for itself. It was against the 'rebel English' that the legislation of Kilkenny was directed, and specifically against their adoption of Irish customs, including the Irish language, Irish dress, Irish games, Irish manners of riding and even working the land, fosterage and above all Irish law. None of these regulations, it must be repeated, was created in 1366, but their codification was an attempt to enforce them. Though this failed they were cited as authoritative by Poynings' parliament (1494–1495) and again by Henry VIII in 1541. Meanwhile between the two real attempted reconquests of Ireland, by King Richard II in 1394 and 1399 and by Henry VIII nearly a century and half later, Ireland virtually enjoyed what was later to be called Home Rule, with its own parliament (established in 1297) and usually administered by the great families of 'loyal English', though their 'loyalty' became as difficult to establish as it was to display towards an England racked by dynastic war. If Ireland had been ungoverned before the arrival of the Normans, after their defeat at the Battle of

Ath-an-Kip in 1270, it became for many centuries ungovernable, at least by foreigners.

This was not because it was in any way invincible. That interesting monarch, Richard II, reasserted his sovereignty in 1394 during a brief interval in the French War. With an adequate army and against very little opposition, he made what was nearer to a royal progress than a military campaign which covered almost all Ireland, receiving a personal oath of loyalty from almost all the Irish or Norman chieftains. He is said to have liked his kingdom of Ireland so well that he returned five years later. The 'ifs and buts' of history are futile though intriguing. Richard, the last of the Plantagenets, patron of Chaucer and Froissart, lover of the arts and of beautiful objects, a cosmopolitan figure more at home in Italian silks and French brocades than in the armour of his predecessors and his knights, was the first prominent Englishman who might be described as a product of the early Renaissance, that delicious springtime of western Europe. Had he remained in his kingdom of Ireland, instead of returning to England to be arrested and murdered by Henry Bolingbroke, who can tell what he might not have made of the gentler kingdom?

For Ireland, which could know no Renaissance since it had never known Greek antiquity, was nevertheless entering upon what, by Irish standards, must be called a variant of a golden age. The age of the bloody sagas was now past, and Irish poets were writing lyric poems of an increasing beauty. In all Europe, perhaps they were the first to recognise and record the beauty of nature and of love. Among them was Gerald Fitzgerald, Earl of Desmond, who died in 1398, and who wrote much in praise of women. I quote his poem *The Dispraise of Absalom*, written in the late fourteenth century and here translated from the Irish by Robin Flower (and quoted from *The Faber Book of Irish Verse*).

> Veiled in that light amazing,
> Lady, your hair soft waved
> Has cast into dispraising
> Absalom son of David.
>
> Your golden locks close clinging,
> Like birdflocks of strange seeming,
> Silent with no sweet singing
> Draw all men into dreaming.

That bright hair idly flowing
Over the keen eyes' brightness,
Like gold rings set with glowing
Jewels of crystal lightness.

Strange loveliness that lingers
From lands that hear the Siren:
No ring enclasps your fingers,
Gold rings your neck environ,

Gold chains of hair that cluster
Round the neck straight and slender,
Which to that shining muster
Yields in a sweet surrender.

Something of the spirit of Provence had reached distant Ireland and the courtly poets of the kinglets were highly honoured and highly rewarded. The spirit and the role of the *file* had never died, and seldom had it been so rewarded. In 1415, the year of Agincourt, it was worth the while of Henry V's lieutenant in Dublin, John Talbot, to plunder them as poets, so rich had they become.

The stonemasonry of the period, or such of it as has survived, is also exquisite, and so, no doubt, were the paintings which, alas!, have not. It is extremely difficult to 'date' Irish music, but it seems that much was created at this time too. It is pleasant, if fruitless, to speculate how an Ireland of Richard II's would have developed, but by the year 1400 he had gone, and shortly after his departure Henry IV recalled his armies to fight in the French War and to postpone the English civil war.

Save Dublin and a narrow Pale, Ireland was abandoned. The annals of 1403 say: 'The Galls were driven from all Ulster, and the North was burned, and the monasteries were despoiled.' The chaos was far from confined to Ulster. A few years later the annals say: 'This Centre was never in so gret a Meschefe as hit is now.' And in 1425 the Bishop of Waterford and Lismore was reporting to Rome the many evil deeds of the Archbishop of Cashel, among others: 'he had taken a ring from the image of St. Patrick and bestowed it on his concubine . . .'

For the Irish return to Irish ways, as the 'loyal English' withdrew to Dublin and an ever-narrower Pale, was perhaps inevitably accompanied by a similar return to pagan beliefs even in areas where they had almost ceased to prevail. John Talbot, who was ennobled as Lord Furnival and later became Earl of Shrewsbury, had proved himself an exceptionally brave and competent soldier in the French War. His act in extracting sums of money from the Irish poets displayed a bravery of another sort. It will be recalled that one of the duties of the *file* in ancient times had been to lampoon his chieftain's enemies, at times even unto death. Lord Furnival's predecessor as justiciar – or lord lieutenant as the chief English executive in Dublin was now usually called – had been a certain Sir John Stanley. He had offended an Irish poet who had lampooned him with the utmost skill and venom: within weeks Sir John was dead. To very many Irishmen, and perhaps to not a few Englishmen as well, the sequence of cause and effect was obvious.

If for the Irish artist in words on wood or stone the fifteenth was in large measure a happy century, this was certainly not true of the Christian religion in Ireland. The fate of so many monasteries has been described in the previous chapter. And the Church in Ireland was essentially monastic in its organisation. In those that remained life was, not invariably, very far indeed from that envisaged by St. Colman or St. Brigid. True, *The Land of Cockaigne* is a long, satirical poem written in Middle English by Gofraidh Fionn O'Dalagh, who died in 1387. The following stanzas are modernised by John Montague (and quoted from *The Faber Book of Irish Verse*). It is not suggested that the reality in any monastic establishment approached such lubricity, but it is certain that no Irish poet could have penned such fantasy either five hundred years earlier or five hundred years later, even in a foreign language.

> The young monks each day
> After meat, go out to play:
> Despite their sleeves and cowl
> There is no hawk or swift fowl
> Faster flying through the sky
> Than these monks when feeling high.
> When the abbot sees them flee,
> He follows them with glee,
> But nevertheless bids the throng
> To alight for evensong.
> When the monks don't come down,
> But further flee, at random,
> He takes a maiden, from the mass,
> And turning up plump white ass,
> Beats the tabours with his hand,
> To make his monks alight to land.
> The monks, all seeing that,
> Drop from the sky, upon the dot,

And ring the wench all about
To thwack her white toute,
And after this pleasant work
Wend meekly home to drink
Going to their collation
In a goodly fair procession.

Another abbey is thereby –
Forsooth, a great fair nunnery,
Up a river of sweet milk,
Where there is a surplus of silk.
When the summer sun is hot,
The young nuns take a boat
And sail upon that river,
Both with oars and rudder.
When they are far from the abbey
They strip themselves naked to play,
And leaping down into the brim
Set themselves skilfully to swim.
The monks, when they this espy,
Rise up, and forthwith fly
And coming to the nuns anon
Each monk grabs him one
And quickly bears forth his prey
To the great, grey abbey,
And teaches the nuns an orison
With jigging up and down.

He that would be a stallion good
And can set straight his hood,
That monk shall have, without fear,
Twelve new wives each year,
While the monk who sleeps the best
And above all, likes his rest,
There is hope for him, God wot,
Soon to be a father abbot.

If it was not only possible but even almost commonplace to
plunder decadent monasteries and even destroy their abbeys in the
fifteenth century without thereby calling down the wrath of God
upon sacrilegious heads, there was little to protect country churches,
in particular those without a resident priest who had no tithes on
which to live. The Irish countryside is dotted with the ruins of little
churches, or shrines, the destruction of which is almost invariably
blamed by local inhabitants on Cromwell or the armies of King
Billy or those of 1798. This may very often be true, but such pathetic

little ruins are also not infrequently to be encountered in places where English soldiers are unlikely to have passed by. Throughout the fifteenth and early sixteenth centuries Irish septs outside the Pale were frequently engaged in raiding one another's territories. Cows would be stolen, crops burned and, on occasion, churches undoubtedly looted and knocked down. Savage bands of gallo-glasses, not infrequently led by a nobleman, roamed the country when not employed by some chieftain, much like the *condottieri* of Italy at that time. Ireland was not alone in its relapse from Christianity in the period before the Reformation. Being cut off from the rest of Europe and lacking even any effective ecclesiastical authority, it would hardly be surprising if the slide towards paganism among the Irish had exceeded that of Calvin's France or Luther's Germany. If any one group of men kept the Christian spirit alive in the wilder parts of Ireland it was the friars from uncontaminated monasteries who, like the bards, had tales to tell, in their case ancient tales of saints and martyrs, and also the Gospels to preach.

If the Irish were losing their Christian faith, this did not mean that they were returning to the somewhat woolly beliefs of their pagan ancestors. The Druids may have often, long ago, become priests, but the priests did not now become Druids. The Vikings and the Normans and the first English settlers had largely destroyed the *tuatha* system. Physically the sept might continue to exist, particularly in the more remote parts of the country, but if so it was as a social convenience, a way of life that suited the people, without pretence to semi-supernatural origin in the remote past. In ancient days sept had fought sept, but on foot and therefore within easy reach of the homeland they wished either to enlarge or to defend. Now they had acquired horses from the Normans, and could create a form of light cavalry, known as hobelers, which ranged far wider and inflicted much greater destruction. English and Welsh farmers who had settled outside the Pale fled back across the Irish Sea in large numbers. Their farms, even if they were not burned, could not be fitted into the *tuatha* system. Petty warfare and looting were so commonplace that the people bonded together in ever larger, but never stable, communities for protection, with some king to lead them and even to settle their internal disputes according to Brehon law. He might be a Norman or he might be a Celt, but his right to tenure was his sword arm, and if there were an Ard Ri he sat forgotten upon a throne somewhere in England. Ireland (always with the conditional phrase 'outside the Pale') might well be in a near permanent state of chaos, though not everywhere nor at all times anywhere, but with the ingurgitation of the Normans now as well as of the Vikings, it was probably more 'Irish' than it had been since first those longships beached on Lambay Island. It was also, after 1536, never to be so Irish again for several centuries, until wave after new wave of foreigners had either receded or remained to become absorbed into the *genius loci* and thus to produce a new sort of Irish man and woman.

9
HENRY VIII'S REFORMATION

For the convenience of schoolchildren, the Battle of Bosworth (1485) has long marked the end of the Wars of the Roses. To contemporaries, however, this was far from obvious. Yet another claimant to the Crown of England (and therefore of Ireland too) had landed and killed its wearer in battle. The claim of the victor, Henry Tudor, was less weighty than that of many of his predecessors and there can have seemed little reason to suppose that Bosworth Field had ended the wars, nor that the Tudor dynasty was to create the modern English nation which was to last as an entity until the present day.

In Ireland the definitive nature of Bosworth was, and rightly, even less self-evident. The Wars of the Roses had scarcely affected Ireland, which had been predominantly Yorkist throughout, and none of the battles for the Crown had been fought on Irish soil. Such effect as they had exerted on Irish life had been largely negative. The mutual self-slaughter of England's chivalry had meant that there were seldom any royal soldiers to spare for Irish campaigns, and the recurrent chaos on the larger island had on occasion drawn English or Norman noblemen, sometimes with Irish mercenaries, to look for loot and power over there. This had scarcely affected the Irish in Ireland at all, save to enable them yet further to decrease the boundaries of the Pale and to increase the equivalent of Home Rule described in the previous chapter. And these circumstances were to continue until well after the end of the century, while King Henry VII consolidated the position of himself and his dynasty in England. During this period he had limited time or energy to spare for Ireland.

This brave and subtle Welshman seems to have had one of the rare, modern virtues, a sense of humour, at least of a practical nature. His financial expert, Cardinal Morton, invented the famous 'Morton's fork' with which to incapacitate the treasonable, or potentially treasonable, nobility to whom, be it noted, the fork itself was a new, foreign instrument for the eating of food, though not for the catching of fish, even very large fish. Morton's variety gave the great noblemen, some of whom were always ready to begin yet again the futile struggle for power, the alternatives of disbanding their private armies or of paying an intolerable tax. In most cases the essential prong of the fork worked: the expensive private armies of 'livery and maintenance' vanished. Then the royal joke, in the form of heavy taxation, could be realised. Henry VII found England in turbulent misery and the exchequer almost bankrupt. He left his heir a rich, and more or less loyal kingdom.

The Irish, however, would not allow him to forget them. When Henry had been but two years on the throne a young man appeared in Ireland purporting to be the Earl of Warwick, nephew of the late King Edward IV whose two sons had been murdered ('the Princes in the Tower') by Richard III and who was therefore the legitimate Yorkist heir to the throne. It was an ill-conceived plan, for Warwick was in fact alive (not being murdered until 1499), and was shown to the people of London in 1487. Lambert Simnel had been trained originally to impersonate one of the dead princes, his tutor being an Oxford priest named Symonds who aspired thereby to win for himself the Archbishopric of Canterbury. Simnel appears to have been a pleasant boy, the son of an Oxford tradesman and some nine years old when Symonds took charge of his peculiar education. No one then knew for certain that the princes in the Tower were dead, and had Symonds succeeded in his original personification of one of them by Simnel, success could only have resulted in acute embarrassment and failure should one or both of them have then emerged alive. On the other hand the fact that neither Henry VII nor Richard III had disposed of young Warwick – a surprising omission on the part of King Richard, though King Henry was far less bloodthirsty – was unknown. His appearance on public display in London cut the ground in England from beneath the Lambert Simnel conspiracy before ever it was launched. This, however, did not deter at least one of the leading conspirators, Lord Lincoln, who had apparently conversed personally with the real Lord Warwick early in 1487. This was at about the same time as, or immediately after, Simnel's appearance in Ireland whither his tutor, Symonds, had taken him.

It was a fairly elaborate conspiracy, involving several thousand German mercenaries to be sent to Ireland by Margaret, Duchess of Burgundy, a sister of the late King Edward IV. As stated, the Irish officers of government were largely Yorkists and whether or not

they believed in the imposture – probably most of them did – unless
Henry Tudor were quickly toppled their own positions of power
were in obvious danger. King Henry had already appointed his
brother, Jasper Tudor, as governor but had retained the Yorkist
Earl of Kildare as his deputy. Only the Lancastrian rivals of Kildare
(principally the Butler clan which held the city of Waterford as well
as Kilkenny and many other strongpoints) and the Italian Archbishop of Armagh were opposed to the conspiracy. The rest escorted
the young Oxford boy to Dublin where he was crowned with a
golden chaplet taken from a statue of the Virgin Mary (this being
itself an act of sacrilege) as King Edward VI (thus assuming the
death of the princes in the Tower) on 14 May 1487. Among those
present in Christ Church Cathedral were the Archbishop of Dublin,
Lord Lincoln, Lord Kildare, the chancellor, the treasurer and
many other magnates, lay and clerical. It is a curious fact, and one
perhaps characteristic of Anglo-Irish relations from many aspects,
that the only coronation of an English king that ever took place in
an Irish cathedral was that of Lambert Simnel.

The rebels, who must now be called Irish rebels, invaded England
with their large number of Duchess Margaret's German auxiliaries.
They were not welcomed by the English of Lancashire, but nevertheless marched on. Finally, near Stoke-on-Trent, they fought a
pitched and bloody battle with the troops of King Henry. Lincoln,
the Irish leader Sir Thomas Fitzgerald, together with the German
general and some 4,000 men were killed. This, incidentally, is
another unique occasion. Throughout the last five centuries one of
the major preoccupations of British governments in time of war has
been fear of an invasion, from Ireland, by England's enemies. This
was the only occasion on which such an event has ever taken place.
It was a fiasco of only a few weeks' duration.

King Henry VII's reaction to his soldiers' victory was as clever as
might be expected from that wily man: Symonds was consigned to
the dungeons for ever; Lambert Simnel was given a job in the royal
kitchens; and the Irish leaders who had survived the battle were
sent home, to be eliminated or forced to accept allegiance one by
one. Henry Tudor had little to learn from his younger contemporary,
Niccolo Machiavelli. And when the next pretender, this time Perkin
Warbeck posing as the younger of the 'Princes in the Tower', landed
at Cork in 1491 he was greeted with courtesy but very limited
enthusiasm by the Irish magnates.

For by then a strange and famous dinner party had taken place in England. In 1489 Henry VII had summoned the great Irishmen to England. Prominent among the servants who waited upon them was a certain Lambert Simnel, whom many of the guests had, with their own eyes, seen crowned in Christ Church. It is to be regretted that we have no record of their expressions as the 'King' they had acclaimed as the Lord's annointed filled their goblets: the expressionless face of another king, at the head of the table, is not hard to envisage. Nor are his intentions in inviting these Irish guests to cross the sea. He would soon have produced peace by royal authority in England. He intended to attempt the same in his other kingdom. And it may be assumed that he wished to examine, and impress, these magnates whom he planned to subdue.

It had taken Henry VII the better part of ten years so to establish his rule in England before he was ready to tackle the same in Ireland. Poynings' parliament met in Dublin in December of 1494 and had completed its work within the following year. This was to establish an entirely new ideological framework for the government of Ireland, which was to be 'whole and perfect obedience' to the government of England, that is to say to the Anglo-Welsh king who now sat upon the English throne. This was a far cry from the theory of two kingdoms with a single monarch, both in theory and, at that time, in practice.

Poynings' most famous law did not abolish the Irish parliament, but it did deprive it of all effective legislative and judiciary decision-making power not derived or explicitly approved from London via the Council of Ireland. The English parliament of the day was in all conscience feeble enough, but the Irish were not even represented there. The Statutes of Kilkenny were reiterated, but teeth were added to them in that Ireland was to be administered by English officials, such as Sir Edward Poynings himself. An Irish grandee might be the titular lord lieutenant or governor but even that only so long as he toed the London line meticulously. Until 1782 Ireland was to be an entirely non-self-governing colony.

Poynings' Law was directed in the first instance not against the 'wild Irish' who indeed were to be left alone to brawl and fight on their pieces of farmland behind almost trackless forests for a further half century. It was the Norman–Celtic nobility that Henry VII wished to emasculate. Since the feudal system scarcely prevailed in Ireland, this was not very difficult. Those who did not melt into the Celtic background were, with some exceptions, particularly the Geraldines, quite easily brought to heel. And this was once again a technological triumph. Poynings and his thousand soldiers had gunpowder and some cannon which even the stoutest Norman castles could not withstand.

What must henceforth be called English strategy was, in Henry VII's time, quite simple. First a solid English base must be established on Irish soil. The Dublin Pale was the obvious choice, but it could no longer rely on a ring of stone forts linked by cavalry. Poynings, who served under a governor who was a child named Prince Henry, later Henry VIII, was instructed to make the whole Pale into a fortified area, with a great ditch and, of course, strategically located castles. This was quite quickly done, and while the Pale grew enough food to feed Dublin, it was, when properly garrisoned, in theory impregnable to kerns, hobelers and even galloglasses. However it was not invariably well protected, and in the thirty years after Poynings it decreased in size by approximately half, losing what is now Kildare and the Curragh as well as almost all the territory south of Dublin.

Nor was the anglification of the Irish administration entirely successful in the early days. The Earl of Kildare retained his status as one in a long line of 'uncrowned kings of Ireland' or at least of the Pale, and there were in effect thus two administrations in Dublin. Since Kildare and his friends were predominantly Yorkist while the Tudor officials obviously were not, friction was latent and was only averted by inaction. Unlike the English, the Irish have never had any great capacity for political compromise. Nor were the early Tudors sufficiently well established to ignore the dangers posed by hostility in the very capital of their Irish enclave. Yet for many years the alternative to tolerance was the risk of civil war in Ireland. Once again, the Irish were in a situation where, had they united, they could surely have expelled the English. That they failed to do so can be ascribed, on the one hand, to the absence of any Irish national concept, on the other to the fact that the only high king they had was also the King of England. In 1541 that King, Henry VIII, struck at his Irish subjects. Their encroachments on his Irish foothold were by then so great as to give him little alternative. Besides, there were other great matters, not of Irish origin, at stake.

The 'great matter' that preoccupied so much of Henry VIII's reign was the dissolution of his marriage to Katherine of Aragon. (It is usually referred to as 'the divorce', and will for convenience be so here: the word was never used at the time, for the simple reason that the concept did not then exist. In brief, Henry wished the Pope to nullify his predecessor's dispensation which had enabled Henry to marry his brother Arthur's widow. Such and similar dispensations and subsequent nullifications were by no means rare for dynastic, political and even personal reasons at that time. Henry's demand was not unreasonable.) Nor was it the root cause of England's breach with Rome.

It was essential, from the English point of view, that a Tudor dynasty be established if England were not to revert to a state of civil war. Queen Katherine bore the King half a dozen children, but save for her daughter Mary, all were either stillborn or lived but a few days or at best weeks. (One boy baby lived long enough to be given the title of Prince of Wales but then expired.) The only precedent for a Queen Regent, Mathilda FitzEmpress, dated from the twelfth century and the period had seen ferocious civil war. By 1514 at the latest, when Katherine was approaching the usual age of menopause, the matter of a divorce was being mooted.[1] This was long before Anne Boleyn had appeared upon the scene, though by one of his many mistresses Henry had an illegitimate son, the Earl of Richmond. In 1519 the matter of the divorce was taken up seriously, by Cardinal Wolsey, who must have told the King that it would not present any insuperable difficulties. The King, who prided himself not without reason on being a very competent theologian, was on the best of terms with the Pope. In 1520 King Henry published an anti-Lutheran book of his own composition for which the Pope gave him the title of 'Defender of the Faith' and to this day British coinage bears, after the monarch's name, the initials F.D., *fidei defensor*. King Henry had requested a title equivalent to that of the Kings of France and Spain, in his case 'His Most Apostolic Majesty', but this was too much for the Pope.

There were then three great European monarchs, Henry VIII, the Emperor, Charles V (who was also King Charles I of Spain) and François I of France, but within three years there were only two, for Henry VIII attempted and failed ignominiously to invade France, while after the Battle of Pavia in 1525 there was one, for the army of François I was utterly destroyed and he himself taken prisoner by the Spaniards. To pay his polyglot army in Italy, Charles I authorised in 1527 that they sack Rome. Pope Clement VII took refuge in the Castel San Angelo, and Rome was gutted. It is said that by the time Charles's soldiers had finished with it, there were but 500 persons left alive in the Holy City. Thus in 1527, almost a decade before Henry laid his hands on the monasteries, there was not a church in Rome that had not been desecrated and even St. Peter's was used as a stables. When Charles called off his ferocious soldiery, Clement VII remained, in all but name, his prisoner. And Katherine of Aragon was Charles's aunt. A papal 'divorce' was dead. And the verdict of Canossa had been reversed.

What Charlemagne had attempted to create, and Dante had sung, was an empire with an elected emperor and a supreme pontiff, embracing all western Christendom. What Charlemagne had over-looked, though Constantine the Great most certainly had not, was that the ancient emperors had been semi-divine and as such, in theory at least, combined both roles in one. What we know about, or can surmise from, his own burial arrangements indicate that Constantine envisaged such a system for himself at least, and pre-sumably for his successors. Had there ever been a united Christen-dom, it is just possible that a papal empire might have come into existence. But by Charlemagne's time the ancient administrative framework of empire had become, *grosso modo*, the framework of a missionary Church that was, in spiritual matters, as monolithic as its predecessor had been in temporal terms. The emperor might be elected, but he was annointed by the pope. And the pope retained enormous spiritual powers in the face of a largely united Christen-dom. Hence Canossa. On the other hand, even if the Donation of Constantine was a forgery, and known to be one as early as Charle-magne's time, what it represented was very true: the emperor was, in theory, supreme, the pope his subject. Christ's saying: 'Render unto Caesar . . .' has usually been interpreted in modern times as an instruction that people pay their legal taxes. For the men of the Middle Ages it had a far more profound, if ill-defined, significance. And by the time of the Emperor Charles V that significance had almost vanished.

For the papacy had become discredited, not merely by the gross malpractices of some priests and monks and by the great schism, when there were two and sometimes three 'popes', but also by the decay of a united Christendom. The nation states of Europe had been or were being born. Though sundry monarchs, including Henry VIII, spoke of leading a new Crusade, what happened? Two years after Pavia, the King of Hungary and the flower of the Hungarian Christian nobility fell to the Turkish sabres at Mohacz. Utterly engrossed in their own struggles the western potentates came to regard the sultan almost as one of themselves, on occasion even one to be emulated. It was Spanish and Genoese, not Christian, seapower that destroyed the Turkish navy at Lepanto, and it was Austrian and Polish armies, not those of Christendom, that halted the Janissaries at the very walls of Vienna a century later. Indeed it is thanks to European national rivalries that to this day the Turks still rule in Constantine's own city.

If the spiritual pillar of Charlemagne's empire had crumbled away, the other, temporal pillar was in scarcely better shape. In theory King Henry VIII (he toyed with the idea) or King François I or even the Earl of Kildare could have been elected emperor. In fact it had become a German preserve long ago and, what is more, in the previous century virtually that of one family, the Hapsburgs. It was by dynastic marriage that Charles V happened to be both King of Spain and Holy Roman Emperor. His territorial possessions were too disparate to be ruled for any length of time by one man. After him, the capital of the emperor became once again Austrian and the effective empire he ruled became a conglomeration of states that straddled the Alps.

From this partial fragmentation of the old order, both lay and spiritual, there were now arising the great nation states of modern Europe. The birthpangs of these states were usually civil wars, and the results were neither linguistically nor ethnically homogeneous, though each of course contained a predominant majority of the one or the other or both. These civil wars, and particularly the Wars of the Roses in England, had dealt a shattering blow to the pyramidal, feudal concept of society, as the old nobility exterminated itself. Simultaneously, and again particularly in Britain, a mercantile middle class arose. The result was that the king became not merely a monarch, but also the actual ruler of the state, governing the people through officials of his own appointment, very frequently drawn from the new middle class, though graced with titles. Also in place of the nobility, of those 'barons' who could unite to force a King John to sign Magna Carta, there was emerging, but feebly, a structural representation of the people which was to become the representative parliamentary assembly. When such a parliament had represented the whole of society it had had a role to play. It was, of course, to have one again. But in the transitional period of Henry VIII its power was usually insignificant save to give its approval to royal edicts and to grant or refuse to grant taxes. England was ruled by its king and by his advisers, the Privy Council with its subsidiary councils such as the Council of the North and the Council of Ireland.

It was against this background – here grossly abbreviated – that

King Henry VIII set about the conquest of the Celtic parts of the British Isles, having failed, in 1522 and 1523, to do more than dent the power of France. He never abandoned altogether his continental claims, but came to rely increasingly on the power of British trade as opposed to English archery. In fact the only powerful weapon of trade he possessed was the exportation of English wool to the Spanish Netherlands, a weapon as likely to boomerang against his own wool merchants as to hurt the subjects of the King of Spain. Although the legend of English wealth and hence of power (*les chevaliers de St. Georges*) remained, by 1525 Henry VIII was broke. He had spent his great inheritance from his father on display, on his fatuous French campaign, and on the creation of the bases which were to build and supply the Royal Navy that, in his daughter's reign, was to defeat Spanish seapower.

The remnants of the empire were to be had, but only by force. Europe was unimpressed by an English king who could not even tidy up his Celtic backyard, and Irish chieftains such as Desmond were in communication, as monarch to monarch, with Charles V and François I. Irish chieftains with a few kerns at their disposal have tended throughout history to exaggerate their own importance to England's enemies, though it was only much later that the fatuous phrase about England's misfortune being Ireland's opportunity was coined. England's enemies have been less impressed. Ireland could be useful to them by rebelling against England and drawing off English or British troops from the serious battle fronts. Neither Spaniards, Frenchmen, Germans nor Russians have ever given twopence for any Irish cause. What they have cared about was Ireland's geographical situation. It also of course suited them that English bullets should end up in Irish bodies, rather than in those of their own soldiers, and that an Irish campaign should absorb England's wealth. For England's enemies Ireland has always been, quite literally, a diversion. But for Henry VIII it was more than a diversion. From the very first days of his reign he had, on occasion, referred to himself as Emperor. Now, in middle age, he needed the title as residuary legatee of Charlemagne's concept. Yet before he could justify his claim to be King, Emperor and therefore self-appointed head of the Church within his empire, he needed to subdue the Scots, the Welsh and finally the Irish. Scotland was a kingdom of its own: he could hope for little more than its defeat in battle and, as was to happen a couple of centuries later, its integration through dynastic marriage into a United Kingdom. Wales was easier. By 1536 he had occupied the Principality, had subdivided it into shires and hundreds, and while his officials did their best to stamp out the language and customs of the country, had agreed to accept some Welsh M.P.s into the English Parliament. He immediately sent civil servants to carry out a preliminary survey of Ireland, with a similar object in view, It is important to remember that by this time the so-called 'Reformation Parliament' (1529– 1536) had passed all of Henry VIII's bills which had thus been written into the constitution with all the legal formality available within Henry's English kingdom. He was head of the Church as well as of the state with the overwhelming approval – in so far as this could be ascertained – of the English people.

As for foreign intervention, this could only come from Spain. In 1538, the monasteries along the southern coast were being demolished to build fortresses against an invasion that was not, in fact, to be launched for another fifty years, while the enormous treasures of the Church had refilled the royal coffers. Henry was divorced, his second wife executed and his third had given him an heir at the cost of her own life, an heir legitimate beyond any dispute, since both his previous wives were dead. A Scottish war ended in triumph in 1542, with the Scots army destroyed, their king dead and on their throne an infant, Mary, Queen of Scots. Henry, who had already begun to act in Ireland, could give his full attention to that country, of which he now claimed to be King rather than Lord by papal approval. This claim had been accepted by the Irish parliament in 1541. As absolute King of England and head of the Church, he intended to establish himself identically in Ireland. It was only now that the real conquest of Ireland, by England, began.

Before returning to Irish matters, one point about King Henry's Reformation must be made. His was a reformation of structure, not of dogma. The dogma of Luther and even more so of Calvin was, in every sense, heretical to Rome. Their teachings were to become popular in England – and more so in Scotland – at a later date. Henry VIII remained, in his eyes, the Defender of the Faith, and although for political reasons he might flirt at times with the German Protestant princes, at home he burned heretics almost as quickly as he executed traitors. He believed in virtually all Roman dogma save in papal supremacy. His Church was not, in his eyes, any sort of alternative Christian church, but remained the Catholic Church. Whether it be the Church of England or the Church of Ireland it claimed Catholicity. They were not then, and they are not now, in any real sense a Protestant church. In his eyes, and those of most of his English subjects, the Church of Rome was merely an alternative, a *Roman* Catholic Church. And when the Pope excommunicated him, the Pope was simply acting *ultra vires*. It was only with the launching of the Counter-reformation (which was in itself primarily a reforming movement within the Roman Catholic Church as well as being an attack on its allegedly Protestant enemies) that England broke finally with Rome, and even in Elizabeth's time it was only the Spanish threat that caused her to abandon the anomalous position chosen by her father and to recognise the Jesuits as political enemies and almost all Roman Catholics as suspect. In a word, the Churches of England and Ireland as originally conceived were not a dogmatic breakaway from Rome, but an administrative one. Thus could sincere men in holy orders be equally loyal to Henry, Edward VI, Mary and the young Elizabeth as their temporal rulers.

There was one profound difference between Henry's Church of Ireland and his Church of England. The latter could quite simply take over from Rome, since the structure of both was episcopal. The pre-Reformation Church in Ireland had been in large measure monastic, in some ways closer to the Greek Orthodox and even to the Coptic Church than to Rome. A Church of Ireland therefore implied the introduction of a new, alien structure in addition to a change of loyalty. Since Henry combined, or attempted to combine, conquest with religious reform, that reform was automatically unacceptable to the majority of the conquered. And as a result, once Irish patriotism was born it was frequently, though far from invariably, linked to the Roman faith.

NOTE
1 See *Henry VIII* by A. E. Pollard (London, 1902)

10

THE IRISH
UNDER THE TUDOR KINGS

It is intended, in this chapter, to attempt some description of the Irish people whom Henry VIII and his daughter, Queen Elizabeth I, attempted to conquer, and largely succeeded in conquering, during the sixty-odd years of warfare that can be dated from 1541 to 1603.

The prime difficulty lies in the fact that Ireland had, long before America, become a 'melting pot', in those days the western extremity of a multiform Europe without integrity of purpose or belief, not yet what de Gaulle was to call the 'Europe of nations' and certainly without any continental homogeneity. In Ireland the 'melting pot' principle had achieved much, most of it destructive, power due to the loss of the old administrative and legal systems, but still had much to achieve. Fragmented as it was, the Ireland that Henry VIII set out to conquer, the Ireland of which he was hereditary lord under the Pope but of which Henry styled himself King in his own right, was not, save in a geographical sense, a country at all. Quite apart from the Scots–Irish tribes that had settled, or been settled, in the northeastern corner of the island and who maintained easy touch with the land of their (partial) forebears, there were enclaves in the west and the southwest where – from time to time, but not usually – Spanish or French was quite freely spoken as the *lingua franca* of the sea-going men and of the merchants who paid them. In the south-easterly towns, and particularly Wexford, the Welsh were as dominant as were the Scots far to their north. The largely anglicised Pale waxed and waned around Dublin as the Irish chieftains chose to attack or were repulsed. These chieftains recognised no suzerainty save that of the sword, preferably their own, but showed at times a certain respect for simplified Brehon law, considerably less (if any) for Roman law, unless there were an English army in the vicinity.

Of all these enclaves or semi-enclaves on Irish soil, the English Pale, based on the Viking strongpoint now called Dublin Castle, was the most important, and this for two reasons: the claim of the King of England to be also Lord or King of Ireland, a claim usually both acknowledged and ignored by the Irish and Norman–Irish chieftains; and the ability of the English to use their Pale as a base from which to send armies in repeated efforts to enforce those claims throughout Ireland, that is to say against the Irish chieftains of various sorts. Until well after the Council of Trent (1545–1563) and the launching of the militant so-called Counter-reformation typified perhaps in its extreme form by the formation of the Society of Jesus of St. Ignatius Loyola (1491–1556), religious matters played only a small part. That there had long been certain divisions between the monastic Irish Church and the episcopal Roman or English Church has been mentioned. The decline of religion during the centuries preceding the Reformation had only served to minimise their importance. As we shall see, however, such division was to be 'politicised', and violently so, in years to come. Indeed throughout modern Irish history (and we may conveniently date this from 1541) Anglo-Irish political hostility has almost always predated Christian sectarianism, though the one has been formidably aggravated by the other. Therein lies the Anglo-Irish (but not the English nor the Irish) tragedy of such long and apparently insoluble duration: that this insolubility lay outside religious differences was proven by historical events, for the German 'Thirty Years War' did not even begin to rage until early in the seventeenth century and left little residue after 1648. There is nothing, save some oratory, that gives to Christianity in Ireland an especially intensive quality save its political connotations. The only spiritual attitude to God that is repulsive to almost all Irishmen is atheism, and the spiritual arrogance that it implies. Since the time of the Druids this has probably almost always been so. For the Irish, magic is preferable to nothing. Despite the variety and multiplicity of the religious causes in which Irish blood has allegedly been shed, the spiritual basis of the Irish has changed little. Indeed the intense attachment which almost all Irishmen have seldom failed to ascribe to their own spirituality might be construed as their introspective astonishment concerning this aspect of themselves.

Long periods of time were to pass before the Spaniards or the French sent expeditionary forces to Ireland, and then it was to invade a British colony rather than to colonise Ireland for themselves. Indeed the English monarchs did not, until Henry VIII, envisage themselves as conquerors. What they did see was that, as

The round tower at Clonmacnois. Round towers were campaniles and also places of refuge from the Vikings. Most religious settlements had one, and many are still standing

Trim, Co. Meath. One of the earliest Norman castles, probably built upon a motte-and-bailey foundation and constantly enlarged. It was virtually impregnable to the Irish, to whom gunpowder was seldom available in any quantity. The great Duke of Wellington was perhaps born here, or more probably at Dargan Castle, now demolished, a few miles away

A stone monk's hut on Inishmore, of the Aran Islands, probably about tenth century. Normally all such huts, and indeed homes, were built to this pattern in wood, and have therefore vanished. But there is virtually no wood on Inishmore, which explains the use of stone

dual monarchs, they might use their power in the one country to assert a similar authority in the other. Ireland, in their view, was supposed to 'pay for itself' (that is to say for English administration) while producing a surplus for the monarch of both countries. Such was the theory according to which English armies – usually of approximately 1,000 men in strength – were sent to exact obedience and taxation from the Irish chieftains. The obedience was almost invariably forthcoming, the taxes not. Nor did the English taxpayers appreciate the demands for money to enable the King of Ireland to pay English soldiers in order that they extract his Irish revenues. The result was that the English armies almost always remained unpaid and soon enough faded away: that the Irish chieftains swore an obedience which they had no intention of keeping, in particular if they could understand its foreign, feudal claims: and that the Pale shrank until in 1535 it consisted briefly of Dublin Castle only. Henry VIII was confronted with the alternatives of pulling out of Ireland (as he had of his French territorial claims, save only Calais and its Pale) or of adopting a forward policy. He chose the latter.

His slight and childhood knowledge of Ireland gave him but little data from which to work. The Irish, he was doubtless told, were savages, primitive tribes in constant internecine combat the one tribe with the other. This was correct. The most petty Irish chieftain had an army of sorts while the King of England (save in time of war or of a feudal 'hosting') did not. These private Irish armies contained two major elements. There were the kerns, who might be described as all-purpose courtiers or even as policemen in time of peace, who were recruited into light soldiers when the chief went on campaign. They did not usually wear armour and the kerns who had horses rode bareback, without stirrups, with a javelin carried overhead, an almost useless form of cavalry against any enemy more formidable than the unhorsed kern. All men except Brehon lawyers, chroniclers, clerics and men of letters (bards and chroniclers) were liable to service as kerns.

Of galloglasses we have already heard. They were originally mercenaries from the Highlands and Islands of Scotland imported into Ireland in the late thirteen or early fourteenth century, but by Tudor times had, save in parts of Ireland, become institutionalised and largely Irish, even forming Irish-speaking clans of their own. They were professional soldiers, some remaining mercenaries, ready to serve any paymaster, even the Crown, some providing private armies for the greatest and richest Irish or Norman–Irish chiefs.

They wore helmets and long chain armour (carried by a servant and a boy when not in battle), and their principal weapon was a heavy battle-axe with a six-foot handle. When the chieftain went forth to raid his enemies, burn their crops and cottages and steal their cows – a highly popular form of activity, half-way between sport and warfare – these heavily equipped soldiers could make mincemeat of mere kerns. And theirs was the pressure that was constantly applied to the Pale.[1]

The result of the original Norman conquest had not been true colonisation. Since they seldom brought their women with them, preferring to marry the daughters of Irish chieftains, they rapidly became hibernicised and the well-known cliché about 'more Irish than the Irish' had a certain truth, since in two or three generations the men might have Norman names, but from their mothers and their grandmothers had acquired Irish customs, morals and very often language: this was especially so the further away they were from English contacts. Throughout the Middle Ages repeated attempts were made by the English authorities to prevent persons of Norman or Anglo-Saxon descent from wearing Irish clothes or speaking the Irish language, these being regarded as indicative of an Irish way of life unacceptable and dangerous to the English: such attempts failed, save from time to time within the Pale.

King Henry was doubtless told quite frequently of the 'land of saints and scholars', although this must have been corrected at once: there were few saints and, indeed, few scholars now. From the time of the great theologian, Duns Scotus (?1265–1308), probably an Ulsterman, to that of Bishop Berkeley (1685–1753) little original scholarship came from Ireland. Indeed Duns Scotus's fame was created in Oxford and Paris, and after his time his platonism was doomed soon to be overwhelmed by the more fashionable theories of the Renaissance, so that his very name, 'dunce', became identified with an inability to absorb new ideas, while what is believed to be his effigy most inappropriately is immortalised on the Irish £5 note.

The poets of the pre-Tudor and the Tudor period abandoned the epic in favour of the lyric form and – a very wild generalisation indeed – may be said to have abandoned force for elegance. Their verses would in any case have been incomprehensible to King Henry, and heard by few of his Irish subjects, though the harpist was a normal figure in a chieftain's court. The music that was composed and sung in Ireland must have been as remote from *Greensleeves* as was Palestrina's organ from Scots bagpipes.

What Henry VIII set out to conquer was his other kingdom, not a rebellious part of his larger one, much as Charles V was then determined to conquer the Basques and François I the Bretons. If Henry were to prove the least successful of these three sovereigns, it was not due to lack of skill, far less of military courage, but simply because he was undertaking a task for which almost every essential was lacking.

He had no money with which to pay his troops or provide for their basic needs, not even food. (The huge treasury that was his father's legacy, he had dissipated.) His predecessors on the throne had so wasted their Irish claims that these were only accepted under the *force majeure* which Henry VIII could not afford. (A remote though capable chieftain, a Fitzgerald Earl, considered himself to be justified in writing to the Emperor Charles V, the most powerful European monarch between Charlemagne and Napoleon, as if he, who styled himself King of Thomond, and Charles Hapsburg were monarchical equals in power and prestige.) Henry VIII did, it is true, build the Royal Navy, but this was directed against the navies of France and Spain rather than for operations in the Irish Sea and, even so, was far from completed in his lifetime. Quite simply, he and his advisers never really grasped the fact that Irish chieftains did not resemble feudal lords, and that the measures which Henry VII had applied finally to smother the Wars of the Roses were not applicable to the powerful Irish warriors who had been waging an entirely different type of warfare. The Irish chieftains were not to be put out of power by threats or even bribes but only by the extinction of the decayed system upon which their power rested. This was not to be achieved until the time of Cromwell and of William III, and perhaps by neither of these, for what has been enforced politically can also be rescinded. How, and how far, Ireland has been conquered emotionally by England or Britain, these are matters which will be discussed later in this book. Military conquest, in the most superficial sense, was always easy in appearance, but proved futile with equal speed. Social conquest usually ended as a complex sort of defeat.

Agriculture, not trade, provided the basic foods, though luxuries such as wine had to be imported and paid for. Again it was agricultural produce that provided the wherewithal, though Poynings' Law ensured that the English Parliament discriminated in favour of the English. With considerable ingenuity the Irish adapted their trade in adjustment to these discriminatory Acts of Parliament. Thus when the export of Irish cattle on the hoof was forbidden, a very considerable exportation of butter was created, particularly to France. When wool was likewise turned into an English monopoly, the Irish took to making knitted garments, and so forth. However, though the various Acts of English Parliaments may have been purely in favour of their own traders, in Ireland they were inevitably interpreted as hostile, and did nothing to increase the popularity of English rule either in the Pale or in the few ports usually controlled from London.

The nature of Irish agriculture varied geographically. There were still almost no roads, save one road that ran parallel to the east coast, and communication was largely by water, for about half the country was still untamed forest or sodden bogland. The Pale and what is now the County Kildare were largely cleared and suitable for crop farming, as the Boyne valley had largely been since time immemorial, but the method of crop farming was in many places eccentric, a field being planted with one crop, usually wheat, for three years and then left fallow for ten. The *betaghs* who actually worked the land are usually referred to by the Irish word: they were in general free men within the tribe, thus being neither serfs nor peasants in the English sense. They usually ploughed square fields which were unlike the more efficient strip farming of the English, and this crop-raising they did either by hand or more rarely with a light plough tied to the horse's tail. The plough itself was of wood and thus the more efficient deep strip ploughing by metal ploughs of the English was impractical. Thus subsistence farming, at least so far as the sept or clan or small community was concerned, was normal, with seldom a bumper harvest to permit export.

As one travelled further west, or up into the mountains, patches of cultivated land became increasingly rare, the way of life more pastoral. The people, too, became wilder: in a state of almost perpetual war a pastoral way of life is much safer than domestic cultivation, since the cattle and sheep can be driven into forest or up hillsides at the approach of an enemy. This is one reason why Tudor armies tended to starve once they had left the comparative wealth of the Pale. And therein lies what the English called the 'wildness' of the wild Irish.

Leaving aside the socially negligible foreign enclaves in the parts outside the Pale and – for the moment – the permanent Scotch–Irish of the northeast, we thus find that the conquest, reconquest and assimilation of and by the Norman–Irish had effected nothing save the partial destruction (and above all the acceptance by all the people) of a debased version of the older Celtic *tuatha* system (which did not accept the possession of land and a hierarchical class structure based thereon from serf to monarch) while the moral authority of the Druids upon which the older system had been based was replaced by monastic Christianity. The ancient septs became, as often as not, scattered groups of farms clustered for protection beneath a castle in which lived the chieftain with his women and his soldiers, 'kerns and idlemen', extracting goods which can be erroneously called rent from the farmers, and from which he would frequently sally forth to attack his 'hereditary' enemies. What would have astounded and no doubt horrified his Celtic forebears was that these enemies were not rarely his own relations. (These 'kings of the nations' as they styled themselves bore some sixty Celtic names, some thirty Norman, or ninety chieftains in a population estimated at about one million.) Such scenes of burning and carnage did not, of course, occur everywhere and at all times, but frequently enough to say that much Irish society, like much Irish monasticism, was reverting into savagery. In 1515 Pope Leo X had appointed certain commissioners to investigate various Irish sees. Clonmacnois and Ardagh, both cathedral 'cities', consisted in the first case of twelve miserable wattle and straw cabins, Ardagh of four. The rest of the people slept with their animals, in the fields. Clonmacnois contained the relics of an Irish saint, but the papal scribe was unable to discover his name. Ross and many other cathedrals were in ruins, the Mass seldom celebrated. Such a situation was far from unusual, as the many reports on other sees show, though they may have been extreme.

Nor was life in the seaside trading towns much happier. 'Coyne and livery' is a phrase that occurs repeatedly in the histories of early English administration in Ireland, always as an example of English oppression and also as something intrinsically nasty. What it meant in effect was an enforcement upon the Irish householder to pay for the English soldiery and, as Irish society decayed, on occasion for a chieftain's kerns. 'Coyne' is a transliterated Irish word which can be translated as bed-and-keep or billeting: 'livery' indicates clothing or embryonic uniforms. Since most Irish homes were one- or two-room smoky cottages often with livestock, the intrusion of this Englishman was in itself bad enough: to pay for him, worse.

Yet the English kings could not afford to occupy Ireland from their own resources. The Crown possessed no army, save for a few hundred Yeomen of the Guard, and no income save for what was drawn from the royal estates and from excise. The cost of the French

Wars ruined the English Crown, even as they ruined France. Armies, as has been shown by Spanish experience in Italy, were tacitly supposed to live on loot: barely feasible for any but very short periods on the Continent, in Ireland it was quite ridiculous. For the King of Ireland to import an army from England in order to assure his rule in Ireland – which meant in the last analysis to extract an Irish profit with English means – was not only fruitless but excessively expensive. The armies sent over periodically by the Plantagenets, ploughboys or wastrels, seldom amounted to more than a thousand men, who deserted for lack of victuals and of pay. The fortified towns became their very temporary bases, and 'coyne and livery' their unsatisfactory system of subsistence. These little English armies might be welcomed by the inhabitants of Dublin, Cork, Wexford or Limerick, but seldom for long. Coyne and livery came with them quickly enough, extracted by the so-called soldiery who, soon enough, deserted or, if lucky, found their way home again.

Their departure did not liberate the townsmen in their insanitary, narrow-alleyed, plague-recurrent little strongholds. All these towns, not least Dublin, were encircled by Irish 'nations', and their survival was dependent on 'black rents' to the 'kings' without the walls. It is quite impossible to adjust the sums paid in such rents to our own currency or even to our own standards, but it is fair to say that they were the utter maximum, that it was certainly impossible to become rich in Dublin or any other Irish town and difficult even to survive unless one were an official. The officials, however, or what we would nowadays call the civil servants, survived and indeed multiplied (a constant in Irish history). The pre-Tudor Dubliners had to support two groups of these persons, since the English saw little reason why they should pay even one set of them.

There were the officials sent out from England, of the Edward Poynings variety, who became of increasing number and importance under the Tudors. And there were the 'loyal Irish', that is to say essentially two great Norman–Irish families, the Butlers (whose *chef de race* was the Earl of Ormond) and the more powerful Fitz-Gerald 'nation' headed by the Earl of Kildare. These magnates also ruled Dublin, the Pale and in theory all Ireland. Throughout the Wars of the Roses the Butlers were, roughly, Lancastrian, the Geraldines Yorkist, and although Ireland's part in these wars was negligible, the king's power obviously went to his supporters, who ruled the Pale on behalf of the lord of Ireland. And of course the king, whether of England or Ireland or, as it happened, both, was in permanent financial trouble, since the enormous crown lands of William the Conqueror were never intended to pay for ever more expensive foreign wars. All the Dublin soldiers and administrators were supposed to be supported by the lord of Ireland's subjects. In fact the citizens of the Pale, and especially of Dublin, were thus burdened with two administrations designed to finance themselves from all Ireland on the feudal basis. Dublin's general misery was extreme. Only in the strongly fortified Dublin Castle did all these almost useless public officials enjoy the good life: it was for them, as well as for the wild Irish chieftains' courts, that large quantities of wine from Bordeaux were exchanged for the hides and hooves of the peasantry's cattle and for the exported portion of the citizens' crafts.

The Irish magnates suffered from, and occasionally enjoyed, much distrust on the part of their feudal masters in England, nor were they the objects of excessive love and loyalty from the Irish, since protection against English and Irish *banditti* was about all they had to offer – at a price.

We do not have the records of most of the people involved. Nevertheless we may assume that such prevalent, petty tyranny may have been less unacceptable to themselves, and perhaps even to some of their descendants, than it is to most Irishmen today, for it was not totally irrational to the basic Irish system of Brehon law. Brehon law was constitutional: that is to say, there was no crime *as such*. All Brehon law was based on what our lawyers call torts; in gross oversimplification the law (or to be more exact the Brehon lawyer) extracted from one man what he owed, by Brehon law, to another, for a multitude of crimes against the person. Again in over-simplification, there was no law other than that of personal offence, namely no state and no criminal code. Furthermore the honour-weight, elaborately established, counted for a great deal in Brehon legislation. Slave girls and cattle were currency. A small farmer might sue a chieftain, but their honour-weight would probably decide the case, while if the small farmer won, this would be usually not only a financial gain but also, and more important, an 'honour-weight' gain to himself and a corresponding loss to his opponent. This did not apparently alter the almost non-existent 'class distinction' but merely the personal status of the men involved: to the feudal, or the modern mercantile mind, this will appear hard to understand. It cannot have been any more comprehensible in Dublin, in 1534, when Brehon law was forbidden and British law ignored. It was then that Silken Thomas appeared upon the scene.

He was then called Lord Offaly, the son and heir to the Earl of Kildare, in his turn the chief of the Geraldine sept or nation. For the better part of a century Kildares, father and son, had been the king's usual Irish governors of Ireland, in particular under the Tudors. They were, indeed, related to the unfortunate Anne Boleyn and thus to the future Queen Elizabeth. However even with such protection when Anne Boleyn was at the height of her power, Henry VIII's doubts were extended to all men of power, and Kildare was summoned to London to account for his stewardship in Ireland. Kildare, with his giddy niece upon the throne and his own record impeccable by the standards of the time, only hesitated briefly before his dangerous voyage. However, to ensure the dynasty – for the Butlers were still very powerful – before his departure he appointed his twenty-year-old son to act as deputy-governor in his absence. He did this in the presence of the Council of Ireland, further admonishing his son to pay the greatest attention to what its members might advise. This advice the young man, known as Silken Thomas, quite refrained from following.

His nickname is said, by some, to derive from his extravagant and flamboyant taste in clothes, by others from the fact that his followers wore a silken plume upon their helmets. Probably both explanations are true. In any event, in 1534 he was informed, erroneously as it happened, that his father had been executed in the Tower of London. Without following that nobleman's advice and listening to the opinions of the Council, he immediately loosed his army of kerns upon the already wretched citizens of Dublin. The officials loyal to King Henry took refuge in the Castle, as did others for obvious reasons, while wood-and-wattle Dublin burned. Among those who attempted to escape was Sir John Alen, the Archbishop of Dublin, an Englishman who had recently been an abbot in England. His ship ran aground and, apparently at Offaly's order, he was beheaded. He would seem to have been the last pre-Reformation Roman Catholic Archbishop of Dublin. Meanwhile Offaly's guns lacked the power to breach the walls of Dublin Castle. In 1535 his father did die in England, apparently of natural causes. Offaly's kerns melted away from the ashes and corpses of Dublin, while such as remained were engaged in war and plunder against Butler territory. Belatedly King Henry sent the largest English army so far dispatched from Britain. As usual, the new Earl of Kildare's Irish allies faded into the native mists, to be defeated in detail. Kildare surrendered, under promise of his life. This promise King Henry cancelled, and also arrested all his uncles. They were executed, though in almost all cases guilty of nothing save bearing the name of Fitzgerald. Indeed, like some modern tyrant, Henry's fury was so great that he would happily have exterminated all Geraldines.

Since that date few Irish leaders have tended to trust the word of English monarchs or of their delegates, deputies, viceroys, lords lieutenant and so forth in Ireland. It is no coincidence that the futile revolt of Silken Thomas corresponds, and not accidentally, with the period when papal supremacy was most in dispute and the King of England and Ireland was assuming for himself all supremacy, spiritual as well as temporal, in both his kingdoms.

Silken Thomas may be a name of elegant charm. Unfortunately the young man left his country in a truly deplorable condition. Henceforth religion and politics were, for centuries, to be horribly and unnaturally confused, and this almost always to the disadvantage of the Irish and very frequently to that of England as well.

NOTE

1 For the scanty facts and statistics upon which the generalisations in this and the next chapters are based, the reader is referred to *A New History of Ireland*, Vol III, edited by T. W. Moody, and *The Beginnings of Modern Ireland* by Philip Wilson.

IRELAND
BEFORE QUEEN ELIZABETH

In the middle of the sixteenth century, then, we have what might be called a triple Ireland that King Henry VIII of England had decided to reconquer (or in the more distant areas from Dublin to conquer) for himself as newly created King of Ireland and therefore the Pope's replacement as head of the English and Irish churches, as Emperor by his own right, a spiritual and temporal heir to Constantine the Great. This conquest he, and his successors, set about achieving. It did not start as a religious war. Whether or not it ever became one – save perhaps in Cromwell's time – is doubtful. Yet spiritual symbols have been repeatedly invoked, up to the time of writing, 1982. There is no sort of 'spiritual thermometer' for the present, let alone for the past and above all for those who are detached from that past. The symbols, therefore, assume an enormous importance to any historian who would attempt to understand the emotions and the motives of men and women, often long in their graves. It may seem to us strange that the precise meaning of the single word *filioque* nearly destroyed the Christian Church more than a millenium ago. It did not seem so to a great many very clever men then. No more did transubstantiation, or even rood screens, in comparatively modern times. Indeed our non-existent thermometer might show that precisely this concern for what the lethargic rationalist regards as trivia indicates where the mercury stands.

In Ireland, in the time of Bluff King Hal, it did not stand very high. Only after a generation and more did the Irish begin to understand the implications of his claim, a secondary claim, to be head of the Church as well as of the state, he and his successors. One of these, his daughter Mary, though she briefly overturned the Protestant Reformation which had taken place, in England, during her brother's brief reign, had pursued their father's policy of conquest in Ireland with extreme vigour and had 'planted' two counties in the name of her husband – who happened to be King Philip of

Spain – and of herself. In theory this replacement, or more often renaming, *betaghs* as peasants or serfs, was a far greater extension of English rule, Pale rule, than anything achieved by her father's or brother's English officials. In fact in large measure it failed. Queen Elizabeth I had to start the whole conquest all over again, for a long time with a marked lack of success, but the religious issue still remained remote for many years. The Irish chieftains continued to judge according to their Brehon lawyers, to steal one another's cows and church plate too. That the kerns, or at least their wives, should continue to honour druidical holy wells and trees is not surprising. Cranmer's magnificent liturgy was as incomprehensible as was the Latin it replaced. In the next century there was little need for the priests to forbid the so-called King James Bible. The greatest work of English prose ever penned was, and has remained, almost unread by the Irish. In so far as the new forms and concepts of Christianity came to Ireland, it was only infrequently that spiritual or intellectual superiority prevailed: rather was it the sword on the one hand and administrative skill, not in ecclesiastical matters so much as in the pacification that should have followed the soldiers, on the other. But because political ends (in their case the creation of a centralised nation state) were basically so vastly superior in English eyes to matters of religion, the great religious struggle of the Tudor and post-Tudor period was secondary to the advance of English armies from the Pale. 'Power tends to corrupt' according to Lord Acton. Physical power undoubtedly corrupts religious intentions and can become a variety of anti-religion. This happened in Ireland, where the spiritual resistance of the sixteenth century was very weak: for neither side was the Christian religion the religion of love.

There is a time-lag between England and Ireland that is quite easy to see in the arts as it is in political and other forms of thought. In the sixteenth century it was wide, perhaps by as much as a century. Quicker communications may well have halved this by the eighteenth century, though 'Georgian-type' architecture endured in Ireland until well into the reign of Queen Victoria. Even in the late twentieth century copies of art that was 'modern' in Paris in 1910 remain 'modern' in Dublin. What has been, in its age, new and exciting in Ireland, for the past few hundred years, has been of individual inspiration and almost always greeted in Ireland with bewildered hostility. In no case is this more true than in the history of the Reformation and of the Counter-reformation in Ireland.

As is well known Henry VIII's religious revolution was essentially fiscal: he wanted monastic wealth, and of course he got it. This enabled him to fund the state for some years. Since few of the Irish monasteries were other than financially decrepit, about a generation was to pass before the Tudors set about acquiring their limited wealth. By then, that is to say early in the reign of Queen Elizabeth I (1558–1603), an Anglo-Irish war for *all* Irish land was in progress: apart from reinforcing English patriotism and, slightly, increasing the Irish variety, religious differences had been thrown into the scale, although with nothing of the intensity of subsequent centuries.

*   *   *

Professor Sir John Percy once, according to Nicholas P. Canny (in his *The Elizabethan Conquest of Ireland*), challenged him 'to make Sixteenth Century Irish history interesting'. Another, German historian, Ranke, once announced his intention of writing history 'as it actually was', by which he meant, in the end, intensive documentation. Since so little Irish history of the Reformation period was then written, let alone printed, it is something of a relief to this writer that this is not a history book. It would be even more of a pleasure if what has been written on sixteenth century Ireland had been done, with brevity, according to Ranke's wishes. The in-numerable volumes and archives about the internal history of the Irish during that century do indeed make excessively boring reading. But, fortunately, since I am not here writing history I do not have to write about obscure and inconclusive tribal battles, nor even about the dissolution of individual monasteries, though both are of some importance. It is, however, once again possible to draw back and view Irish affairs against the vastly important spiritual, potential and social conditions of a Europe in one of its very major crises, or to be more exact to bring up again the words *cujus regio, ejus religio* which spell both the end of Christendom as a unit, and authorise the concept of monarchy 'by the grace of God'. This concept of sovereignty was highly transitory, for the power of the merchant was already on its way to European dominance. The Irish, as usual, were half a century or so behindhand. But in this case, at least, the English attempt at the reorganisation of society in Ireland was even more out of date. When feudalism was dying or dead elsewhere in Europe, the Tudors were attempting to impose it upon the Irish.

Modern historians, and those the most acclaimed, have accepted Ranke's view as to the purpose of their eminently important pro-fession. What they tended to overlook is that they will usually only have access to those aspects of the past which the past has chosen to leave them, until this century that means 'the written word'. But ideas are promulgated and circulate, almost invariably, long before they are committed to paper. Furthermore, in dealing with the Irish people at the time of the Reformation, extraordinarily little was put down in writing, and for the great majority of the Irish people virtually nothing. In such a desert of 'facts' folk memory may be a substitute, provided it be treated with extreme caution. But, in the affairs of large parts of Ireland, such as Connaught, even the verses of the bards are lacking. Indeed the Tudor conquest must have been incomprehensible inside any logical framework, to most, perhaps all, of the people involved. The dates and names of skirmishes, decisive though some of these may have been, can hardly equate to the destruction of one subculture by another. Certainly the man who grazed his cows in the less stony parts of the County Clare cannot have expected that his descendants' affairs were being decided, in Latin and German, in Trent or Augsburg, in Rome or later in Westphalia. Indeed, few men can have realised even in those distant and sophisticated places, that they were instrumental in much of Europe's future outside their primary considerations.

For the trouble with Ranke's stern – and in our century ever more accepted – admonition to the writers of history is intrinsic. All that we know of what 'actually happened' is what was written down at the time. But ideas, movements, theories have usually come to maturity before anyone commits them to paper. We may know a great deal about Victorian politicians (but never all); about the Irish peasantry in the sixteenth century we know almost nothing. Outside the Pale, illiteracy was almost general, the chroniclers employed to laud their chieftain, even place names dubious among bog and wolf-infested forest. The dreary chronicle of monastic decay is documented, the movement of English armies is so to a lesser extent, the statistics of corrupt revenue officials give an indication as to the economic situation, the human imagination (not missing from these) and analogy must give us the rest. It is therefore with some trepidation that I return to Europe, of which Ireland has always been an obscure, but not invariably unimportant, part.

Ireland has always been something of an *Alice in Wonderland* place (a book that, according to his widow, was Charles Stewart Parnell's only reading: very apposite) and Ireland's first, virulent conquerors were therefore, appropriately, the last Tudor queen who maintained the Roman Catholic faith and her husband, King Philip II of Spain, who was the prime supporter of what has been called the Roman

Catholic Counter-reformation. This hyphenated word is itself grossly incorrect. Yet in the story of the Irish people, it cannot be omitted. But if its Irish implications are to be understood, as they must, then the concept itself must be clarified in non-Irish terms.

The social hierarchy called feudalism was both practical and efficient in times of tranquillity, assuming that all the elements in the hierarchy, from king to serf, accepted their role, both upwards in form of obedience and downwards in that of responsibility. The system of primogeniture was intended to give a permanence to a society so organised for the common good. Since there could be no passing from one class to another, in theory there could be no Marxist class-war. The cement of this hierarchical construction was a common religion. And as head of a universal church, the pope should decide between the monarchs who headed each hierarchy and thus there need be no 'national' wars at all, for the idea of nationhood was tied to that of religious hierarchy. Feudalism replaced anarchy and was generally accepted by those who lived according to its guidelines: little more can be said for any social system before or since. But, like them all, its lifespan was limited by external circumstances and human folly. It was based on landed property, that is to say on ownership and sub-ownership, usually in the form of very long leases. For this reason, among others, it was not attractive to the Irish, for whom the Celtic hierarchy was based neither on primogeniture nor on the ownership of land.

Feudal Europe has been compared to vast estates, each the property of its monarch who could sell or give leases to his principal subtenants, but who had no income save what he derived from those leases or from the produce of such land as he retained for himself. It was contrary to all legality that the citizens of the Pale and even of Dublin itself should pay 'black rent' to the Irish chieftains who hovered about its borders. Since the time of King John an attempt to enforce the English feudal system, dividing the land into shires which were subdivided into hundreds, had been tried periodically, using in the first instance the Norman conquerors and to a lesser extent the Irish chieftains as the primary subtenants. Outside the Pale, and even to a large measure within it, English, Vikings, Normans and Irish were prepared to swear allegiance to the King as lord of Ireland, but as Ireland relapsed more and more into barbarism, the lord became the Ard Ri to most of his subjects with virtually no power out of bowshot where his armies stood, save to a limited and spasmodic extent in the Viking ports. His deputies could not police the great hinterland where the Norman chieftains assumed Celtic modes and language and where each was only as strong as his own armies. He might form alliances, even with the English, in his interminable destructive wars with his neighbours. His religion was a Christian overlay of paganism, remotely controlled from the great monasteries. He dressed, rode, fought increasingly in the Irish fashion and Irish became his first language. Money scarcely circulated outside the ports. Most of the populace lived a life of isolation, the only strangers they saw being either enemies (to be dealt with at once) or bards or friars. From that period the Irish have inherited, at least in part, two attractive characteristics, the one being a tolerance of individualism to the point of eccentricity, the other a comparative (comparative to the English, that is) absence of class distinction and class consciousness.

Once Henry VIII had decided to conquer the country of which he had appointed himself King, he was immediately confronted by lack of an army with which to subdue even the Normans, the least alien of his rural 'subjects'. Those who lived in the more remote districts, such as the de Burgos (hibernicised Burke) of Connaught and Ulster, had in general become completely Irish, but those who lived within reach of Dublin, generally known as the 'Old English', and henceforth so referred to here, had retained links with the larger island. Henry's fury directed against the Geraldines shows that he regarded them less as foreigners than as traitors, and ever since the Statutes of Kilkenny repeated attempts had been made to compel them to speak English and to behave like Englishmen, while in Dublin and the Pale equally futile attempts were made to expel the Irish altogether, attempts which if successful would have deprived the growing city of its embryonic urban proletariat. But above all King Henry, like his predecessors and his heirs, was determined to suppress Brehon law and substitute the law of England based on Justinian as codified in large measure by Edward I. In effect these legal systems, at the personal level, were not very different. However crime in the abstract scarcely existed in Brehon law. And this of course produced a weaker legal state. It may be from this difference, quite apart from 'conqueror's justice', that some of the people of Ireland have seldom accepted and often denied the validity of the Crown (or now of the Irish Republic *per se*) as the supreme adjudicator of any legal action. It is, by the way, extremely hard for any person brought up to conceive of 'law' as a superhuman force to understand a legal system based upon individual relations, for better or worse. The ancient joke about the Irishman who asked two combatants whether this was a private fight or if anyone might join in is perhaps a faint echo of once very important an issue

The law, then, but equally important and concurrent the title to land. There were two English policies. The gentler at first glance was 'surrender and re-grant': the chieftain surrendered all rights in his territory, and was given a feudal title and the land of his county together with all feudal rights thereto. This was done in terms of peace or at least semi-peace. The other English form of colonisation in Ireland in the century and a half after Henry's VIII's actions was far more obviously brutal and was based on war. It is called plantation, and is precisely the same colonisation programme that was being pursued in Virginia. Basically, unpaid soldiers, and others to whom the Crown owed benefaction, were to be given land from which the rebellious Irish or Amerindians were expelled (save perhaps as serfs). In Virginia this worked, painfully to all save the merchant adventurers. In Ireland it did not.

In clearing the land of his enemies and in granting feudal titles to the Irish or Old English chieftains, Henry VIII could and did expand the Pale. His daughter, Queen Mary I, however, went beyond this. She 'planted' what had been Ossory land and other territory with unpaid English soldiers and, to a lesser extent, with what we would call carpet-baggers. But the expulsion of the Irish was a failure. Either they did not go at all, being needed hands to till the land, or they bought out the soldiers, who happily returned to England with most of their pay now in their pockets. King's County (the King in question was Mary's husband, Philip II of Spain) and Queen's County were a colonial failure, though not a catastrophe, and plantation as an English policy in Ireland was not abandoned. Indeed this policy of stealing land and enforcing an alien culture was not to reap its full harvest until it was inflicted upon the least anglicised provinces of Ireland, Ulster, in post-Tudor times. That sour harvest has not yet been stored in the granary of history.

* * *

On the Continent of Europe the Lutheran and Calvanist Reformation had so undermined, or loosened the fabric of, the already antiquated feudal system that civil war had resulted. Luther had thrown in his very considerable weight against the proto-communists of the Peasants' War and a *modus vivendi* arose, at Augsburg in the 1550s, the basis of which was *cujus regio, ejus religio*, which in plain English means that the religion of the ruler of a state decided that

Kilcooley Abbey. A fifteenth-century carving of an abbot, perhaps also a bishop. The angel above his head is waving a censer

A farm in Gougane Barra, Co. Cork, until recently utterly remote. It was here that St. Finnbar, one of St. Patrick's earlier disciples and Bishop of Cork, had his 'lone retreat' on an island in the lake. It can now be reached by road, but in 1918–1920 it was inaccessible, except by foot over the mountains, and the IRA used it as a sort of headquarters. Here there are still some trees

Dungiven Priory, Co. Derry. An early figure of a galloglass, one of the Scots–Viking professional soldiers who came to Ireland as mercenaries. Whether or not he is wearing chain armour, as he would in battle, is hard to say. These were by far the most formidable soldiers that the Normans and later the English had to face in Ireland *(Department of the Interior, Northern Ireland)*

of the state he ruled. Occasionally this was applied in reverse. Thus the Huguenot claimant to the throne became a Roman Catholic with the title Henri IV on the very pragmatic political grounds that 'Paris is well worth a mass.' In effect, the Pope had compromised. He retained his claim as Christ's Vicar; he renounced the Canossa victory save in such countries and territories where the head of state recognised papal authority as supreme in the religious field. King Henry VIII was among the first to deny this supremacy. His motives, save for the much exaggerated Anne Boleyn affair, have been much misinterpreted. He wanted monastic wealth, and he got it. From that vast source, he extracted immense power both in the form of cash and in the form of loyalty from those rich men who had bought and built on previously monastic lands. All this happened in England long before the Henrician Reformation was imposed upon his other kingdom, Ireland, save that he became head of the Church in his second kingdom: that there was little money to be picked up from Irish monasteries hardly made it worth his while to 'nationalise' these. His interest in Ireland was one of conquest, not religious reform, and he created the rich County Kildare as a result. The Irish clergy, or at least those who came under his control, seem to have had little if any objection to his administrative reforms. In his time bishops counted for little in the Irish monastic church: who appointed them, whether it be London or Rome, was a remote and uninteresting matter. Towards the end of his life, King Henry (as Pope of England, a title he never in fact assumed) was ever more opposed to Lutheranism, and in Ireland it was far from difficult for the monastic priesthood to accept his ultimate authority, which in any case was almost never exerted. Titles mean little to Irishmen. His monument, in Ireland, is the County Kildare and the safety of Dublin, which was soon to become the second city of Britain, a great port with a population, by the end of the Tudor century, of some 50,000 souls.[1] It was a Christian city but never, in Tudor or Stuart times, a Geneva or a Lisbon, rather a formulation of Tudor theological ambiguity. From that day to this Dublin is a city in which sectarian views have never had much political or even social clout.

The brief reign of the boy-king, Edward VI (1547–1553), saw a violent attempt to make England an extreme anti-papist country. It also saw the theological rule of Cranmer. Little of this reached Ireland, and the accession to the throne of Queen Mary, a very devout Roman Catholic, threw the whole mechanism of Church and state into violent reverse, in England. In Ireland this meant very little, and in any case her reign too was a very short one. There are the tombstones of clerics which bear silent witness to priests who accepted both Roman and English Catholic clerical appointments. Meanwhile Queen Mary pursued her father's policy of conquest from 1553 to 1558. When Queen Elizabeth I dangerously succeeded her half-sister, the axiom *cujus regio, ejus religio* prevailed. The true religious views of the Great Queen are, like those of most of us, buried in her breast. Her primary motives however are obvious: she intended to guard her Crown of England and, if possible, succeed her father in the conquest of her Irish realm. For a couple of decades these two ambitions were neither complementary nor divisive. It was the Spanish threat, as represented by the Counter-reformation, that gave her dual policy an almost absolute unity. But Queen Elizabeth's was, as European monarchies go, very poor.

One huge economy she had inherited from her half-sister. Queen Mary had lost Calais and its own Pale to the French, and therewith England's last foothold on the Continent. This fortunate defeat permitted Elizabeth to regard her realm as purely insular, and to devote her meagre resources to defence against the Spaniards and to the pursuance of her father's Irish policy. Though Ireland remained a net loss to Queen Elizabeth's exchequer, it provided one gain of great importance to the other, major aspect of her international policy. The great Irish forests were systematically felled (while those of England were spared) and from their oaken planks were built the ships that permitted Elizabeth to carry on her father's policy. The wooden walls of England were in very large measure of Irish timber, manned to an increasing extent by Irish crews. The English forests she did her best to preserve, as part of her Tudor heritage. In Ireland itself the rolling blue hills, the gorse and the silvery streams we know so well emerged slowly from their primaeval covering. The untamed island became slowly susceptible to roads – though hardly in Queen Elizabeth's time – and thus to central government. Many of the ships that chased the Armada were of Irish oak. But this could scarcely be entered into Elizabethan accountancy. For her, Ireland was extremely costly and her numerous despatch of expeditions there would hardly have been possible if her half-sister had not lost the vastly expensive and really useless enclave around Calais.

NOTE

1 All population figures for Ireland up to 1841 are suspect. Maurice Craig, in his authoritative *Dublin 1660–1860* gives a far lower figure. I am guessing at what would now be called 'greater Dublin'.

THE FIRST TUDOR INVASIONS

The very word 'Reformation' has been consistently and deliberately misinterpreted since Luther's time. It was his wish to reform the Holy Roman Catholic Apostolic Church, a reform that was desperately needed were the Church not to sink among corruption and temporal values. What in fact Luther, Calvin and Zwingli achieved was the creation of other, Christian hierarchies and dogmata which inevitably became hostile, in varying degrees, to Rome. Rome, in the arrogance of its princely clerics, pronounced these devout reformers heretics. Itself little more than a Spanish political enclave for a generation, the Vatican allowed the Spaniards (who were still ending their own *hijaz* against the Moors) to create what might be regarded as policy, and while the Roman Inquisition withered away a new, Spanish Inquisition acquired a considerable reputation for the burning of heretics and above all of Protestants. The Lutherans and Calvinists, who had never wished to destroy Christianity, became 'the enemy' while the Turks advanced into Europe. At last, in the middle of the sixteenth century, the Council of Trent set about a long overdue and very real reformation of the Roman Catholic Church, in administrative and financial purity little less extreme than, though different from, the desires of Luther himself. The Romans had left it too late, the Spaniards were too strong, and the Lutheran heresy – if it ever was a heresy – had become a schism, still unhealed and nowhere less so than in Ireland. It is therefore incorrect to speak of 'a Reformation' and of 'a Counter-reformation'. Nor was the theological iniquity of the *cujus regio* doctrine allowed to prevent its political acumen in ending, at least for the time being, the schismatic wars. All this was, in 1558, very remote and apparently irrelevant to most of the Irish scene. The planters of King's and Queen's counties were in part papists – a word just coming into its own in England – but this was of small importance. They represented Tudor might, intent on permanent conquest. What they wished to conquer was another question. In the north the O'Neills wished to conquer the O'Donnells to their west and the Roman Catholic

Scots MacDonnells to their east: the O'Briens and the Butlers wished to beat the Fitzgeralds. The English were simply another, and completely misunderstood, factor in an Irish equation that had then proved insoluble for several centuries. It was not to be solved – if it ever has or will be solved – for several more. Certainly the injection of the religious, or to be more exact sectarian, element did nothing to help and a great deal to hinder mutual tolerance among the Irish.

✻ ✻ ✻

The great difference between the Reformation in England and in Ireland is one of comparative simplicity. Henry VII having broken the power of the great noblemen, to the general relief of the English after the Wars of the Roses, left his son an inheritance which Henry VIII, after his early follies, was determined to make into a firm, rich dynasty. Religious matters were subservient to this main purpose which, with the hindsight of history, we can see as the end of feudalism, the rise of nationalism and the coincident emergence of a 'middle class', of a mercantile society to be ruled either by an absolute monarch or by a representative parliament, essentially of mercantile middle class and landed gentry in composition. In the following century Richelieu imposed the first on France, while in England a civil war decided in favour of the second choice of government. In neither of these great countries, be it noted, was the religious issue of paramount importance.

To Ireland the Reformed Church came in the company of no sort of peace nor of patriotism or national unity. To a country that did not then exist, it came on the swords of foreign conquest and to chaos and misery it added but more of the same. There is no reason, no cause-and-effect, why this should have been so. The Church, in Ireland, was at least as badly in need of reform as was that in England. The condition of many monasteries has already been described, in what was essentially a monastic church. The morality it induced was at a very low ebb, even in the Europe of the Borgias and the Medicis. Sexual morality had, if anything, declined with the decline of the old Gaelic system under the Norman hammer. The second Earl of Clanricard, a Burke who died in 1582, had at one time four legal wives: a certain Turlough O'Donnell had ten. John, Lord Leitrim, had a son by his sister. Pope Clement is said once to have suggested bigamy to Henry VIII as a solution to his dynastic problem: as Lord of Ireland, this would have been possible in Brehon law. If the highest nobility behaved in this way, it is not difficult to imagine the influence on their social inferiors.

Murder was so common a crime, at least among the powerful (and we know little concerning anyone else), that a 'natural' death was almost unnatural. Some such murders were almost routine – the Castle had upon its staff a man known as Bottle Smith, the official poisoner – while other deaths were carried out with abominable and subtle cruelty.

An oath was virtually valueless, as all knew, yet they were demanded, more as superstition than as a religiously binding contract.

All this can be traced to two principal sources. The first and best documented is the decay of the Roman Church and the failure to replace it with the English variety. To give but a few random examples: in 1576, in the County of Meath, so close to the Pale as to be under some measure of civilised control, there were 224 benefices of which 105 belonged to the Crown and *none* had a resident clergyman. At about the same time the Bishop of Killaloe was an undergraduate at Oxford, while the Bishop of Cork sold the livings at his disposal to any purchaser, lay or cleric, and, in a sermon preached before the Lord President, explained that this was his sole income. Those were Protestant incumbents. Their Roman Catholic predessors had been expelled and either became tramps (the tinkers are often descendants of the men broken in the Tudor wars) or sometimes spread the Gospel. They had, however, in general been little better than the Protestants who succeeded them. Many of those who took the ambiguous saying of Jesus (Matthew XIX, 12) seriously, not infrequently compromised by being maritally celibate but by keeping 'harlots' instead.

As has been already stated, Henry VIII wished for administrative, not theological, reform, and to this day the Church of England is 'officially' the Holy Catholic and Apostolic Church. To call a Church of England (or of Ireland) cleric a Protestant is likely to be answered with a reproof. And such was Henry VIII's basic view. In his old age he was increasingly pro-Roman and anti-Lutheran, and despite the vast wealth he had derived from despoiling the English monasteries, and much less from the Irish ones, he would certainly have liked to make an arrangement with Rome, probably not unlike that of the Gallican Church in France. But it was too late. He was therefore not particularly pleased when a sycophantic Irish parliament, in 1541, pronounced him King of Ireland. He had previously been merely the Pope's liege-lord there, and since he was now in a state of excommunication he could hardly expect His Holiness to ratify this new title. Characteristically, after some grumbling, he accepted his new monarchy, but Ireland remained, in theory, a separated kingdom until the Act of Union of 1800. (This fiction is comparable to the claims on the English coinage that the monarch portrayed was also King or Queen of France.)

With his death, and during the short minority of his son, Edward VI, Cranmer's Reformation had full freedom of action in England and Ireland exemplified by the introduction of a new prayer book in 1552. It was not a popular revolution in either country, and a description by a highly biased observer, the recusant Bishop of Ossory, is probably typical of Irish reaction in that part of the island which was under English control and which had therefore been forcibly re-romanised on the accession of Queen Mary.

> On the twentieth day of August, was the Lady Mary with us at Kilkenny proclaimed Queen of England, France and Ireland with the greatest solemnity that there could be devised, of processions, musters and disguisings; all the noble captains and gentlemen thereabout being present. What-a-do I had that day with the prebendaries and priests about wearing the cope, crosier and mitre in procession, it were too much to write. On the Thursday, which was the last day of August, I being absent, the clergy of Kilkenny, by procurement of that wicked justice Hothe, blasphemously resumed again the whole Papism, or heap of superstitions of the Bishop of Rome; to the utter contempt of Christ and His holy Word, of the King and Council of England, and of all ecclesiastical and political order, without either statute or yet proclamation. They rung all the bells in that cathedral, minster, and parish churches . . . they flung up their caps to the battlement of the great temple, with smilings and laughings most dissolutely . . . they brought forth their copes, candle sticks, holy-water . . .[1]

This was in accordance with the Royal Proclamation, published three years after Queen Mary's accession to the throne, but by then the policy it outlines was rigidly in force and the Fires of Smithfield were consuming the heretics.

> Instructions given by Philip and Mary to the Lord Deputy, Lord Fitzwalter and the Council. [28 April, 1556. Cal. Carew MSS. I. 252–3.]
> Our said Deputy and Council shall, by their own good example and all other good means to them possible, advance the honour of Almighty God, the true Catholic faith and religion now by God's great goodness and special grace recovered in our Realms of England and Ireland; and namely they shall set forth the honour and dignity of the Pope's Holiness and See Apostolic of Rome, and from time to time be ready with our aid and secular force, at the request of all spiritual ministers and ordinaries there, to punish and repress all heretics and Lollards and their damnable sects, opinions, and errors.

Very few if any suffered a heretic's fate by burning in Ireland, for there were many precursors of the Vicar of Bray, ready to turn a cat in the pan once more when Elizabeth came to the throne in 1558.

It is one of the curios of history that had Queen Mary's pregnancy not been an illusion, and had she borne King Philip a son, who lived, that boy might have been King of England, Ireland, Spain, Portugal, the Americas and the Low Countries. The idea of so vast an empire must have occurred to King Philip, for with almost indecent haste he proposed marriage to the young Queen Elizabeth. Her own position, when first she came to the throne, was far from secure. She had not then been excommunicated, and almost the prime trump in her hand was, in fact, her hand in marriage. She was to dangle the prospect of matrimony over many heads for an almost indecent number of years, but she can hardly have taken King Philip's indirect proposals very seriously. He was, for one thing, her dead half-sister's ex-husband, though no doubt the Pope would have obliged in some way or other. (As already mentioned, an earlier Pope, in similar circumstances, had probably suggested bigamy to her father.) More important, the overbearing manner of Philip's grandees in London when he was Mary's King consort had thoroughly alienated the English: in a country that was increasingly turning towards Protestantism and was becoming ever more nationalistic, the return of King Philip might well have jeopardised Elizabeth's monarchy. Among other qualities inherited from her father, Queen Elizabeth was well able to keep her own counsel. The Spanish marriage faded into the mists.

Again, like her father, Queen Elizabeth's attitude towards the religious question, which was becoming ever more acute, remained in some measure ambivalent and certainly took second place to her patriotism. The nature of her agnosticism, if that be the word, will remain forever a mystery. She was, however, no bigot. Her principal admiral, Lord Howard of Effingham who fought the Spanish Armada in 1588, was a Roman Catholic. She had no desire to create martyrs – traitors and spies were another matter – and she lit no Smithfield fires. What she desired was a united, loyal and solvent kingdom. Her religious attitude, too, was much like that of her father. Only in 1559, that is to say the year after she became Queen, did she restore, in modified form, the prayer book of 1552, and accept from the English Parliament her father's supremacy of the Church of England.

She had inherited from her grandfather, Henry VII, an acute

awareness of the importance of money and from her sister an almost bankrupt kingdom. If there was one firm element in her sometimes vacillating policies, it was that her exchequer should do well. Whether it were Drake's circumnavigation of South America or her administration in Ireland, these were supposed to be profitable to the government of England, profitable in cash rather than in glory. If, like her grandfather, she was accused of being financially mean and even petty, this meant nothing to her. She had known poverty, both nationally and personally, and she knew that it was the basis of nothing in statecraft. With such a point of view the growing mercantile class was in full agreement. It was, after all, their business to make money.

Throughout the sixteenth century it became increasingly obvious that the two principal adversaries in the Wars of Religion were Spain and England. Spain was, in appearance, immensely rich, but the Spaniards did not 'make' money: they stole it in enormous quantities from central and southern America. To be more exact they stole its symbols, gold and silver, and this they used to create immensely powerful armies and navies. When the money had been spent, the wars won or lost, there was nothing left save memories and monuments. It took a long time before the world realised that the Spaniards had wasted a century plundering the Americas while they left their own country to decay. Of all their victories, perhaps only Lepanto, which freed the Mediterranean of the Turks, was permanent. Spain has remained among the poorest countries of Europe, ruined by bullion.

This vast influx of gold and silver affected all Europe, in that it led automatically to a decrease in the value of precious metals and hence to inflation. This was one reason why Queen Elizabeth was parsimonious. England had no money to waste on wars, and unless Queen Elizabeth's fabulous navigators and pirates, Drake, Hawkins, Raleigh and the rest, brought home a profit they received small thanks. But the worst English headache was Ireland. Ireland was supposed to produce money for the English exchequer. Instead, it was one perpetual expense. Spain at least made money out of its principal European colony, Sicily. In one year, a typical year, the English extracted some £3,000 out of Ireland at a cost of £18,000 to the English exchequer. The comparison with Northern Ireland today is obvious, the causes very different.

❋　❋　❋

Despite the brief restoration of the Roman Church under Queen Mary, Tudor policy towards Ireland remained little changed. (Queen Mary, for instance, did not restore confiscated Irish monastic lands.) The Normans had attempted, and failed, to bring their own feudal methods of government to Ireland. They had succeeded, in very large measure, in destroying the old *tuatha* system, but in the process had themselves become Irishmen over the generations: in response the old Irish clans or septs had become small quasi-feudal military societies. This cross-breeding was eminently unsatisfactory. In ancient days, as has been remarked, the elective 'kingship' of each social and economic unit seems to have produced little friction. Without feudal primogeniture the position of *tanaiste* or successor was not automatically settled by birth. No more, on the other hand, was it purely elective. Polygamy added to the semi-feudal confusion, and tanistry led to internal warfare within the socio-economic unit. The Tudors were determined to abolish it, and with it fosterage, but to little effect. The chieftain, with his galloglasses and his kerns, accepted from the feudal system a far more complex system of taxation in order to support his armed forces. And in the almost constant inter-tribal warfare slaves and itinerant labourers appear upon the scene. By the time Henry VII won the Battle of Bosworth, Ireland was in very bad shape, but at least it was run by its own people or by Norman–Irish who were little different. Repeated attempts to turn the Irish into provincial Englishmen by banning national customs, national law, national games, national dress and even the native language had failed repeatedly. For nearly a century the English, while never renouncing their claim to all Ireland, were prepared to leave the Irish alone.

The Tudors introduced reform at several levels. Sir Edward Poynings had made the basic constitutional and administrative changes. Irish administration and legislation – which in his time meant little more than the Pale – was in theory independent of, but in practice subservient to, that of England and henceforth the administrators were increasingly, at last almost entirely, Englishmen. This most important step was taken further by Henry VIII who was so shocked by the Silken Thomas revolt that he seriously contemplated genocide of the entire Geraldine family or clan. If he failed it was for lack of means, not an excess or even a modicum of morality. Meanwhile his servants enlarged the Pale, principally by the reconquest of Kildare and points south, thus linking the towns and the trading ports, and renewed attempts were made to ban Irish ways and above all Irish law in that part of the island (a small part) controlled from London.

This attempted anglicisation of Ireland was continued, despite the re-introduction of the Roman faith, by Queen Mary. The expansion, now westwards, continued and from the territories of Offaly and areas to the east were carved two English-style counties named King's and Queen's counties with the English appendages of sheriffs, taxation and so on. Two county towns, or to be more precise castles, were founded: Philipstown (now Daingean) in what is now County Offaly and Maryborough (now Port Laoise) in the renamed County Laois. And two new elements were introduced or, to be exact, became elements of practical policy.

The first of these was the policy of 'plantation' which served a dual purpose. Instead of being given money, the English soldiers were paid in land. There was, almost up to this century, an almost perpetual shortage of ready money in Ireland, since currency was the easiest form of wealth for transference to England, and it would be no exaggeration to say that this form of payment by land was an extension of coyne and livery. A second proposed advantage was the planting of Ireland with a loyal English peasantry and yeomanry. It was no doubt intended to duplicate the ancient Roman colonial system, but this it failed to do. The dispossessed Irish attacked the planters and most of the surviving soldiers were only too willing to sell their land and go home, cash in pocket. Some, however, remained and added another element to the already mixed population of English-occupied Ireland into which they soon sank without trace. Indeed the profession of soldier – for galloglasses at least were mercenaries, often prepared to serve a new chieftain or even the English – came into existence long before it did in England. As late as Charles I, the king had to rely on the then grossly impractical feudal system of 'hosting' while within a very few years Irish soldiers of fortune were serving in almost all the armies of Europe.

A more complex procedure, at a higher social level, was known as 'surrender and regrant'. Briefly, an English army would occupy an Irish territory, usually by conquest, and the local chieftain would swear loyalty to the English Crown. He would then surrender his Irish title and his land and be given a feudal title with all the appurtenances of rule inherent therein. English law would replace Brehon law and a new English barony or county would be created. The trouble with this three-card-trick was simple. The Irish kinglet owned no land to surrender: it belonged to all his people.

And these foreign titles meant far less than the old Gaelic kingships, no matter how puny these might be, to all the free Irish. Nor
was an oath of loyalty extracted under duress regarded as valid.
As soon as the little English army had moved on, therefore, the Irish
usually ignored the whole transaction. As will be seen, the climax
to this was to come in Ulster.

In fact it was not possible, by any legal or administrative trickery,
to turn Irish-speaking Irishmen into English-speaking colonials or
second-class Englishmen. The Irish roots were too strong, the culture
despite all the batterings it had taken was too deeply seated. The
only true method of total conquest was genocide, and in a country
largely covered with bog and forest this was not feasible with the
petty, unpaid armies at the disposal of the Tudors. Nevertheless it
was tried, under Queen Elizabeth and her successors.

❋ ❋ ❋

Even if the system of 'surrender and regrant' was largely unacceptable to the sixteenth century Irish, the fact that it was accepted
at all shows yet again the decay of the old tribal 'kingships' in favour
of feudalism. This was due in part to Norman influence and, in
Leinster at least, to the increasingly less pastoral nature of the Irish
themselves. The gradual clearing of the primaeval forests and the
drainage of boglands, though very far from complete, permitted
farming as we know it on a much larger scale while the English
soldiers built a few, inferior roads. That both remained, by English
and continental standards, extremely primitive, meant nevertheless
that the septs became inevitably more attached to the land that
they tilled. Furthermore 'territories' grew larger, contacts between
neighbouring *tuatha* closer, both in a hostile and in a friendly way.
They would frequently band together, sometimes temporarily,
sometimes on a more permanent basis, in self-defence. This meant in
turn that the leading family would have numerous client families.
Such a family would need more in the way of taxes to support its
position and to pay its courtiers and soldiers. Although land did not
become property, and Brehon law continued to be basically concerned with people rather than with things, and though there was
still no concept of 'country', the old system was very much in decay.
In the towns, and particularly the trading ports, it was dead save
perhaps in those inland 'towns' which were built about the castle of
the leading chieftain. In effect the Irish continued to fight one
another, and to fight the English, more and more in defence of, or to
augment, their tribal territories. The result was that whereas the

Tudors had destroyed feudalism, in fact if not in name, in England, in Ireland they were introducing a form of debased feudalism, in name if not in fact. This was intensely unpopular among the Irish, and since the English were also introducing a state religion, this unpopularity spread to religious innovation too. Even as early as 1553 we have seen the manifest rejoicing in Kilkenny at the re-imposition of the old religious order. And such joy was certainly not confined to that one town.

NOTE

1 Vale, who was of English origin, had originally been educated in the Romish religion and became a Franciscan, but later became converted to an extreme form of Protestantism. He was nominated to the See of Ossory by Edward VI in 1552. He was extremely unpopular in his diocese, on account both of his innovations and of his overbearing manner, and at one time his life was actually in danger. In his 'Vocation' he compares his sorrows and perils in Ireland to the sufferings of St. Paul. He left the country shortly after the accession of Mary, and proceeded to Switzerland. He returned to England on the accession of Queen Elizabeth, but never to his Irish diocese. (See Ware's *Bishops of Ireland*, ed Harris.)

13

CONQUEST

Gloriana. The Virgin Queen. It has been said that part of the mystique which was neither *sui generis*, nor derived from her many victories on land and sea, was somehow a vague inheritance from ancient deities, from the devotion her subjects used to give to the Blessed Virgin Mary, to Aphrodite, to Brigid, to Rhea herself. Such fulsome glorification was doubtless diluted by a considerable dose of cynicism in England: in Ireland, her second kingdom, it was not accepted at all save perhaps by those, like Edmund Spenser, whom she planted there.

From the time of the Elizabethan conquest until 1922 (and perhaps in years to come) the English attitude towards Ireland has almost always been a pendulum swing between 'coercion and conciliation', as it becomes known much later. The one meant, quite simply, conquest and in the last as in the first (Elizabethan) analysis genocide. The second meant benevolent despotism, with or without Irish middlemen and executors. Neither was tempered to assume, a horrible and almost meaningless contemporary phrase, the 'Irish dimension'. Indeed the very use of those two meaningless words means the discussion or decision of Irish matters in English terms. Since these have no universal validity, and coercion means the imposition of alien values, which can only be done eventually with weapons, the nice distinction between compulsion and coercion becomes blurred as does the swing of the pendulum.

Elizabeth accepted her father's role and decided to use her first kingdom, England, in order to conquer her second. No means were to be spared and none were. Sir Henry Sidney, father of a nobler son, and others set about the conquest of Munster, the unoccupied parts of Leinster, and Connaught. They succeeded in the generation after 1569, and murder or massacre was their principal means. We have descriptions of the defeated, starving Irish, creeping back from their thorn-infested forests, their mouths green with nettles and grass. English chroniclers speak of cannibalism. In the Low Countries the tyrant Alva spared women and children: not here, in Ireland, did the English regard such Catholic vermin as worth a bullet, if a knife would do. The Irishmen fought back, but lacking weapons and armour were useless. Yet enough Irish found cover in bog and forest to preserve the race and the language. Huge grants of land were given to the latter-day Conquistadors, Sir Walter Raleigh alone received some quarter of a million acres, with which he could do little since he lacked labour. Spenser, another enormous beneficiary, wrote part of the *Faerie Queen* in his castle of Kilcolman, and in his affected, convoluted and obscure style attempted, in Book Five, to describe an Irish kinglet's court. Such had obviously entertained their conqueror and despoiler, but either their ways so bewildered him or his verse style is so grotesquely hard to understand that there is little knowledge here to be gleaned.

How, in fact, were the Irish living before the Elizabethan tornado hit them? There is no simple answer, since that large, roughly circular area was not a country and in no sense a unit, nor ever had been. Many would and do doubt if it is one now.

There is, or was, a certain intrinsic homogeneity in each of the four provinces. Leinster, based on Dublin and the Pale, was more subject to foreign influences and, including the coastal parts down to Cork and southeast Munster, might well in due course have become an intrinsic part of an English-speaking realm. Indeed some would say today that Dublin has more in common with certain western English city-ports than with certain western Irish ones. However, only a few miles to the south of Dublin and virtually in central Leinster the Wicklow hills provide some of the roughest, wildest and least easily controlled areas in all Ireland. While slightly further to the south the inland city of Kilkenny, the ancient capital of Butler country, is very Irish indeed. To this day, in fact, even as one is almost never out of sight of the blue-and-green rolling Irish hills, so the cities – Dublin in particular – have only in this century begun to transform parts of Ireland from a rural to an urban atmosphere. And in the sixteenth century it must not be forgotten that those lovely, feminine hills were still very largely bog and forest and almost without roads or bridges.

Between Leinster and the river Shannon, the Province of Munster (later including Clare) was seldom controlled by Dublin. It was here that the 'kingdoms' of Celts and Normans were most intermixed. Throughout all Ireland population had been increasing and by the middle of the sixteenth century had surpassed the level reached before the Black Death. This had two obvious results. Hostility between adjoining tribal states was rife. And attempts were made to grow more food, either crops or cattle, by pushing back the forests. Save for the chieftains' courts, virtually all the people lived on a subsistence diet, and a low subsistence at that. Poverty was great, nor was wealth created by robbing neighbouring tribes and, often, burning their standing crops. Yet the people do not, so far as we can judge, appear to have been particularly unhappy with their condition. How could they, since they knew no other? The 'golden age' was, as almost always and almost everywhere, far in the past. But there was much singing and dancing and much telling of stories in the wintertime. Apart from the chieftains and their courtier-warriors, there was very little class distinction and, since money was rare, what there was derived from status, from honour-worth, more than from any other source. Just as I feel in no way inferior to the landlord from whom I rent a furnished room, since the house belongs to neither of us, nor towards the civil servant of the inland revenue, since it does not become his money when it ceases to be mine, so the sept that paid its tax or tribute – usually in kind – to their chieftain or to his agent was in no way demeaned thereby: it remained the property of the sept. Only the servile element, who by definition were not members of the sept, usually paid in labour, but even here any sort of 'class distinction' was blurred, though to this day it is an insult to call an Irishman 'a peasant'.

For the purpose of transacting business of all sorts, the sept would meet once, more rarely twice, a year. Taxes would then be paid and the Brehon lawyers would decide cases between parties that had not called for more immediate legal intervention. The king would be among his own people and he would provide them with a feast, much as he would do after a victorious battle. These were among the rare occasions when meat would be eaten in large quantities, and the drinking was heavy. (The Irish had invented the distillation of spirits from fermented liquour approximately in the seventh or eighth century: curiously, the habit had not spread to Cognac and other continental points until several hundred years later.) No wine was produced in Ireland, so far as we know, but a great deal was imported for the chieftains and their friends, both from France and from Spain. The ordinary people drank a form of beer, probably cloudy and not to our taste, but there was so much fresh water in Ireland, almost everywhere, that poteen and water was probably the normal drink, and was certainly drunk to excess on feast days.

A curious feature of these feasts – so far as this writer knows, one unique to Ireland – was the 'faction fight'. These presumably derived from rivalry between septs that had melded down the years. They were not, however, usually inspired by hostility, but rather were traditional, following on the feasting, perhaps the declamation of poems, the dancing and the love-making. The time had come for a fight, perhaps for several. A coat would be trailed, the heavy-handled blackthorn sticks brought into action but seldom, it would seem, with lethal intent, and a few dozen men would be at one another to the applause of their women. Limbs might be broken, but deaths would seem rare. It would appear to have been formalised, but not as formal as its sporting successors, hurley in Ireland or hockey in England, for there was no ball and no referee. Then, when they had had enough, it would end as quickly as it had begun and the antagonists, their arms around one another's shoulders, would pull out their leathern bottles and drink one another's poteen. Of course not all such faction fights ended in so amiable a fashion: in which case, perhaps next year . . . Some of the factions became rooted family fights, their origin, a stolen cow perhaps or a dis-honoured maiden, long forgotten, and were even transferred across the Atlantic. Very rarely, in the wildest and most remote parts of Ireland, their inheritance lingers on, but with extreme discretion. These are private matters, not the concern of the Royal Irish Constabulary a century ago nor of the *Garda Siochana* today. It might scarcely be an exaggeration to suggest that secret fighting is an Irish, or perhaps a Celtic, speciality. There is, or was, faction fighting in Scotland and Wales. To the knowledge of this writer this never was, and certainly is not today, a phenomenon of the English countryside.

These tribal meetings were also, in a way, fairs. The so-called 'grey merchants' – who obviously dealt mostly in coin – would travel from one to the other, their wares on pack-mules and their information as good as they could make it concerning the state of peace or war upon their future tracks. For many an Irishman they were his contact with the world outside his own tiny community, and from them he could buy those few necessities his little society did not produce for itself, as well as adornments for his women and luxuries for his table. These grey merchants were not popular. In view of the way they had to trade, their profits must needs be very great. If the little community lacked cash, the agricultural goods they must accept were cumbersome. And, perhaps inevitably among poten-tially hostile strangers, they were scarcely in a position to refuse at

Patrick Sarsfield (?1660–1693), also the English Earl of Lucan, though he preferred his Irish name. He was James II's most efficient commander. In command of Limerick in 1691, he surrendered to King William, though the king's signature was dishonoured by the London parliament. By the terms of the Limerick Treaty, he was allowed to leave Ireland with 12,000 men, and join the Wild Geese in the service of France *(Franciscan Community, Killiney)*

Merrion Square, Dublin, one of the few late eighteenth-century squares that have remained intact. Note the beautiful fanlights over the front doors, which are among the visual joys of Dublin

Aghadee House, Co. Waterford, one of the many Georgian mansions that either fell into decay during the nineteenth century or were burned in the 'Troubles' of 1918–1922

least limited credit which entailed usury in some form or other. They thus became the forerunners of the much hated 'gombeen men' of Irish story and legend. They came to fulfil the role of the Jew in Europe, needed, insulted and at times persecuted, for there were virtually no Jews openly in Ireland until Oliver Cromwell rescinded the anti-semitic laws of Edward I. (To this day the Jewish population of Ireland is small, and anti-semitic feeling too. Otherwise Dublin could scarcely have elected an orthodox Jew as Mayor, which happened a few years ago. Even in view of their small numbers, Jews are not unduly prominent in the professions, and although Dublin's walls have probably the richest and most varied *graffiti* of any city anywhere, this writer has yet to see a scribble that was in any way anti-semitic.)

West of the Shannon, that is to say in the Province of Connaught and the County Clare, the basis of life in pre-Elizabethan Ireland was little different from that of Munster, save in so far that the land is much poorer, the mountains rocky and seldom suitable for agriculture, while even as pasturage most of it is poor. The Norman penetration, too, was less, though the Burke clan was powerful in parts. The great Celtic families, however, had in large measure preserved their territories, and Dublin was so far away that, except on the rare occasions when an English army marched through the province, the Celtic or Norman chieftains could and usually did ignore directives from that distant place.

Ulster was, and has remained, unique.[1] Owing to the poverty of communication so frequently stressed, that part of Ulster east of the river Bann is closer to Scotland (and was certainly so five hundred years ago) than it is to the great majority of Ireland. So, too, is and were much of its population. The English never conquered the Scottish Highlands, where live the cousins of the men of Antrim and of Down. The peculiar fate of these Scots–Irish will be discussed in the next chapter. Meanwhile, in pre-Elizabethan times, the great family of Ulster was the O'Neills, for centuries titular High Kings of All Ireland, a family that might be described as proud, clever, unscrupulous and very brave.[2] It is improbable that some members of this great family ever renounced in their hearts their almost hereditary Irish claims, save perhaps at times to the Stuarts.

❋ ❋ ❋

It is not intended here to attempt any detailed military analysis of the intensely complicated Elizabethan wars. They consisted of at least two wars or series of wars, the first primarily against the

Geraldines in the south, the second against the O'Neills, principally in the north. However alliances were far more complex, and fluctuated far more, than that. At most times there were groups of Irishmen to be found on the English side, while others remained 'neutral', and the English fell out with one another though not to the point of going to war. The first of these two wars, the one in which the O'Neills were not directly involved, lasted from 1565 to 1576. In it England's enemy was the Geraldines above all, and it was really an armed punitive progress through Leinster, Munster and southern Connaught. It remained inconclusive so long as English power did not encompass all of Connaught and of Ulster. Hugh O'Neill fought, won skirmishes, even received some aid from Spain until he surrendered in 1603. With very great reservations, his can be considered the first Anglo-Irish war.[3] It must, however, be remembered that this war was fought by the English against only one of the four Irish provinces.

* * *

In the opening years of Queen Elizabeth's reign, after a certain amount of local brawling which was of little interest outside Ulster (Shane O'Neill established his supremacy over the Scots settlers in Antrim) Ulster enjoyed a long period of comparative peace and good government. Indeed it was Shane O'Neill's boast in 1561 that some seven hundred farmers had moved to his Ulster from the maladministration of the Pale. The Crown was unable to prevent his predatory attacks on his neighbours to the south and west, nor were attempts at intervention by the Earls of Kildare and Ormond of any avail. He was now in a virtual state of war with England, and in contact with the French court, canvassing a French expeditionary force to Ulster, but this came to nothing. It was a see-saw of diplomacy and war, of victory and defeat. In 1563 Shane was expelled from Armagh, but in 1566 he returned and burned it. Queen Elizabeth decided that she had had enough of him, and declared that he must be 'utterly exterped'. However, it was Hugh O'Donnell, his neighbour to the northwest, who defeated him in battle. He fled to his Scottish enemies in Antrim, who murdered him and handed his head to the English. These pickled it, sent it in a barrel to Dublin, and impaled it on a castle spike. The scene shifted to Munster.

The Earls of Desmond controlled territory and people from Dungarvan to Kerry and from Limerick to Cork, and this junior branch of the great Geraldine family (the senior was 'ruled' by the

Earl of Kildare) overawed MacCarthys, O'Sullivans and others. They were in fact the most powerful people in southern Ireland, usually at loggerheads with the Butler Earls of Ormond. It was Elizabethan policy generally to keep one or more of these magnates in London, technically as guests but actually as hostages or even prisoners.

They offered hostages of another sort. Though they did not, by tradition, own lands they did control large areas of territory, usually subdivided and from which they extracted the equivalent of rents, and they usually possessed castles. These were, of course, both immovable and destructible. If they incurred the royal wrath, and the Queen was not in an exceptionally parsimonious mood, a column of soldiers with modern equipment and arms, could be sent against the offender to burn his crops and destroy or seize his castle. But Queen Elizabeth wished to go much further than this. She wished to administer Munster (which was now divided administratively into the two provinces of Munster and Connaught) using English methods, English law, new English religious ceremony and, for the time being at least, English civil servants. In fact, during approximately the first half of her reign, her reaction to the O'Neills was essentially defensive, to the Geraldines offensive. That she sent over a number of very brutal but not particularly efficient men to 'govern' Ireland is hardly surprising: it was a brutal age, and these executives were not of any particular nationality. (If this comment should sound unduly anti-English, it must be recalled not only that such were soldierly morals during the sixteenth and seventeenth century Wars of Religion, but also that a large though statistically unknown portion of the English soldiers were Irishmen.) In one of the most destructive acts of the revolt Sir Edmund 'utterly despoyled' the annual fair at Enniscorthy and 'ravished killed or spoyled' the merchants and their families who had travelled from Wexford to attend it, or so the Mayor of Waterford informed Sir Henry Sidney in 1569. It is hardly surprising when we learn that the inland towns of Munster, all small, were more or less destroyed during this dreadful period.

It is curious to think of Shakespeare's contemporaries as being also those of the Franks and the Goths, yet in fact it had only taken the English horde a thousand-odd years longer to cover almost as many miles, while the annihilators of ancient Rome had also had as contemporaries St. Augustine and many more while Cervantes was a sixteenth century Spaniard. Yet Roman society and its successor states had possessed a strength and a solidity that Celtic society lacked. Furthermore the Irish, while retaining much that was very ancient and indigenous, had suffered some four centuries of semi-feudalism. Tanistry had decayed, but primogeniture had not replaced it. While two Christian rituals competed (and were indeed in large parts of Europe coming to war) in Ireland ancient myths remained vivid: neither Church could aspire to omnipotence, though they too were forming up for war. The great Norman families, thoroughly hibernicised though most of them were, still sometimes preserved a certain residual loyalty to the English Crown. Two forms of law claimed jurisdiction. Through the interstices of these decadent social and religious orders, where monogamy, inheritance and the celibacy of clergy constituted many a gap, there appeared a Renaissance man, a certain Fitzmaurice FitzGerald, usually referred to as Fitzmaurice.

That he was a Geraldine is almost certain, that he was 'legitimate' or not meant little. His putative cousin, the Earl of Desmond, was a 'guest' of Queen Elizabeth's in London, the strongest nobleman in Munster but, it seems, a somewhat vacillating character. Yet he gave his name to the Desmond war or wars, having spoken out against the O'Neills. In fact it was his cousin Fitzmaurice who led the Irish in their defence against the first *razzia*, and was defeated. Various forms of English government were inflicted on Munster, but Fitzmaurice slipped the noose repeatedly. The province was destroyed and English officials exchanged a 'pardon' to 'rebels' in exchange for sacks full of heads. The forests ceased to retreat and began to advance, not now the old hardwood forests but masses of overgrowth and undergrowth that swallowed up tilled fields. The Irish starved, the English did little better. Yet, suddenly, there was Fitzmaurice with his kerns and his galloglasses. Bitterness, on both sides, grew. All over Europe this was becoming identified with Protestantism on the one hand, Catholicism on the other. Munster was no exception.

In 1567 the Irish Act of Conformity (to the state Church) had been passed, preceded by its legal arm, the Court of High Commission in 1564, and since the Earl of Desmond refused to conform he had become one of Queen Elizabeth's 'guests' in London, as was a young man named Hugh O'Neill. Almost immediately the first English freebooters began to arrive in Ireland, and to carve out estates for themselves. And almost at once the Munster Irish began to 'rebel' against their infiltrators. Briefly, Butlers and Geraldines

combined against these alien impositions and colonisations. By
1569 the greater parts of Munster was in revolt against the rule of
Sir Henry Sidney. Inland and even coastal towns such as Cork,
Kinsale, Youghal and Kilmallock were attacked by the Irish,
briefly united in Munster under the leadership of MacCarthy and,
above all, of a somewhat curious figure, of whom unfortunately we
know very little, the Fitzmaurice already mentioned.

Fitzmaurice was in a stronger position than most of the other Celtic
or Norman leaders, in that owing to his anomalous birth he had
neither castle to destroy, cattle to hough, nor crops to burn. He also
seems to have been well informed about international events. He
sent the papal appointee to the bishopric of Cashel, who bore the
same surname as this writer, to King Philip in 1569 with a plea for
help, for the despatch of an army to Ireland there to appoint a
governor and expel the heretics. But all hope of a reconciliation with
Elizabeth had not yet been abandoned in Rome and the papacy put
no pressure behind such a venture then. Perhaps the Armada was
already in Philip's mind, but if so it was to be many years before it
put to sea, and then its purpose was not to 'liberate' Ireland but to
carry Parma's troops from the Low Countries to England. In any
event, by then Fitzmaurice had long fled to France (1575) and the
Rock of Cashel was much the ruin that we see today.

Queen Elizabeth, like all second-generation revolutionaries, was
most anxious to prove the legitimacy of her claim to power over all
counter-revolution. Though the feudal hierarchy was almost dead,
in Ireland it still had some reality in some Norman eyes. The
wretched Earl of Desmond was therefore sent to Munster, which he
was to govern under the closest English control. Instead, he found
himself at the head of the remnants of his cousin's rebellion, in a
land reduced to a desperate desert. He was swept aside, and the
English moved on in to Connaught. The sickle had almost encircled
the island, and the O'Neills had shown no inclination to intervene.
The most important member of that family was, in fact, another of
Queen Elizabeth's 'guests' throughout most of his childhood and
youth: he had availed himself of the opportunity not only to dress
in a fashion as gorgeous of those of northern Italy and Paris but also
to learn the cruel lessons of statesmanship that had long been
practised in the Italian city states and that Machiavelli had put on
paper many years before. He returned to an Ulster that was almost
intact, and he played many a diplomatic card before the cruder
English in Dublin and London compelled him to resort to force. He

won some battles, but he lost more, and when at last a Spanish expeditionary force came to his assistance, in 1601, it landed in Munster, not as requested in Ulster. Hugh O'Neill marched with his troops the length of the island: he was too late. The Spaniards and the Ulstermen were defeated in detail. In 1603 O'Neill sued for peace, that is to say he surrendered. He had fought beside his old enemy, O'Donnell, and the surrender included them both.

Unlike our contemporaries, however, Renaissance politicians and soldiers avoided such words as 'surrender' while seeking for the reality behind them. The failure of the Spanish expedition and the almost total defeat of the Irish spelt victory for Mountjoy's forces after sixty years of indecision. When the Irish could no longer fight, an ancient form of society had passed beyond decay. The English must have realised this, and enforced a treaty which was not, in their eyes, so humiliating as to compel further Irish resistance. The old formula of surrender and regrant was produced. The O'Neill ceased to be that and became the Earl of Tyrone: the O'Donnell the Earl of Tyrconnel. To English ears this was little more than a translation of titles: to the descendant of Niall of the Nine Hostages such a translation meant precisely nothing at all, save the surrender of his real title. To his people it meant even less. Tyrone County belonged to the Earl: O'Neill territory had never *belonged* to any particular O'Neill. He was surrendering, for a tinny title, what was not even his: such was the value of his earldom. And with the foreign, meaningless title came all the trimmings, foreign law, foreign customs, foreign religion. In our jargon the surrender was, in effect, unconditional.

Hugh O'Neill maintained that he would have continued to fight had he known that the great Queen had died a few days before he signed the treaty. Presumably he imagined that the extinction of the Tudor line and the accession of James VI of Scotland to the throne of England as James I would have led to a change of policy towards Ireland in general and Ulster, with its Scots–Irish element, in particular. He would have been wrong, for the early Stuarts strengthened, if anything, the Tudor policy of conquest. For four years Tyrone and Tyrconnel attempted to carry out their new tasks, while James I set about the plantation of Ulster with Lowland Scots and Englishmen. This meant the dispossession of Irish farmers. Why should these families move off land which had never belonged to Gaelic chieftains? These found themselves in an impossible position, obligated by English law to enforce an alien way of life on their own people. For four years they attempted the shameful if not the impossible, and then in 1609 they slipped away by sea, with their families and their closest associates, Tyrone to die in Rome, Tyrconnel perhaps poisoned by an English agent in Madrid. The Flight of the Earls can be described as marking the end of overt Gaelic society in Ireland. It also set a precedent. Save for a brief period when James II was attempting to reconquer England via Ireland, the Irish were left without temporal leaders, to be administered by foreigners in a language and according to a code of law they did not understand. Furthermore the abortive Spanish expedition to Munster had made the English even more conscious of the danger posed to their nation by the proximity of Ireland and the illegal Roman Catholicism of its people. For a long time Ireland was to be run almost exclusively by Englishmen and Dublin became a garrison city. The whole country might as well have been placed under martial law, for such was effectively its condition. Ireland had been conquered.

NOTES
1 Without false modesty, I would refer the reader to my own *Red Hand: the Ulster Colony*.
2 The reader is referred to *The Great O'Neill*, by Sean O'Faolain, a most readable book.
3 The subjugation of the south is well summed up, and briefly, by Nicholas P. Canny in *The Elizabethan Conquest of Ireland*.

14

'THOROUGH'

It was, I believe, Max Weber, the father of sociology, who first spoke of the Protestant work ethos. By this is meant, if the somewhat hermetic phrase is correctly understood, a state of affairs whereby the Roman Catholic finds salvation in pràyer, the Protestant in good works. This concept has been repeatedly applied to the population of Ulster after 1607, the Scots–Irish being the 'Protestants', the Irish-speakers the rest. It is, unfortunately, pure nonsense. Long before John Knox (c. 1505–1572), the eastern Ulstermen had been Christians, far more closely related to their fellow Scots than to their Irish cousins. In this and the last century the competition in Ulster has been to acquire jobs, not for the one who can perform them the better.

It is unlikely that John Knox ever visited Ireland, but the influence of his religious teachings was great among the Scots there. On the other hand as Knox moved from Lutheranism to Calvinism – at no time was he a firm adherent of either dogma – he and his followers became increasingly antipathetic to King James VI/I. In effect Knox was the creator of Presbyterianism, which King James rightly interpreted as republicanism, as: 'No bishop, no king.'

The fact that there was a fairly large Scottish population in eastern Ulster long before the Reformation is frequently forgotten. They are sometimes referred to, with a subdued sneer, as Scotch–Irish which is correct, for they were both, but this should not imply any form of patronage either from the Irish or from the Scots, let alone from the English. These aboriginal Scots–Irish, whose fore-bears had twice crossed the narrow sea, do not seem to have been a particularly pugnacious or expansive sort of person, and those who visit the beautiful glens of Antrim today will find there farmers little changed from what we know of their ancestors, or, indeed, from their very remote cousins in other, rural parts of Ireland. In 1610, however, their loyalties were to King James and their religion was therefore either to his Established Church or to the much 'lower' forms of Protantism which Knox had acquired in part from

Calvin. In this they were not very different from that English puritanism which was a rapidly mounting force in almost all parts of England proper. And since they had not been tormented by the Elizabethan soldiery they had no reason to equate English domination with the state Established Church. In fact, as Presbyterianism, as well as other forms of autonomous Christianity, spread to 'planted' Ulster, those who embraced these faiths became known as Nonconformists and were subject to religious legislation almost to the same degree as were the Roman Catholics, their most bitter theological opponents.

The splendour of Queen Elizabeth I's personality, the achievements of her reign and the brilliance of her advisers did not provide the blubber-lipped, homosexual foreigner, James, with an easy inheritance. His new English subjects might sneer at him as 'the wisest fool in Christendom', but if his conversation seemed to many foolish, his brains were very real. And almost the first problem he had to tackle was the problem of defeated, leaderless Ulster.

Since he had had no direct personal connection with the cracking of this last, and toughest, Irish nut, so his difficulties in dealing with the shell and the meat were all the more complex. He looked first to precedents, but the plantation of King's and Queen's counties was not a happy example. Nevertheless it was applied, and the unpaid soldiery were paid off in land. As before, the normal reaction of the English was to sell up and go home. But now they did not sell to the Irish, totally impoverished by the wars. Nor were those who remained particularly successful: the training of a soldier and that of a farmer are very different. And the Ulster Irish, whose history was so different from that of the inhabitants of the other provinces, showed little inclination to move away. This was their land, or at least family land, and while they would remain upon it as indentured tenants, or even as casual labourers, it was still, in reality, their land. Great Englishmen, who had served Mountjoy in his defeat of O'Neill, were given great estates: many of their descendants are there to this day. But the influx that purchased smaller farms came from Scotland rather than from England. And in his dual capacity as King of both countries, this did not increase King James I's popularity with the English.

There was then only one town of any real commercial value in Ulster: the port of Derry. Belfast in those days was a negligible fishing village and was to remain so for some two centuries. In order to balance the influx of colonists, Derry was sold to a consortium of

London merchant companies and hence acquired the name of Londonderry. A condition of sale, however, was that the merchants should build, or rebuild, the town's fortifications. But the merchants proved little more efficient as military engineers than had the soldiers as farmers. Only when the penalty clause was invoked by Strafford did they set about making Londonderry into a fortress, and history has shown that they were almost too late. While the rest of Ireland slowly recovered, and the 'New English' (or 'New Scots', though the phrase is rare) set about restoring the devastation of the Elizabethan wars, the Irish in Ulster made little attempt to accept the new society and the new administration. There was still no Irish patriotism in sight, but the island was slowly regaining its economic strength and, to the distress of London, returning to its old ways. A people, like a person, can reach a low point at which the only ways are upwards or out. Ireland, still an agricultural country at last at peace, could *only* recover if it were to survive. On the other hand many historical examples have shown that when nemesis appears to have been reached, further decline into chaos is still possible. The Irish people in 1600 had owned most of Ireland; even though by 1641 some two thirds of their land was now owned by the Old English or the New English,[1] they still vastly outnumbered their conquerors, and were once again ingurgitating them into a warlike Irish tribal culture, even if, by defeat, Ireland had been spared the worst horrors of the European religious wars. Their literary culture, too, was enjoying a silver age.

Yet from the English (or perhaps one should henceforth say British) point of view the main purpose of the Irish colony, even though it was now conquered and at reluctant peace, was not being met. It was not a net financial asset to the London exchequer. The Stuarts could never control their parliaments of merchants and landowners as the Tudors had done, and as Queen Elizabeth I was finding increasingly difficult towards the end of her reign.

Since the Crown was far from self-supporting, and since almost all major finance bills, such as taxes, customs and excise, were the prerogative of Parliament, the burgeoning mercantile class had ever-growing power in the state. Furthermore it will be recalled that by Poynings' Law even in most Irish affairs ultimate authority rested with the Privy Council in London, which in its turn was answerable to Parliament in general and increasingly to the House of Commons. In the early seventeenth century that House was not, in our sense, a house of representatives of the people but rather spoke for property, landed and increasingly mercantile. The long inflation of the previous century was drawing to a close and the period of what was later to be named mercantilism was beginning to flourish in northern and western Europe. However, and quite separate from this, religious conflict was becoming overt war upon most of the Continent. At the risk of a very wild generalisation, it may be said that the adherents of the Roman Church tended to cling also to a modified form of rural feudalism (in France, for instance, autocracy) while the new mercantile classes (as in England, the Low Countries and the Hansa communities) preferred the comparative self-government of parliamentary representation. In England these two forces were to find themselves very roughly opposed in the Civil War, though none had anticipated this.

The effect on an impoverished, conquered and in some measure still a chaotic Ireland was obvious. Ireland had very little mercantile infrastructure and the year 1614–1615 showed a mere 143 ships trading in and out of the country, of which less than a hundred were of Irish registration.[2] These Irish ships were usually of small tonnage, for the Anglo-Irish route. Spanish, English, French and the larger Irish ships imported wine. (That same year showed a total of a little less than 400,000 gallons, surely a remarkably large consumption for a population of perhaps a million souls.) Salt was also a commodity in considerable demand in Ireland, since this was needed not only for domestic purposes but also for salting the fish, particularly salmon, which was one of Ireland's principal exports. Hops were also imported in large quantities, for the making of beer. When it is recalled how much poteen was being distilled, it would appear that the Irish were scarcely an abstemious people. Statistics are scarcely available, save spasmodically. Too much attention should therefore not be ascribed to them in any attempt to describe the Irish way of life. It does, however, seem that in 1632 the main agricultural exports were the by-products of a pastoral way of life: cattle, wool, hides, tallow and butter, linen yarn and rugs, as well as some coastal fish, such as herrings and pilchards, and timber.

This in turn would indicate that when the Irish were attempting to rebuild their agriculture, which must precede the rebuilding of their ruined little towns, their experience of the almost perpetual wars and lack of administrative control led them to eschew tillage (too many standing crops had been burned by Irish and English alike) and to devote themselves to cows and sheep, which could be driven into the forests or to rocky mountains, out of the reach of soldiers. Also Sir Walter Raleigh had introduced the potato, that most ominous of tubers in Ireland's history, but throughout the seventeenth century its cultivation was not particularly widespread and it was not until the eighteenth that it assumed a great and finally preponderant and disastrous importance.[3]

The division in Ireland had not, if it ever has, become a purely religious one as yet. However, with the Thirty Years' War bringing chaos to Europe, it was tending that way. The Roman Church was a bond between the 'Old Irish' and the 'Old English', though this bond was not as yet political. The 'New English' – who must now include the Scots – were in Christian terms the very antithesis of the Roman Catholics, but Archbishop Laud's Conformity Bill made them, no matter how reluctantly, in some ways the politico-emotional friends of their Catholic fellow-Irishmen. Furthermore Henry VIII's original motive, the financial one, in the dissolution of the monasteries and that of his successors in the nationalisation of the Roman Church did not work satisfactorily in Ireland: too much church land was sublet in various complex ways to and through laymen or lay and monastic corporations which made straight confiscation both legally and politically very difficult, if not impossible. During one year of this period we have figures of Irish moneys: £60,000 paid by the exchequer for expenses in Ireland, £40,000 extracted from Ireland in the form of taxes etcetera. Even if these figures were unusual – and there is no reason to believe they were excessively so – a colony that only produces two thirds of its cost is hardly a viable economic concern: it is in this proportion that such finances can best be assessed, since the translation of the £ symbol from one century's currency to that of another is usually almost meaningless.

❋ ❋ ❋

When Thomas Wentworth, later Earl of Strafford, was sent to Ireland as lord deputy in 1633, he came as the King's man. As Archbishop Laud in spiritual, so Wentworth in temporal matters saw it as his duty to find, in his case in Ireland, 'the opportunity and means to supply the king's wants'. His Irish appointment he regarded as only a stepping stone to absolute, efficient government in England, again in no interest save that of the King. In his own words he intended to govern Ireland 'thoroughly', before going on so to govern England. Had he succeeded during his short life (1593–1641) his achievement in Britain might well have been equivalent to that of his contemporary, Richelieu (1585–1642) in the creation of monarchical autocracy. But Strafford served Stuarts, not Bourbons, and in Ireland he served his King in a land where law, administration and what is generally called 'civil service' were only beginning to recover from chaos. Whether Richelieu would have done any better in Ireland – an almost equally foreign land to them both – is problematical.

The problem was, of course, financial. The change from the feudal to the mercantile systems, in both countries, implied a fundamental alteration in both the means of government and in the methods of exchange. Any French comparison can here be dropped: indeed there can be little, save the men in charge, that invites comparison between the kingdoms of Ireland and of France, since the first was a fiction in its comparison and relationship with the second. Wentworth, an administrator of proven ability, was sent to Ireland in order thoroughly to reorganise a confused, impoverished and non-national state, and to do this for the benefit of the English King. If one were to draw another comparison, with another contemporary, John Winthrop was sent to America in order 'thoroughly' to reorganise the Bay Colony of Massachusetts: but since Winthrop scarcely had to consider the wishes and history of the Iroquois and other Indians, his was an easy task. A century and a half were to elapse before his English colonists became consciously Americans. At no point were the Amerindians taken into account, nor was such culture as they possessed to influence, save in utter superficiality, that of the colonists or, later, of the immigrants.

Wentworth had served his apprenticeship for his Irish undertaking in northern England, where the new religion had never enjoyed great popularity. Recusancy (that is to say, originally attendance at Roman Catholic church services but later extended to include abstention without good reason to attend Laud's Established Church of England) was an offence for which a fine was imposed. In large parts of the north this had lapsed in particular with regard to the new and growing Non-conformist churches. Wentworth saw to it that the recusancy fines were collected, the money of course going to the royal treasury. In Roman Catholic Ireland this would amount to a very large sum. He also rationalised the system of customs and excise and indeed the law generally, always in the royal favour.

He appears never to have given a fig for popularity as such, and his methods made him many enemies. However, with the growing of the King's power, and Charles I's personal indebtedness to him, Wentworth's transfer to Ireland was most definitely a promotion, since his powers there would be virtually absolute within the limits of Poynings' Law: but few men in London were prepared at this time, 1633, to cross swords with the viceroy.

A visit to London's National Portrait Gallery shows how different is our image of seventeenth century men and women then and those of their predecessors. Very rarely did a great portraitist of the English sixteenth century so delineate a character that one feels one might have met him, frequently. The same applies to literature, and this is perhaps why Shakespeare's plays (when they work, which is not always) are so superior to those of earlier, brilliant writers. Renaissance man is 'one of us'. In Chapter IV of the *New History of Ireland* (Vol. III, ed T. W. Moody) Aidan Clarke describes Wentworth thus:

> A self-contained man of marked intelligence and overbearingly forceful character, remarkable executive abilities, and natural insensitivity, he was an authoritarian by inclination as well as by conviction. As an administrator, he possessed vigour and mastery of detail, made decisions clearly and unhesitatingly, thought constructively and connectedly, and was committed to success by pride and ambition. As a politician, his tactical judgment was excellent, but his manipulative skill imperfectly concealed an inability to compromise and a total incapacity either to understand or to acknowledge the legitimacy of an opposing point of view. Both as an administrator and as a politician he was dangerously prone to simplify, because he could not objectify, the analysis of problems in the interests of preconceived solutions.

This character, a modern character, rings true just because it is not a synopsis of his actions and his career. Such was the man sent by Charles I to govern, or rather to reorganise and place a government upon, Ireland. He was closer to a forceful American businessman sent to reorganise the European division than to the noblemen of some near-anonymous Mortimer family or even to Poynings. His resemblance to these earlier deputy viceroys lay in the simple fact that he, like they, failed.

Not that the Wentworths were in any way *nouveaux riches*, let alone Tudor social upstarts. For centuries they had owned vast estates in the north of England, had held half a dozen titles and been related by marriage to various royal families during the Wars of the Roses, had held high office and in due course been imprisoned or executed in the Tower. Yet they were not merely a feudal noble family but also foreshadowed the later landed gentry of the highest and richest class. It would have been difficult to find a more competent administrator to disentangle the Irish confusion that followed the conquest. And there were not a few in England who were pleased to see him go.

Of the great Duke of Wellington, some private soldier is said to have remarked that he was a beast, but a just beast. Such might well have been an Irishman's description of Thomas Wentworth (created Earl of Strafford in 1640). He was in Ireland for a mere six years, but during that time he more than doubled the state's income from recusancy fines and taxation, sorted out the currency and proclaimed, as he had done in England, the absolute sovereignty of the monarch on behalf of the people. 'Whoever,' he had said, 'ravels forth into questions the right of a king and of a people shall never be able to wrap them up again into the comeliness and order he found them.' On this basis in Ireland, he ordered that all the grand juries of all the counties inevitably find for the King. When Galway (and Galway alone) demurred, he fined the county sheriff £1,000 for summoning such a jury and summoned the jurymen to the castle chamber to answer for their offence. In Ulster, where the London city companies had not fulfilled their contracts to fortify Derry and other places, he confiscated some of their property.[4] King Charles had promised that no colonists be forced into Connaught, but this Strafford ignored. He created an army in Ireland, and the Puritans in the English Parliament – his most bitter enemies – maintained that its ultimate purpose was the invasion and the infliction of royal tyranny on England. Summoned back to England by Parliament, he was impeached, although Charles I promised him, more than once, that 'upon the word of a king, you shall not suffer in life, honour or fortune,' and finally hesitated to sign the Bill of Attainder, which was in fact Strafford's death warrant. That tall, stooped and in appearance almost morose man had a greater sense of honour and of responsibility than his royal master. Foreseeing civil war, he requested the King to sign the bill that would lose him his life and thus 'establish that blessed agreement which God, I trust, shall for ever establish between you and your subjects'. He was beheaded in May 1641, on Tower Hill, after receiving a blessing from the High Church Archbishop Laud, who was himself executed a few months later. By then most of Ireland was in rebellion, governed neither by King nor by Parliament, while the tortuous Civil War was fought out on the larger island. Not until Cromwell had won it, and himself ordered the beheading of the King, could English eyes be turned to Scotland and then, in 1649, to Ireland. Save for some of the nobility and for some of the Puritans, the English Civil War was of little interest to the Irish, though the nobility did incline towards the Cavaliers, for to a very limited extent it was a class as well as an administrative war. But 'class' in Ireland was primarily ethnic.

* * *

Just as Strafford was not the first, and far from the last, English administrator to lose his reputation or even his head as the result of his activities in Ireland, so the chaos and civil war that followed close upon the Englishman's departure were very far from unique.

That the Irish were a disparate collection of tribes before ever the Vikings put to sea has been stressed: that the break-up by them and the Normans introduced a bloodier hostility between those tribes than such known by Cuchulain, Finn and the rest has also been, I hope, made plain. But now there was injected into this individualistic mayhem the European dimension of religious war. Vague, or less vague, ethnic and linguistic alliances only served to aggravate and embitter what, to most foreigners, must seem a permanent and pointless hatred among fellow-Irishmen regardless of ethnic origin. Had there been two sides, a victory no matter how bloody might have put an end to it. Unfortunately there were usually at least three (in a country that had no retrospect of unity) and at no time was this more obvious than in the dreadful years between the execution of Strafford, in 1641, and the arrival of Oliver Cromwell, in 1649. And neither solved any sort of Irish problem.

The Christian theologians have rightly described the Trinity as a mystery, and have sternly warned against the attempt at its 'solution'. In Ireland, in the late fifteenth and early sixteenth centuries this mystery was superimposed, with immense force, upon the religious beliefs of the Irish. It was not, and never has been, a simple dichotomy, between Roman Catholicism and Protestantism, for there have since then been at least two major non-Roman forms of Christianity, which for abbreviation may be termed the Established Church and the Non-conformists. The animosity between these last two has frequently been at least as bitter as that of either of them to the Church of Rome. As we are all reminded daily in 1982, these animosities have now been going on for well over three hundred years. None can admit that its truth may be less absolute than that of the others. He who does so is liable to the most fearful punishments, culminating of course in Hell itself. Attitudes have improved, in part through lethargy, since 1641, but such were they then.

Goethe is quoted as having remarked that of tyranny and anarchy he preferred the first: one tyrant is preferable to the hydra-headed

Henry Grattan (1746–1820), founder, father and leader of the first post-Williamite Irish House of Commons. Only Protestants of some means might vote for, or sit in, it, though such was not Grattan's ideal. It lasted for a mere eighteen years, being absolved by the Act of Union of 1800

Theobald Wolfe Tone (1763–1798). A Dubliner by birth and lawyer by choice, he was much influenced by the French revolutionaries and the American, Tom Paine. He was instrumental in creating the non-sectarian United Irishmen who were eventually massacred in the '98 Rebellion. He was by then in France and took part in a small French invasion, which failed. Captured, he avoided the death penalty by suicide. He left a heritage of violence and atheism (*National Library of Ireland*)

Daniel O'Connell (1775–1847). This not altogether happy monument of Ireland's great patriot, 'the Liberator', stands at the end of the street now named after him. He abhorred violence and won the Catholic vote for his co-religionaries. He had seen revolution in action, in France, and founded a non-sectarian Irish constitutional party to obtain Irish freedom alternative. With Strafford gone – to face principally his enemies' accusations of tyranny in Ireland, for there were none in England – Ireland very rapidly became an anarchic place. The Elizabethan wars had not been forgotten, and for neither the first time nor the last the Irish wanted the English out. However a great many of them were in Ireland precisely because the island had been conquered by the English. The families of some had been there for so long (the Vikings and Normans in particular, who had never been English at all) that loyalties were strange. The 'Old English' had usually continued to adhere to the Roman faith. The 'New English', those planters from the Elizabethan wars and their successors and supporters, had been tending more and more, particularly in Ulster, to extreme Low Church faiths and were therefore as religiously alien to the Established Church as were the Romans, and equally unpopular with the government of Charles I. Yet they had almost all been planted on Irish farms, confiscated from Irish farmers. And the Irish farmers, papists almost to a man, intended to get them back. This, in 1641, they proceeded to do.

W. E. H. Lecky (1838–1903), probably the greatest of Irish historians, estimates the massacre of Protestants by Catholics in 1641 at some 4,000, and perhaps twice that number were expelled from their farms. In the hysteria of the age, these figures were undoubtedly much exaggerated. But the massacre happened, principally in Ulster, and the border counties: it has never been forgotten.

With the exception of the Pale, a large area based on Cork, and strongpoints dotted throughout the country, from 1641 to 1649 the Kingdom of Ireland became a confederacy of Roman Catholic Gaelic–Norman chieftains with no effective central administration. This confederation of Kilkenny received support from Richelieu, both in money and arms, and many Irish soldiers who had emigrated to France and Spain returned, in particular Owen Roe O'Neill, who was an experienced and most competent senior officer. Save for the brief Jamesian episode this was the last time that the Irish were to rule the majority of their country, and the inspiration came from the Roman Catholics of Ulster, where the recent settlers, the 'New English', were in large measure expelled before they had set down roots, and where most of the killings took place. The number of these was grossly exaggerated both in England and in the more remote parts of Ireland.

Although there was little in common to the principal types of

Irishmen – namely the Celtic-speaking Old Irish, Old English and Norse, and the New English or 'planted' families – save for the language and Roman Catholicism common to the first three, and a growing 'Irishness' common to the mixture of these people in the Viking-created cities, the decade of the 1640s saw even more prolix divisions in the larger island.

Before returning to Irish affairs, it would be as well to attempt an almost absurdly brief résumé of events on the larger island, in particular as these affected Ireland and the Irish.

What began as a struggle for power between king and certain elements of the new governing class that had come into existence with the decay of feudalism, and which are usually referred to as 'Parliament', scarcely fits into the Marxist framework of historical fiction. If there were a class distinction between the opponents, it was primarily between the rural proletariat and the nascent urban proletariat, above all London. In so far as it was a religious war, much the same applies, for in general the countrymen tended to be High Church (and thus more sympathetic to the few Roman Catholics who still existed in England): much the same applied in Scotland, whether the Highlanders continued to be Roman Catholic adherents of a Celtic-speaking liege-lord, while the far more numerous, and geographically more dangerous, Lowlanders had embraced Knox's teaching. The sects of religious fanatics, and they were many, in both Scotland and England abominated one another. Thus, with scarcely excusable roughness, were the lines drawn when the war in England started. To make matters even less simple, it was triangular. King Charles, being also (and quite independently) King of Scotland, attempted and failed to subdue his Scots subjects. Parliament looked to them for religious (which in this context meant military) support. And across the Irish Sea there was an almost entirely Roman Catholic Irish army, originally Strafford's creation, which in fact played no part in the Anglo-Scots wars worth mentioning but yet which could never be left out of anyone's calculations.

The end of the war found a very different situation. The hitherto obscure country gentleman, Oliver Cromwell, was Protector or dictator of both England and Scotland, having cut off Charles I's head and soundly defeated the Scots with his New Model Army, a most formidable force, created, trained and usually led to victory by himself. The confederate Irish army, loyal to the Stuarts, was still in existence. A maritime war with the Dutch was to come. Cromwell decided that, after Scotland, Ireland must be dealt with.

First, however, he disposed of his proto-communists, the Levellers and such, who, like later adherents of such creeds, had imbibed their ideas from war-torn Germany. It was not easy to rid himself of them, since in some ways he still needed those fanatical and experienced soldiers in his negotiations with the still living King Charles and with the Scots. However, he skilfully established his omnipotence, and then turned to Ireland.

His methods were more than thorough. His propaganda weapon was the rising of 1641 and the grossly exaggerated massacre, for which he held virtually the entire Irish people responsible. In 1664 he landed at Dublin with 20,000 men, an enormous army for the period. The gallant but ill-trained Irish armies, lacking real leaders or even a unified government, won some battles but were no strategic match for his veterans whose brutality inspired terror. When Drogheda failed to surrender, he threatened the inhabitants with total massacre. Here there seems to have been some confusion. Drogheda is divided by a river, and when the Irish forces on one bank surrendered it is alleged that Cromwell, still meeting resistance on the other side, ordered the annihilation of the entire population. At Wexford he had no such excuse. The city had surrendered, but his soldiers were tired, hungry and angry. He ordered another total extermination. He then sailed for home, leaving his son-in-law, General Ireton, in charge of the defenceless provinces. So great is the shadow of hate and horror that Cromwell's name still inspires in Ireland that it is hard to realise he was there for only a few months. But he left orders behind him. These included the transportation, more or less as slaves, of many thousand Irish men and women to the West Indies, while perhaps as many as 30,000 former Irish soldiers, the first of the 'Wild Geese', were allowed to join continental armies. In ten fearful years the population of all Ireland had fallen to some half a million souls.

Cromwell's final 'Act of Settlement' was passed by the London Parliament – which by then represented little more than the army – in 1653 and working with their usual thoroughness its conditions were fulfilled in some five years: the Irish-speakers were, at least in theory, expelled from all towns including Dublin. The poor, with possessions of less than £10, were excluded from these Settlements: they were in any event needed as labourers in all Ireland. For the rest, Ireland was divided into two parts, that west of the Shannon including Clare and the Province of Connaught which were to remain Irish, and the remaining twenty-six counties which were to be

English, and which were so divided up by a certain Sir William Petty among English landowners. (He became extremely rich in the process and was ennobled as Lord Shelburne. It is perhaps not unsuitable that what was once a charming and elegant Dublin hotel of that name has now all the graces of an English Trust House.)

The Kingdom of Ireland was abolished and the twenty-six new English counties were given some representation in the moribund London House of Commons. All Roman Catholic church lands and property were seized, but tolerance was extended to other faiths, including the Jews. Ulster probably suffered most, since there was a great influx of Scotsmen to join their relations. Ireland in 1658 must have borne a considerable resemblance to Poland in 1943. One wonders: if Cromwell had possessed Zyklon B and the other marvels of our century, would he have been more successful than his Nazi imitators . . .

NOTES
1 Moody, T. W. (ed). *A New History of Ireland*, Vol. III, ch. VI.
2 Kearney, Hugh F. *Strafford in Ireland*.
3 According to the *Encyclopaedia Britannica* he brought it from North Carolina to his enormous Irish estates in 1585 or 1586, though another variety or varieties of the tuber may have been introduced by others into Italy and Spain at an earlier date.
4 Kearney, op. cit.

15

THE WARS WITHOUT ROSES

As has been postulated earlier in this book, the visual arts of the Irish, in common with those of the other Celtic-speaking peoples, tended from the very beginning towards the abstract or at least towards the symbolic. To the early Celt, realistic sculpture, for example, would appear virtually pointless. What is the purpose in making a stone or wooden reproduction of a man or woman if the real man or woman already exists? Nor were their 'gods' of the type that call for the honour of immortalisation in some other material, save perhaps by way of explanation. Thus we have a very early three-faced god from central Europe, but it is neither an object of beauty nor of reverence. Only with the Graeco-Roman influence of Christianity do we get representations of St. Patrick and his peers, but remarkably few of these. And then we get the great High Crosses, unique to Ireland and astonishing in their massive beauty.

These, however, were almost certainly didactic in purpose, or at least originally so. Each panel tells a biblical story or incident, and was undoubtedly used by the priest to make explicit what he was relating to his illiterate flock. Most of these can still be deciphered as coming straight from the Old Testament or the New, even though time and weather have much coarsened their surfaces. Their usually enormous scale is perhaps fortuitous in that it would have been well nigh impossible to carve, in stone, such biblical scenes on smaller scales: this does, however, explain why the Vikings did not steal and only very rarely tried to smash them. They were just too big.

Apart from dolmens, cromlechs, stone circles and other such monuments, the High Crosses, carved almost entirely towards the second half of the first millenium, are the earliest Irish sculpture that has survived. In our late twentieth century the general terms used for art forms have become transformed, perhaps to their original meanings. Thus piles of what, to the ignorant, appear to be rubbish are described as sculpture. In total reverse stone circles of even such a monument as New Grange might be called 'sculpture' or 'artistic creations', concepts unknown to those who made them. This writer prefers to regard Stonehenge as nearer to an astronomical observatory than to a work of art. That it may well be both leads to such complexities of thought concerning artefacts of every sort than he draws a quite arbitrary line between objects created to please man or God (the gods is perhaps more appropriate) and those with some ulterior purpose such as cooking ovens or piles of old rubbish.

Were the High Crosses originally painted? The evidence is entirely negative, in that no scrap of paint has been found in their proximity. On the other hand, so far as we know, all early sculpture, Greek or Gothic, was painted. And certainly the Irish of the period were far from lacking in the painter's skill as the Book of Kells, the Book of Durrow and others, all roughly coeval with the High Crosses, show. To this writer it would seem unlikely that they were not painted, and fantastic in colour they must have looked. Yet their siting would argue against this. The two High Crosses at Monasterboice, in the Boyne valley, are already so close together that violent colouring – and we know from the manuscripts how addicted to violence those monks were – would have been confusing in works of art whose obvious purpose was quite the reverse. We can only speculate, both about the monks who built them and how. Our speculation becomes even wilder when we consider those small gargoyle-like fertility sculptures, known as Sheela-na-gigs, which may be of Norse or Norman origin or may be copies of wooden Celtic originals. They add an odd leer to a few ancient Christian churches.

So much has been written about the famous illuminated manuscripts that there is little to be added here. They are virtually the only works of early Irish pictorial artists to survive. Even in Byzantine Rome no work so exquisite has survived, and from what has one may doubt whether there was a great deal *to* survive. This is not to denigrate the superb work of many Byzantine artists, but merely to point out how such supreme and lifelong endeavour succeeded at the very other end of Europe, sprung, like Athene, from little save, in their case, the Christian faith.

For there is a direct ancestry to the very beautiful church ornaments that survived the Vikings in the exquisite pagan jewellery of an earlier age, the so-called Tara brooch, the multitude of golden torques and much else. There was a lot of gold in the Irish rivers and to this these earlier craftsmen added exquisite enamel work, silver work and precious stones. To this day these superb works of art, religious as well as pagan, turn up in the Irish soil from time to time, though it is rumoured that there are more of them in Scandinavia than in Ireland.

Of pre-Stuart Irish painting we know very little. What has survived, and it is not much, is both weak and ineffectual. It is impossible to see in these fragments the hands of the masters of Kells and Durrow. It is probably a mistake to make the attempt. There is no reason why a miniaturist should also be a master of church murals. And even the work of the muralists has almost entirely vanished in the wars, the persecutions and the destruction of churches.

Nor are the churches that much richer. The pre-Christian and early Christian Irish did not leave any architectural heritage at all, for the very simple reason that they built in wood. Only on such remote early monastic island settlements where there was no wood did they build dry-stone cells that are still standing and that were obviously copies in other material of the wooden 'beehive' houses in which, had they not become monks, they would have lived. (A photograph of a stone monk's hut on Inishmore, of the Aran Islands, appears on page 138.) Since the heating and cooking were provided by a central fireplace, these little homes very frequently burned when they did not simply fall down with age. They were the highly practical dwellings of a pastoral people, since they could be easily moved at the dictates of the seasons. Being without any form of drainage, they were less useful in the Viking towns, but seem to have been used nevertheless. Indeed, when the Normans arrived and began to build stone castles some fifty years after their arrival – they had used motte-and-baile strongpoints to begin with – the Irish regarded these new foreigners as fools: why build an immovable building? Only when the Normans, now as conquerors, began to toss Irish men and women over their new ramparts, did the purpose of stone become apparent. And the very early Norman castle at Trim (p. 138) is among the finest examples.

That there were stone buildings in Ireland before the arrival of the Normans, and perhaps before that of St. Patrick himself, is shown by the existence, usually as ruins, of the very earliest monastic foundations and of the churches or shrines. So little remains of the most ancient monasteries (many of which were certainly wooden and had probably, as has been said, often served as druidical training colleges) that it is not possible to speak of 'Irish style'. As for the earliest churches, usually attached to the monasteries, these are invariably very small shrines, intended no doubt for special divine services on the part of a few of the monks themselves. Large congregations worshipped outside in the open air. The idea of a cathedral does not seem to have occurred in pre-Norman Ireland though their skill in monumental building at a very early date shows that they did not lack the ability. Do we see here another example of the influence of Egypt and Byzantium on the very earliest Irish Church?

The monumental stone buildings that they did not produce in the pre-Norman but in the Christian period are the very well known and most spectacular Round Towers. There are a couple of smaller versions of these in Scotland and, I believe, one in Brittany, but otherwise they are entirely Irish (see p. 137). They are almost invariably, perhaps totally so, connected with a monastic settlement, though this may well have vanished by now.

For a long time, indeed throughout the eighteenth century and much of the last, there was dispute between antiquarians concerning the purpose of these Round Towers. It was not merely that they were almost uniquely Irish, but also that there were so many of them. Our ancestors were even worse at dating ancient objects than are we, but they did know that the ancient, early Christian Irish were not addicted to stone work, and even an ignorant eye can see how skilled the masons of those towers must have been.

One theory which I have mentioned, propounded by some bitter Englishman, was that the sly Irish deliberately built these incomprehensible huge stone pencils in order to bewilder honest, straightforward English antiquarians a thousand years later. A more plausible explanation is that they were hiding places for monastic treasures. The only entrance is usually some dozen feet above ground. When the fearsome Vikings appeared, these treasures would be taken up high and the last monk would pull up the ladder while his colleagues, already installed on high, would pour boiling oil or something of the sort on the howling savages below. This may well have happened more than once – there is little other explanation for the height of the entrance unless there were once penitential steps up to it or, less likely, that there had been prototypes in wood – but to build so many, often so far inland, seems strange.

The most probable explanation is that they were originally *campaniles*, or perhaps they were a combination of *campanile* later adjusted to be a warning tower, and a place of refuge. They remain something of a mystery, and perhaps the hybernophobe Englishman was right after all. It would be a remarkable act of prescience, a skill not unknown to the Irish.

Since the pre-Viking Irish did not build towns, they obviously did not build fortified ones. And when, with their Viking admixture of blood and talents, they set about this, the speed with which the Normans traversed the island would indicate that the fortifications can scarcely have been formidable. Indeed, even when in later centuries the Irish, by merger or reconquest, obtained Norman castles they do not seem to have been able to keep these in order: ruined castles are almost as much a part of the landscape as are ruined churches. It was using Irish labour and, if they existed, Irish military architects that the London companies failed until penalised to turn Derry into Londonderry.

Wooden, inflammable, medieval Dublin certainly did not prosper in the sixteenth century. It was not even the capital of a semi-state, and its Viking citadel was described in 1684 by a member of the Butler family as 'the worst castle in the worst situation in Christendom'. That Silken Thomas had failed to capture it, a century and a half before, speaks more of his tactics and of Norman military builders' skill than it does of Irish military ability. It happened to be a better strongpoint than Drogheda or Kilkenny, both of which had served as Ireland's capital and seat of parliament in the recent past. Yet when the Normans built beside their motte-and-baile fortress, which preceded their stone castle here as elsewhere, the Cathedral of Christ Church they had constructed what is now the Dublin building that has been in constant use longer than any other. When the Normans built Wood Quay on the wreckage of Viking ships, they made Dublin both a port and nationally pre-eminent city. At the time of writing the officials who now rule Ireland are abolishing Wood Quay in favour of yet more bureaucratic offices and thus reducing Dublin once again from its eminence as a cathedral-dominated capital city to a congeries of ugly, unproductive buildings. Dublin, as a great city, had a very short life,[1] almost all of which belongs in the later part of this book.

There were, of course, a few stone houses apart from the castle and the cathedral in this mess of narrow donkey-tracks and Gaelic wigwams. These, however, were seldom if ever inhabited by the rich and the powerful and were therefore built, particularly in the sixteenth century, to house merchants impoverished by every ingenuity of rent and tax. They were copies of the residences of their English equivalents, without any ideal of permanence nor of aesthetic virtue. They have therefore almost all disappeared. An exception, worth a visit, is the inn called The Brazen Head, in Bridge Street.

Its owners claim that it is of early Norman origin, and it is logical that some such place of lodging and nourishment should have existed south of the ford while the bridge was a-building. In fact it is now, more or less, a seventeenth century building, complete with courtyard and stabling, worthy of any small provincial town through which water flowed. If this was, as is said, Dublin's finest inn, all five senses recoil at what the others must have been like. On the other hand there is very little evidence that it has been cleaned since Norman times. Nor is there much else to show that medieval Dublin was very different from any contemporary provincial town, dirty, plague-ridden, unsewered and of course unlit.

The great guild halls that existed in pre-Cromwellian Dublin have left little trace behind, though the control of the skills and crafts, from apprenticeship upwards, was very tight indeed. The Tailors' Hall was, it seems, much the largest and parts of it are standing today. But did they need halls of grandeur? This was a Viking fort that had, more or less fortuitously, developed into an Irish town. It outgrew its walls quite fast. So did most of northern Europe's cities. But unlike many another, Dublin's centre never was and never will be its gloomy Viking fort. The city, of which that fort or castle forms so insignificant a part, was to become a great port, where the language of almost all the people was for several centuries Irish and the manners and morals of its inhabitants much the same until the English took it over. By then Oliver Cromwell had been dead for nearly half a century and even his head, on its spike in distant, foreign London, had rotted away.

* * *

Oliver had left his brother, Henry, in charge of the Irish administration and this man proved to be the less brutal of the two. When Scots and English restored the Stuarts to their thrones, in 1660, Charles II re-appointed the Duke of Ormonde to the vice-royalty he had held before the Civil War, the tenth member of the Butler family to hold that or a similar post. For the rest King Charles's policy in Ireland, as in England, was one of pacification and not revenge. Charles II wished to be King of all his people, not merely of the Cavaliers. This, however, meant that he must refrain from restoring all the rights and properties that the Cromwellians had seized during their brief period of military and administrative triumph. The grossest of these, much as 'Hell or Connaught' – Ireland had been on the whole royalist, but had seen no battles – could be easily rescinded and were. Church and monastic property, on the other hand, were not restored even when the confiscations had been by Cromwellian and not by ante-bellum order. Similarly little private property, either in Ireland or in England, was ever restored to its rightful owners. This undoubtedly caused much less ill-feeling among former Cavaliers in Ireland than it did in England, the concept of property being so different in the two countries. The religious question was more difficult. Until his deathbed Charles II was an Anglican and the head of a Church which at the very end of his life he renounced. In Ireland the hardships and cruelties inflicted by the Cromwellian Congregationalists and other forms of Protestants were not forgotten but, perhaps fortunately for the restored regime, they seldom conformed to the established Protestant Church, which was therefore re-instated. Although the Religious Wars had now reached Ireland, where perhaps 75% of the population were determined Roman Catholics with the leadership of a very much revitalised priesthood, usually trained abroad, the Established Church was acceptable, if ignored by the mass of the people. Furthermore, the Duke of Ormonde, who was of a mixed Roman and Anglican background, had seen, during his long exile, the happy effects of Louis XIV's tolerance of the Huguenots.

'In good King Charles's golden days' a very hard line was drawn between Roman Catholicism and the Protestant faith in Ireland, most especially in Ulster, but it was in general a peaceful line. And for a quarter of a century Ireland prospered as it had never done before. Tribal war virtually ceased, and unburned crops filled the granaries. It must have seemed to most Irishmen that in the Stuart dynasty they had at last found a line of kings that could and would care for them, with the exception of the most violently bigoted Non-conformists of the north, perhaps for all of them. The forests withdrew before the axe, the bogs beneath the spade, and physically Ireland began to resemble the country that we know today. In country houses that were no longer small fortresses, the harpists played and the poets recited. Trinity College, which Queen Elizabeth had ordered founded for her Protestant Irish subjects in 1577, was at last enabled to take its place in the scholarship of the world. Dublin was still a most inelegant city, but it was not now one without any learning. Galloglasses were becoming figures of the past, while trade began to produce a middle class, principally Protestant but not entirely so. Roads were built, by our standards very few, but lavish compared to what had gone before. Ireland, as a real country, was beginning to exist.

There is a much told story about King Charles II. When warned
of an assassination plot he is said to have remarked that no one could
possibly wish for his death in order that his brother, James, might
become king. Yet, Roman Catholic or not, his tolerance was not
limitless. He did, after all, sign the death warrant of St. Oliver
Plunkett, whom he well knew to be the Primate of All Ireland. The
fact that St. Oliver had many, bitter enemies within the Church
itself, hardly excused the killing of a man whom the King must have
known to be innocent. His loyalties, in fact, were limited. As the
Wars of Religion reached their conclusion of exhaustion, he spoke
for most of Europe when he spoke for tolerance. Whether Elizabethan
and Wentworth's and Cromwellian cruelty had made tolerance a
possible policy in Ireland is, of course, problematical. There is some
evidence, from the age of Charles II, that it had, that the Irish are
not born to be religious fanatics. Certainly they have proved as much
on the rare occasions when the foreigners and their compatriots have
permitted them to treat one another with civilised decency.

James II was in every sense a disastrous monarch. Among other
defects, he was an anachronism. What Bloody Mary had failed to do,
he attempted a century later. The great men of England first
shrugged their shoulders: then they decided that he must go. He
went, and they summoned his elder daughter's husband, William
of Orange, ruler of the Netherlands, to take his place.

King William III, as he then became, was a Protestant soldier
whose life-work was the frustration of King Louis XIV from conquering the Netherlands in the Roman Catholic interest. (King
Louis found no incompatability in his alliance with the Grand Turk,
who was even then besieging Vienna: in effect the Wars of Religion
were over, while the dynastic wars had begun.) James II had of
course taken refuge with the French King and with his help was
proposing to reconquer England via his other, Roman Catholic,
kingdom of Ireland. King William, on the other hand, intended to
defeat his prime enemy, using English resources, and therefore set
about the expulsion of James from Ireland. The famous Battle of the
Boyne was therefore in essence not an Irish civil war at all, but a
battle between Louis XIV's mercenaries, most of whom were both
Irish and Roman Catholics, and the Dutch troops of General
Schomberg, whose allegiance was to William of Orange, most of
whom were Protestants. Schomberg had landed, in the north where
he might expect the least opposition, in the autumn of 1689. He
spent that winter in reconnaissance and training. He also recruited a

few thousand Protestants, ex-Cromwellians' sons or grandsons. Unlike the Ironsides or even Schomberg's men, they were not experienced soldiers. The Battle of the Boyne was won by Dutchmen: it was lost by Irishmen, because King Louis's troops and above all their artillery were, as usual, too slow in their arrival. James placed little if any trust in his Irishmen. Their bravery might well be beyond dispute: their tactics were deplorable. But to this day those Orange-men (as they came to call themselves) when speaking of Boyne Water should recall that a fair mixture of Dutch gin is needed to make a really palatable drink.

The Boyne was not the decisive battle, save in so far that King James deserted his own Irish army. Riding on the fastest horses back to Dublin, he is said to have remarked, 'The Irish are running', to which some Irish lady is said to have replied: 'But Your Majesty won the race.' He returned to France, there to become for the rest of his life King Louis's pensionary. He does not appear to have given any further thought to the Irishmen whom he had left behind him.

When King William won the Battle of the Boyne, he won Ulster, a fact which Ulstermen are most reluctant to forget. It was not, however, the decisive battle of the war, for this took place at Aughrim in the summer of 1691, just one year later. King William had returned to England, leaving a Dutch general, Ginkl, in full authority. Although Louis XIV had withdrawn the few troops he had sent in the previous year, he had despatched arms and armament and a first-class general named St. Ruth. St. Ruth trained some 14,000 Irish troops and commanded them at Aughrim, which is in the western midlands of Ireland and thus a place of the greatest strategic significance. It seems that St. Ruth's death in battle caused the Irish to disintegrate, some falling back on Galway, others on Limerick. In the words of the old Irish lament it was from the Irish point of view 'a great disaster'. Yet from every other point of view what then happened is of far greater importance. The Scots and English Protestants, even though numerically only in the ratio of about 3:2, would eventually have conquered the Roman Catholic Irish, presumably after an even bloodier war. They might then have driven the Irish not merely to Connaught but out of Ireland altogether, as Louis XIV had done with his Huguenots in 1685.[2]

As it was, the new Irish leader, Patrick Sarsfield, an incarnate mixture of Norman and Celt, withdrew westwards and prepared to surrender. He was not a surrendering sort of soldier, but Ginkl's terms were moderately attractive, certainly more so than those

Louis XIV had inflicted on his Protestants. There was to be religious and legal tolerance, no property confiscation or other repetition of Cromwellian harshness, and those Irish soldiers who wished to emigrate were to be helped so to do: others (and we must here recall the mercenary nature of galloglasses) he would accept into his own army. The treaty was signed on the famous Treaty Stone outside Limerick in late 1691, endorsed by the parliament of Ireland and counter-signed by King William in his capacity as King of Ireland. One clause was from the English point of view far and away the most important. What was left of the Irish army consisted of some 15,000 men who still accepted orders. Of these some 11,000 sailed to France with Sarsfield, and 1,000 enlisted with Ginkl, while the remainder either went to their homes – if these still existed – or became the first of those rapparees and tories and highwaymen who recur so monotonously on Irish roads throughout the century to come. There was now no Irish army of any sort in Ireland. Three points, which are not fantasy, must here be borne in mind.

The English statesmen, with their representative assembly called the House of Commons, had appointed William of Orange their King. They neither liked him nor saw any reason why they, the masters of England's wealth, should honour a document to which he had put his signature. On the other hand they, and the persons of property whom they represented, had developed a strong dislike of the Irish. This was not that Ireland was any sort of a threat to England: it was quite the reverse, and English apprentices and ploughboys strongly resented being conscripted to fight in that barbarous, incomprehensible land of bog and forest. Fynes Morrison, Mountjoy's secretary and intelligence officer a century before, waxes more than irritable at the habit of the Irish of misleading his English soldiers both as to directions and to distances.

With the last Irish army gone – paradoxically a real French army arrived at Limerick a few days later, but Sarsfield, that honourable man, did not break the treaty and sent the French away – Ireland was at the mercy of the London merchants, many of them ex-Cromwellians and contemptuous of any royal signature. The London Parliament repudiated the treaty that the Dublin parliament, Ginkl and King William had signed, and, in accordance with which, Sarsfield and his soldiers had left Irish soil. Not only did these parliamentarians repudiate the treaty: they immediately began contradicting it with their Penal Laws against Roman Catholics. Since property was wealth, in Ireland, by the time they had done –

that is to say by the end of the century – 75% of Ireland belong to 5% of the population. The English legislators were far more thorough than either Strafford or even Cromwell had been.

They were also far nastier. In another book[3] I have speculated concerning the resemblance between the Irish Penal Laws and the Nazi anti-semitic Nuremberg Laws, and showed the probability that the German legislators knew and not infrequently copied their English predecessors in the classification and humiliation of second class citizens. I shall not repeat these arguments here, save in one or two respects. For the Nazis, a Jew was always a Jew. For the English, a Roman Catholic who changed his religion reaped an immediate benefit in that he became heir to all his father's property, thus disinheriting his siblings, surely an especially vile appeal to cupidity. The head of a Roman priest brought in the same reward as that of a wolf, £5, but this seems to have seldom been claimed, for the Irish were rallied behind their priests. The emigration of Sarsfield's armies, and particularly of its officers, following upon the Flight of the Earls and the first great emigration of Wild Geese in 1649, had left the Irish with little temporal leadership, so that inevitably the people looked for advice to their priests, often the only educated men they knew. The Church responded to this need by establishing Irish seminaries in Douai, Salamanca, Rome and elsewhere. These vicious laws – their application lapsed during the middle of the century – had among other motives the total elimination of any Irish aristocracy or property-owning class. No Roman Catholic might attend a British university, which applied to Protestant Non-conformists though these could take a degree in Scotland. Many Irish Catholics therefore attended continental universities and since medicine was one of the very few professions they might practise, in Ireland, many took medical degrees. No Non-conformist (which of course included Roman Catholics) might vote for, let alone sit in, either the Irish or the English House of Commons nor might Roman Catholic peers vote in the Lords. In some important families it became the habit for one member to attend one Protestant service, thus preserving the property and rights of his whole family in his own person. Such are the mendacities to which penal laws may force honourable men to stoop. Not all would do so. Thus Lord Gormanston was the premier viscount of Ireland, but he refused even token renunciation of his faith. Lord Dillon therefore became the premier viscount, even though his family had sailed with Sarsfield and he and his descendants were in command of a regiment in the French army throughout a century during which France was almost constantly at war with England: they were Roman Catholics, but had preserved their property and rights by the device described above.

One of the meanest of the Penal Laws forbade ownership of a horse worth more than £5 to a Roman Catholic. Any Protestant had the right to a compulsory purchase of such a horse, and many exercised that legal right.

It must, however, be said that after the first fury, and the many ways in which the Penal Laws were being flouted in increasingly obvious fashions, they tended to be more and more ignored. By the time they were abolished, in 1793 (save the laws of franchise), they were in effect defunct, for power had passed into Irish hands, not so much the old Irish, Norman or Vikings but the Cromwellian, Williamite and post-Williamite settlers whose home had for several generations frequently now been Ireland. These were usually designated Anglo-Irishmen in the mid-nineteenth century and I fear I must use this ridiculous phrase here, though these men made a very real contribution to Ireland's (or part of Ireland's) liberty from English rule. No one, so far as I know, has ever referred to George Washington or Abraham Lincoln as an Anglo-American.

＊ ＊ ＊

During the Second World War it was expected that after the destruction of twelve years of Nazi censorship a great deal of hidden literature and perhaps of painting would emerge. In fact the total was little better than nil. Tyranny and war do not produce a climate in which the arts can flourish. Thus Elizabethan, Cromwellian and Williamite wars, by destroying the patrons destroyed the society in which the Irish arts were rooted. These had seemingly included little that was visual or architectural, and most of this vanished while little new and noteworthy was produced. Music and poetry are more durable, and of Irish music I shall have more to say later. What happened in the field of poetry is a little easier to describe.

Irish poetry is almost utterly different from that of the English, save that in both cases the poets have expressed what the prose writers, as any student of prose-and-verse can show, cannot achieve. Since the Romantic period this has been frequently described as 'emotional' expression, its opposite presumably being logical. But Irish poetry was never an alternative to logic, and the emotional content of ancestor-worship and enemy-hatred produces emotions rare in great English verse. Furthermore the grammar and the syntax of the two languages are utterly different, so that the basis of the poems has been virtually untranslatable, save into prose via its own prose. An Irish poet, perhaps like any major poet, expressed his ideas in a way that was unique. It was also, and in larger measure than pre-Renaissance English poetry, tighter in form and more ruled by precedential poems, for Irish poetry was an essential part of each little Irish community or kingdom. Finally, what made these poems the alternative to prose was, by the very nature of the language, quite different from the same process in England. The difference was far stronger than that which the French feel when reading Shakespeare or the English Racine. Of these, both had roots of a sort in Rome and Greece.

The effect of the sixteenth and seventeenth century chaos upon the Irish poets was, at first glance, surprising. The Irish poets looked back from the disgusting present to a past that was immortalised in its poetry, and the result was a form of Celtic classicism which had nothing to do with the Graeco-Roman variety. Simultaneously this influx of Saxons brought them into contact with the non-Irish world of other emotions. It is said that in its death throes Irish poetry was at its greatest.

Perhaps the *Lament for Art O'Leary* (see pp. 229-37), written by his widow, can best express both these emotions and the near-impossibility of rendering them into English even by so fine a poet as Frank O'Connor.

Among the more inexplicable reactions of the eighteenth-century Irish is their attitude towards the Stuarts and towards the French. The Stuarts had treated their Irish subjects little better than had the Tudors, and had brought upon them far worse disasters. James I had planted Ulster and well laid the road that Oliver Cromwell was to follow. Charles II had given the Irish almost no retribution, though thereby perhaps a period of peace. James II had called on Irish Roman Catholic loyalty, had received it, and had ridden away to personal safety over the corpses of his followers. It is hardly surprising that the crushed Irish showed no enthusiasm for the 1715 fiasco invasion of Scotland by his son, and little less for that of his grandson in 1745.

Yet there was always the muttered hope that the Stuarts, with French support, would destroy the English tyranny. Many thousands of Irishmen fought for the French (and for the Spaniards, Austrians, even Russians) and it is said that at Fontenoy, in 1745, the Irish won the battle for the French, their only real victory between Louis XIV and Napoleon. It is said, that is, in books of history not written by French historians.

As for a French invasion, with the eclipse of Spain as a major power, the Irish ascribed a positively mystical importance to such an event. 'The French are on the sea,' and sometimes they were and more often they were not. But is the song of the San Van Voght a mystical, mythical memory? Had not the Danaans come, long, long ago? Might they not come again, with names like Hoche and Humbert and even Wolfe Tone? They would surely bring priests, as well as their terrible guillotine, and cut off the Protestant heads and the Mass need no longer be celebrated under hedgerows.

Stuarts and the French haunt the imagination of the Irish peasanty. Others had very different projects.

NOTES

1 Craig, M. *Dublin 1660–1680*. This fine portrait of a city is well worth reading, whether or not the reader be interested in Irish matters as such.

2 Those for whom imaginary history is distasteful rubbish had best skip this note. James II wins the Battle of the Boyne and installs a Catholic tyranny in all Ireland, with French support. Five or so years later King William invades and after a lengthy, bloody war expels French and Irish alike. These are deported *en masse* to America, and Ireland becomes as English as Cornwall. A predominantly Roman Catholic America, with French backing from Quebec to Louisiana, overthrows the pitiful English rule without a war. An Irish- and French-speaking U.S.A. refuses to accept the atheistical revolution in 'the motherland' and after yet another civil war declares its independence as a fief of Rome according to the Donation of Constantine. Ireland is by now, as neutrals tend to be, an extremely rich and powerful English-speaking power. Now, fantasise . . . And forgive this fantasist . . .

3 *Miss Finnegan's Fault*.

4 For both the quotation and the drawing the author is indebted to Harold Orel's *Irish History and Culture*.

16
ASCENDANCY

It is now nearly two centuries of haze and propaganda that separate the eighteenth century from ourselves. That the haze be any thinner than the difficulty in understanding what happened in the seventeenth century is in part due to the immense garrulity of the eighteenth – an enormous amount of which was committed there and then to paper – but perhaps even more so to our interest in 'ordinary life' as it once was lived. For this we have, very largely, Marx and Engels to thank. A skilled story-teller, such as Sean O'Faolain, can exhume enough facts about the Great O'Neill to make him a living character (in his *The Great O'Neill*): of his ostler, we and I must assume O'Faolain knew almost nothing. This, I think, is what Ranke meant – 'as it actually happened' – but what he found concerns almost solely famous men and great events. The rest, that is to say the rest of humanity, disappears into a mist of nonentity, pierced only by an occasional flash of fortuitous lightning. We are left with an atmosphere of emotion, part of the time in question but equally part of a later age. Nowhere is this more true than of eighteenth century Ireland, where a high percentage of the people were illiterate and where an absurdly large percentage of the documents either originate from, or were intended for, London, where people administered a foreign land that spoke a foreign tongue. In effect, we do not know eighteenth century Ireland, though perhaps we know a certain amount about it and its inhabitants.

A minor impediment to the understanding of dead centuries is precisely our unshared simplicity of numbers. We speak and write about the '30s, the '50s and so on – I have done so here myself – almost as if a new epoch began whenever a zero replaced a nine in our Christian calendar, and all the more so when a double zero replaced a double nine (though some tedious haggling goes on in the correspondence of *The Times* as to whether this century did not start on 1 January 1901). Other European nations speak in what are both more vague and more accurate terms, with reference to real events. Thus the English twenties and thirties become a period *entre deux guerres*, the mid-nineteenth century becomes the period of the *Risorgimento*, and the years between the dismissal of Bismarck and 1914, or maybe 1916, are *die Zaiserzeit*. Nowhere are our puerile mathematics more misleading than in any attempt to unify the century between the Battle of Aughrim and the Act of Union, yet this period filled precisely one century, the eighteenth. Therefore, since such is our usage, let us imagine that it has some sort of reality, but with the strongest possible reservations.

Ireland was completely conquered, Irishmen not to the same extent. After the Williamite wars the English, very simply, enforced the Penal Laws, made normal English law paramount, and divided most of the land among their more powerful supporters. There was to be no Roman Catholic religion and its adherents, together with the Non-conformists, were penalised in a multitude of ways. The Irish language, that is to say a nation's soul, was to be obliterated.

Whether or not a nation can have 'a soul' is a matter for the theologians: what even the smallest and weakest can possess is a self-conscious dignity and self-respect, and these can be destroyed, in particular if they be incarnate in its leaders. When the century started a disproportionate number of the nation's leaders had fled overseas – with the intention, it is true, of returning, while never entirely losing touch with the people whom they had left behind. The conquerors very rapidly occupied the vacant places of power and wealth, though seldom those of honour and respect and loyalty.

So it was now. Men who had done little to deserve it were elevated to great landowners: Ireland was carved into shires and baronies, and the old 'plantation' system was attempted yet again, but usually with the same results, for the Irish were seldom physically expelled, since the intrinsic value of their labour had been recognised, but their position as tenants and subtenants was an almost insoluble muddle. 'The land' had never belonged to an individual, but grazing and farming rights had increasingly become the subject of legal tenure of immense and varied complexity. Now all this was supposed to be changed, but was not, since before it can become effective the law must be accepted, and two legal systems in two languages still overlapped. Nor was that the end of it. Over it all there loomed the far from inactive power of distant London. When the Irish built up a decent woollen export industry, enough to frighten the English wool merchants, the exportation of wool from Ireland was forbidden. Flax was grown in its place, but not in the same places where the sheep had once grazed. There was, in fact, no basic

agricultural stability and thus little incentive to improve farms
(though this was done more than the nineteenth century historians
were prepared to acknowledge) and there was a growing number of
Irish labourers who in turn often became beggars, highwaymen,
rapparees and tories (these last were real: it was their enemies who
applied the term to English politicians of what we would call 'the
right').

There is perhaps a more important confusion concerning our idea
of the Irish eighteenth century that should be mentioned and, if
possible, explained. The terrible Wars of Religion were over, save
perhaps in Ireland where a Protestant dominant class ruled over the
Roman Catholic masses. But even in Ireland it was becoming
evident that hostility, let alone massacre, was both wicked and out of
date. Within a generation these emotions that had inspired, and
been inspired by, those laws were falling into desuetude. The
Williamite soldiers had knocked down far more churches than ever
had the Cromwellians but by 1750 at the latest it was not difficult for
a Roman Catholic to participate in the Mass in most of Ireland.
However the priests who came to Ireland from their seminaries in
Louvain and elsewhere were very serious men who had risked much
and were prepared to risk more. This was equally true of the friars
who trod the dusty or muddy paths of Ireland where few priests
went. This must not be confused with Jansenism though it too was a
grandchild of the Council of Trent and of the whole ill-named
Counter-reformation movement. Since it was the priests, or more
frequently the lay teachers, who taught the children in their hedge
schools, it was to be another generation that profited from their
instruction. Similarly, and indeed almost simultaneously, the Non-
conformists received a great religious revival in the form of John
Wesley's Methodism. If the Roman Catholics had become lost sheep
without pastures, the Calvinist Congregationalists had reached a
form of spiritual brick wall: if salvation is by Grace alone, then why
all the fuss about human behaviour? Wesley's oratory explained to
his huge numbers of followers what salvation meant and how it could
be achieved. Meanwhile the Anglican Church, the Church of
Ireland, slept in comfort and spent its tithes. As John Betjeman once
wrote:

> Within that parsonage
> There is a personage
> Who owns a mortgage
> On his lordship's land.

Against this background of nascent puritanism, which did not really flower until the following century, when it affected Scotland and Wales even more more strongly than it did Ireland, we see the Irish eighteenth century through what might be called a nineteenth century filter. Even now, close on a hundred years after its decay, the imprint of Victorian morality, particularly sexual morality, remains so great that we tend to regard it as a normal code for the western, Christian world, even today when we are busily dismantling so much of its apparatus. From the High Victorian point of view, the avowed morals of contemporary England would indeed seem debased, those of the previous century, in particular France, even more so. Their very religion made them aware of sin, and it is not coincidental that the favourite form of entertainment of the new middle class was, now, the novel. This, in turn, was usually centred about adultery or fornication, activities to which the newly rich mill-owners and steel magnates can only have devoted a very small portion of their time and energy.

Nor is there any obvious connection between the industrial revolution with its new cities and the almost obsessive middle class sexual morality that accompanied it. In any case these affected Ireland less than the rest of Europe, and it may therefore be assumed that Victorian middle class morality was, like so much else, an import. The indigenous Irish were preoccupied with other matters, yet they left their stamp upon our view of their forebears.

It is a distorted view, and inevitably so. The poor, the simple, the weak leave little mark in their passage through life. Save when there is some major personal catastrophe or even a national disaster, the workingman does his work, returns to his home each evening, has a springtime of gaiety and love, and eventually is succeeded by his sons and daughters. Here lies no story for the Victorian novelist, and therefore no novel: only a few entries, perhaps, in the parish register at best, in those of the criminal court at worst.

> For forms of government let fools contest:
> What e'er is best administered is best.

Alexander Pope's well-known axiom may well be true within the tribal or national unit. At some future period it may have a universal validity. Unfortunately, when first formulated at the beginning of the eighteenth century it was contemporary with the early European colonies. The 'administration' of foreigners takes on a very different hue from that of one's own people, especially when such administration is largely in private hands. In an agricultural country this can become, quite simply, the exploitation by the landlord of the people who work 'his' land. Should that landlord prefer to live abroad, he exports at least some of his profits. Many of the new landlords in Ireland already owned property in England, and the 'absentee landlord' became an important and undesirable figure. Just as medieval monarchs had attempted to use Irish revenues to buttress their English monarchies, so the new English landlords used such profits as they could extract from their new Irish estates for their expenses in England. There was an almost constant flow of money eastwards and a recurring shortage of currency in Ireland. The number of 'absentee landlords' was never as large as some Irish nationalists have painted it, nor did all of these people neglect their Irish estates. But they, and particularly their agents and sub-agents, were very frequently harsh and grasping men. Their reputation is not savoury, and their behaviour in these early days of *laissez-faire* was backed by the state. On the other hand it was certainly not unique. The same business interests which advised George I, George II and, after 1760, George III concerning Ireland were also advising them about the thirteen American colonies, and in both cases their interest was identical: to extract the maximum wealth in return for the minimum cost in defence against Red Indians, Frenchmen and other foreigners. In Ireland this keeping of the king's peace by the militia put an end to those inter-tribal wars, which had been such a curse in previous centuries. Only in Ulster did these linger on, in particular in those areas where Protestant Scots–Irish and Roman Catholic Irish were in competition, primarily for land.

The nineteenth century's popular version of the previous century's story was in part, then, based on the middle class morality of the new rich, the products of the industrial revolution. There was, however, far less of this in Ireland than in England herself. The ports, however, had begun to grow, in large measure because of the greater proximity of Cork, Limerick, Galway and Londonderry to America. Throughout the eighteenth century the American trade prospered, at least until 1776, and though Irish exports as such were never very great the provisioning of ships for the long transatlantic journey was profitable. Cotton came in from the southern American colonies, and although the English attempted to monopolise the making of cotton goods by law they were not entirely successful. No more did they succeed in the prevention of smuggling, both ways, between

Munster and the continent of Europe. Indeed it is said that the Kerrymen ceased bothering to make poteen, since smuggled brandy was so plentiful and cheap. Furthermore the very children of the Englishmen who had been given larger or smaller estates in Ireland began to think of themselves as Irishmen often reluctant to enforce laws passed solely to benefit the English financially. The so-called Ascendancy might and usually did remain Protestant, but by the middle of the eighteenth century it was ceasing to be English. And there was also a small Irish middle class coming into existence, based not only on land but also on an astonishing creation, or perhaps even a revival, of high craftsmanship in the use of glass, silver and wood. Much of this was exported, legally or otherwise, and Cork silver or Waterford glass paid for many a Kerryman's cask of brandy. This creation of Irish industry was helped and encouraged by the Huguenot exiles who were encouraged to come from France to Ireland. Many of these had been bankers and some returned to that profession thus removing what had been a virtual monopoly from London and giving the Irish one of the essential bases on which to construct their economy.

Throughout almost all Europe the nineteenth century was the age of nationalism, and Irish patriots – in particular perhaps the 'Young Ireland' publicists of the 1840s, whose beliefs and propaganda were to become a sort of doctrine as the century progressed – saw in every anti-British act of the previous century a gesture for Irish freedom. This was certainly not so, either on the smallest or the largest scale. Swift might speak of an 'Irish nation' as early as 1720, he was surely speaking as a clergyman, not as a patriot, for though he despised the way the Irish poor were treated he showed elsewhere a marked contempt and even dislike for 'the Irish'. Until the French Revolution, and the prospect of a similar, atheistical terror in all Ireland, there were no Irish patriots of the type envisaged or invented by Young Ireland. The Irishman may have disliked a tyrannical landlord and ruler, to the extent of shooting his agent and cruelly wounding his cattle, but so have most peasantries, at most times, save perhaps times of war, in most countries. That is not patriotism.

Without wishing to diminish in any way the Irish patriotism of the original Wild Geese (did not Sarsfield himself, dying for France at the Battle of Landen in 1693, say: 'Oh, that this was for Ireland!') their contribution to Irish history remained slight during their existence which ended with the French Revolution. Very few of the old Celtic or Norman leaders remained in the conquered country, and it is rare that liberators with a foreign base can free their country of origin. Since in those distant days leadership was usually the prerogative of the governing class, it was from the new men of power that the first stirrings came, though it was the old which was to produce Daniel O'Connell, in himself a link between the Roman Catholic aristocracy and the Wild Geese. But his time lay in the next century.

Henry Grattan (1746–1820) was very much a man of the Protestant Ascendancy, but not of that rip-roaring, drunken, fighting, heiress-abducting and practical-joking Ascendancy portrayed in their memoirs by Sir Jonah Barrington and others. This type of stage Irishman certainly existed, particularly in the backwoods, but he had scarcely the time to spare from his cards and his claret to run his estates, let alone to create a country out of a colony. The men who created 'Grattan's parliament' were in large measure drawn from the legal professions and were usually second or third generation Irish Protestants.

The opposition (that is to say the opposition to the London-imposed government and its supporters) had been led by Henry Flood (1732–1791), a most powerful orator and, it seems, most honourable man, the son of a judge and himself a lawyer. In October 1775 he accepted a sinecure, Vice-treasurer of Ireland, from the government, a non-job worth £3,500 a year. This was quite correctly interpreted as a bribe and a large one. He was therefore no longer acceptable to the opposition, though he proved a sad disappointment to the government since he continued to vote against them in the House and there is no evidence that he 'earned' his bribe outside it in any way. But it is typical of the way Ireland was being run that no one seems to have doubted why he was given this sinecure. In fact it was removed from him after six years, but by then his political career was virtually over, for Grattan had succeeded him as leader of the opposition which was rapidly becoming a very powerful movement.

The Irish are not by nature revolutionary. Few agricultural people are, since the farmer would reap where he has sewn and will be inclined to accept his status as he must accept the natural elements. Conquest by foreigners is another matter altogether. In fact the two not infrequently go hand in hand, but certainly not always. Nor have the Irish as yet produced any revolutionary theorist of note, preferring to accept the theories at second hand or not at all. They are a people much given to violence but save when directed against the British or their servants this violence is both easily aroused and quickly appeased. They are a charitable people, capable of intense cruelty, yet they seldom bear grudges for long and they do not usually generalise. The enemy of yesterday can easily be the welcome guest of today, and they see little connection between British soldiers, to be murdered, and British tourists, to be entertained. This is in itself a wild generalisation, but one which is true and which those who dislike the Irish condemn as 'two-faced' or worse. It certainly makes the Irish an exceedingly difficult people for foreigners, that is to say Englishmen, to govern or understand. It also explains the absence of indigenous revolution. Neither 1641 nor the rallying to King James was revolutionary. The first, partial revolution bears Grattan's name and was based on imported American ideas.

If we compare the American and the first Irish (Grattan's) revolution, we find very close parallels and we also find that the American colonists anticipated the Irish colonists by about a decade or more. Indeed, without the American precedent, it is almost certain that Irish history could not have taken the course it did. Utterly different as the two countries have become, if we cast our minds back a couple of centuries the resemblances are striking.

With a few exceptions, both were ruled by the descendants of colonists, who had won them in bitter wars with the native inhabitants. Both had built on the English model of representative parliamentary government by and for those colonists and their descendants to the exclusion of other groups of people (in Ireland of the Roman Catholics, in America of the aboriginal inhabitants and of imported Africans). In *The Federalist Papers* America is described as an essentially agricultural and maritime country, industry and manufacture being left primarily in British hands. This was willy-nilly true of Ireland, though here there was relatively more manufacture and owing to intense competition rather less maritime activity. Both countries had prospered greatly in the first half of the eighteenth century, due to the hard work of the colonists. Both saw themselves milked by taxes imposed from London, where neither had any say in government, nor representation in Parliament. Both were ultimately dependent for protection (the Irish from their native majority: the Americans from the French and to a lesser degree from the Amerindians) upon the might of Britain, in the one case its army and in the other its navy, but in normal times both were capable of self-protection. Briefly, neither wished for a breach with Britain, but for a far greater or even a total control over its own mercantile and financial affairs.

In 1768 there were the first Boston riots, and two years later in that same city the Redcoats fired on the mob, that is to say on their own people. As Voltaire sagely remarked, the world would never be the same again.

By 1782 the British regiments normally stationed in Ireland had been withdrawn for combat in America, while the Royal Navy was not doing well in a war with France. To replace the British garrison, Grattan mobilised what has been called the rooted garrison, that is to say the Protestant landowning class. Virtually the entire male Protestant population of the appropriate ages became the only armed force in all Ireland, and, apparently to the surprise of the British, Grattan demanded a free Irish parliament. The British were in no position to risk another war, on their own doorstep, and in 1782 at the Dungannon Convention he made his demands, which were granted. For a moment, perhaps the last, all Ireland appeared to be free.

It was a brief moment: Grattan's parliament had a briefer life than Latvia between 1918 and 1940. It had many faults. For the greater part of the Irish population had no vote, and Grattan could not get his parliament to grant them emancipation. Two thirds of the seats were owned by patrons. Corruption was commonplace. And finally King George remained King of Ireland and England. Since no bill could become law without his signature, his ministers in London continued, diminuendo perhaps, to control Irish affairs. Above all – and this is important in Irish eyes – Grattan's parliament lacked all dignity, personal abuse being a regular substitute for reasoned debate. And in 1783 a peace treaty was signed between Britain and America. Only commercially did the Irish Protestant gentry profit, industrially and agriculturally, from Grattan's parliament: many of their beautiful Georgian houses and much of Dublin's finest architecture date from its time. A legend and an illusion have remained. Even the concept of a free Ireland is better than what went before or what was to come after.

※ ※ ※

Meanwhile the mass of the population, perhaps some two millions in 1700 and perhaps four a century later, had little save spasmodic interest in the politics of their country (but remember to beware population statistics for Ireland. This increase seems almost unbelievable, and for the next half-century even more so). Since the new idea of an Irish nation was of such recent vintage, this is hardly surprising. Their landlords remained the same, and the changing face of the countryside was too gradual to be noticeable. The system of land tenure remained grossly loaded in the favour of the landlords, and the poor had virtually no redress against exploitation. Only in Ulster did the Scots–Irish create 'the Ulster custom' whereby leases were longer and more favourable to the farmer.

Statistics are often misleading, usually boring, but in the matter of the Irish population of great importance matched only by their unreliability. Learned men have guessed that there were perhaps two million Irishmen, in Ireland, after the Williamite wars and that of these perhaps 15–20% were Protestants, mostly in Ulster but scattered throughout the whole country, usually in dominant positions, so that they owned perhaps as much as 95% of the land, though a high proportion of this was stony or otherwise agriculturally almost valueless. But it was on such land that a great many of the Irish lived, particularly in the northwest where the potato provided an easy if monotonous sustenance with minimum labour, perhaps as little as a few days in the year to feed a family. This has been named the 'conacre' system, very brief leases providing a subsistence of food if the potato flourished, the rest of the crop of grain or cattle being the landlord's property. But the potato, even the hideously named 'lumper' which was the cheapest and quickest, is susceptible to several sorts of blight. Therefore in regions of Ireland, throughout the eighteenth and early nineteenth centuries, there were many of these small farmers who could not properly feed their families, while growing food for their landlords to eat, sell or export.

Most of the conacre farmers lived at this bare subsistence level, their food being their potato crop, their lease being for eleven months only since a year would have given them some security of tenure. To improve the property would, for the more hard-hearted owners, merely serve to increase the rent. The 'Ulster custom' permitted longer rents or the renewal of short ones at the same price.

The conacre farmer lived, at the best of times, just above the starvation level and with no incentive to improve his little farm. This was not the case with all landlords, but with enough to provide the basis of the land war. Semi-secret societies, the White Boys, Ribbonmen and so on, sabotaged their landlords' property, burning ricks and maiming cattle, not for their own prosperity but for motives of simple revenge.

The homes in which these poor and often hungry families lived were frequently built of turf, mud cottages with perhaps a chimney but with no windows or a floor, other than trodden earth, perhaps covered with rushes if they grew in the neighbourhood. If the family owned a pig, hens or other livestock, these usually lived with them, the 'Paddy and his pig' of English humour. For some reason unknown to this writer these dwellings were referred to as 'cabins', and in some cabins the women of the house would grow one fingernail to unusual length for the purpose of peeling the potatoes, for there was usually no cutlery nor even furniture, save perhaps for a chest. Occasionally the cabin might have two rooms, or be divided in two by a hanging blanket, but privacy was really nil, as was any form of sanitation, water being fetched from a well, spring or stream. In virtually all such dwellings the language spoken was Irish, though sometimes a little English was understood or misunderstood.

A stranger to the west of Ireland has described one such home as he found it early in the following century, that is to say before the Great Famine. It is unlikely to have changed greatly in the previous hundred years.[1]

> In the evening I found myself still far away from Clifden in a heavy rain, so I asked at a little cabin by the roadside for hospitality, and was welcomed cordially. There was only a kitchen and one room. In the kitchen were a cow, a calf, a dog, three or four hens and a cock fluttering noisily about, and in a corner a coop full of chickens. Here I slept on the ground near the ashes of the glowing peat fire; and in the other room slept the family – the father and mother, two girls and a boy. The silence of the night was broken from time to time by the thud and splash of dung on the mud floor, and the crowing and clatter of the fowls woke me early. There was one chair, one bench, and several boxes to sit on, but no table; and some rude harness hanging from pegs on the wall was the only ornament. "Michael, rise up!" shouted a man's voice, about seven o'clock, and a boot, as it seemed, struck violently against the wooden partition. Michael lounged in, and rekindled the peat fire from the dying embers. In a few minutes in came his mother, and milked the cow in front of the fire into a series of dirty-looking little tin pots, that reminded me of old tomato cans. She then fed the calf on some milk and raw potatoes, and in a little time gave me a cup of excellent tea and a piece of potato bread.

Half, or rather more than half in the west, lived in this type of dwelling during the Ascendancy period.

The Irish are a talkative, even a garrulous people, yet they can be also remarkably secretive. Secret agrarian societies sprang up across the whole country, usually unconnected the one with the other and directed against a particularly unpopular landlord or even in some areas against landlordism as such. They were aimed against the landlord's cattle, his fences, sometimes against his house, and served to restrain malpractices by members of the property-owning élite, a duty which we regard as the duty of the law. But in eighteenth century Ireland the entire legal apparatus was part of the Protestant Ascendancy's property. Neither the methods nor the motives of the agrarian gangs were attractive, but their own laws had been abolished and replaced by nothing. It was as inevitable that maladministration by foreigners should produce this unattractive type of agrarian crime as that 'Reconstruction' would bring into being the Ku Klux Klan. England could not 'police' Ireland two hundred years ago, even if the idea of a policeman's role had then existed. It was up to the 'rooted garrison' of Protestant landowners to look after their own, using if need be the militia they officered, in England's interests of course since it was thanks to a series of English governments that there was anything in Ireland for them to look after. They did their best, in general with success. Taken all in all, one may speculate that save for its very beginning and its very end the eighteenth century was the least unhappy that Ireland had known for a thousand years.

Yet these poor 'conacre' farmers did not belong to the lowest economic level of society. Their cousins, who could not find even a conacre farm, walked the roads and often begged. They added massively to the vast number of beggars that already infested the roads of Ireland and, even more, the streets of the cities. These itinerants, as they are nowadays politely called, had their nucleus in the tinkers, which is nowadays an insulting word. But the tinkers themselves had once upon a time been rated very highly in Irish society. It is said that St. Finn Barr's father was a tin smith, perhaps the oldest itinerant trade plied by man and, by its nature, he carried his skills to his clients rather than the much later blacksmith to whom the horses were brought. The tin smiths became the tinkers, and business deteriorated so that they became, on occasion, beggars or even thieves. (They must not be confused with the gypsies, whose life-style resembled their own and who also exist in small numbers in Ireland, but who often still speak Romany and are seldom Christian.) To the tinkers were added those 'broken men' of the Elizabethan and other wars, men and women with no pretension to mend a tin pot or kettle. And to these again must be added the farm labourers unable to find work. They walked the roads, in the hope of finding even conacre work, and as that hope lessened they became part of that huge army of beggars upon which every foreign visitor to Ireland in the eighteenth and nineteenth centuries commented.

They were at their most in and around the cities, particularly Dublin. Throughout the eighteenth century there was an enormous increase of the Irish population. All our statistics are doubtful, but it would seem that the population doubled during the century and doubled again before the Famine of 1848. This would mean a subdivision of all, even conacre, land holdings and an even vaster increase in those without work at all. A more classic incidence of economic misery would be hard to envisage, even if public and private charity had been more lavish and more acceptable.

With the stabilisation of Irish society towards the end of the last century most of these people have vanished from the streets and roads. Only the tinkers, now called itinerants, remain, and so far energetic efforts on behalf of the civil authorities to give them permanent residence and to educate their children have shown little success. The beggarwoman, with her property baby, still accosts the foreigner at Dublin's street corner: the Irish have, in general, little time for these vagrants. They have, on the other hand, no apparent objection to these profiteers from human sympathy and state welfare being kept in some style by the tourist. A tourist is, after all, not a real human being but a source of income.

In the eighteenth century what education the poor received was almost always from their priests, since Roman Catholics were barred not only from the sole university, Trinity, but also from most of the schools. However the brighter children, and particularly those with moneyed parents, were helped from their 'hedge schools' to centres of higher education abroad. Indeed the coming and going between Ireland and the Continent was great at all levels. Smuggling was a major industry in the south: so too was the recruitment of soldiers for the Irish units in the French and Spanish service. The authorities, whether they be British or Grattan's, attempted to stop both these activities, but with little success. Some British may have wished to close the rift between the main country and its colony: other interests of administrative and industrial power, English and Irish, were not unhappy to see it widened, and in Ireland at least quite a number of the colonists were not dissatisfied to watch their colony of adoption developing, on the American style, into a country in its own right. To this end 'Grattan's parliament', at least in its early years, undoubtedly contributed.

But if it gave Ireland a government, it did not give that government Ireland. It represented, in an increasingly corrupt fashion, a minute proportion of the population, and what is more, a proportion which was almost always of foreign origin and spoke a foreign language. Grattan himself was well aware of this and desired that the franchise, limited financially among the Protestants, be extended to a growing Roman Catholic middle class. For here he was confronted with a problem which never worried Jefferson or Hamilton: no American of any importance then suggested that the Amerindians should participate in the government of the United States. But how to define Irishmen suited for admission to the organs of government? That a Catholic middle class was growing was obvious. According to the Penal Laws it was an illegal growth: those laws were dead or dying. A £10 franchise was not hard to come by and in the eighteenth century enfranchisement of the Roman Catholics, in any circumstances, must mean what it has come to mean, the government of Ireland by the Roman Catholic majority and therefore, for the comparatively newly arrived Protestant landlords who sat in Grattan's parliament, their own expulsion, probably sooner rather than later, leading inevitably to civil war, a British reconquest, and an end to their concept of an independent, self-governing Ireland, self-governing, that is, in their terms not ours, a government of Protestant property owners independent from but closely linked to England. Educated Irishmen, like the educated founding fathers in America, accepted Plato's view that democracy was the lowest form of government ever conceived.

I was once privileged to see Stendhal's private library, with his annotations. Among his books was a positive hagiology of the joys that the Austrian empress, Maria Theresa, brought to her northern Italian territories. At the end Stendhal had simply written: *'Puis vint Bonaparte'* ('Then came Bonaparte'). One might write such a postscript to Grattan's parliament of Protestant landlords, some drunk, some sober, some devoted to improvement of their lands, some to its exploitation for expenditure elsewhere: *Puis vint la terreur*, not in Ireland yet but in Paris, in 1793.

NOTE
1 Salamen, Redcliffe N. *The History and Social Influence of the Potato* (Cambridge, 1949).

The statue of Charles Stewart Parnell (1846–1891) stands at the far end of O'Connell Street. His mother was American, while paternally he was descended from a member of Grattan's cabinet. Elected to the Westminster parliament, he used his position there solely to further Irish independence, constitutionally. His career was ruined by a sordid divorce. Soon enough the 'uncrowned king of Ireland' died

Irish emigrants' arrival in Liverpool – a painting by Erskine Nichol which exemplifies the nineteenth-century 'Paddy' image *(National Gallery of Scotland)*

17

THE CULTURAL ECLIPSE

Ireland was conquered – as it then seemed finally and for ever – in the Williamite wars, and the first half of the eighteenth century saw the consolidation of that conquest by the English rooted garrison. The departure of Sarsfield and almost the entire native or Norman aristocracy together with most of their fighting men left the Irish without any Celtic temporal leaders. The Penal Laws were, for a while, almost as successful in depriving them of an effective Roman Catholic hierarchy, though even these cruel laws could not change men's beliefs. A very few old Irish noble families retained their land, usually in the more remote corners of the island, just as brave priests continued to celebrate the Mass among the ruins of their churches and monasteries or even in unsanctified, secret places. Just as the soldiers won commissions in foreign armies (four de Lacey brothers who left with Sarsfield became field marshals in the French, Spanish, Austrian and Russian service), so seminaries or Irish colleges for training the Irish priesthood were established or enlarged on the Continent, at Louvain, Douai, Salamanca, Rome and elsewhere. But even as the brave priests, risking martyrdom, had to return to Ireland in disguise, so the few members of the old Irish ruling class had to be as inconspicuous as possible on the lands they had almost miraculously preserved. The concept of a myriad of local kings, each with his court and courtiers, had been destroyed forever. We hear no more of Brehon lawyers, nor of courtly *filidh*.

This does not mean that Irish poetry did not continue to be composed and sometimes be written down in the Irish language, nor Irish bards to wander across the west. Perhaps the most famous of these was the blind harpist, Turlogh Carolan (1670–1738), patronised by the MacDermott Roes who owned an iron foundry in County Roscommon. Equipped by them with a horse and a servant, he travelled principally through Connacht and Ulster, and his compositions are tantamount to a reference book of the old Irish families who had survived and whose praises he sang. He became a famous national figure, much loved, and his funeral was attended by an enormous number of mourners from all over Ireland. Nor was he a simple peasant bard. Of the fifty-odd compositions that have survived and are attributed to him, some are said to show the influence of the then new 'Italian' style of music popular in the more advanced musical circles of Dublin. Nor was he a unique phenomenon. And later in the century it became fashionable for the descendants of Williamite settlers to have a harp and perhaps a harpist, even as their own nineteenth century descendants would have a pianoforte or perhaps a harpsichord in their drawingrooms.

Dublin, indeed, was a very musical city, and we read of concert halls so crowded as to be dangerous. Handel's *Messiah* was first performed here on 13 April 1742, and he was so gratified by the appreciation his works received that he returned to Ireland more than once. But Dublin looked, perhaps, more to the Continent than to the hinterland. Yet it provided more than just audiences for foreign composers. To mention but one Irish composer of the end of this period, John Field (1782–1837), the son of a violinist, was one of the earliest composers of the nocturne if he did not perhaps invent this form of composition. He certainly exercised a great and acknowledged influence on Chopin, and was patronised by the Tsar of Russia. He died in Moscow, where there is a street named after him. Music has continued to be much loved and played in Ireland to the present day. The late Sean O'Riarda (1931–1971) is recognised as a major composer on an international scale. His music derives from his profound knowledge of what remains of old Irish modes.

However much the poets of the seventeenth century may have observed the traditions of the past, these could not outlive the total and final destruction of the society which the poets expressed. Professor McLysaght maintains (in *Irish Life in the Seventeenth Century*), in his masterly fashion, that that society had decayed beyond the point of no return by the time of Charles II, but it was the Williamite conquest which gave it its *coup de grâce*, for all Ireland was henceforth under close English rule, all the professions save medicine were closed to Roman Catholics, and all property owners or lessees, regardless of religion, were forced to pay tithes to the Church of Ireland clergy.[1] The Irish spirit, in appearance at least, was broken for the first half of the century, and the Irish gave no assistance, either in 1715 or in 1745, to the Jacobite invasions of Scotland by the Stuart claimants to the Crown.

Yet there was what might be called a silver age of Irish-language poetry during the second half of the century as the Penal Laws were relaxed. Indeed the very disappearance of the courtly *filidh* was not an unmitigated disaster, for they had largely become, as artists, what Malraux – as quoted earlier in this book – called the practitioners of an 'aristocrat' type of art. It is very difficult to compare the poetry of two countries, and in particular of Irish with English poetry, but one may say that the standard short Irish poem, the *aisling* (literal translation: 'vision') of the Irish poets towards the end of the Irish cultural hegemony might be thought of as the lesser and less circumscribed equivalent of the English sonnet. Perhaps the two greatest Irish poems of what, with all reservations, I have called the silver age are Merriman's *The Midnight Court*, an earthy, even at times a bawdy, dramatic poem, much translated into English, and the intensely moving *Lament for Art O'Leary* written by his widow. I intend to quote this poem in full, despite its length, but a brief explanatory note is needed.

Eibhlin Dubh O'Connell was an O'Connell of Derrynane. (A quite surprising number of known Irish poets were women.) Art O'Leary was one of the many Irishmen who served in foreign armies, the descendants of Sarsfield's original Wild Geese. He was a cavalry officer in the Austrian army, and as such owned a beautiful horse, which he brought to Ireland on a visit in 1775. The Penal Laws, though less and less applied, were not abolished (save for standing in political elections) until 1793. One of these, as we have seen, laid down that any Irish or English Protestant who 'conformed' might buy for £5 or less any horse belonging to a Roman Catholic. Such a one demanded Art O'Leary's horse for £5. The Austrian officer whipped him thoroughly with his riding crop. For this crime he was arrested, and shot by English soldiers. (It is not improbable that he was in Ireland recruiting for the Austrian service: by that late date a judge would scarcely have imposed the death sentence solely on such a charge, but he was legally quite entitled to do so.) The following lament was written by his widow and sister. The twentieth century illustration by Jack Yeats, reproduced here, is in this writer's opinion almost as poignant as the poem itself, here translated in part of Eilis Dillon and in part by John Montague and taken from the latter's edition of the *Faber Book of Irish Verse*.

LAMENT FOR ART O'LEARY

I

HIS WIFE: My love forever!
The day I first saw you
At the end of the market-house,
My eye observed you,
My heart approved you,
I fled from my father with you,
Far from my home with you.

II

I never repented it:
You whitened a parlour for me,
Painted rooms for me,
Reddened ovens for me,
Baked fine bread for me,
Basted meat for me,
Slaughtered beasts for me;
I slept in ducks' feathers
Till midday milking-time
Or more if it pleased me.

III

My friend forever!
My mind remembers
That fine spring day
How well your hat suited you,

Bright gold-banded,
Sword silver-hilted –
Right hand steady –
Threatening aspect –
Trembling terror
On treacherous enemy –
You poised for a canter
On your slender bay horse.
The Saxons bowed to you,
Down to the ground to you,
Not for love of you
But for deadly fear of you,
Though you lost your life to them,
Oh my soul's darling.

IV

Oh white-handed rider!
How fine your brooch was
Fastened in cambric,
And your hat with laces
When you crossed the sea to us,
They would clear the street for you,
And not for love of you
But deadly hatred.

V

My friend you were forever!
When they will come home to me,
Gentle little Conor
And Farr O'Leary, the baby,
They will question me so quickly,
Where did I leave their father.
I'll answer in my anguish
That I left him in Killnamartyr.
They will call out to their father:
And he won't be there to answer.

VI

My friend and my love!
Of the blood of Lord Antrim,
And of Barry of Allchoill,
How well your sword suited you,
Hat gold-banded,
Boots of fine leather,
Coat of broadcloth,
Spun overseas for you.

VII

My friend you were forever!
I knew nothing of your murder
Till your horse came to the stable
With the reins beneath her trailing,
And your heart's blood on her shoulders
Staining the tooled saddle
Where you used to sit and stand.
My first leap reached the threshold,
My second reached the gateway,
My third leap reached the saddle.

VIII

I struck my hands together
And I made the bay horse gallop
As fast as I was able,
Till I found you dead before me
Beside a little furze-bush.
Without Pope or bishop,
Without priest or cleric
To read the death-psalms for you,
But a spent old woman only
Who spread her cloak to shroud you –
Your heart's blood was still flowing;
I did not stay to wipe it
But filled my hands and drank it.

Version: Eilis Dillon

My love and my delight!
Rise up now, straight,
And come on home with me,
We'll have a beast slaughtered,
Call friends to the feast,
Get the music started.
We'll get ready a bed
With crisp linen sheets
And bright speckled quilts
To bring out a sweat instead
Of the chill that grips you.

HIS SISTER: My friend and my treasure,
There's not a shapely woman
From Cork of the sails
To the bridge of Toime
With her bit of money gathered
And her herd of cattle
Would go to sleep in her room
The night of your wake.

HIS WIFE: My friend everlasting!
You must never believe
The gossip that's flying,
That slanderous story
That I slept at your wake.
It wasn't real slumber
But your children were unhappy
And needed me near them
To lull them asleep.

Neighbours, don't listen
To such lying tales!
Is there a woman in Ireland,
Who, at each day's end,
Stretched at his side,
Who bore his three children,
Would not lose her mind
After Art O'Leary, who
Lies spent here with me
Since yesterday morning.

My long lasting sorrow
That I was not at your side
When the bullet was fired
To take it in my right side
Or the folds of my linen
And you would still be at liberty,
O smooth-handed horseman!

HIS SISTER: My sharp, bitter grief
That I wasn't near you
When the powder blazed
To take it in my right flank
Or the fold of my gown
And you would have gone free,
O grey-eyed horseman!

HIS WIFE: My friend, my true fortune!
It's poor treatment to put down
A soldier, cowled in his coffin;
A stout-hearted chevalier
Who fished in the streams
And drank in the halls
With warm-breasted women.
A thousand laments –
I've lost my companion!

My love and my delight,
When you went out the gate,
You turned back quickly,
You kissed your children,
You kissed my fingers
Saying: 'Eileen, get up
And put your things together
Carefully and quickly,
I'm leaving from home
And it's not sure I'll return'.
I could only mock such talk,
You'd said it so often.

My friend and my choice!
Bright-sworded cavalier,
Put on your courtly suit,
Put on your black beaver,
Pull up your riding gloves,
Lift up your riding crop –
Your mare is waiting
To strike the path east
Where the trees will thin out
The streams narrow to a trickle
The men and women salute you –
If they still have the old ways,
Though I fear they've gone.

My love and my companion
It's not my dead kindred
Nor the death of my three children
Nor Donal Mor O'Connell
Nor Conall whom the tide drowned,
Nor the woman of twenty-six
Who crossed over the sea
To be the friend of kings –
It's none of these I'm calling
But Art who was mown down last night
At the inch of Carriganima
And lies with me here
With no one to wake him
But the dark little women of the mill,
Not a single one weeping.

HIS SISTER: My love and my treasure,
My bright-breasted pigeon!
If I come to mourn you
Without my escort,
It's no shame on me,

For they lie locked
In a sleep without waking,
In narrow coffins,
In closed vaults.

But for the smallpox
And the black death
And the spotted fever
That proud hosts of riders
Would be clattering
With bridles ringing
To join the cortège
Of Art of the white breast.

My love and my delight!
Friend of the wild horsemen
Who hunted the glens
Till you turned their heads
Home to your hall where
Knives were sharpening
Long tables being laid
For the roast beef,
The sucking pig and bacon,
The countless ribs of lamb,
With yellow oats pouring
To make the horses snort
And stable boys who
Would never go to bed
But fodder the beasts
If they stayed for a week
With my much loved brother!

My love and my calf!
A vision broke through
My dreams last night
As I lay in bed late
And lonely, in Cork:
That lime-white courtyard,
The fair stronghold
Where we played together
As children was fallen,
The hounds voiceless,
The birds songless,
While you were found
On the bare hillside
Without priest or cleric
But an old, old woman
To spread her cloak

Where the earth held you —
Art O'Leary —
Your life blood pouring
Over your linen shirt.

HIS WIFE: My love and my secret,
How well they became you,
Your five-ply stockings,
Your knee-high boots
And three-cornered Caroline,
With a light whip
For a frisky gelding:
Many's the modest, mannerly girl
Turned to gaze after you.

My steadfast love,
When you rode into town,
Sturdy and strong,
The shopkeepers' wives
Bowed and scraped
Knowing only too well
How good you were in bed,
What a fine cavalier
And sire for children.

If my cries could reach my kindred
In far, famed Derrynane
Or Capling of the yellow apples,
Many's the supple, spirited rider
And women with spotless kerchiefs
Would be here without delay
To weep upon your brow,
Art O'Leary of the smiles!

So part of my heart goes to you
Bright women of the mill
For your skill in lamenting
The brown mare's rider.

Christ himself knows
I'll have no hat on my head
No linen next my skin
No shoes on my feet
No supplies in my house
No harness for the mare
But I'll spend all at law
And I'll cross overseas
To speak to the king
And if no one pays heed

I'll return on my own
To the black-blooded clown
Who stole my precious one.

My love and my treasure,
Your stacks are roped,
Your cows heavy with milk
But sorrow in my heart
All Munster can't cure,
Nor the druids of the past.
Until Art O'Leary comes again
This sorrow won't lift
That lies across my heart
Like a rightly-locked trunk
With rust on the hasps
And the key thrown away.

So stop your weeping now
Women of the soft, wet eyes
And drink to Art O'Leary
Before he enters the grave school
Not to study wisdom and song
But to carry earth and stone.
                    Version: John Montague

Need any more be said about the old Irish aristocracy's attitude towards the English-imposed administration in their country?

* * *

From quite a different quarter, and in a most unusual fashion, the late eighteenth century saw a great revival of interest in Irish poetry. Ossian was a legendary third century figure in the Finn cycle, a poet killed in the Battle of Cabra, who languished for many years in fairyland before being re-incarnated in time to be baptised by St. Patrick. A minor Scots poet and translator from the Gaelic, James Macpherson (1736–1796), collected some fragments of ancient poems, added much material of his own to their translation and published this opus as *The Works of Ossian* in 1765, parts of which he had already had printed. Although immediately recognised and denounced as a fake by the great Dr. Johnson himself, 'Ossian' enjoyed immense popularity not only in Scotland, but almost everywhere else in Europe. Indeed the work broke the near monopoly of literary forms which the French then enjoyed. Johann Wolfgang Goethe, who in 1765 was sixteen years old and so, when the German translation appeared, stood on the threshold of his career as a great lyric poet, was much influenced by this bogus Ossian when it appeared in German. Its complete breaking of the French classical mould helped him, Schiller and others to create the *Sturm und Drang* ('Storm and stress') movement in German literature which, in due course, led directly to the Romantic movement in Germany, England, finally in France and the rest of Europe.

In Ireland Macpherson's partial forgeries had, of course, no influence on the Irish poets who knew the Fenian sagas in their original language, but their vast success did make the children of the Williamite settlers aware that what their parents had called, and treated as, savages, were in fact the heirs to a great tradition. It was then that the harps appeared in the drawingrooms of the Ascendancy. More important, perhaps, it encouraged Scots and Irish scholars to collect, maybe just in time, and commit to paper much that would have otherwise been lost as the songs and poems of the Cornish have been lost. Furthermore, this recognition of an indigenous Irish culture made it easier for an increasing number of the Cromwellian and Williamite settlers' descendants to identify themselves with the land of their birth, even if they did not know the language of the people whom they controlled. The importance of this identification cannot be exaggerated. Though some stood out against it, the majority of the so-called Anglo-Irish became quite rapidly Irishmen, and, like the Normans and the old English before them, Irish patriots. If there were a roll call of Irish patriotic leaders from the time of Flood and Grattan to the present day, the number of Celtic names would probably be in the minority.[1]

❋ ❋ ❋

Irish literature written in the English language is usually reckoned to have produced its first major writer in Jonathan Swift (1667–1745). The Dean would probably have denied that he was an Irishman, and might well have forestalled the Duke of Wellington's famous epigram, when his own Irish birth was mentioned, that to be born in a stable does not make a man a horse. But Swift combined love, pity and hatred for the Irish in their misery, a mixture that has constantly recurred among Irish writers to the present day. Such a love-hatred is the very essence of James Joyce's *Ulysses* and repeated by his pupil, Samuel Beckett, in other forms. Here is an extract from Beckett's *Watt* which, though ostensibly about the Irish weather, can with a minimum of effort to be turned into the reason why Beckett abandoned the Irish scene and even took to writing in French.

The crocuses and the larch turning green every year
a week before the others and the pastures red with
uneaten sheep's placentas and the long summer days
and the newmown hay and the woodpigeon in the morning
and the cuckoo in the afternoon and the corncrake in
the evening and the wasps in the jam and the smell of
the gorse and the look of the gorse and the apples
falling and the children walking in the dead leaves
and the larch turning brown a week before the others
and the chestnuts falling and the howling winds and
the sea breaking over the pier and the first fires and
the hooves on the road and the consumptive postman
whistling *The Roses Are Blooming in Picardy* and the
standard oillamp and of course the snow and to be
sure the sleet and bless your heart the slush and every
fourth year the February débâcle and the endless April
showers and the crocuses and then the whole bloody
business starting all over again.

After Swift, the eighteenth and nineteenth century literary sky
contains almost as many Irish as English stars, though few of them
spent much of their adult life in Ireland. (To call these writers
Anglo-Irish is somewhat absurd. Was Henry James an Anglo-
American novelist or T. S. Eliot an Anglo-American poet, or for that
matter Dylan Thomas Anglo-Welsh or Burns Anglo-Scots? A
writer's work is stamped with the loves and revulsions, the rhythms
of thought and emotions that are imprinted for ever upon him in his
early years.) Thus Goldsmith's *Deserted Village*, though it is given no
precise location, is recognisably an Irish village: the contrast with
Grey's almost contemporary *Elegy in a Country Churchyard* shows how
Irish Goldsmith was. W. B. Yeats spent the greater part of his life
away from Ireland, Robert Graves virtually all of his, yet no one
but an Irishman could have written quite as they did. This is even
more true of the theatre than it is of prose or verse. Leaving aside
contemporaries, too close to us for judgment, it has been maintained
that *all* English language playwrights whose work has lived beyond
their own time, since and including Congreve, were Irishmen. The
explanation may be that in ancient days Irish poems, whether epic
or lyric, were written to be heard, not read.

And it must be repeated that Irish literature, of which only a
fragment has come down to us, had reached the heights of poetic
expression before ever Spenser or Shakespeare put pen to paper.
Spenser's long years in Ireland produced many an echo of that older
culture in the *Faerie Queen*; indeed its very title might have come from

an *aisling*. Some have even found Irish echoes in Shakespeare's plays, though it is hard to accept, as has recently been proposed, that he was himself an Irishman by the name of Nugent: it is less difficult to believe that Lear was once O'Leary, for dangerous women occur repeatedly in ancient Irish sagas.

Another aspect of the Irish spirit impregnates the thinking of Bishop Berkeley (1685–1753), born at Dysart Castle in the County Kilkenny. His philosophy is often described as entirely novel, even eccentric, in its emphasis on the intangible, crudely expressed in the phrase 'mind over matter', for it is the mind which creates through perception. This is no great leap from early Irish mythopoesis which endows fairies and even waves of the sea, among much else, with a concrete reality of a transcendental nature. When Christianity is added to this, and God becomes the Supreme Reason, eternity and infinity cease to be incomprehensible on the divine ground. Kant acknowledged his debt to this Irish thinker, as did Hume. With such a philosophy the Bishop could not ignore the plight and abject poverty of so many of his compatriots, and in the three volumes of *The Querist* (the first of which appeared in 1735) he continued the work of Swift's *Drapier's Letters* (1724) and the Dean's other bitter polemics to improve the miserable circumstances in which so many Irish men and women then lived.

Edmund Burke (1729–1797) was born in Dublin and attended Trinity College, to become, in England, perhaps the most influential political thinker of his day. While he favoured the American revolutionaries he loathed the French Jacobins. Nor did he hesitate to speak his mind in the London House of Commons, though his oratory is said to have been harsh and his gestures awkward. He never lost his interest in Irish politics, and sent his somewhat ineffectual son to run a political society devoted to Roman Catholic emancipation. He himself played little direct part in Irish politics, remarking that most Irishmen were more interested in potatoes than in popes. In his writings, however, he has been said to have laid down the theoretical guidelines of the future English Conservative Party. Though they must have disagreed frequently, he was one of Dr. Johnson's intimate circle, 'the Club', which included – as well as Boswell – Goldsmith, Reynolds and Garrick and the Irish actor, Foote. He brought to England the prevalent, rather flippant attitude among the Irish governing class towards money and debt, which was not appreciated in England.

❋   ❋   ❋

Trinity College, Dublin, had been founded by Queen Elizabeth I to provide an education for the sons of the Protestant gentry and nobility. By the eighteenth century many, if not most, of the Oxford and Cambridge colleges were in an advanced state of intellectual decay, providing little save sinecures for the fellows, who gave few if any lectures and admitted the minimum of undergraduates. Trinity and Edinburgh University then provided the best higher education to be had anywhere in the British Isles, and Dublin is also said to have had finer schools than could be found at the time in England.[2]

The eighteenth century was a great period everywhere for the foundation of learned societies. The two most important in Ireland were both in Dublin, and both still exist. A Philosophical Society had been founded in 1684, modelled on the Royal Society in London, but it was a victim of the Jacobite war. It was not until 1785 that a successor, the Royal Irish Society, was created in order to promote the study of 'science, polite literature and antiquities', its guiding spirit and first president being that great connoisseur and patron of the arts, Lord Charlemont, whose fine town house is now the Municipal Art Gallery. Much earlier a somewhat more specialised society had been founded for 'the improvement of husbandry and other useful arts'. That was in 1731, and at one time it was in Leinster House, sold to it by the third Duke of Leinster and now the seat of *Dáil Eireann*, the Irish Republic's parliament. When George IV became its patron, in 1820, it became the Royal Dublin Society. It is a very large society indeed and soon exceeded, but has never abandoned, its original purpose. It is now located in Ballsbridge, which until quite recently was almost the southernmost part of Dublin. It developed a fine library, from which the nucleus of the National Library on Kildare Street was extracted, and now a theatre that is also used as a concert hall. It is probably best known to the outside world for the Dublin Horse Show, where an annual *dressage* competition is held to which many countries send teams to compete for the Aga Khan's Cup and other prizes. This is perhaps the only occasion when the President of Ireland and the government stand to attention when *God Save the Queen* is played in honour of the British team. But the Spring Show, principally of cattle, is perhaps of greater importance to the Irish. When the famous agronomist, Arthur Young, visited Ireland in 1776 he spent much time with members of the Society. He regarded Irish agriculture as, on the whole, less skilled than that of England, but he did meet a great many 'improving' landlords. These in turn relied largely on the Society for information concerning the latest developments in agriculture.

* * *

There was never much painting done in Ireland, and what there was in the eighteenth century is derivative in large measure of the English school of portrait painting. Names such as Barry and Nathaniel Hone mean little outside Ireland, and the attempts of Lord Charlemont to encourage the visual arts by a school came to very little. He, Lord Moira and a handful of other great collectors bought their pictures – not infrequently fakes – from abroad. I recall an exhibition, some thirty years ago, of paintings from Irish country houses, most of which were marked, optimistically, as 'attributed to'. These included one of a large yellow dog attributed to Titian.

Indeed it can be said that very few of the Irish have a much developed visual sense. This can be seen, most easily, in the course of a stroll down Grafton Street, the most fashionable shopping street in Dublin today, its Bond Street or Fifth Avenue or Rue de la Paix. The display of expensive goods in the shop windows would, in almost all cases, be deemed deplorable in a village grocery. The Irish also have a love of garish colours which may derive from the vivid green of the grass and of the sky when it is blue. But both in Irish women's clothes and in juxtaposed village house fronts these very frequently clash in a manner that is almost painful to the eye. And nowadays not only the hideous orange but also the siting of the street-lights uglify even the finest streets.

For eighteenth century Dublin, in particular the then newly developed part south of the Liffey, was most beautifully laid out and built. The main streets are usually wide, as becomes a capital city, the houses beautifully proportioned, the fan-lights above the front doors rightly famous for their elegance. In recent years, however, much of this Dublin has gone, deliberately demolished by speculative builders to be replaced by modern office blocks in almost all cases as boring and in some as offensive as the work of most contemporary architects in all Europe, the horrible heritage of Le Corbusier. These monstrosities may be lost in London or Paris, where the architecture is so varied: forced upon the almost uniform beauty of certain eighteenth century Dublin streets and squares they are positively offensive to the eye. Meanwhile the streets and squares of the same period north of the Liffey have in most cases degenerated into slum

This picture portrays the extreme penury of an Irish 'cabin' in the mid nineteenth century *(Graves Art Gallery, Sheffield)*

Such is the exterior of such a cabin of the time in Co. Galway

Once Ireland, or twenty-six counties of it, was free, Irish politicians took over. Here is the late Eamon de Valera's first cabinet, 1932 *(National Library of Ireland)*

tenements, soon to be demolished. If either the architects or the
town planners of today knew how to see, official vandalism on this
scale would never have been permitted. Efforts by Princess Mariga
Guinness and her Georgian Society to stop this process may have had
a little success, at least in awakening a glimmer of awareness on the
part of the authorities, but not enough to prevent the continuing
destruction of one part of Ireland's heritage. Yet the mass of the
people obviously notice nothing strange in all this, for this is a
democracy and the bureaucrats (for whose housing many of the
worst monstrosities are being or have been built) are answerable in
the end to an electorate, which apparently neither sees nor, if it
does, cares.

✳ ✳ ✳

The greater part of the memorable architecture of Dublin dates
from the eighteenth century. Little in stone is older, and this is true
of Ireland's other towns and cities, save Norman castles and the
ruins of once great abbeys. In Dublin the Castle, much rebuilt, and
the two cathedrals, both 'restored' almost out of recognition in the
nineteenth century, are almost all. Kilmainham Royal Hospital
dates from the seventeenth century, during which the ruins of what
was once a Priory of the Knights Hospitallers were rebuilt by Sir
William Robinson as a home for old soldiers on the model of
Christopher Wren's Chelsea Hospital. It later became a museum.
Trinity College was almost entirely rebuilt in the eighteenth century
and later. The Phoenix Park (the largest urban park in Europe)
contained a private house that later became the vice-regal lodge and,
later still, the presidential residence, again much altered in the
eighteenth and nineteenth centuries. Under the vice-regency of
Ormonde, in the time of Charles II, what might be described as the
first piece of town planning took place. Dublin then was so ram-
shackle, verminous and inflammable that the city fathers decided to
build a new city to the south and east of it. Almost their first act was
to enclose common land and let lots facing on to what is now
St. Stephen's Green. Dublin had a rapidly growing population and
from 1660, when it may have amounted to some 30,000, increased
perhaps to as many as 60,000 by the time of the Jacobite war.
During this time Ormonde began to build the quays, one of which
bears his name today, and enclose the sprawling Liffey, though it
continued occasionally to flood the low lying areas of the town for
many years. Bridges were also built, most of them originally of wood.
Two or three Church of Ireland churches dating from this period

have also survived, though much 'improved',[3] and a few houses o
the nobility, now gone. A certain Viscount Fitzwilliam of Merrion
was among those who bought long leases from the municipality on
what was then undeveloped land.

The first Irishman who might be termed an architect and not
just a builder was a man named Burgh (pronounced 'Birr') who
built, among much else, the rightly famous and magnificent Library
of Trinity College, which was opened in 1732. He, too, has a quay
named after him. He also built St. Werburgh's Church, but not
the church we now see, for it was rebuilt forty years later. Early in
the century the Gardiner family built in the area of the street named
after them, which included Mountjoy Square, two sides of which are
still intact. They employed, among others, a German architect
named Richard Cassels who worked in Dublin from 1729 until his
death in 1751. It was the Gardiners who created Sackville (now
O'Connell) Street, originally built as a square, by Lord Drogheda,
and called the Mall. Near its centre is the General Post Office, made
famous in the Easter Rising of 1916, and opposite it was Nelson's
Pillar (blown up by the government in 1966, after the admiral's
statue had been badly damaged by *plastiqueurs* said to have been
employed by the new I.R.A.). This is generally regarded as the
centre-point of Dublin, and it is here that mobs demonstrate while,
on formal occasions, Irish dignitaries review parades.

At a slightly later date the Grafton St.–Dawson St. area was built
up on what had been Molesworth land, and, under the supervision
now of the admirable Wide Streets Commission of 1756, the Merrion
Square–Fitzwilliam area was built. The width of the streets is
important and elegant, even when jammed with traffic as some of
them so often are. It can thus be seen that in some respects the town
planning of Dublin preceded by half a century the wishes of the
Prince Regent in London and the work of Haussmann in Paris.
For the further development of Dublin – which has little to distinguish it from other cities in Britain – the reader is referred to
Maurice Craig, op. cit.

Three more great eighteenth century buildings must be mentioned,
the work of an English architect, born in 1743. John Beresford
brought Gandon to Dublin in 1781, to build a new Customs House,
which he did in the teeth of formidable opposition from the populace,
the Irish parliament, facing Trinity College, and the Four Courts.
He did much other work in Ireland, where he died in 1823. Fortunately a fine architectural draughtsman, James Malton, produced

a series of etchings of Dublin's architectural beauties which he published in 1792. Thus we can see how beautiful were parts of the city, and almost all built during this one century. If this seems to contradict my earlier comments on lack of visual powers on the part of the Irish, it must be pointed out that neither Cassels nor Gandon were Irishmen, though their patrons were. And the many beautiful Georgian houses that dot the Irish countryside and have survived political arson show that, architecturally at least, the Irish Ascendancy knew what was good.

NOTES
1 Irish-language prose was not considered, until recent times, to be an artistic medium at all.
2 Maxwell, Constantia. *Dublin under the Georges*. The late Professor Maxwell's work is a masterly and readable account of the period.
3 Craig, Maurice. *Dublin 1660–1680*.

18

GRATTAN'S PARLIAMENT

The Penal Laws (unlike the Nazis' anti-semitic Nuremberg Laws, which in some ways they resembled) were not a code of laws drawn up after King William's victory over King James, though their purpose was roughly the same. To start with, the London Parliament disowned the fair Treaty of Limerick that King William had agreed with Sarsfield. The Penal Laws then derived from a series of Acts of Parliament, passed either in the English or the Irish parliament over a period of years with purpose: to punish, degrade and render politically impotent the Roman Catholic and, to a lesser degree, the Non-conformist populations of Ireland. Behind them all lay the ancient Poynings' Law which made any act of the Irish parliament invalid should the Westminster Parliament so decide. These laws were passed, in Dublin or in London, in a spirit of vengeance and malice. It was not illegal to be a Roman Catholic or a Presbyterian, so long as the adherents of these forms of Christianity were deprived of all political and almost all economic power and above all to prevent them from educating their children into the Roman faith. This last was perhaps the most important of the Anglican and Church of Ireland's ambitions, since had it succeeded it should, in theory, have destroyed the Catholic religion in one generation not merely in Ireland, but also in Scotland after the creation of the United Kingdom in 1705 and indeed in England itself.[1]

They were, then, in Ireland, directed primarily against the Roman Catholic majority, which was overwhelming in all Ireland save among the Scotch–Irish in eastern Ulster (who were predominantly Presbyterians) and in Dublin, where it has been estimated that perhaps 50% only of the inhabitants were Roman Catholics. In all Ireland it has been estimated that the percentage of Roman Catholics remained at about 85% who owned in 1700 some 15% of the land, which by the end of the century had shrunk to some 5%. One reason for this decline was a particularly nasty law whereby a Roman Catholic was compelled to leave his land, in equal portions, to all his sons. However, should the eldest son turn Protestant, he inherited the lot. This unsavoury appeal to material gain and denial of spiritual belief was, however, increasingly ignored. The eldest son would pretend to be a member of the Church of Ireland, would attend a Protestant religious service or two, and would continue to be a Catholic. Another trick to foil the English was for a man to give or sell for a pittance his land, in his lifetime, to a Protestant friend, who would then give it back, after his death, to the donor's eldest son. (Sometimes this did not work out. In my own family, the chief of Clangibbon made such an arrangement with Lord Kingston. The story is murky, but it appears that by the time FitzGibbon died, Kingston had succeeded his own father as Lord Kingsborough, and the new Lord Kingston did not feel bound by his father's promise. There could be no appeal to the courts, of course, and the grandfather of that John FitzGibbon, who in the 1790s was Lord Clare and perhaps the most powerful man in Ireland, was reduced from being the White Knight and a great landowner to being in reality what he had always been in pretence, a small farmer. Thenceforth his son, and I think his grandson, the future Earl of Clare, chose the safer method of sham Protestantism.)

Direct persecution of the priesthood was not particularly successful.[2] According to Miss Wall, despite the Banishment Act of 1691 and the departure of the bishops and many of the clergy, about 1,000 diocesan priests were permitted to remain. She writes: 'Despite the savage laws on the statute books, the Catholic Church was reorganized and reformed; and before the middle of the century the hierarchy had been restored to its full strength for the first time since the Reformation.' The creation of Irish seminaries in the Low Countries, France and Spain served to train Irishmen for the priesthood and, until it was safe for bishops to return to Ireland, these men were ordained on the Continent before coming back to celebrate the Mass. It was only when those foreign seminaries were overrun by the atheistical and violently anti-clerical French revolutionary armies, and almost all the Penal Laws had been repealed, that Lord Clare set about arranging for the foundation of Maynooth. His uncle had been ordained after training at a continental seminary.

It was the intention of the Irish Protestant governing class to keep all political power in their own hands. Catholics were therefore debarred from all positions of authority, from the House of Lords down to that of justice of the peace. They had no vote in parliamentary elections. The law courts were closed to them, save as defendants, or, perhaps, plaintiffs in civil cases against another

Catholic. Judges, barristers and even jurymen had to conform to the Established Church. In fact the only profession open to them was medicine. Since Trinity College would take none save members of the Church of Ireland, and there was no other centre of higher education in Ireland, even that had to be studied abroad, for Oxford and Cambridge were also closed to Roman Catholics. Many went abroad allegedly to study medicine, but in fact to get a degree in some other subject. Lord Clare's father (whom the Provost of Trinity, John Hely-Hutchinson (1724–1794), described in a letter as 'a notorious Papist') was such a one. He returned from Paris, where in theory he had studied medicine, 'conformed', and made almost as much money at the bar as his father or grandfather had lost to Lord Kingston. It goes without saying that no Catholic could hold a commission in the militia or the yeomanry, which became in effect the private armies of the great Protestant landowners. High administrative positions in business, which were rare, were seldom given to Roman Catholics. Indeed, well into our century it was the policy of Arthur Guinness Ltd. not to promote Roman Catholic administrative staff above a certain level, while to this day St. Patrick's Hospital, endowed by Jonathan Swift in his will, cannot be headed by a Roman Catholic. Nevertheless, an Irish Catholic middle class was beginning to appear, particularly in the cities.

The second method of keeping the Irish down was to force the closure, by Acts of the Westminster Parliament, of Irish industries that were in competition with their English equivalents. Thus was a flourishing trade in finished woollens forbidden to the Irish. So heavy a duty was imposed on the importation of hops, that most Irish breweries had to close. An Irish merchant marine was smothered at birth, and in this mercantile age, by dint of the British Navigation Laws, all goods to or from Ireland had to be carried in English bottoms. Heavy taxes were levied on Irish silver, glass and furniture which were being made with ever greater skill early in the century. (It is often said that the Act of Union of 1800 killed these skilled trades by destroying the domestic market, but they had been moribund long before that.) Taxes were levied ruthlessly, and so were tithes to support the Established clergy. In fact it was this same ruthless commercial exploitation and taxation of a colony that caused Americans to begin to stir against English rule in the 1760s. The Americans, however, were two thousand miles away, the Irish Sea, at its narrowest, only twenty miles. And even the Boston massacre did not lead to immediate revolt. But the course of

Grattan's polite revolution in Anglo-Irish relationships was directly inspired by the American example of 1776, as we shall see, though the situation was quite different in the two colonies.

The attempt further to degrade the Irish by denying them education was in some measure flouted by Roman Catholic teachers, who held classes where there were no schools, out of doors in fine weather (hence the name: hedge schools), in a private house when the weather was foul. Few of these teachers were priests, but all were Roman Catholics and they both preserved Irish traditions and prevented a nation from being utterly crushed. A respect, even a reverence, for learning was part of the Irish tradition.

* * *

But perhaps even more important than these examples of deliberate tyranny by the masters of Ireland was the miserable condition of the masses.[3] The reasons for this were manifold. Only one derived directly from the Penal Laws: the compulsory break-up into smaller and ever smaller segments of farmlands in Roman Catholic hands, by the inheritance law. But this only accounted for a very small percentage of Irish agricultural land. The big farmers found it increasingly profitable to turn their land over to grazing. This meant the eviction of many tenants when their 'conacre' leases fell in. (In Ulster the 'Ulster custom', which was a custom without the backing of a law, allowed longer leases.) This did not therefore stop Lord Downshire from clearing his huge estate in the mid-eighteenth century and these and similar evictions led to the first great Irish emigration to America, and Non-conformist Irishmen provided an important part of Washington's armies. They also provided many of the 'Indian fighters' in and from the Alleghany Mountains, where their descendants can still be found. (The brutality of Ulster life gave these emigrants a good background for the genocide of many Indian tribes. This emigration, estimated at 50,000, was of course very small when compared with the much larger emigration of the nineteenth century when almost all Ireland was struck by famine.) In 1778 Arthur Young reported that within the past quarter of a century rents had doubled. In many cases a landlord, or his agent, would increase the rent if the tenant had himself improved the little farm. The result of this was that the cottier would have to grow most of his produce, in particular grain, in order to pay his rent, leaving only enough land and time to grow potatoes for himself and his family: potatoes and skimmed milk were the staple diet of Munster and Connaught, Leinstermen being slightly richer on the average. The casual labourer, that is to say the great majority of a rapidly expanding population, earned, in 1782, some 6d. a day, which had not increased since the time of Elizabeth I, though the price of all commodities had grown vastly, and casual labour was dismissed at once when not required. Perhaps even more hated than the landlord or his agent was the gombeen man who would give credit, usually in the form of food, to these wretched peasants at a high rate of usury. That he performed a useful function in the more remote communities by bringing salt and clothing was not realised by the people who saw him solely as the exploiter of this misery.[4]

The condition of the peasantry continued to deteriorate throughout the second half of the eighteenth century. An English traveller named Bush, who visited Ireland in 1764, is quoted by Lecky as writing: 'What dread of justice or punishment can be expected from an Irish peasant in a state of wretchedness and penury . . . ' and twenty years later John Fitzgibbon, the attorney general, who cherished no sentimental views about the working class, said: 'I am very well acquainted with the Province of Munster' (he not only had his country house near Limerick, but as a barrister had travelled the Munster circuit more than once) 'and I know that it is impossible for human wretchedness to exceed that of the miserable peasantry of that province. I know that the unhappy tenantry are ground to powder by relentless landlords.' It was from such powder that many of the beautiful Georgian houses were born and drew their sustenance.

And all through the eighteenth century the population was growing, while the land available to grow food for those who worked it was decreasing, more and more being exported in the form of grain or meat to finance the landlords, not a few of whom were absentees. Many had properties in England as well as Ireland and used their Irish incomes to finance their standard of living across the Irish Sea.

There was no form of poor relief in Ireland, as there was in England, and since the landlord class totally controlled both the administration and the judiciary, there was no one to whom the grossly impoverished rural proletariat could appeal for help.

Such was the background to the almost senseless violence of agrarian crime in rural Leinster, Munster and Connaught. This usually took the form of nocturnal attacks upon the property of the landlords, sometimes of a particularly unpopular and exacting landlord, sometimes on landlords in general. Cattle, sheep and horses were killed or mutilated, outbuildings set on fire, less often the landlord's own mansion. One group of these law-breakers was called Whiteboys, since they wore a white coverall that enabled them to see one another in the darkness and to distinguish them from the landlord's loyal servants, whom they occasionally murdered. The name spread to the perpetrators of all such agrarian crime, and the story may be true of the absentee landlord who sent a letter to his tenants saying that if they thought they could intimidate him by murdering his agent, they were very much mistaken.

It has been estimated that some 400,000 Irishmen emigrated throughout the century, mostly to France where they enlisted in the Irish brigades of the original Wild Geese. (I have seen the figure of 2,000,000 given in this context, but this is surely too high to be credible.) Some went to Spain, Austria and Russia, and a great many to England. A roll of the Cheshire Regiment towards the end of the century shows a marked predominance of Irish names. And still the Irish population at home continued to grow. Some two millions in 1700, within the century it had doubled. The reason for the contemporary population explosion in England has been ascribed, by Carr-Saunders and other experts, more to a drop in the death rate, particularly among infants, due to improved medical practice and above all to Jenner's discovery of vaccination against smallpox. But there was little, if any, improvement in the medical services available to the outlying peasantry of Munster and Connaught, yet it was precisely here that the population exploded with the greatest violence.

In the cities, or towns, of Ireland there was a small urban proletariat, a mass of beggars, and the beginnings of a middle class, both Protestant and Catholic. Far from all the landlords were brutes and extortioners, and as the grandchildren of the Williamite officers reached manhood there was an increasing desire for a better form of government than then prevailed in what these young men regarded as 'their country'. Their inspiration came from the American Colonies, their political theories from the France of the Enlightenment, and their opportunity from the American War of Independence. They were of three sorts. the new upper middle class, descendants of immigrants who had done well as represented by Grattan and the Speaker of the Irish House of Commons, John Foster; the old English or Norman–Irish who had conformed, such as some of the Butlers, Plunkets and Geraldines; and the descendants of more recent conquerors, Elizabethan, Cromwellian or Williamite, such as the Beresfords, to name but the most prominent political family among many. All were Protestants, though a few were secret Catholics, including probably the future Earl of Clare, and, like the leaders of the American Revolution, what they desired was not a social revolution (Paine's *Rights of Man* was not to reflect either their or their American counterparts' views) but rather the transfer to themselves of the power that had long lain in London. Their leader was Henry Grattan (1746–1820) when Henry Flood (1732–1791) accepted a sinecure from the government, presumed to be a bribe from the Castle for services which he never, in fact, rendered. However, by the time the Castle withdrew this sinecure, Grattan was firmly established as leader of the opposition.

This was not an opposition in the British or later the American sense, in that it was not an alternative government which could replace the government in office should the Irish parliament or electorate so decide. For the government of Ireland was not based on the Irish parliament, but rather on the Castle, that is to say the vice-regal court, and on certain men appointed, by the viceroy or by London, to certain offices of state, such as the Under-secretary, the Lord Chancellor, the Chancellor of the Irish Exchequer, perhaps half a dozen in all. And the amount of power that they exercised was in large measure dependent on their personalities and political skill. Thus was governmental policy hammered out, largely behind closed doors. The opposition simply consisted of those men in parliament or in public life who disagreed with Castle policy. They were not, in any real sense, a political party, though at times they acted as one.

Such a time came in 1772 when the Patriot Party was formed, under the leadership of Grattan, whose aim was to give to the Irish parliament control of Irish affairs. What they wanted was not revolutionary, in that it was not directed against the King of England and Ireland, but was very close to what was later to be called Home Rule, with one important reservation. The exercise of power was to remain, at least for the time being, in the hands of the Irish *Protestant* landowners, with their rotten boroughs and the other unsavoury methods by which the English upper and middle classes preserved political power. It is true that Grattan himself, and some others, wished to extend the franchise to Catholics of property, but this was not to be for many years.

The English army in Ireland was withdrawn to fight the Americans and the French. There was no police force in those days, and quite apart from the danger of a French invasion, internal safety was in great jeopardy from highwaymen, tories and rapparees, with which neither the militia nor the yeomanry could cope. Therefore to protect Ireland both internally and externally the Patriot Party in 1778 called into being the Volunteers. Virtually all young Protestants joined up, to protect their property. What they lacked in military skill, they more than made up for in enthusiasm. Since they never met an enemy, it is not possible to judge how they would have fared. But in Ireland, for the next few years, they were virtually the only armed force. And as England was losing the war in America and the naval war with France, London simply could not afford to disregard their demands.

The situation developed fast. The repeal of the Penal Laws was begun, with Gardiner's Relief Act for Catholics in 1778 and the repeal of most of the restrictive acts concerning trade in 1779. In 1780 the Test Act, which was aimed against the Dissenters, was also repealed. Most important, in 1781 much of Poynings' Law was repealed, and the Westminster Parliament could no longer veto Acts of the Irish parliament. In 1782 there was the great Volunteer Convention at Dungannon. Gardiner's second Relief Act for Catholics was passed and, most important of all, Irish parliamentary independence was established and confirmed in January of 1783 by the British Renunciation Act. Grattan himself would have liked to see full enfranchisement given to the Roman Catholics, even as the repeal of the Test Act had given it to the Presbyterians and other Non-conformists, but here his followers overruled him. They intended to keep the monopoly of power, to paraphrase another Irishman speaking a century and half later; what the Volunteers in their splendid uniforms wanted was a Protestant parliament for a Protestant oligarchy, Home Rule by a small minority with ultimate recourse to their King and the Protestant forces of his other kingdom, across the sea. For the first time, Ireland had become a nation with its own capital and parliament and all the trappings of government. Yet since the franchise was still closed to Roman Catholics, it was in large measure an emotional and less a political nation. And the Viceroy did not and could not replace the King as head of state, but merely as head of the administration. The two Irish Houses of Parliament, the Lords and a very corrupt House of Commons, might turn bills into acts: there were still two hurdles before they became law, the Viceroy and the King. And the King, in his capacity of King of England, was himself not yet a purely constitutional monarch, but subject, in London, to the wishes of his English ministers, who thus, at third hand it is true, continued to have the final say in Irish as well as in English affairs. What Grattan's parliament could, and immediately did, do was to repeal all or almost all of these discriminating Acts of past English or British parliaments that had limited Irish trade, that is to say had interfered with the profits and well-being of the Protestant landowners and merchants who made up the Irish parliament. A growing minority of merchants were Roman Catholics: they too profited by the loss of power of Westminster in regulating Irish affairs.

But government remained with the Junto, as it was called, in Dublin Castle, which could both overrule the Irish parliament and, with its enormous powers of patronage, could influence the members of that parliament directly. In the 1790s, that is to say within a decade of its creation, the Irish parliament was to be faced with another decade of violence and terror which, in the end, killed it. Had it been spared that second decade, the Irish state might have worked out a *modus vivendi* that could take root and flourish. We shall never know, for events not of its own creation overtook it.

In Ulster the Scots and English, who had long been settled there, and who had been much re-inforced by the plantations, primarily of Scots, by James I, Cromwell and to a lesser extent by King William, had never become assimilated into the original Irish population. Nor had the rural proletariat been reduced to the status of the basic inhabitants of the other provinces, due in some measure to the 'Ulster custom' which, by giving the farmers greater security of tenure, had produced a yeoman class that both disliked and distrusted the Roman Catholics, with whom they competed for land. In 1641 the Roman Catholics had attempted to massacre the Scotch–Irish, and eight years later Cromwell had exacted his revenge. When the dust settled, eastern Ulster, that is to say that part of the province east of the river Bann, was predominantly, in some areas such as north Down entirely, English-speaking Nonconformist. To the west of the Bann, Irish-speaking Roman Catholics predominated. There was between these homogeneous areas a belt of mixed origins, where hostility prevailed, most particularly in the endless quest for land by a growing population. Within each area was a mixed city, Derry in the west and the new city of Belfast in the east. Here the root causes of mutual hostility were the search for homes and the search for jobs. Proximity did not lend to tolerance, but quite the contrary. Belfast, which in 1750 had been little more than a fishing village, was the first city to be built for the new industrial proletariat, first linen (brought in by the Huguenots), then cotton, then ship-building being the major industry, and by 1790 was the second largest city in Ireland. When, at a slightly later date, the great English industrial cities were built there was some attempt to provide rudimentary comforts. Belfast was built as a large slum of back-to-back houses, housing the maximum number of workers in the smallest possible area. At first essentially Non-conformist, it soon experienced an influx of unskilled Irish labour who were discriminated against and who, for obvious reasons, chose to create ghettoes for themselves. Derry, it will be recalled, had been sold by James I to a consortium of London companies, and Londonderry was a walled city which had resisted a half-hearted siege by the Jacobites in 1690. Here the new Catholic influx lived in slums outside the walls and worked largely in the linen industry. In the agricultural zone where the two populations competed for land, feelings were bitter. The Presbyterian farmers and farm labourers had their own equivalent of Whiteboys. Called Oakboys, in 1763 these made a first brief appearance in Counties Armagh, Tyrone and London-derry. In 1770, when Lord Donegall 'cleared' his estates in County Antrim for grazing, the Steelboys appeared by night. The movement spread as other landlords copied Lord Donegall. The evicted Presbyterians now lusted after Roman Catholic farms. In the 1780s, the Roman Catholics banded together to resist the attacks of the Presbyterians intended to drive them out, and to retaliate. Originally called the Defenders, for they were on the defensive against dawn raids by the successors to Oakboys and Steelboys, now called Peep o' Day boys. The situation deteriorated and the armed Volunteers, usually of a higher social standing, became almost indistinguishable from the Presbyterian mobs. The Roman Catholics copied their enemies and were soon enough raiding and burning Presbyterian farms and homes. In September 1795, at the Diamond, County Armagh, a pitched battle took place between the two peasant factions, the Defenders were roundly defeated and in the following months thousands of Roman Catholic families were forced to flee from the southern districts of Ulster.

Within twenty-four hours the Protestants of the area founded the Orange Order, which included an officer-class Church of Ireland element as well as the far more numerous Non-conformists who had been Peep o' Day boys. The Orange Order created Orange Lodges all over Ireland, but it was only in Ulster that they were immed-diately – and have remained – of great political significance.

It was therefore extremely difficult, in Ulster, for Tone and McCracken to create an inter-denominational Jacobin (i.e. terrorist) organisation. And from then until today all attempts to reconcile the two Ulster communities with one another have failed.

For the so-called Battle of the Diamond, the exchange of a few shots at extreme range, led to much greater and more horrible events.[5] But the important fact is that since the division was essentially religious, neither side was susceptible to Jacobin atheism.

In 1792 Wolfe Tone, a Dublin-born Protestant with an English law degree, was chosen to succeed Richard Burke, Edmund Burke's only son, as Secretary of the Dublin Catholic Committee, a pressure group intent on winning ever more concessions, economic and political, for the Roman Catholics of Ireland. 1793 saw the passage of Hobart's Catholic Relief Bill, which gave the Roman Catholics virtually all the rights of the Protestants save only that they might not vote nor sit in Parliament. Tone had wider ambitions. Almost at once he got in touch with the Protestant leaders of a revolutionary tinge in Belfast, of whom the most celebrated was to be Henry Joy McCracken, and it was decided to create a Society of United Irishmen. Tone returned to Dublin and was joined by James Napper Tandy and, a little later, by Lord Edward Fitzgerald, a younger son of the Duke of Leinster and a revolutionary. The Hon. Simon Butler, another aristocrat, was the first chairman of this new inter-denominational society. Tone writes, in his *Autobiography*: 'To my own past, I think it right to mention, that, at this time, the establishment of a Republic was not the immediate object of my speculations. My object was to secure the independence of my country from any form of government, to which I was led by a hatred of England, so deeply rooted in my nature, that it was rather an instinct than a principle.'[6]

In 1793 and 1794 a number of prominent members of the Society were tried on various charges and these men were usually encouraged to emigrate. By 1795 the Society had become frankly revolutionary, though secretly so. It was, from the beginning, riddled with informers, agents of the government. From then, until 1798, it was the policy of Lord Clare (Lord Chancellor) to urge its more prominent leaders that they emigrate, which a great many of them, including Tone, did. For the course of the French Revolution had made the United Irishmen infinitely more dangerous as that Revolution was carried by French arms into Italy and Germany. In 1793 Tone had written in his diary: 'The King of France was beheaded on the

21st – *I am sorry it had to be done.*' (Whether the emphasis is Tone's or his editor's, I do not know: it is not mine.) Two weeks later Hobart's Catholic Relief Bill was passed. Meanwhile, on 1 February, France had declared war on Britain and Holland. Holland was rapidly overrun. The United Irishmen began to look to France for help, and Dublin Castle to look ever more carefully at the United Irishmen. In July of 1794 Robespierre was beheaded and the worst of the Terror was over. This, however, was not immediately realised, certainly not by Tone who, on advice, had left for America in May of 1795. In February of 1796 he arrived back in Europe, but now it was to France where he had come explicitly to organise French military support for a revolution by the United Irishmen. He was wearing a Jacobin cockade in his hat, but this he rapidly removed.

Carnot and Hoche naturally saw the situation the other way about. They received Tone and noted what he said. Plans were already under way for an invasion of Ireland, and a rising of the populace could only help this undertaking. Tone probably exaggerated the number of United Irishmen who had been recruited into the movement, but certainly even the true figure was very large and, in general, very ill-armed. In Catholic Ireland the bishops and the clergy knew the atheistical content of the French Revolution, but the simple countrymen believed – despite what their priests might say – that the French were coming not only to destroy the English, their clergymen and the hated tithes, but also to restore the old religion. In any event it came to nothing.

A large French French fleet, with Tone aboard, sailed into Bantry Bay in December 1796. Waiting for his commanding general, Hoche, the senior officer, Grouchy, did not disembark at once. Hoche had, in fact, been blown way off course, and two days later a rapidly worsening storm arose. It reached near-hurricane force, and Grouchy saw no choice but to cut his cables and let the storm carry his ships back to France. Had Grouchy landed, there was precious little to stop him from marching straight to Dublin, to the applause of the Irish people.

The Castle was badly frightened, as were the landlords. Most of the United Irishmen's leaders were known to the government and they were now arrested, although Clare almost implored Lord Edward to leave the country. As for their followers, nicknamed Croppies because they wore their hair short in imitation of the French revolutionaries, a veritable reign of terror was imposed by the British General Officer Commanding, a bad soldier named Lake.

First in Ulster, and then throughout Leinster and Munster, he used the most cruel forms of torture to extract not merely information but also such weapons, usually pikes, as the Croppies might possess. This went on for over a year, until the United Irishmen became an unled mass of almost unarmed men, bitter and filled with hatred.

In 1797 a second expedition, organised now by Bonaparte, set sail in what was virtually the whole Dutch navy. They were rapidly blown to bits by Admiral Duncan's men o' war at the Battle of Camperdown. And even after that, Pitt could spare few troops for Ireland, since Bonaparte was massing an Armée d'Angleterre in the French Channel ports, together with troop-landing craft and a naval escort. Nor did he take Tone or Tandy, who was now also in France, into his confidence when he decided that an invasion of England was too dangerous and turned his eyes to Egypt, and eventually India, instead.

It is not the purpose of this writer to tell again the story of the '98. Without any central leadership the counties rebelled in sequence, the Ulster Protestants last of all and then for a mere three days, since they had heard correctly that in the south it had become a sectarian war and their co-religionists were being murdered by a mass of peasants, often led by priests. It was all put down quite quickly, when the very capable General Cornwallis arrived to be both Viceroy and commander in chief.

After the mass uprising had been crushed, a small French force arrived at Killala, in the extreme northwest, won a battle, but found the Irish peasantry useless as soldiers and soon surrendered. With another French general named Hardy was Wolfe Tone, who was arrested, tried for treason, and condemned to death. He forestalled his execution by committing suicide in a Dublin prison.

An even smaller force landed, with Napper Tandy. He was so drunk that he had to be put back on ship, and the last French expedition sailed away from Ireland.

All this happened beneath the ominous shadow of reports that Bonaparte was embarking his Armée d'Angleterre at Toulon, with destination unknown. It was only when the news at last came on 2 October of Nelson's astonishing, total victory at Aboukir Bay that England felt reasonably safe, at least for the time being. Many years later, Napoleon on St. Helena was to admit his mistake and say that he should have gone to Ireland.

The only result of all this slaughter – between 20,000 and 30,000 Irishmen had been killed – was to foster sectarian hatred, which had seemed to be dying down, and to make it inevitable that the government of Ireland be reorganised. For several years an Act of Union had seemed the last resort. Now it appeared to Pitt and the Castle as the only contingency left. It had, after all, worked with Scotland. The Ascendancy might object, but they could be bribed with money and titles. Complete emancipation of all Irishmen would give satisfaction to the Roman Catholic middle class, and this was promised. The Act of Union was passed through a lethargic Irish parliament in 1800.

Unfortunately King George III was, at the time, more or less sane, or at least as sane as he had been when he lost the American colonies. His obstinacy was now almost beyond belief. To give total emancipation to his Roman Catholic subjects would, he said, be a violation of his coronation oath. He said it again and again.

And so an Act of Union was passed in which most of the Irish population, who then numbered perhaps a quarter of the population of the whole, new United Kingdom, had no representation in Parliament. Throughout the nineteenth century, Ireland remained in fact a colony while in theory an intrinsic part of the United Kingdom. As Abraham Lincoln was to remark, no nation could hope to survive 'half-slave, half-free'. The Irish were not slaves, but most of them were not allowed to participate in legislation for some thirty years, and by then the purpose of the Union, the destruction of Irish nationalism, could no longer be achieved. Jacobinism would probably have been worse.

What, then, was achieved? The answer is hard to find. Certainly sectarianism, particularly in Ulster, and dislike concerning the payment of tithes in all Ireland, increased, but that might have happened in any case. Irish nationalism became, at times and among a small if conspicuous minority, tinged with social revolutionary republicanism, as it is today in the I.R.A. But such might have occurred had there been no '98 and even no Act of Union.

In his one famous poem – famous at least for its first line – John Kills Ingram (1823–1907) wrote in 1843:

> Who fear to speak of Ninety-eight?
> Who blushes at the name?
> When cowards mock the patriot's fate,
> Who hangs his head for shame?

The answer to these rhetorical questions is, well, nobody. If nobody talked much about '98 until the members of the Young Ireland movement decided to celebrate it at about the time Ingram wrote his poem, it is because in an Ireland dominated by that great man of peace, Daniel O'Connell, there was very little to say, certainly nothing more by Ingram, who devoted a long life to scholarship in Trinity College, of which he became in the end vice-provost.

And what about figures in the Irish patriots' pantheon? Who knows or really cares about Napper Tandy, and if everyone knows his name that it is because someone 'took him by the hand' in that fine song *The Wearing of the Green*. Even Wolfe Tone himself, recently immortalised in a remarkably ugly piece of sculpture on St. Stephen's Green and christened by the irreverent Dubliners Tonehenge, no Irish politician of any party seems able to make a speech without some reference to him. Yet for nearly half a century after his death he was forgotten. Nobody even knows for sure where he is buried. Annually those same politicians and many other make a pilgrimage to his father's grave in Bodenstown, because it is assumed, on no evidence, that he was buried there, since he is not known to have been buried anywhere else. Lord Edward is remembered for his good looks, his charm of manner and his beautiful French wife. As a political leader he was a complete failure, and in any case was dead before the '98 erupted. Who else? Does anyone who is not a historian even know who Henry Joy McCracken was? Yet he perhaps, more than Tone or Tandy or Lord Edward, might have changed Ireland for the better. But then Irish history, more than the history of most countries, is intermingled with mythopoesis.

NOTES

1 There was never an established Church of Scotland. The Welsh bishops of the Established Church were under the control of Canterbury. In the course of the eighteenth century the Welsh became predominantly Wesleyan Methodists. In Scotland (the only part of the United Kingdom exempt from the payment of tithes in that century) the Highlanders were, in general, Roman Catholics, the Lowlanders Calvinist Presbyterians. It is curious that among the Celtic peoples of the British Isles no matter what form their religion took, a high degree of puritanism prevailed. One possible explanation of this may be that the Celtic peoples were more hot-blooded in the lusts of the flesh and were tinged with a psycho-physical manic-depression, both of which needed to be held on a tighter spiritual rein by their priests or pastors if stability were to be preserved – in contrast to the more stolid nature of the basically Anglo-Saxon English. Such vast generalisations must, however, be made with every possible reservation.

2 See the contribution by Maureen Wall to *The Course of Irish History*, ed T. W. Moody and F. X. Martin, and her monograph entitled *The Penal Laws, 1691–1760*.

3 For a study of the period, W. H. E. Lecky's *History of Ireland in the Eighteenth Century*, first published in 1892 (and republished in recent times by the University of Chicago Press), is still the wisest and deepest. I have drawn on the revised edition of 1902.

4 The gombeen man was seldom, if ever, a Jew. There were, and are, indeed, very few Jews in Ireland. During the Russian pogroms of 1881–1901 some 4,000 arrived, entirely in the cities, and there were mild outbreaks of anti-semitism in Cork and

Limerick, always among the roughest cities in Ireland. But in Dublin, in 1876, a Jew named Harris had been elected Mayor, though he died before he could assume the office. Robert Briscoe (1895–1969), another Jew, was Mayor of Dublin in 1956 and elected again in 1969. Dr. Barnardo's father was a Dublin Jew named Barnardi. Many Irish patriots, recognising the similarity of the plight of the Jewish emigrant to that of the Irish, spoke out against anti-semitism: these included O'Connell, Justin McCarthy, Parnell and J. E. Redmond. On the other hand Arthur Griffith, the original founder of Sinn Féin, was mildly anti-semitic. In 1904 it was a Redemptionist priest, a certain Fr. Creigh, who had preached against the Jews in Limerick and stirred up anti-semitism there. Michael Davitt protested, but 80 of the 120 Jews sold their little shops and departed. For details of this see *The Jews of Ireland*, by Louis Hyman.

5 For a history of the Ulster problem the reader is referred to my own book *Red Hand: the Ulster Colony*. In the decade since that book was written the situation has, of course, deteriorated very greatly, while remaining in essence the same.

6 The version of this *Autobiography* – which is in reality a biography based upon Tone's diaries and writings, edited by his son – on which I drew is that edited by R. Barry O'Brien.

19

DANIEL O'CONNELL

The Flight of the Earls in 1607, of Sarsfield and the Wild Geese in 1691, the steady drain of emigration to join them throughout the eighteenth century, the complete failure of the '98 resulting in the death or disappearance by transportation or flight of its generally middle class leaders, the suicide of Grattan's Protestant parliament in 1800, all these dissimilar tragedies had the same effect of depriving the Irish of leadership from within their own people. Even the Non-conformist preachers were bought out of any attempt at a renewal of United Ireland. In 1802 the government of the United Kingdom agreed to pay each Presbyterian minister £50 to £100 p.a., provided they were satisfied concerning his loyalty. They almost invariably were, and so the gulf between Protestants (with their Orange Lodges) and Roman Catholics, particularly in the north, widened. Throughout nineteenth century there were sectarian riots, often causing deaths, in Ulster on the average of one every seven years. In the early years of that century Westminster was prepared to vote for a familiar scheme which would, in effect, have given the Roman Catholic priesthood and their flocks all that was won by the Emancipation Act of 1829, but with one proviso. Pitt had, verbally at least, promised emancipation as the palliative of the Act of Union. With his death in 1807, renewed attempts to pass the necessary legislation got under way, led by Henry Grattan who was by then a United Kingdom M.P., but one clause was unacceptable to the Roman Catholic bishops, and this they made clear in 1810. London had no wish to appoint Roman Catholic bishops, who had been and are invariably papal appointments, but they wished to preserve for the monarch (that is to say for the government) a right to veto such appointments. Clearly the Irish bishops could not accept, nor be bribed into accepting, the right of any man to overrule the pope in any circumstances. Grattan, who had consistently advocated Catholic emancipation throughout his long public career, first in the Irish and now in the United Kingdom parliaments, introduced a bill in 1813: it was almost passed when Canning added a clause concerning the royal veto. Grattan thereupon dropped the bill. In 1814 Monsignor Quarantotti (acting for the Pope, who was still a prisoner of Napoleon's in France) came out in favour of the veto, but by then the Catholic party in Ireland had split between Grattan, Lord Fingall and other remnants of the Catholic aristocracy in Ireland on the one hand, and Daniel O'Connell on the other. In any case after Waterloo Pius VII returned to Rome and cancelled Quarantotti's decision. O'Connell spoke for the people, those others for the peers and the M.P.s. We can here see, in religious matters, the displacement of power by the oligarchy to power by the people, largely led by their priests. The eighteenth century was truly dead, and the nineteenth was being born, and in 1820 the great Henry Grattan himself died. By then O'Connell was providing the Irish with a new sort of leadership, and Maynooth was providing the priests who were to be, in many respects, his lieutenants.

But before embarking upon this new phase in the story of the Irish, there is one incident which, for its mythopoetic qualities, must be mentioned, even if merely as a pendant to the '98.

In 1795, hearing of disloyalty to the Crown among the undergraduates and perhaps some of the fellows of Trinity College, the Chancellor of the University, Lord Clare, carried out what is officially known as a visitation. Backed by the faculty and scholars he interviewed, personally and in public, each member of the college. Each had to swear an oath to answer all questions fully. This, Tom Moore (the poet and composer) refused to do. When Clare asked him his reason, the young man replied that he feared lest he be asked questions which might incriminate others. Clare agreed to put no such questions to him, Moore took the oath and was exonerated of being a member of United Ireland. When the name of Robert Emmet was called, there was no reply. He had gone underground, where he remained for many years. In 1803 he, and a few friends including his brother, made a histrionic gesture of rebellion. It had no possible hope of success, and Daniel O'Connell described the affair as a brawl, but it was one in which lives were lost, including that of the Lord Chief Justice. Condemned, inevitably, to death, Emmet delivered a most passionate, moving and patriotic address, now part of the Irish heritage. He was then publicly executed.

His brother escaped to America, where he enjoyed a long and successful career at the bar. His sweetheart, Sarah Curren, daughter of the famous barrister John Philpot Curren, married a British officer in Cork and moved to England, where she died in 1808, a very different tale from the love-lorn maiden, *Far from the Land*, of Tom Moore's famous song. This song, however, *should* have been true, in that romantic age. Unfortunately there is little that the most skilful romantic poet can extract from the cold facts of history. Moore himself also removed to England, where in due course he achieved fame, fortune and the close friendship of Byron. It was no doubt Moore's accounts of Irish affairs that led Byron to write:

> I met with death upon the way
> He had the face of Castlereagh.

Somewhat later, in 1811 or 1812, Shelley, who had the not uncommon poet's wish to be a man of action, came to Dublin and rented upper rooms on Sackville (now O'Connell) Street. From these he scattered leaflets urging the Irish to rise up in arms in the name of religious freedom and repeal of the Union. Nobody, in or out of government, appears to have paid any attention to him or his leaflets whatsoever.

* * *

One figure dominates the Irish story from the time of the Union until the Great Famine that began with the potato crop failure of 1845. And Daniel O'Connell's background and upbringing are highly relevant to his politics.

The O'Connells were an old Irish family, aristocratic chieftains though never of the stature of the great Irish families such as the O'Briens or the O'Neills. It is perhaps this comparative obscurity, together with the geographical remoteness of their central base, Derrynane on the Kerry coast, whence it was easier to travel by sea to France than by road to Dublin in the eighteenth century, that had enabled them to survive the Elizabethan, Cromwellian and Williamite wars with this land, and the way of life of their clansmen, more or less intact. (To their east, on the Kerry mountains called the Reeks, the McGillycuddies were similarly fortunate.) In addition to the normal wealth derived from O'Connell land and fisheries, they profited from a brisk trade in smuggling. By the time Daniel, the future 'Liberator', was born in 1775 the landlords of English descent had no hesitation in buying their French silks and their brandy from smugglers or their middlemen. The O'Connells were well off.

Daniel's father, Morgan, played almost no part in his son's life. For his first four years he was boarded out with a peasant family, and we may therefore assume that his earliest language was Irish. He spoke it fluently all his life, and it was perhaps these earliest years that gave him a keen and profound insight into the mind of the Irish countrymen, then far and away the most numerous, and least politically powerful, of his compatriots. After returning briefly to his parents' home at Caherciveen, he was sent, more or less as foster-son, to his uncle Maurice, the childless head of the family who lived at nearby Derrynane. Whether this was a deliberate continuation of ancient Celtic fosterage or mere practicality, we cannot tell. Perhaps it was both.

This Maurice O'Connell, nicknamed by all 'Hunting Cap' since he wore that form of head-dress on all occasions, played a far more important part in Daniel's life than ever did his father. So, too, did another uncle, also named Daniel, who had gone to France to join the Wild Geese of the Irish Brigade in 1761. He enjoyed a distinguished military career, becoming a colonel at an early age and being ennobled as a French count in 1788. He was usually referred to, at least at Derrynane, with which he maintained close contact, as 'the Colonel', though in fact he ended his long military career as a lieutenant general under Louis XVIII and Charles X. Like so many of the Wild Geese, he had served with the British during the Revolutionary War, and it was only the French revolution of 1830 that led him finally to resign from the French army, perhaps the very last of the Wild Geese to wear French uniform. As not only a soldier but also a courtier under Bourbon monarchs, he could hardly accept to serve under King Louis-Philippe, the son of Philippe 'Egalité' duc d'Orléans (who had voted for his cousin Louis XVI's execution), and therefore the half-brother of the illegitimate Pamela de Genlis, wife to Lord Edward FitzGerald of '98 fame. In their different ways, and alien spheres of life, both Hunting Cap and the Colonel were proud men, fully aware of their station in society. In his dislike of Jacobinism, which they both shared, Hunting Cap was a keen supporter of the Act of Union, as indeed were the Vatican and the Irish bishops.

Young Daniel was taught in the hedge schools of the period, but Hunting Cap saw to it that his education was not neglected. Besides being steeped in Irish language and legend, he learned a very pure English, the language of the Derrynane household, as well as adequate Latin and even some Greek from his teachers. But Hunting Cap desired more for his nephews, and in 1790 he was sent to the Colonel, in France, for further and more formal education. He, and his younger brother Maurice, went first to Louvain, then in 1791 to the English school at St. Omer and in 1792 to Douai where there was a famous English seminary. The political situation in France was deteriorating fast, and at Douai the O'Connell boys, obvious *aristos*, were beaten up by a gang of revolutionary youths. The Colonel decided it was time they went. On 21 January 1793, the very day that Louis XVI was executed, they left France for England. Daniel O'Connell had seen bloody revolution (though not, as some have suggested, the Paris Terror) in a foreign country. He was to see it in his own, five and a half years later, and from these experiences as well as from the mouths of his uncles, he derived a profound and rooted hatred of violence in any form. It is perhaps this conviction that makes him, and his successors, such a relief in his country's sad and blood-stained history.[1]

In London, Daniel's younger brother joined the army and was soon shipped to the West Indies, where he died two years later. Daniel himself entered Lincoln's Inn as a member-student, and also in 1794 registered for King's Inns, Dublin, his obvious destination as a future barrister. In London he read that seminal book of the age, Tom Paine's *Rights of Man*, flirted with the ideas of Rousseau and the Encyclopaedists, and temporarily lost his faith. From 1796 until 1803 he described himself as a Deist. In 1803 he returned to the Church, but he was always careful not to confuse politics and religion, describing himself accurately on one occasion as 'a Catholic but not a Papist'. This could only appeal to the Irish clergy, who had always preferred not to be involved in the papacy's Italian problems, most of which in the nineteenth century were concerned with the nascent Italian nationalism and the existence of the Papal States. He was to maintain this attitude, and it is perhaps to him that the absence of sectarian emotions in most of Ireland can be traced. As his personal lawyer, he employed a Protestant. As late as 1836 he, Michael J. Quin and the Rev. Nicholas (later Cardinal) Wiseman founded a quarterly entitled *The Dublin Review*, a forum for Catholic writers on general topics and for religious polemics. When Quin withdrew from the editorship, O'Connell (then at the height of his reputation) suggested that a Quaker, William Howitt, replace him.

In 1844, when the revolutionary Young Ireland movement was beginning its advocacy of violence, O'Connell in his old age composed a proclamation for general distribution.

> I tell you solemnly that your Enemies, and the *Enemies* of Ireland are desirous that there should be a breaking out of Tumult, Riot or other outrage. Be you therefore perfectly peaceable . . . obey my advice. No Riot, no tumult, no Blow, no Violence.

This was the same man who had described Robert Emmet's attempted uprising of 1803 as 'a street brawl'. He had been admitted to the Irish Bar in April of 1798, and so he knew what he was talking about. He wanted, all his life, religious liberty for all. The Orange Lodges, particularly those in Ulster, therefore hated him and at least once burned him in effigy. On one occasion, when he was talked into preparing a sort of Pilgrimage of Grace to Belfast, he realised that this would be met by violence and that he could not answer for his supporters' reactions. He therefore called it off. Similarly, his Monster Meetings, attended by as many as half a million persons, were entirely peaceful. When the biggest that he summoned, to be held at Clontarf near Dublin in advocacy of repeal of the Union, was declared by the Castle to be illegal on the very day before it was due to be held in 1844, and when perhaps three quarters of a million people were already on the roads to attend it, he called it off. And that really marked the end of his successful political career, as he must have known it would. Three years later he was dead, in Genoa, on his way to Rome.

* * *

Forty-two years after O'Connell's death, that is to say in 1889, William Ewart Gladstone, who as Prime Minister had introduced his first Home Rule Bill four years earlier and who was to introduce his second four years later, took the opportunity to review, in *The Nineteenth Century*, an edition of O'Connell's letters. He wrote what was, in effect, an essay of the very highest praise: 'Almost from the opening of my Parliamentary life I felt that he was the greatest popular leader whom the world had ever seen.' He regarded him, he said, as greater among Irishmen than Swift or Grattan and comparable only to Edmund Burke.

The Act of Union had not been immediately unpopular either among the mass of the Irish people or among the Roman Catholic clergy. Indeed the poor and the downtrodden could scarcely imagine a worse rule than that they had suffered under, when their rulers were also their oppressive landowners and the supporters of a hostile Church to which they must pay tithes.

Tithes were the most immediate cause of dislike. Of a rising population in 1800 of at least 4,000,000, only 800,000 belonged to the Church of Ireland. To minister to their spiritual needs, the Church of Ireland required four archbishops, eighteen bishops, many deans and other clergy in every diocese, and fourteen hundred parish clergy. To support this army of clerics the peasantry had to pay one tenth, not of their produce but of that portion of the produce which did not go to the landlord. Similar extortions were made in the towns. But it was believed that this would all go, once the Act of Union was passed.

Economically, the earliest years of the Union were not too bad. For most of the first fifteen years the Continent was closed to Britain. Irish food was needed, as were Irish men to fill the battalions and man the ships of Great Britain. But Ireland was not, in fact, treated as just another thirty-two counties of the United Kingdom. The Westminster Parliament, in which sat some eighty Irish Protestants, passed discriminatory laws against Irish industries. Furthermore, Britain was enjoying, relative to Ireland, a great boom as the industrial revolution got fully under way. True, the poverty in English cities and villages was, by our standards, atrocious: by Irish standards England was a land of plenty. Ireland lacked the coal, iron and perhaps above all the risk capital that made an industrial revolution possible. Most of the Irish had only the land to live off, and as the population grew, the land per family became less and less, despite increasing emigration to England and then to America. In most of Ireland, and particularly in the west, families were reduced to a steady diet of potatoes and skimmed milk. And almost every year the potato was subject to blight, in some area or other, though never until 1845 in all Ireland at the same time. All visitors commented on the appalling number of beggars, everywhere. Only the drunken stupor of raw poteen could give a little respite. And then, with a blinding hangover, the wretched paterfamilias found the tithe-proctor at the entrance to his single room mud cabin. And gradually all this came to be blamed upon the Union.

In 1808 O'Connell became leader of the Catholic Committee, but there was little that this could do. In the panic that ensued after the '98, the strictest laws against 'combinations' were strictly applied. Dublin ceased to be a capital city and became a garrison town, with, it is said, a higher proportion of prostitutes than any in Europe. Disease of every sort was rampant, as was crime. Is it any wonder that men of property chose to sell up and move to England? True, the Catholic professional middle class was on the increase, but they seldom chose to identify themselves, save in church and perhaps at the races, with the beggars and thieves and whores all about them. At the beginning of his political career, O'Connell expressed grave doubts concerning the ability of the Irish to govern themselves. It is surely to his credit that he did not allow such doubts to hinder him in his search for peace and prosperity in a free Ireland. But first, he decided, must come Catholic emancipation. Once Ireland knew religious freedom for all, and had learned to know it by peaceful means, then would be the time to talk of real self-government. To attempt these two aims in reverse order might simply lead to another '98, if a failure, or a Paris Terror, if a success. Indeed, before the repeal of the Union he foresaw the abolition of tithes, universal suffrage, an elected House of Lords, the abolition of slavery, and the repeal of the Corn Laws.

There was little that the Catholic Committee could do, and in 1812 it decided to broaden its base by 'aggregate' meetings, to be addressed by O'Connell, his loyal lieutenant Richard Lalor Shiel (1791–1851) so far as emancipation went but in politics a Unionist, and others throughout Ireland. In that same year occurred the Magee case. John Magee (1780–1814), who owned and edited *The Dublin Evening Post*, wrote and published a pro-Catholic article which the newly appointed Secretary of State, Robert Peel, decided to use (claiming that it was a libel on the Viceroy, the Duke of Richmond), for his own political ends. O'Connell, by now a very successful barrister, defended Magee, also for political ends. (He and Peel were lifelong enemies: O'Connell referred to the austere English statesman, whose smile is said to have resembled a glint of sunshine on the handle of a coffin, as Orange-peel.) In his plea for the defence he not only quoted the whole of Magee's article, thus ensuring it a vast readership which it would otherwise never have had, but also engaged in demagoguery of language directed less at the (Protestant) jury than at the general (Catholic) populace, whom it delighted. It earned him, however, a mild rebuke from Hunting Cap who said, in effect, that he expected his nephew to speak in public like a gentleman and not a rabble-rouser. The Colonel, back in Paris, wrote to much the same effect. And, curiously perhaps, Daniel O'Connell took note of what they said, and henceforth he usually spoke with greater moderation. Poor Magee lost his case, but O'Connell was the darling of the Irish people. He had, in fact, discovered his true career.

An unfortunate side issue involved him in a duel. Duels were even more commonplace in eighteenth and early nineteenth century Ireland than in England or France. O'Connell had referred in rude terms to Dublin Corporation and a member of the board of aldermen challenged him. O'Connell had neither named the man, who was called D'Esterre, nor referred to him anonymously. He tried to appease the alderman, but to no effect. The duel took place and, to his horror, O'Connell's bullet killed him. He gave his enemy's orphaned daughter an annuity for the next thirty years, and when the widow became involved in a legal action he, probably then the most expensive barrister in Ireland, fought and won her case without charging any fee.

He was nearly involved in another duel with Peel, but Mary O'Connell (his lifelong wife and also his cousin) intervened, and it came to nothing. Duelling had always been illegal, but soon after this the law enforcement officers (the police force created by Peel and known in England as 'peelers') actually enforced this law, so that duelling soon disappeared from the English and even from the Irish scene.

It was a miserable scene. The end of the Napoleonic Wars in 1815 had seen a severe drop in the price of food, Ireland's main source of income. In 1821 and 1822 the potato crop failed in large parts of the country, and there was much starvation. In 1825 a Select Parliamentary Committee reported that in some provinces the land allotted to a farm worker, from which he was supposed to feed his family, amounted to as little as half an acre. Apathy prevailed.

Only one ray of hope lit the mournful Irish scene in 1823. Lord Mornington (the Duke of Wellington's elder brother) sat in Dublin Castle: of Irish birth and upbringing he could not ignore the misery of the Irish. But when the Duke became Prime Minister, he resigned, if only temporarily, for he knew that they disagreed concerning Catholic emancipation. (Many years before the Duke had sat in Grattan's parliament as Arthur Wesley, the original spelling of the name. John Wesley, the great Methodist preacher and reformer, was a distant relative.) And O'Connell had virtually abandoned his law practice in order to devote all his time to forwarding the aims of the Catholic Association.

He now solved the Association's finances in the most ingenious manner. Those members with money were asked to contribute a guinea a year: those without were asked to give one penny a month to their parish priests, all of whom were honorary members. With a population approaching seven million, this produced a sizeable income, out of which O'Connell paid himself what he had been earning as a barrister – £7,000 p.a. – and supported a small full-time administration. The rest went on charity, for the Association had categorised itself as such, thus gaining immunity from the 'anti-combination' laws. But the Association was really a one man band.

In a by-election of June 1828 he stood for Parliament for the constituency of Ennis, in Co. Clare, where his opponent was a popular landlord named Vesey Fitzgerald. Thus the issue was purely a religious one, for as a Roman Catholic O'Connell was not eligible to take a seat in the House of Commons. He was, however, elected, and the Duke of Wellington was far too sensible a man not to see what this meant. In 1829 he passed the Roman Catholic Emancipation Bill, which really gave the Irish all that they could aspire to, politically, within the Union. (The repeal of the Test and Corporation Act, in the previous year, had given the Catholics and Nonconformists much else.) There was, however, a sting in the tail. Enfranchisement had hitherto been limited to 40s. freeholders, that is to say to males owning property to that amount. The argument behind this is that unless a man has at least a small stake in the country, he has no right to help choose its rulers. This was now raised to £10, and with a stroke of the pen the majority of the emancipated Irish were immediately disenfranchised. Nevertheless it was a vitally important step, and one for which almost the entire credit must go to Daniel O'Connell.

He was the hero of the Irish Catholics, and of not a few Protestants as well, as he now turned his attention to repeal. But not for the first, and certainly not for the last time, in Irish history, victory resulted in a most vicious split among his supporters. Repeal meant little to the mass of the people, tithes a great deal. The Tithes War is generally dated as having begun in 1830, and to have gone on, in one form or another, until the disestablishment of the Church of Ireland in 1869. Its warriors had inherited all the tricks of the Whiteboys, killing tithe-proctors and landlords' agents, cruelly wounding their livestock, a war fought in darkness and with no real leaders. For such methods were of course anathema to Daniel O'Connell, yet it was hard to persuade the English and even many of the Irish landlord class that he had not only no responsibility but no real ability to curb such violence. He tried to divert the energy thus expended to repeal, and the Monster Meetings he now held would, at least to an outsider, indicate that he still had immense power, but he himself knew that it was not so.

All that he really achieved, as more and more Roman Catholic M.P.s appeared upon the benches of Westminster, was to start the creation of an Irish party. In return for small favours for Ireland, he could offer a few votes to Melbourne or Lord John Russell. He never, however, developed this political lever as Isaac Butt, and even more Parnell, were to do. It was a cynical manoeuvre, whether at parliamentary or constituency level, and Daniel O'Connell was not the sort of cold-blooded, scheming politician successfully to use it. He was far more at home orating, in his enormous overcoat or cloak, to a huge outdoor audience than whispering the right word in the proper ear at a corner of the corridors of power.

Surely one of the reasons for the peaceful nature of his Monster Meetings was his alliance with Father Theobald Mathew (1790–1856). On 10 April 1838, this most remarkable priest signed a pledge of total abstinence with the words: 'Here goes, in the name of the Lord.' His temperance campaign was almost unbelievably successful in a country seldom known for its sobriety. By 1844 it is believed that half the adult population had taken the pledge. A figure that cannot be disputed is that the revenue from excise duties on spirits had fallen from £1.4 million to £0.8 million. It is perhaps not surprising that the crime figures fell in proportion. Father Mathew worked closely with the Non-conformist temperance clubs, with whom he shared teetotal club-houses throughout all Ireland. He took no direct part in politics, but accepted Daniel O'Connell's warm friendship and admiration. 'Ireland sober, Ireland free!' was probably a slogan coined by the Liberator. We know that sobriety marked his Monster Meetings, which would almost certainly have been chaotic Donnybrooks on a gigantic scale, had it not been for Father Mathew's crusade.

Father Mathew took his movement to the Irish in England and America, also with considerable success. Rome offered him a bishopric, but this he declined for reasons of ill health. He returned to a very different Ireland in 1851, retired to live with his brother, and died in 1856.

The date of his statistical triumphs is 1844, as the reader will have noticed. O'Connell's last Monster Meetings were held at Dundalk, Navan, Tara again, Dublin, Cork, Wexford and Galway in 1845. In the spring of that year the potato crop looked remarkably healthy. But then their tops began to wilt, and when they were dug they were, or rapidly became, a putrid, stinking mess. The Great Famine had hit Ireland: the old Ireland, even the new Ireland of O'Connell and Father Mathew, were dead. From a population estimated at perhaps close on nine million souls in 1845, it had dropped to four and a half million by the end of the century, and only since 1961 has it ceased to fall and begun to increase in all Ireland. The Famine, starvation and the resultant emigration had reduced the population by one half in a decade or so.

This seems a convenient moment in Irish history to explain, in inevitable oversimplification, the attitudes of the Irish who desired independence, that is to say the repeal of the Union, and of the English governments who wished to preserve that Union, though in both countries the campaign had precedents long before the Union of 1800. However, it is of the last two centuries that I here write.

The British attitude and treatment of the Irish alternated between coercion and conciliation, between 'killing Home Rule by kindness' and filling the jails with rebels, guilty of treason-felony or worse.

Similarly the Irish, who wished to rule themselves, either resorted to violence (the United Irishmen, Young Ireland, the Fenians, the I.R.A.) or they attempted to achieve their aims through constitutional means (O'Connell, Parnell, Redmond). Often both methods were being tried simultaneously, nor did the Irish action or reaction necessarily correspond with the British offer of either stick or carrot. It is this absence of continuity in either country, and even necessarily of symmetrical action or reaction, that makes the history of Irishmen's attitudes towards the London government so difficult to grasp. From the Irish point of view, vacillation in London is almost equally incomprehensible. It was difficult to understand in 1845: it remains almost equally so today, particularly in the Six Counties of Ulster that are a province within, but not of, the United Kingdom. That both sides, that is the Irish and the English, accuse one another of duplicity goes without saying, though it is almost never attempted. That Irishmen and Englishmen of different persuasions accuse their compatriots of treason or cowardice also goes without saying, and is almost always equally untrue. The permutations of these – at least four – factors produce a well nigh innumerable series of similar or dissimilar problems. And it seems highly improbable that, on their own, any form of a solution can solve one or two of them without exacerbating others.

NOTE

1 There are many lives of Daniel O'Connell, as well as his own letters and other writings. Perhaps the most readable, and the least partisan, biography is modestly entitled *Daniel O'Connell, An Essay* by Raymond Moley. Dr. Moley was himself a very experienced politician, writing in extreme old age.

20

FAMINE

Europe reacted against the discipline of the Enlightenment, which catered admirably to man's or woman's desire for reason but which thereby pushed aside both the spiritual and the emotional, these being inaccessible to the firm rules of Reason. The political result of this reaction took two forms, primarily, of romantic nationalism, an emotional response that could give the satisfaction of action later; when its end had been achieved, this emotion was to be replaced, at least in the teachings of some intellectuals, by the equally dangerous theory of class warfare. Meanwhile the spiritual *lacuna* created by the post-Cartesians, first expressed in the violent anti-clericalism of the French Revolution, was to be filled, particularly in Protestant Europe, by a renascent puritanism, by respectability and by its handmaiden, hypocrisy. In Ireland, nationalism was first expressed by the Young Ireland movement, while Maynooth produced many priests whom one might call Jansenists. But it must be emphasised that both these forces, nationalism and strict morality, particularly sexual morality, were more the product of the *Zeitgeist* than of purely (or impurely) Irish creation.

Bismarck, Cavour, even Kossuth and Napoleon III were far more successful practitioners of nineteenth century nationalism than were Daniel O'Connell or the hydra-headed Young Ireland movement. In the first place, and very prominently, looms the question of a national language. In 1844 the great majority of the Irish people were speaking their own, ancient language but they were also in large measure illiterate. O'Connell, a fluent Irish-speaker, preached a doctrine also popular in Wales at the time: English was the language of the educated, of the law courts and of Parliament. Therefore the quicker the Celtic languages were abandoned, the better. And so it worked out, despite the lingustic nationalism of later generations: the native language has degenerated, both in form and geographically, until we have the paradox of a 'Welsh Wales' and an Irish *Gaeltacht* kept alive by various measures of artificial stimulus among a shrinking and not so well educated

The Glen of Aherlow, Co. Tipperary. Note the square fields, but above all the distant hills which seem to form the backdrop to almost every Irish landscape – blue, green, purple, grey, these gentle contours are perhaps the most striking and beautiful aspect of the Irish countryside *(Irish Tourist Board)*

The devotion of Irish pilgrims has not changed. This photograph, taken in 1980, speaks for itself

It is estimated that when Pope John II visited Ireland in 1979, some $2\frac{1}{2}$ million people attended his great open-air Masses. Perhaps the most spectacular, as it was the largest, was held in the Phoenix Park, Dublin, and is shown here (*Irish Tourist Board*)

Yet the Christian faith has not become omnipotent. These decorations to a holy well at Doon, Co. Donegal, contain rosaries and plastic madonnas, but much that is older

proletarian population or among patriotic and well-educated linguists. I am told that much the same applies in Scotland.

The nationalism of the nineteenth century required linguistic identity. For nations already established, such as France or Spain, Holland or Denmark, such an identity of language was taken for granted. Among subsequent nation states, whose evolution was the most important political event of nineteenth century Europe, the Germans went so far as to claim, in the end, that everyone who spoke their language was one of them. The Poles had both a language and a religion with which to identify themselves. The Italians, very unsuitably, invoked the history of Rome as a unifying bond between, say, Venice and Naples. But even in Sicily the Tuscan tongue was not totally incomprehensible. Only the Irish had no single accepted national language – this was to be invoked later as an adjunct to their nationalism, though never in all Ireland and never as a living tongue among the educated and professional classes – and, what was perhaps worse, very little national history save wars of rebellion against Britain. (The magical stone, it may be a meteorite, on which the Kings of All Ireland were to be crowned, had never been used for that purpose. Stolen by Edward Bruce, it became the Stone of Scone. Stolen by the English, it is part of the coronation ritual. The only monarchs of All Ireland to be crowned upon it have created a nice or nasty paradox, since they were the kings and queens of the United Kingdom, George IV, Victoria, Edward VII, George V and VI. The Stone, however, having been briefly purloined by Scots nationalists, remains in Westminster Abbey, while most of Ireland is of course a republic.)

O'Connell was a patriot – in this writer's opinion the greatest whom modern Ireland has produced – but he was not a nationalist. He advocated the repeal of the Union, and indeed went to prison in 1843 for so doing, but he would have been quite content to see an all-Ireland, as opposed to a Protestant-minority, government in Ireland and did not baulk at the prospect of the same German king or queen reigning over Britain and also over his own independent, self-governing country. At one time he even advocated a federal state, consisting of Ireland, Scotland, England and Wales, though with the burgeoning of the new British Empire this was not practical politics.

Young Ireland, on the other hand, while perfectly prepared at first to make practical use of the old warrior and of his far less formidable son, was the child of romanticism, not of Enlightenment,

and was therefore bound eventually to collide in bitterness with
O'Connell's point of view. Its birth may be dated 1841 and its
death the Famine of the late forties and its own fatuous attempt at
revolution in 1848. However, from its ashes there arose all the
violent revolutionaries of modern Irish history, the I.R.B., the
Fenians, the Invincibles, the I.R.A. of 1916–1922 and the I.R.A.
of today.

Its place of birth was the Historical Society ('the Hist'), a political
debating club in Trinity College, Dublin, founded under another
name by the great Edmund Burke in 1744, a society of which several
Young Irelanders were auditor or at least member in the late 1830s
and early forties. Trinity at this time was open both to Catholics and
to Protestants, and therefore so was 'the Hist' and Young Ireland.
In casting about for a history (that is to say: a legitimacy) they
therefore picked on the United Irishmen and perhaps above all on
an almost fictional Wolfe Tone. But in the half-century that was
passing since 1798, much had changed in Ireland. In particular the
Scotch–Irish of Ulster had even less wish now than they had shown
in the previous century to cast in their lot with what they regarded
as a backward, priest-ridden Ireland. The Orange Lodges had
acquired almost total dominance in Protestant Ulster and they were
soon to call themselves Unionists, for they would far sooner be ruled
by a Protestant parliament in London than by what must, demo-
graphically, be in due course a Roman Catholic parliament in
Dublin. This, of course, has never applied to *all* the Protestants of
Ulster, but it certainly did and does to the Presbyterian proletariat.
They did not want the Catholics to own farms, and to this was now
being added a wish that the Catholics should neither have jobs
in the growing shipyards of Belfast nor in the mills based on Londonderry. The Orange Order did not even wish Catholics to live in these
cities. The successors of the galloglasses, they were prepared to fight,
and did. For reasons of self-defence the Roman Catholics tended
more and more to create ghettoes for themselves in the cities. In the
country there was a Roman Catholic drift towards the west and the
south of the Province of Ulster, where they could find some safety in
numbers. And they too were prepared to fight for their homes. The
fact that a few middle class undergraduates of differing persuasions
were prepared to dream of an independent, united Ireland, and
very rapidly to gain control of most of the press in which to forward
their ideas, was a very long cry indeed from an always problematical
United Irish Movement. Yet as propagandists they were very good.

And it was on this fallacious, one might even go so far as to say mendacious, disinterment of quite recent Irish history that they built their short-lived edifice. In a time of intellectual drought, they could count the best of Irish writers, in prose and in verse, among their members.[1] For a good poet or journalist, facing almost no opposition, it is not always necessary to tell the truth in order to convince. And Daniel O'Connell was too old, too tired and too sick to shout them down. Indeed, when he made his last speech in the House of Commons, the other members could barely hear that once stentorian voice which, in its time, had been listened to by hundreds of thousands in the open air.

The attempted risings of 1848 and 1849 were both a complete fiasco, one of them being sardonically dismissed by cruel Irish tongues as 'the rising in the cabbage patch', which is precisely what it was. To have expected a sick and starving peasantry, anxious only to flee the accursed land, to follow Young Ireland's leadership, as their grandfathers had in some cases done, was an example of grotesque self-esteem. Indeed those who were grandsons of the men of '98 knew only too well what had happened to their forebears. The British government never took Young Ireland seriously, the leaders being usually sent to prison or transported. One did rather well in Australia, and accepted a knighthood. Another fought with the Confederate Army in America. A third, John O'Leary, lived to a ripe old age and inducted W. B. Yeats into the I.R.B. It was for Yeats' couplet, however, that he is best remembered:

> Romantic Ireland's dead and gone
> It's with O'Leary in the grave.

Young Ireland was, essentially, a futile copy of almost equally futile bourgeois revolutionary movements in Europe and of the Anglo-Irish Chartist demonstrations in Britain. If it had an intellectual concept, this was hardly Irish. In France, throughout that century, the thermometer of revolutionary thought gave the Presidency of its Second Republic to a famous Romantic poet, himself then middle-aged and writing far beyond the inspirations of his youth. Wordsworth, had he been so inclined, would have filled Lamartine's role well in England. In Ireland it was a gaggle of journalists and minor poets of whom only one, Thomas Davis (1814–1845), has achieved much posthumous praise, and even in his case more for his politics and propaganda than for his poems.

Throughout Europe the bourgeois 'revolution' of 1848 was, at its best and most successful, little more than a deathblow to feudalism. Karl Marx recognised it, quite correctly, as a transference of power into the hands where economic power already lay. His error was in the assumption that it would be succeeded in the most successful capitalist states by a transfer into the hands of the working class, from which the surplus values enjoyed by the bourgeoisie derived. In Ireland, however, the Famine put paid, for at least a generation, to Marxist, Rousseau-ist, or indeed any other form of revolutionary action. For the Famine was indeed a stunning blow. Among semi-educated Irishmen it is, to this day, held to be the most wicked example of English crimes against the Irish people, worse than the Elizabethan wars, worse even than Cromwell, worse than the Penal Laws. But was it?[2] Were the English to blame?

From early in the previous century there had been repeated failures of the potato crop from a number of causes, in Ireland, such as dry rot and curl and even the fluctuations of the Irish weather (for none of which London could surely be held responsible) and the crop failed in various districts of Ireland: 1728, 1739, 1740, 1770, 1800, 1807, 1821, 1822, 1830, 1831, 1832, 1834, 1835, 1836, 1837, 1839, 1841, 1844. Few of these failures were more than regional and none total.

Furthermore, the population of Ireland had exploded, by a figure which Cecil Woodham Smith estimates at 172% between 1779 and 1841, the first reliable census, also of 1841, being almost certainly an underestimate at some 8,000,000: by the time the Famine struck the population of Ireland was probably somewhere between nine and ten millions. The population of England and Wales had meanwhile increased by about 88%. The Irish had very little in the way of medical centres, particularly in the west where the population explosion was greatest, and until 1838 no Poor Law to provide for the totally destitute. Therefore such land as the Irish might obtain, by conacre or any other means, was subdivided again and again among their children, and this process had been going on for a long time. It was the fallible potato that made this possible. A family, in a good potato year, could live off 'lazy bed' potatoes grown on as little as three acres of land. Potatoes, however, do not keep, and if the family was evicted for failure to pay the rent (usually in the form of grain) or if the potato crop failed, the result was starvation. Many landlords constantly threatened eviction, as the only way of extracting rents, but few carried the cruel process through. Meanwhile for their tenants wheat or barley was not a food but was the rent. Indeed in the west the Irish forgot even how to grind grain into meal. In the wildest parts, where they did not farm for a landlord, they had also forgotten the elements of ploughing and sowing, for 'lazy bed' potatoes required only a spade and a few days' work in the year. Potatoes and skimmed milk formed their well-balanced, if monotonous, diet. They had almost no knowledge of money and there are cases of a labourer, who happened to have acquired a five pound note, pawning it rather than spending it, thus giving the interest to the hated 'gombeen man' who might let him have a little food on credit in a bad year. But each year before the Famine some two and a half million beggars were added to the already enormous begging population, between the finishing of last year's potatoes and the harvesting of the new crop. Such was the poverty in the west that fishermen had no incentive to fish the abundant herrings: they could not afford to pay the gombeen man for the salt with which to preserve their catch. Yet those who survived, and increased in numbers to such an astonishing degree, seem to have been both healthy and happy. It is not in such a population that a romantic revolutionary movement will find recruits. The relationship between rich and poor, between the landlord class and the rural proletariat, was probably more remote, and especially in the west, than at any time in recorded Irish history.

How much were the English, and specifically their elected U.K. government, to blame for the truly atrocious misery, how much the landlords – in popular legend not infrequently or quite incorrectly confounded with the Parliament at Westminster – and how much the unanswering dead? Statistics are here even less useful than usual. Certainly we know that within a generation the population of Ireland was halved, and within a century reduced to what it had been before the 'explosion'. This was due, in large measure, to emigration, particularly to the United States via Canada, at first in the hideous 'coffin ships' of legendary truth. They, and their descendants, have preserved a picture of famine atrocity that has served to finance every anti-British movement and that has always affected Anglo-American relations at the highest levels of government.

But to what extent, to what even approximate extent, were the British government to blame? The answer to this question is almost entirely dependent on another: how much is, or should, any government be responsible for the welfare of the citizens? In the mid-nineteenth century the dominant political ideology put this at the minimum. Until very recently, in the late twentieth, the reverse has been accepted doctrine, at least among intellectuals. Yet it is surely fatuous to expect that the Peel administration of the early 1840s should have worried itself about the way of life of unnumbered and voteless persons living in the almost roadless wilderness of Mayo or Sligo. Situations of extreme crisis, as Ireland was to become, may have called for drastic action even then, and so it did though to an extent that a century later was regarded, by Englishmen, as totally inadequate. Meanwhile a much greater shift in the British economy was producing views that might have been productive of revolution (the Chartists) and thus of civil war. The most responsible English politicians were entirely aware of this crisis in Britain's future.

The Corn Laws had been devised to protect English agriculture by taxing imported basic foodstuffs to a level that did not make American or other foreign wheat competitive economically with home-grown crops. The Corn Laws applied, of course, to Ireland as part of the United Kingdom, but could hardly have been repealed unilaterally even if Grattan's parliament had still sat on College Green. Meanwhile the enormous surge of the industrial revolution had called into existence in Britain a vast urban proletariat which, by the accepted doctrine of the age, had to be fed as cheaply as possible if wages were to be kept low and the mills of heavy and light industry to flourish. This could not happen without the repeal of the Corn Laws, while in an open market it was then believed the British farmers could not compete with the huge, new crops from the Dakotas and elsewhere. It then seemed – erroneously as it happened – that the great traditional power of land was headed for a direct collision with the new and increasing power of industry. Karl Marx, who never visited a factory, from his table in a Soho pub saw it coming and, beyond it, the successful revolution of the urban proletariat against its exploiters, the new bosses. Benjamin Disraeli, from the diningrooms of the old aristocracy, saw much the same, and decided that the ominous proletariat could be cynically persuaded to support the older order. In England the Chartists, who were that proletariat, seemed to be far more powerful than actually they were. An argumentative Irishman from the County Cork, F. E. O'Connor (1794–1853) became their leader and led them to their failure of 1848 and himself to a lunatic asylum four years later.

Peel, the Tory Prime Minister in 1845, had been for at least three years considering, ever more seriously, the need for repeal of the Corn Laws, though his party represented above all the landed interest in England and Ireland, and even within his cabinet such a possibility was viewed, by almost all his ministers, with emotions ranging from distaste to horror. Were there to be famine in Ireland, it would be tampering with the accepted economic ideology of the age – to which Whigs and Tories alike subscribed – to interfere with the workings of the free enterprise market by the distribution of free food in Ireland, even were such food available rapidly and in bulk. The nearest that he dared approach such a heresy would be to cheapen the price of basic foods, and that could scarcely happen only in one part of the United Kingdom. Assuming that the threat of famine was very real – and many anti-repealers believed it was being exaggerated for political purposes – public works and the repeal of the Corn Laws were the only palliatives. Both were tried, but too late. Yet as early as the autumn of 1845 Peel, as well as certain landlords and their agents, had begun to buy Indian corn in fairly large quantities. Peel, without awaiting Treasury approval, had told Baring's, the bankers, in November to buy, secretly, £100,000 worth of Indian corn in America. He did this without first going to the Treasury, thus avoiding red tape and ideological dispute.

He chose corn because it was the cheapest food available. Also, since it was not usually sold in Europe, its distribution to the Irish would not interfere with any normal market. However, since the value of the potato crop lost in 1845 has been estimated at no less than £3,500,000 in the currency of the day, this, together with the smaller reserves of food bought by some landlords or their agents, could scarcely affect the famine at all. Without awaiting the repeal of the Corn Laws a Relief Commission for Ireland was appointed, modelled on that created for Irish Famine Relief in 1836–1839. Since state charity was anathema to the doctrinaire Treasury, in particular to Charles Edward Trevelyan (in effect its permanent head) and to the principal economic adviser to the government, Nassau Senior, public works had to be organised on a massive scale to provide financial relief to a people who had little idea of money at all, and no shops in which to spend it. This took the form of road building above all, and Ireland, which had always suffered from a dearth of roads, soon had almost too many, some leading virtually nowhere. Poorhouses, too, had to be built in large numbers for those too weak to work owing to starvation and its handmaiden, typhus. The slowness with which these rather feeble attempts to deal with the horror were put in motion meant that during the winter of 1845–1846 perhaps as many as a million people died or emigrated. Nassau Senior estimated that, in any event, there were a million Irish too many.

But, for the Irish, perhaps the most bitter memory was to be the export of food from Ireland throughout the Famine. As has been explained, the Irish countryman grew wheat and tended sheep or cattle wherewith to pay his rent. Undoubtedly many landlords used this food to feed their tenants: it is equally beyond doubt that many continued to export it. In the west and southwest, which were the worst hit, landlords were rare or even non-existent. Had all the food in Ireland been simply given to the people it would still not have compensated for the potato crop. However, it is ineradicable folk memory that the English, in the form of 'planted landlords' many of them absentees, exported food while the Irish starved to death. The fact that many good landlords ruined themselves in helping the people with food or with money to emigrate plays no part in this collective memory, particularly perhaps among those who emigrated during these frightful years. The situation became, inevitably, simplified to a formula: the English created the Famine and then watched the Irish die. For in 1846 the potato crop failed again. And the 'coffin ships' continued to carry the sick, the dying, often the dead, in the most appalling conditions to Canada, since the United States would not allow direct entry to these horrible, overcrowded vessels. It was only in the 1850s that Ireland began, very slowly, to recover. But the flood of emigration continued.

Since the potato blight had also hit America and the Continent of Europe, how could any United Kingdom government have fed the starving population, particularly those in or from the west? Ideology forbad massive public charity, even if the English had been prepared to feed the Irish and grew sufficient food so to do. Nor did the English like the Irish, whom they regarded as dirty, feckless and rebellious. We can detect a faint parallel today in Poland and Russia. Owing to the dictates of Marxist–Leninist ideology, the Soviet Union cannot even feed itself: why should it feed its Polish 'colony'? According to the prevalent Communist theory Poland, which in pre-Communist days was a net exporter of food, should be able to feed itself. The Polish hatred of their Soviet conquerors has roots deep in the history of the two countries, as had the Russian contempt for Poles. True, the food shortages in Poland are, at present, scarcely comparable with the Irish famine. However the Irish tragedy was not man-made. Yet it could no more be cured without a basic change to the free enterprise market system, than can food shortages in Eastern Europe be righted without scrapping the very basis of the Communist political system with regard to the nationalisation of the land. It is safe to say that the Poles blame the Russians and their measures for empty shops and long queues, just as the Irish blamed and still blame the English and their 'rooted garrison' of landlords for the Famine. While in Ireland, hatred of the English has almost vanished, among the descendants of the immediate Famine victims who survived in America, it too has survived, and any anti-English movement can still rely on fairly massive support from the Irish–Americans.

Although it is not the purpose of this book to discuss the Irish diaspora (perhaps the greatest apart from the Jews) there is another fact that casts light on the Irish in Ireland immediately before the Famine. On their tiny plot of land, the Irish countryman usually only knew how to grow potatoes in 'lazy beds', his wife only how to boil them. She did not know how to grind wheat or corn into flour, and lacked even the simplest tools for this purpose. Her husband, unless directly employed by a landlord, did not know how to plough, sow or tend the land: the only instrument he or his forebears had ever handled was a spade. True, the peasant's cry in Ireland, as in Russia in 1916, was for more land of his own. Yet when the Irish emigrants reached America in and after the Famine, with a whole empty continent in front of them, they did not, like the Germans and Swedes and even Italians, go west. They remained, huddled, in the appalling slums of Boston, New York and Philadelphia. There were, of course, many exceptions, but the rural Irish populace that escaped the accursed land became the urban proletariat and, quite rapidly, its saloon-keepers, capitalists and politicians. To give a family from the Burren or from Connemara a farm of, say, three hundred acres in 1850 would have been in most cases futile: they quite simply would not have known what to do with it. Only quite slowly, with the Encumbered Estates Act and the Land Acts of 1881 and 1891, did Ireland become in large measure a country of self-supporting farmers, while emigration remained the safety valve against any future population explosion.

There is such an explosion going on at present. It is said that half the population of the Irish Republic is under twenty-five years of age, but the safety valve has been sealed down by mass unemployment in Britain and America. It is not for this writer to attempt to foresee what this will mean. We cannot even be sure that the current Welfare State ideology will be, in a crisis, more successful or less harmful than nineteenth century economic liberalism or twentieth century state capitalism calling itself totalitarian communism.

The Famine destroyed the Ireland that had been growing since, perhaps, the Elizabethan wars and certainly since the Williamite reconquest. Yet it had destroyed only about one half of the Irish – and that over a period of years which followed the natural disaster – but it did have an almost immediate effect upon the survivors in Ireland. In the first place there was the sexual morality of the Irish.

I am here treading upon the most treacherous slopes which would have been equally so had I been alive at the times in question, and were I not writing about a nation that contained as many geographical and cultural fissures as did the larger, class-dominated society of nineteenth century England. (Though in Ireland, as will be seen, if it has not shown already, class was also important.) But first I should ask the reader to bear with me while I make a wild and sweeping generalisation.

The Irish, by comparison with their European and American neighbours, run to extremes. Briefly, they either work very hard or almost not at all. They seldom work at half-steam. Thus while a good Irish surgeon or pilot is second to none, a bad Irish doctor or lawyer cuts a deplorable figure. At a far lower level, Irish labourers in large measure built the British and American canals, roads and railways with great efficiency, speed and exertion. At home the Irish builder is often lazy and unreliable. For to work hard, in his own village or community, is not praiseworthy but rather shows a materialistic ambition for wealth, and therefore superiority, which can be resented. Perhaps what I have written earlier about the ancient Celts, whose values were accepted, if slowly, by subsequent immigrants or conquerors, helps to explain this obvious phenomenon noted by so many. To dismiss it as fecklessness, as has so frequently been done by English writers, is to show a profound misunderstanding of the Irish ethos.

Secondly there is little geographical unity of values in Ireland. Quite apart from the Scotch–Irish of Ulster, the attitudes, perhaps even the morality, of the stony, boggy west and southwest is different from that of the richer midlands, and both are at variance with those of the cities, in particular of Dublin. Under British rule, physical force imposed a measure of political unity, but this was always regarded as transient: the priests of the Roman Catholic Church imposed moral values which were, until very recently, acceptable to virtually all Catholics. But once again a reservation must be made. When Daniel O'Connell described himself as a Catholic but not a papist, he was speaking for almost all his compatriots. The greatest dogmatic link with Rome, the episcopal authorities, were never taken as seriously by the people as the bishops perhaps desired. When the secular aristocracy had fled, been debased or killed, it was to the parish priest that the Irish looked, and not always with love, for leadership, both spiritual, and, on occasion, political. The, usually Protestant, landlord class seldom succeeded – save as individuals – in replacing the old Irish aristocracy. And this was true of both the rural and the urban workers. Throughout the last century and this to have 'a brother, a priest' gave and gives great social status, even though the priest may be an economic burden on his family.

And this leads directly to sexual morality both before and after the Famine. Since the facts from which any generalisation can be drawn are, here, rightly enclosed in intimacy, the writer must draw upon very secondary sources. There are, however, a few sources that appear to be more direct. The tendency to puritanism of the Irish Roman Catholic clergy has already been mentioned. There is some evidence that the teachers at St. Patrick's College, Maynooth, were early on tinged with Jansenism, which can be described with some crudity as a puritanical movement within the Church. The teaching at Maynooth not only directly affected the future priests in their parishes – it was subsidised and to an increasing degree until 1869 by the British government – but even more so it affected the people through the Reverend Mothers and the religious orders which controlled almost all Irish education. Thus the Irish who passed their schooldays in the first half of the nineteenth century were made well aware of the sins of the flesh. Living, as so many of them did, in most crowded conditions, with the flesh of others always omnipresent, the only sure refuge, other than the nunnery, from hell-fire was early marriage. There have been many comments on the purity of Ireland's women. Nor can the Jansenists of Maynooth be held in any way responsible for the coffin ships of the Famine. Nevertheless the priests did, beyond doubt, contribute to the population explosion that had already occurred and that added to the misery. The girls had married at fifteen or so, the boys a couple of years later. The families of such marriages might be enormous.

The tendency of the Irish to exaggerate, to 'go the whole hog' has been mentioned. This also applied to the girls. Not all listened to the Reverend Mothers, and though each village might have its local prostitute, popularly known, at least later, as 'the village bicycle', the Roman Catholic countryside had little to offer to the 'fallen woman'. She might, on occasion, even be denounced by name in her parish church. Furthermore, her village was not prepared or able to support her. As already mentioned, Dublin was a garrison city, and soldiers want women. Nor was Dublin, for many, the ultimate ambition. Beyond lay London and much else. Some of Europe's most famous courtesans were of Irish origin, from *la belle Murphy* who so pleased Louis XV to Marie Gilbert (who called herself Lola Montez), a Limerick girl who made and lost fortunes and even thrones (1818–1861). The purity of Irish women, in Ireland, is probably true: the legend of the Irish barmaid who did more than serve drinks to her clients from St. Petersburg to San Francisco has also a credibility. The Irish indeed run to extremes.

* * *

There are two by-products of the Famine which should here be mentioned. The worst hit areas were precisely those where Irish was still the principal language. It was not regarded as an intrinsic part of the national heritage: as the previous chapter has shown, even so undoubted a patriot, and Irish-speaker, as Daniel O'Connell regarded it as an incumbrance to national renaissance. This psychological wound was exacerbated by the physical destruction of so many monoglot Irish-speaking communities in the Famine and the emigration that followed. The very sturdy attempts, after independence, with full governmental backing in the schools and the civil service, to revive Irish as the first language of the people have largely failed, save perhaps among extreme patriots and not always then. The Irish language has continued to decline. Worse, its study has come to be regarded as a chore by most of the people. They put up with the Irish lessons in school, but it seems to lead nowhere except into the civil service (for which it is compulsory) and once they have got the desired job as clerk or postman, most Irish men and women will forget the language as fast as ever they can.

A certain amount of literature has been written in the Irish language, but it is usually read mostly in English translation. Some of it is very good, but the great names of modern Irish literature are almost all those of Irishmen who wrote in English. It is principally among some scholars and some anti-English revolutionaries that the language was deliberately fostered. Had it not been for them it is fairly safe to say that the Famine would have killed it off by now, save in certain remote pockets of the rural population.

* * *

Another result of the Famine was the change in marriage patterns. Before 1845, and again since about 1965, the Irish married young or very young. In the intervening period they married late or, to a degree higher than anywhere else in Europe, often not at all. Neither the landlords nor their tenants wished ever again to see families attempting to survive on an acre or so of land. Most of the children would emigrate: one son would work for his father, and at his death he would inherit the small farm – and marry.

Yet the innate gaiety of the Irish, the singing and dancing and story telling, did not die out. Another horror, and in this case an entirely man-made one, was to deal a far more serious blow to the gregarious and natural cheer of the Irish: the international drivel of the television set. It has almost stopped conversation – though not drinking – in the pubs. 'Romantic Ireland's dead and gone.' In my own local pub I met a very old, very alert man who had known John O'Leary. In his opinion Yeats had got his dates wrong. O'Leary, the Young Irelander of long ago, died in 1907, but what Yeats regretted had by then been dead for half a century.

NOTES
1 See Dennis Gwynn's *Young Ireland and 1848*, which opens with an adequate bibliography.
2 The most scholarly history of this, known to me, is *The Great Famine* by Prof. Desmond Williams and Dudley Edwards. The most readable (which relies largely on that volume) is *The Great Hunger* by Cecil Woodham Smith. Liam O'Flaherty's novel, *Famine*, is the greatest work of a great writer.

21

PARNELL

No figure bestrides the second half of the nineteenth century in Ireland as Daniel O'Connell had the first. Charles Stewart Parnell (1846–1891) came nearer than any other but for reasons that were very different and with constitutional results that were, by comparison, almost negligible.

Indeed Ireland had been struck such a blow by the famine and by the emigration that ensued that it may be said, in many ways, never to have recovered. The advocates of physical force to free the country from English rule proved once again their ineffectiveness in the Fenian uprising of 1867 which in fact had been scarcely more an uprising than had the attempts of Young Ireland in 1848–1849. The Fenian newspaper, *Irish People*, revived in some measure popular patriotism, and the execution of two Fenian prisoners during a foiled prison break gave Ireland the 'Manchester martyrs' to add to the long list. But the activities of James Stephens (not to be confused with the poet of the same name), O'Leary, O'Donovan Rossa, Kickham and their followers did not cause the British enough anxiety to warrant repression on any large scale. The Irish Republican Brotherhood, the secret society dedicated to revolution, remained underground for nearly half a century.

Furthermore the I.R.B. suffered from the grave disadvantage of operating largely from abroad, particularly New York, whither John Devoy (1842–1924) had emigrated after serving a five year sentence for his part in the Fenian uprising of 1867. He there joined, and soon led, *Clan na Gael*, the powerful and (what was equally important) increasingly rich Irish–American association that funded newspapers and periodicals both in America and in Ireland. Every Irish movement for independence and for land reform was connected with *Clan na Gael*, with the obvious disadvantages inherent in long and slow communications.

Nor were conditions in the old country propitious to the use of physical force. The British not only used the country as one of their principal military bases (while Irishmen of military age were steadily leaving, to inspire all those songs of lament and departure we know so well) but had also established a formidable police force of a type unknown in the rest of the British Isles.

The Royal Irish Constabulary had been established early in the century and by 1867 was a formidable quasi-military force, armed and living usually in barracks. It had a high *esprit de corps*, was immaculately turned out, and had as little in common with the English bobby-on-his-beat as Bismarck's 'barracks police' had with the man in control of traffic at street corners. It still survives, in the form of the Royal Ulster Constabulary, and like them it was responsible primarily for anti-republican activities in the countryside.

A second police force, the Dublin Metropolitan Police, was an independent body but also under control of the Castle and was reponsible for law enforcement in and about the capital. Its first three divisions were each assigned an area of greater Dublin to police (this number was later increased) and its fourth, D-division, was a detective force directed against mafia-type criminal organisations and against anti-British political ones.

Behind this again was the Irish Special Branch (now known simply as the Special Branch) which was an active counter-insurgency agency. It was very efficient, and infiltrated almost all anti-British political movements. It has been said that wherever there was an Irish gunman there was also an informer. If not himself a member of the Irish Special Branch, he was almost certainly in its pay. Only the I.R.B. seems to have been immune to its activities. Thus was Ireland very effectively policed throughout the second half of the nineteenth century. Furthermore, not only was the population of Ireland shrinking in absolute numbers, but even more so in relationship to the population of the United Kingdom as a whole. Nor was that all. Antipathy between the Roman Catholics and the Protestants of Ulster had been increasing. There were, in Ireland, about one million Orangemen and families who were absolutely loyal to their concept of the Crown. Any thought of re-creating a United Irish Movement directed against London was, by 1867, quite ridiculous. Even among the majority nationalism was less violent: the ideal of Home Rule had replaced Independence, and Home Rule meant little more than a glorified provincial status (such as the Six Counties were to enjoy from 1920 to 1974) with no real control over national finance and none over defence or foreign policy.

No, the great Irish problem was no longer strictly political but economic. Irish energy was largely directed towards a solution of the land question (which scarcely affected prosperous Belfast) and this was far from insoluble. As already shown, often bad administration together with massive overpopulation overtaxed the system in force and, culminating in the Famine, had reduced rural Ireland, already poor enough, to penury. Many of the landlords were in debt so heavy that any prospect of solvency in the foreseeable future was nil. This problem was attacked, as it were, from both ends.

In 1849 the government had passed an Encumbered Estates Act allowing for the purchase of such estates for resale. Within ten years some £23 million had thus been paid. The old estates were sometimes broken up and sold on a long-lease system to tenant farmers. Unfortunately, more often they were bought by new English or Scots landlords as an investment. These often had even less interest in their tenants' welfare than had their predecessors. Since, despite the flight from the land caused by the Famine, its distribution often made little economic sense, and since the American Civil War had only postponed the massive importation of cheap wheat, the new landlords set about rationalising their estates – regardless of the people – drastically. This meant evictions on a scale far greater than had prevailed before the Famine, and eviction meant emigration or starvation.

Michael Davitt (1846–1906) had been a Fenian since the age of nineteen, and in 1868 he became organising secretary of the I.R.B. Arrested in 1870, he served seven years in Dartmoor Prison, and then went to America where he worked with John Devoy. In 1879 he returned to an Ireland where many of the countrymen were in revolt, ill-organised and using the usual traditional methods of killing landlords' cattle and rick-burning. That year saw the worst harvest in Ireland since the Famine. Davitt immediately organised the Land League to which almost the entire peasant population adhered. Its methods were simple: no rent and the boycotting of landlords and their agents. With Parnell's backing in the House of Commons, Davitt was almost immediately successful. (In 1880 there were 2,590 agrarian crimes, and between 1874 and 1881 some ten thousand evictions. This movement, heir to the Whiteboys and the Ribbonmen, was known as Captain Moonlight. Even the highly efficient R.I.C. could hardly arrest two or three thousand men a year, nor the prisons house them. A high proportion of the evicted were prime recruits for Captain Moonlight.)

In 1881 Gladstone passed his first Land Act: it was not satisfactory, and though amended at once, the land war continued until at last,

A barefoot pilgrim at Croagh Patrick in 1980. Note her feet

'Idlemen' have been referred to. They have not vanished. This photograph was taken at Macroom, Co. Cork, in 1980

Irishmen of tomorrow – youths in Armagh, 1980

in 1891, the Land Purchase Act arranged that tenants should eventually own the land they worked. Since then, and particularly since the improved bill of 1903, rural Ireland has been largely a land of peasant-proprietors, at least until very recent times, under pressure from the European Economic Community. But for a while it seemed that at long last the Irish land problem (and with it the 'Irish question') had been solved. And in the countryside William Ewart Gladstone became the most popular Englishman of all time, whose fly-specked photograph can still be seen in many a village bar.

* * *

So much has been written about Charles Stewart Parnell that I do not intend to do more than recapitulate his story here.[1] A good landowner in the County Wicklow, a Protestant educated in England, with a marked aversion to public speaking and, it is said, a poor orator, he was hardly the man to succeed O'Connell as 'the uncrowned King of Ireland', yet that is what, for a while, he became. His principal claim to fame is that he made of the Irish M.P.s at Westminster a coherent, obedient political force. It will be recalled that O'Connell had laid the foundation for this and he had been succeeded as leader by the pleasant but not very effective Isaac Butt. Another character of importance was Joseph Gillis Biggar (1828–1890), a Belfast man but a nationalist, converted to Roman Catholicism in 1877. He used his seat in Parliament frequently to hinder government, by filibuster means.

Parnell was elected M.P. for Meath in 1875 and with Butt's death four years later became the leader of the Irish party at the early age of twenty-three. His great-grandfather had been Chancellor of the Irish Exchequer, had opposed the Catholic Relief Bill of 1793 and the Union of 1800. His mother was an American, the daughter of Commodore Stewart who had fought the British at sea in the war of 1812. It has been frequently said that Parnell inherited strong anti-English tendencies from his mother, but this is now considered doubtful. They were never particularly close – she was an eccentric as were other members of the family – and the fact that he was educated in England, spoke and looked like an Englishman, would indicate that whatever anti-English feelings he may have inherited from her were negligible. That the Ireland of his childhood was grossly ill-administered was obvious, even to many Englishmen, and Parnell was Irish. His own estates in Wicklow were well run, as were those of Lord Powerscourt next door, and indeed the whole of County Wickow was, by Irish standards, prosperous. The condition of the greater part of the country was deplorable, which was not unconnected with the prevalence of absentee landlords, and when the boy returned to Ireland for his holidays the contrast with England must have been striking.

He was a new and very young M.P. when the situation was deteriorating into the Land War of 1879–1882 and the word 'boycott' was added to the English language. Captain Boycott, of Lough Mask House, Co. Mayo, personified the landlord class, apparently at its worst. In his district no man or woman would talk to him, no servant would work for him, no shop would deal with him. This new tactic was so successful that it was much copied. Furthermore the courts and government offices were boycotted in large parts of Ireland. Davitt's Land League established another precedent by setting up its own courts of law. Obstruction, rather than violence, was the essence of Parnellite tactics, and Parnell was President of the Land League.

The British response was initially clumsy. In October 1881, Parnell was arrested and lodged in Kilmainham prison, in considerable comfort be it noted, for he was after all a Member of Parliament. The Land War was aggravated, and in March of 1882 Gladstone, the Prime Minister, came as near as a man in his position could to accepting defeat. He and Parnell agreed the 'Kilmainham treaty', the Land War petered out and land reform was pressed forward. It was a great victory for Parnell, and perhaps equally so for Davitt, through the latter had wished to see the land nationalised rather than gradually distributed among those who worked it. Yet his Land War had changed the face of Ireland.

❋   ❋   ❋

Furthermore, and for the first time in a century, the Roman Catholic Church (though not its Primate, Cardinal Cullen) had largely abandoned its neutral or even reactionary stance and had come out for the Irish in their misery. The archbishop of Dublin had spoken, and the parish priests could now express what most of them must long have felt. Gladstone sent an emissary to the Pope, but he returned from Rome with, as they say, a flea in his ear. The papacy might commit itself to oppose atheistical Jacobinism, as it was to do to pagan Marxism, but it was not willing to use its influence in favour of a Protestant British government against an ill-administered Roman Catholic people.

Gladstone's Disestablishment of the Church of Ireland, in 1869, had given more temporal authority, and perhaps in some cases an increased sense of responsibility, to the Roman Catholic priesthood. From experience they had learned to be particularly circumspect in their handling of political issues. The cries from the Presbyterian north that 'Home Rule meant Rome rule' made them even more cautious than they might otherwise have been. And this was an issue that the Church preferred to leave to the politicians, above all to Parnell. The fact that he was himself both a landowner and a Protestant only served to strengthen his position.

As a politician, and indeed as a man, he was unscrupulous save in his devotion to the Irish cause, and with the land question on the way to solution this meant primarily Home Rule. In manner cold and haughty, in debate disdainful, logical and full of cool scorn, he was almost the opposite of O'Connell. He could treat the British House of Commons with the same casual contempt that Lord Clare had used to the old, corrupt Irish House of Lords. He was not a particularly brilliant speaker nor even a highly educated man – his widow has written that he read *Alice in Wonderland* over and over again, and very little else – yet his manner commanded respect and attention from Irish and English alike. He does not seem to have sought nor inspired affection or even deep friendship. And his love-life would appear to have been limited to his long affair with, and subsequent marriage to, Mrs. Katherine O'Shea. Since her first husband, always referred to by his quondam military rank of Captain, was among Parnell's principal political lieutenants and protégés (though a man of much smaller talent than he claimed) it is not irony that the careers of both men should have collapsed in the stuffy hypocrisy of the Victorian divorce courts: indeed it is perhaps surprising that Parnell's lasted for as long as it did, for his political morality, in an age when that noun was so highly prized, scarcely exceeded that of his private life. The fact that for a decade he was 'the uncrowned King' of Ireland is due in part to a long and rooted desire of the Irish people to have a king of their own: but in the shorter term it was due to Liberal expediency and to the apparent admiration of Gladstone, whom Parnell was at all times prepared to betray. After the divorce Gladstone's verdict only reinforced that of the judge: Parnell's public career was finished, and within a year he was dead.

His only real, public triumph was the 'Kilmainham treaty', which was a very important step towards ending the Land War. But in that 'war' the real victor, on behalf of the Irish countrymen, was Davitt. That Parnell should have given him the full backing of the Irish Parliamentary Party undoubtedly reinforced Davitt – and the Irish – but this indicates little more than Parnell's political sagacity. As President of the Land League, he rightly claimed and got much credit, but the battle was fought and won by Captain Moonlight, and the high degree of discipline shown by Davitt's followers. Had Parnell failed to give parliamentary backing to the Land League, his place in history would have been as obscure as that of Dilke or Butt.

His second claim to fame is that he somehow manoeuvred Gladstone and the Liberal Party into favouring Irish Home Rule, and that he used the Irish Party in the House for this purpose. This is twice untrue. Gladstone was quite capable of making up his own mind, after having consulted others whose opinions he respected. He once remarked to a friend of mine, the late Basil Throckmorton, that it was Lord Acton, the famous historian, who had persuaded him in favour of Home Rule. Nor was Cardinal Manning's influence in this direction negligible. That the votes of the Irish Party were a bonus to Gladstone's Liberal governments goes without saying – as does the fact that the Grand Old Man publicly acknowledged this – but neither their value nor Parnell himself persuaded him to put forward his two Home Rule bills.

The weakness of Parnell's party in public affairs was shown quite clearly when he attempted to adopt Tammany tactics (Tammany Hall was not an Irish invention, but was rapidly taken over by Irish–Americans) to the Westminster scene. Using the ubiquitous O'Shea, by that time almost certainly a *mari complaisant*, as his intermediary with Joseph Chamberlain, the radical Tory, Parnell attempted to see what the value of the votes at his disposal was to the Conservatives. The party of Benjamin Disraeli was not run on principles of high morality and did not rely on the Non-conformist vote. The only result of Parnell's political *léger-de-main* was, quite soon, to induce Lord Randolph Churchill to 'play the Orange card', in 1886, thus reinforcing a profound division in Ireland which already existed, and ensuring for close on forty years that Irish political issues would be decided by English Conservative–Unionists. Parnell's attempt at political thimble-rigging was thus of direct harm to his country, his party and ultimately to himself.

Besides, while the Liberal Party might use the Irish Party to forward their aims, the Irish could not get what had become their real prize and ambition, namely Home Rule. The House of Lords was not utterly conservative, with either a small or a capital C, but the Unionists could be sure of a majority there, and in the last century that meant that any bill passed in the Commons could be quite simply thrown out in the Lords, as were Gladstone's two Home Rule bills. Nor did Parnell have any influence in the Upper House. The Irish peers most certainly did not favour Home Rule, and a large number of English peers who owned estates in Ireland were equally reluctant to see any form of internal power revert to Dublin. Indeed, the Home Rule issue became, if not the very essence, at least the symbol of constitutional reform in the early twentieth century. Meanwhile, in Parnell's time, a Liberal-dominated House of Commons could pass Irish Home Rule bills until it was blue in the face, certain that they would be thrown out by the Lords. The British political system of the last century was not susceptible to Tammany methods. And if Parnell did not know this, then he did not know anything about the political system that his haughty, chilly manner appeared at times almost to dominate.

Two actions, one private the other public, had won him Gladstone's esteem. In May of 1882, that is to say the year after the 'Kilmainham treaty', the newly arrived Chief Secretary, Lord Frederick Cavendish, and Mr. Burke, the Under-Secretary, were murdered near the Vice-regal Lodge in Phoenix Park. Their murderers were members of a secret gang called 'the Invincibles' who had, apparently, no connection with the I.R.B. and certainly none with Parnell. He was, however, so horrified by this atrocity with which he knew his name must be connected as an Irish patriot leader, that he went to Gladstone and, with obvious deep emotion, offered to resign his seat and retire from politics. Gladstone was no doubt better informed about 'the Invincibles' than was Parnell, and was moved by the Irishman's altruistic gesture of self-sacrifice in their communal attempt to improve Anglo-Irish relations. He persuaded Parnell not to resign.

The second such episode began in 1887, when the London *Times* published an article inspired by Richard Pigott, a former nationalist, entitled *Parnellism and Crime* which linked the Chief's name with the diminished agrarian terrorism that he had absolutely renounced (though on occasion he had threatened to call on Captain Moonlight's assistance). Parnell sued *The Times* for libel. He also insisted on a parliamentary commission of enquiry. *The Times* published a letter, alleged to be by Parnell, approving of the murder of Burke. In fact it was all forgery, and Pigott shot himself. Parnell was completely exonerated in the spring of 1890.

In the autumn of that year Captain O'Shea sued his wife, Katherine, for divorce, naming Parnell as co-respondent. The case was not defended. There was really no defence possible. Mrs. O'Shea (who was never called Kitty and whose husband pronounced his name to rhyme with 'me') had been Parnell's mistress for many years and at least two of her children (the first-born died as an infant) were his. In return, to put it crudely, Parnell had given O'Shea political protection within the Irish Party. Though O'Shea's own sexual morals were negligible, Parnell preferred that the woman whom he addressed as 'Wifey' should not file a counter-case. Neither man comes out of the affair with any credit, but for Parnell it meant the end. Gladstone could not afford to lose the Non-conformist vote by an alliance with a condemned adulterer. In Ireland the majority of the priesthood was likewise repelled. After long and agonising debate the Irish Party dismissed him as its leader. He tried to fight back and failed. As soon as the law allowed he married Katherine, but within a year he was dead. The Irish Party was split, and with it the Irish people. Only very briefly, in the early twentieth century, did the old constitutional party play a part of any significance in Irish affairs, for the Parnellite split dismayed – disgusted would not be too strong a word – the Irish by its fruitless attempts to achieve any real means of political change from the Westminster Parliament, while Parnell's and Davitt's alterations to the land situation had taken much of the violence out of the countryside.

❊ ❊ ❊

The violence that in the 1890s was brewing in the cities, not merely of Ireland, hardly enters the history books until the page is turned to the next century. And of all the countries of Europe, Ireland was perhaps the least infected by the Marxist myth that on one fine, communist day, history would cease. If that myth, as propounded by the moderately well self-educated socialist James Connolly (1868–1916), a journalist and lecturer, was acceptable in Ireland, this may have been because the Irish were enjoying the period of superficial calm that appears when the tide is on the turn. In the 1890s, and for almost all the first decade of the new century, Irish parliamentary tactics were valueless: not only did the Irish Party remain in some measure split over the Parnell issue, but the huge Liberal majority of 1906 did not need their votes. The more important issue, land, was being solved. In a brief golden age the Irish saw their wishes being fulfilled without the need of violence. For a while their patriots were men of letters, historians, linguists, anti-quarians, playwrights, even athletes. And, for a while, they could coexist without hostility, even with mutual esteem, between Celt and Anglo-Saxon, since both were Irish. Joyce's *Ulysses* was almost contemporary with *The Real Charlotte* by Somerville and Ross: neither of these masterpieces of English literature is particularly kind, or unkind, to the Irish among whom both books are set. The ill-named 'Celtic twilight' seems to have been rather a robust mid-morning. The opening of Lady Gregory's and W. B. Yeats' Abbey Theatre, in 1904, hardly bespeaks the closing of the day.

It was the age of the camera, of the snapshot pasted by female hands into the family album. Can we glimpse a few? The Kildare Street Club, Dublin's most famous, and probably in the running for the most boring too, was then located at the corner of Kildare Street and Nassau Street, Victorian red brick without, tokens of Imperial grandeur within. On the far side of Nassau Street are the grounds of Trinity College. There cricket (the most English of all games) was played and thence the most forceful of all English batsmen, G. L. Jessup, hit a six through an *upper* window of the Club.

Another snapshot, and it is of the ladies playing croquet (always pronounced 'croaky') in long dresses that are rumoured to have permitted a certain *léger-de-pied*. The sun shines (did it never rain in those days?) and soon Bridie will be bringing out the tea, with cucumber sandwiches and cherry cake.

And then we are at the races, Galway, Leopardstown, Fairyhouse, the list is very long, and neither class nor origin is of any interest to anyone – this is no Ascot – as the silken jockeys crouch over their animals' necks and the crowd roars.

We turn the page and see, alas only in black and white, the huntsmen at the meet, stirrup-cup in hand, Galway Blazers, Scarteen Black and Tans, and in the upper corner the houndsman with his beautiful great brutes.

And the picnic on Dollymount Strand, from a humbler album perhaps, with the children clutching hard boiled eggs and sardine sandwiches as they stare at the mysterious little box that will, who knows?, immortalise them forever.

The suitable expressions of respect, even devotion, at Clonmacnois or Glendalough, with the birds wheeling above the holy place.

The ass has always walked the boreen. It is not worth a photograph.

That is Queen Victoria, the little old lady in black in the back of the carriage. She might be a hundred years old.

And those are her soldiers, the Leinsters, the Munster Fusiliers, the VIIIth Irish Hussars, the Ulsters, marching smoothly down to Kingstown, which some old-fashioned people called Dunleary, on their way to beat the Boers.

It was a fine heifer, my uncle's. It won a prize at the R.D.S. Spring Show in, I think, was it 1898?

No, I never knew Percy French myself, but of course a lot of my friends did. And Count John McCormack, how we all loved his marvellous voice, a great man too.

That Oscar Wilde business? Well, if you're asking me: I wonder if they'd have sent him to gaol if he hadn't been Irish? His father, Sir William Wilde, now there was a great man, a great eye-surgeon combined with a great antiquarian. As for his mother, well now, there were a lot of people admired Speranza. But if she hadn't dressed her son up as if he were a daughter for all those years, who knows? No, I never read her poetry. Did you?

Bernard Shaw? Sure didn't he know how to cod the English? Used to live near Dalkey, yes, that's right, the old number eight tram. That's me, standing alongside it. Now you'd never see *him* taking the tram. Taxi or private cars, that was Mr. George Bernard Shaw's style.

Goodnight, now, and the best to all the family. Safe home.

NOTE
1 The best biography known to this writer is *Charles Stewart Parnell* by F. S. Lyons, the former Provost of Trinity College, Dublin.

22
WITHOUT END . . .

Maurice Paléologue, the distinguished French diplomatist, remarked early in this century that while a long series of Balkan and Russo-Turkish wars were marking the slow disintegration of the Ottoman Empire, and while what was then the next war would basically be concerned with the end of the Austro-Hungarian Empire, the one after that (which he did not live to see in 1939) would mark the end of the British Empire. It is dangerous even for a man of Paléologue's vast experiences and knowledge to make such wild generalisations, but his was not too far from the truth.

In retrospect that atmosphere at the end of the last century and early in this, at least in Europe, was macabre. They had coined for themselves the phrase *fin de siècle*, which implies more than *Yellow Book* decadence and French symbolism and the break-up of the Renaissance tradition in the plastic arts and twelve-tonal music and even Yeats' *Lake Isle of Innisfree* period. Only in the English speaking countries was there a marked decline in sexual and financial morality and an increase in vulgarity and display. The general artistic revolution was regarded by many less as a decay than as a new beginning, a gust of fresh air blowing through the Paris salons and the Viennese concert halls of the West. Much ostentatious religion had come to be regarded as hypocrisy or even as jobs-for-the-boys. The division of wealth in the industrialised countries was patently grotesque, as Karl Marx had realised a generation or two ago, though his anticipated solution of revolution–socialism–communism has remained very wide of the mark as was his forecast of an inevitable Anglo-American war for raw materials and markets. We know what did happen in the first three quarters of this century and it is easy enough for us to poke fun at our ancestors: no doubt our descendants, if we have any, will do the same to us. Meanwhile this atmosphere of *fin de siècle* was very real, and is most beautifully described in its high society manifestations by Barbara Tuchmann in her book, *The Tower above the Town*. When the 1914 war broke out, it seems to have come almost as a relief from tension and foreboding.

A Viscount Grey might lament that all over Europe the lights were going out. The officer class jumped on to their chargers, usually in equally high spirits, while the masses yelled: '*Nach Paris!*' and '*A Berlin!*' Even in Ireland a gentle poet, patriot, schoolmaster and linguist, Padraic Pearse, could speak of the necessity that blood must flow – for Ireland, of course. While in Ireland the Great War appeared to put an end, or at least into cold storage, the interminable Orange question.

Home Rule had been passed through both Houses of Parliament and was due to become law in June of 1914. As is very well known, Carson, Smith and others raised the standard of rebellion in Ulster and found a considerable measure of sympathy among some senior British officers, particularly those stationed at the Curragh. First Protestants, then Catholics began to form private armies, with guns bought from Germany. But with the outbreak of the war, Home Rule was postponed until its conclusion and both Redmond's Irish Parliamentary Party and Carson's Orangemen agreed to fight the Germans rather than one another. The I.R.B. was less than satisfied with this arrangement, and proceeded to make plans for a rebellion while the war was in progress.

John Redmond (1856–1918) had succeeded in 1900 in cobbling together the political party that had split over the O'Shea divorce. He was however never its leader as Parnell had been but he immediately proved himself to be a hard-working, conscientious patriot. Serving on the Land Conference of 1902, which produced the Land Act of the following year, the system of tenant land purchase was virtually completed. Another thorny problem, involving the churches, had long held up the foundation of national universities, but this too he helped solve in 1908. Finally the Liberals, who could and did ignore the Home Rule issue after their massive victory in 1906, needed the Irish M.P.s' votes after 1911, and Redmond secured the passage of the Home Rule Bill in 1912. The violent opposition of Carson's Orangemen took him by surprise and the Irish National Volunteers (some of whom later became the old I.R.A.) took their orders from the I.R.B. rather than from him. His British patriotism in 1914 was also not to the liking of all Irishmen. He then proposed that the security of all Ireland be entrusted to his and Carson's forces, and that the British army be withdrawn. Asquith's government snubbed him: nor would it permit the formation of Irish divisions, though a 36th (Ulster) Division was created (and virtually annihilated at the Battle of the Somme, in 1916). In fact John

Redmond never gained the very real credit due to him both from the Irish and the English and is now almost a forgotten figure. Had the British given the Irish Home Rule, as and when promised, instead of making them fight for it, the Union might have endured and Maurice Paléologue been proved mistaken. True, he had got his war wrong, but a British Empire with a hostile or even a neutral Ireland was no longer a great power. Super-patriots such as Carson not infrequently cause almost unlimited harm to the country or cause they would serve.

*   *   *

The Irish are said to have long memories, but these are highly selective. British maladministration (not infrequently confused with the Viking and Norman conquests of the Celts) is never far from the surface: failure amounting to betrayal by Irish patriots' Spanish, French and German allies are glossed over, while Irish 'liberals' today appear to prefer Russian imperialism to repeated and un-requited American support. In his doctrinaire adherence to 'neutrality' De Valera's policy may have cost the lives of many U.S. sailors who were in fact protecting Ireland, while – final grotesquerie – as First Minister of a neutral state he formally regretted Adolf Hitler's death, surely the only person in the world so to do. Having sworn an oath which he said was meaningless, he had clambered to power over the corpses of dead comrades who had fought the British on Irish soil while he quarrelled and begged in the United States. From 1914, for some forty years, the stupid or gross performances of so many Irish public men was in marked contrast to the quiet dignity of the great Irish majority.

*   *   *

Nevertheless a brief résumé of what has been blasted upon such an orchestra of brass may be needed. The British had declared war to save 'poor little Belgium' from the Kaiser. The 'poor little Irish' wanted to be rid of English monarchy. Q.E.D. they went to war for their own purposes, as every nation always does. And England's 'rooted garrison' of landlords and such led the kerns for their own, materialistic purposes. It sounded fine, and hundreds of thousands volunteered: the War Memorial to those who died is totally neglected, behind the Phoenix Park. It did not ring the same echo in the ears of the I.R.B., either in Dublin or New York. Sir Roger Casement set off from America to Germany to see what he could muster in the cause of Ireland.

But the shadowy I.R.B. and its overt force, the Irish Volunteers who had refused to accept Redmond's lead and who were now under command of a great scholar and linguist, Eoin MacNeill, were far from being the only Irish patriot force. Another quasi-revolutionary was Arthur Griffith (1871–1922), also an intellectual and a journalist who edited *The United Irishman* and, after 1906, *Sinn Féin*, which is usually translated as 'ourselves alone' but more accurately 'we ourselves'. A somewhat superficial study of Hungarian history had led him to believe that Irish aspirations might be modelled on those of Hungary in 1848 and that they were not met satisfactorily by the Home Rule Bill of 1912. Griffith supported the creation of the Irish National Volunteers in 1913, and was involved in the importation of foreign weapons. Quite incorrectly, the name of Sinn Fein (*anglice*: Shinners) was applied to the entire Irish rebel cause, of which it never formed more than a fragmentary minority.

Another, and quite disparate, force was James Connolly's (1868–1916) Irish Socialist Republican Party. He founded Ireland's first Marxist newspaper, *The Workers' Republic*, in 1896, and in 1910 published a book entitled *Labour in Irish History*, in which socialist ideas then fashionable are fused in a not altogether convincing amalgam. He spent most of the new century's first decade in Britain or America, where he made himself famous or notorious, according to taste, by helping to found the Industrial Workers of the World, popularly called and not to their advantage 'Wobblies'. The United States was a stony ground in which to sow the seeds of emotional, international socialism.

While he was abroad a great labour orator, James Larkin (1876–1947), had founded in Dublin the Irish Transport and General Workers Union (1909). It was modelled on the British trade union of that name, and Larkin, who was Liverpool-Irish, had already made a name for himself in the Belfast dockers' strike of 1907. His great moment came in 1913, with the appalling hardships of strikes and lockouts in Dublin. Connolly, now back in Ireland, describes this struggle as a draw, but said that the workers had thereby won strikes that could never be denied them. (This phrase, hard to understand, is not atypical of his style.) Connolly then created yet another private army, the Citizens' Army, which was intended to fight the class war (in many ways a new importation into Ireland) but which was inevitably swept up into the events to come. Larkin withdrew to the United States. He spent some time as a 'political prisoner' in Sing Sing, but was released by Governor Al Smith in 1923. Connolly had long been dead and Larkin's attempts

to create an Irish Socialist Party had only a limited appeal to his
compatriots, and that largely among the intellectuals who took
their ideas from Britain and other foreign countries. Perhaps its
growing popularity among such people in England in the years
between the two world wars made it, if anything, less attractive to
what was still a basically rural Ireland.

* * *

The Gaelic Athletic Association was another nationalist body
which could surely have never existed in any other period than the
late nineteenth and early twentieth centuries. It did not merely
encourage team games of, presumably, Irish origin but actually
forbad to its members English games such as rugby football or
cricket. De Valera, who had been good at rugger, gave it up for
nationalistic reasons, while a later Taoiseach, Jack Lynch, won
many votes for his enthusiastic support of the Cork hurley team,
of which he has been a member for many years. If all this sounds
quite dotty, it was not so when the British army, in 1920, opened fire
on the patriotic crowd watching an Irish game at Croke Park. It
was not the Russians who introduced politics into sport in 1980: the
Irish had done so at least eighty years before, and such emotions
are still not difficult to evoke. The Irish needed neither Adolf Hitler
nor English soccer hooligans in order to learn how mass hysteria
can be created by 'sportsmen' and used by 'politicians'. Few of us
can avoid politics altogether: fortunately almost all of us can spurn
spectator sports. Yet those men of good will who enjoy watching
such games must be pleased that some Irish teams ignore, and better
always have ignored, Lloyd George's division of the island. Meanwhile in Ireland to sound derogatory about the G.A.A. is not unlike
being rude about the Monarchy in England, or the Constitution in
the U.S.A.

* * *

Patriotism and nationalism are by no means synonymous nor
contemporaneous. In a country with as confused a history as that of
Ireland – and few countries have not – they can often collide.
Ultimately this can lead to a pointless civil war, from which the
outcome is said to derive a purpose, whether or not this really
occurred. Perhaps in no new country of our century has such a
post hoc propter hoc been more misleading than in Ireland. In any
attempt to explain this, a brief resumption of the situation between
1914 and 1922 is necessary, banal though it must be to most readers.

In 1914 most Irish patriots, regardless of their religion, were anti-German, and the young men proved so by enlistment. Irish nationalists (who of course were also patriots) took another view. This was particularly true of Irish–Americans, many of whom had inherited a real hatred of England, and all of whom had a vote. After the experience of Carson's attempt to dictate British policy in Ireland, and following on the British government's very peculiar, if not actually dishonest, refusal to enforce the Home Rule Act of June 1914, such Irishmen were prepared, in some cases reluctantly, to mount a rebellion in Ireland. The secret society of Fenian origin, the I.R.B., was the organising force. The Irish National Volunteers, led by the brilliant scholar in almost all nationalist fields, Eoin MacNeill, had, in so far as it had broken with John Redmond, provided a physical force in Ireland itself.

Meanwhile the Irish people in their overwhelming majority were increasingly uninterested in revolution. Into this complex amalgam must be added the Presbyterians of Ulster on the one hand and James Connolly's small new socialist Citizens' Army on the other. In 1915, the Irish revolutionaries were controlled, in Ireland, by Pearse and Connolly. Their finances came from Devoy and his friends in America. Their arms were being secured, from New York, by Sir Roger Casement in Germany. The Irishmen who were to use them were supposedly under the control of MacNeill, in Dublin. The date for this most complicated operation was to be the Easter weekend of 1916. The British authorities in Dublin Castle knew almost all about it, and almost any staff officer must have known that it was doomed.

When Casement landed from his U-boat in the extreme southwest, and was almost immediately arrested, and when the German vessel carrying arms scuttled itself off Cork, it was obvious to MacNeill that the whole operation was a fiasco. He therefore cancelled – in the public press – his orders to rise. Pearse overruled him, at least for the Dublin area, and the Easter Rising took place. With a minimum of speed and efficiency the British authorities – who were so convinced it would not now happen that most of their officers had gone to the races – crushed it within a week. It did not exist outside Dublin, with which the First World War British generals dealt in the only way they knew, artillery and gunboats. Perhaps at most some five hundred Irish Volunteers took part, and half as many of Connolly's men. When the prisoners were marched off to prison, the Irish populace booed and spat at them. Quite quickly all the rebel leaders were tried by court-martial and shot. The only one to be spared the death sentence was Eamon de Valera, almost certainly because he had been born an American citizen (though it was not he who brought this up). The Easter Rising was, in fact, a total failure. Only the cruelty of the death sentence is said to have revived Irish memories of long ago. But, though this contributed, it did not create a new form of Irish patriotism. The cause was far less altruistic.

Two British armies had by late 1916 died in France, the B.E.F. and Kitchener's Army. In that war of attrition numbers were paramount. Therefore in 1916 the British government introduced conscription. But in Irleland, perhaps even more than in England, almost all who wished to fight for what seemed to some an increasingly dubious cause had already volunteered. Only the reluctant could be conscripted. Therefore the people of Ireland began to see that perhaps the men of 1916 had been right. And soon enough the names of those killed in action and those executed joined the long list of patriotic martyrs, going back to Emmet, Tone and far beyond. In the awful Europe of 1917–1918 ghosts walked while men died.

In Ireland the result became apparent in the 1918 elections. *Sinn Féin* candidates, now taking on a republican line, stood in almost all the constituencies, and almost all of them were elected to Parliament, where, as republicans, they refused to take an oath of allegiance to the Crown and thus their seats. Furthermore, in Ireland the tactics of political (though much less of personal) boycott were adopted. Government began to collapse, or at least to become increasingly difficult to enforce. The police became the target of Irish patriots, not a very difficult target. To re-inforce them, in 1919, Lloyd George invented the Black-and-Tans, an auxiliary to the police force, so called because their uniform were in part army khaki, in part R.I.C. dark blue or black. They were the redundant soldiery of the First World War, men without peacetime experience and therefore without jobs. Their behaviour in Ireland was as abominable as it was inefficient, for the Irish had produced a guerrilla leader of extreme skill in Michael Collins, who commanded the Irish irregulars, the I.R.A., against the British army. He won no great battle (he fought none) but he rapidly gained control of all those parts of Ireland where no British soldiers stood.

During most of this time de Valera was gathering funds in America. As the only surviving commandant of 1916, he was recognised by the Irish as the Irish Head of State, and Arthur Griffith even resigned his Presidency of *Sinn Féin* in his favour. Collins served him loyally, even delivering by hand letters to Mrs. de

Valera, living in Greystones (some twenty miles south of Dublin), when the British had put an ever higher price on Collins' head, dead or alive. I mention this detail because it had subsequent significance.[1]

The Anglo-Irish War petered out in the usual stalemate of ruined cottages, burned mansions, hungry people, and recrimination. In 1921 de Valera, the accepted (by the Irish) new President of a free Ireland, sent Collins and others to London in order to negotiate a treaty with the Lloyd George cabinet. In Ireland there was a great sigh of relief, save from the extremists. The I.R.A. was running out of guns, ammunition and money, for quite a few of the millions collected by de Valera had disappeared, though certainly not into his pockets. Lloyd George had pre-empted the treaty by creating a province out of the United Kingdom in Ulster, in great haste, in the previous year. King George V had opened its mini-parliament in the ostentatious splendour of Stormont. Lloyd George now offered Collins, Childers, Griffith and the other Irish delegates dominion status, that is to say rather more than Home Rule but continued British sovereignty. On the other hand, he threatened to put a third of a million Black-and-Tans (which were probably available) into a total defeat of Irish independence. Collins had the status of Irish plenipotentiary, but when he accepted the lesser evil he was disowned by de Valera. By a narrow margin, he won the crucial vote in the Irish parliament, *Dáil Eireann*, in early 1922. The result was a civil war in which Collins was soon murdered and his extremist republican enemies defeated. Ireland had never before known civil war, and its residues are still with us. So, of course, is Lloyd George's invention of his northern Irish semi-state. In the last twelve years it has caused more loss of life than both the Anglo-Irish War and the Irish Civil War combined.

❋   ❋   ❋

In the Irish Free State, as it was then called, public life enjoyed for a decade the tranquillity of exhaustion. To judge by the writers of the period 'enjoyed' is scarcely the correct word. The government of W. T. Cosgrave (1880–1945) had little interest in the feelings of the young, republican writers from whom we derive our vision of that age. It was certainly not a happy one for revolutionaries, nor for Ireland as a new semi-nation state. De Valera and his party, by refusing to take the oath to the monarchy, debarred themselves until 1927 from taking their elected seats in the Dáil. In 1932 he formed his final government. The economy was stagnant, poverty atrocious, artistic creation at a veritable nadir, and traditional Irish gaiety

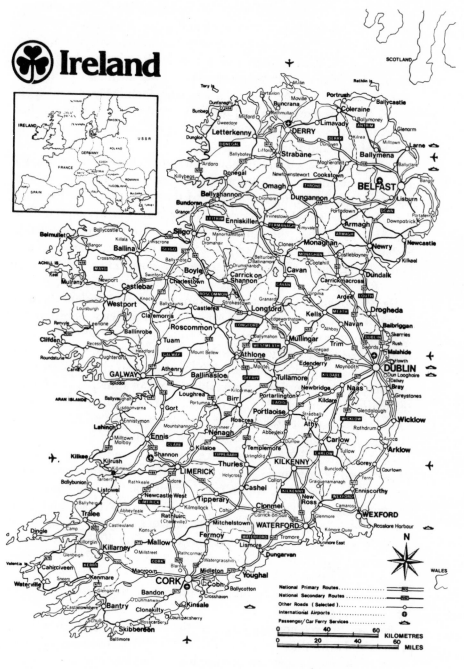

Ireland

IRELAND

SCOTLAND

National Primary Routes.....................
National Secondary Routes ....
Other Roads (Selected).....................
International Airports ....
Passenger/ Car Ferry Services ....

0   40   60
KILOMETRES

20   40   60
MILES

N

WALES

Because of the small scale of this map not all place names or routes can be shown

Cartography prepared by Michael D. Gleeson   © IRISH TOURIST BOARD commercialised upon the stages of London, New York and, regrettably, Dublin. Synge was dead and gone, long ago: the 'great Irish playwright' was, and for tourists has unfortunately remained, Sean O'Casey. The greatest perhaps of Irish painters, Jack Yeats, the brother of his country's greatest poet, was turning to a style of explicit anger. Oh, there were others who should have been mentioned, but it is dangerous and misleading to write about one's close contemporaries, before the sands of time shall have done their own rough shifting and selection.

In 1927 de Valera decided that he, and his followers, could achieve a most convenient compromise: by taking the obligatory oath of loyalty to the British monarch, he and they could take their seats in the Dáil, while simultaneously abstaining from perjury on the theological ground that the oath was enforced and therefore invalid. So back they trooped, the party that was to be called *Fianna Fáil* and that after the next election was to be the government of the Free State/Republic for most of the succeeding period.

De Valera had wished to create an agricultural Ireland, deeply religious and speaking the Irish tongue. His secondary ambition was to cut all economic, and even more so all political, dependence on Britain. His third was to establish Irish sovereignty over the whole of Ireland, that is to say to abolish 'Stormont' and all it represented: but here he was cautious, probably not out of timidity but from a reluctance to introduce a further million Protestants into what would then be an all-Ireland state of only about four million citizens. He was therefore consistently and even brutally hostile to the 'new I.R.A.' who were ready to use force in order to re-unite all Ireland. Expert and experienced politician (both in Ireland and internationally) as he was in the thirties, for him political solutions were far more an end than a means and were, in any case, inferior to spiritual and social matters. In the thirties and forties, such an attitude was very very much at variance with that of most prominent politicians, anywhere.

＊　＊　＊

It is not here intended to discuss most recent Irish history, save in very general terms.

Poverty in Ireland was acute in the thirties, in part due to de Valera's 'Tariff War' with the British. In 1937, however, this was settled. The most important by-product of this was that Ireland had had to become largely self-supporting. This in turn gave the de Valera government the ability to adopt a policy of neutrality in the 1939–1945 war. There was little emotional neutrality among the Irish. Over 140,000 men with addresses in the Free State volunteered for the British forces. How many Liverpool and London Irish volunteered is not known, nor is the number who joined the American forces. But it is generally believed that more Free State than Six County citizens, proportionate to the populations, volunteered and fought and died.

Owing to its neutrality Ireland did not benefit from Marshall Aid. Only in the fifties did a new Irish government, headed by Sean Lemass, abandon de Valera's rural dreams and set about enticing industry and capital into the west's poorest country. Although the Irish 'economic miracle' was the last to occur, it was none the less startling. A large free trade zone built around Shannon airport was very successful, but the chief demographic change was a shift from the land to the new industries in the Dublin area. No serious attempt was made to anticipate this. The old centre of Dublin was spottily demolished, and concrete office blocks appeared in the Georgian streets of what had been one of Europe's most beautiful cities, while the sprawl of huge housing estates covered the green fields and blue hills that had everywhere been its back-drop. Pollution soon followed, both of the air, the sea and the rivers. Dublin was not well served either by its city corporation or by its county council.

In his determination that Irish neutrality be preserved, Eamon de Valera was quite ruthless in his treatment of the 'new' I.R.A. which had become in increasing measure communist-infiltrated. Not only was it declared an illegal organisation (which it never was in Britain) but active members were promptly arrested. De Valera was not impressed by hunger strikes: the strikers were left to die. After the war there was a mild revival of I.R.A. activity in the fifties, but it never amounted to anything. Until 1969 it seems that the I.R.A. was virtually dead. What has happened since then in the north is common knowledge, and not fit for discussion here, since at the time of writing there is no outcome in sight.

Perhaps de Valera's other great contribution to the making of modern Ireland was his 1937 Constitution. It was designed for the rural, religious Ireland he still desired, and is, I am told, not altogether satisfactorily drafted from a legal point of view. It is one of the major stumbling blocks to a unification of all Ireland, and will almost certainly be scrapped. But it performed a great service in its time, in that it gave Irishmen and Irishwomen a definite status vis-à-vis the state.

One gets the impression that Ireland, a republic now for twenty years, is on the whole a happy and united country, apart always from the nagging misery of the north. But like the other nations of semi-Americanised Western Europe it has been steadily losing its own unique character and charm. After all, a traffic jam of Toyotas and Mercedes outside a slab of office concrete in what is still called Merrion Street, is exactly like such a jam in Bristol or Toulouse or Genoa. While the pub conversations for which Ireland was once rightly famous are not possible with a television set blaring about football in the corner.

Yet in the opinion of this writer, despite those infections of our *Zeitgeist*, it is still the most attractive place he knows in which to live. Voices are still soft, wit still cherished, the rain pours down and the food is deplorable, but sure you can't have everything now, can you?

NOTE

1 Some years ago, having realised that so many persons involved were still alive, I abandoned a biography of Michael Collins in favour of a novel, in which he is never referred to by name. I believe that it is historically as accurate as was then possible. It is entitled *High Heroic* (a quotation from Robert Browning).

FURTHER READING

A bibliography on the subject of this book would be twice as long as the book itself. Most of the books referred to in this list of suggested further reading in fact have full bibliographies themselves.

Bury, Prof. John. *Life of St. Patrick* (Dublin, 1905)
Butler, Hubert. *Ten Thousand Saints* (Kilkenny, 1972)
Canny, N. P. *The Elizabethan Conquest of Ireland* (Brighton, 1976)
Craig, Maurice. *Dublin 1660–1860* (Dublin, 1980)
Curtis, Edmund. *History of Medieval Ireland from 1086–1513* (London, 1968)
de Poer, Maire. *Early Irish Art* (Dublin, 1979)
de Poer, Mair & Liam. *Early Christian Ireland* (London, 1978)
FitzGibbon, Constantine. *High Heroic* (London, 1969)
—— *Miss Finnegan's Fault* (London, 1953)
—— *Red Hand: The Ulster Colony* (London, 1971)
Gwynn, Denis. *Young Ireland and 1848* (Cork, 1949)
Harris (ed.). *Ware's Bishops of Ireland*
Henry, Françoise. *Art Irelandais* (in several volumes). Works available in English include *Irish Art in the Romanesque Period* (London, 1974) and *Irish High Crosses* (Cork, 1978)
Herity, Michael, & Eogan, George. *Ireland in Pre-History* (London, 1977)
Hyman, Louis. *The Jews of Ireland* (London, 1972)
Kearney, H. F. *Strafford in Ireland* (Manchester, 1959)
Lecky, W. H. E. *History of Ireland in the Eighteenth Century* (Chicago, 1972)
Lyons, F. S. *Charles Stewart Parnell* (London, 1977)
Maxwell, Constantia. *Dublin under the Georges* (London, revised ed. 1961)
McLysaght, Edward. *Irish Life in the Seventeenth Century* (Dublin, 1950)
Moley, Raymond. *Daniel O'Connell, An Essay* (New York, 1974)
Montague, John (ed.). *The Faber Book of Irish Verse* (London, 1974)
Moody, T. W. (ed.). *A New History of Ireland* Vol. III, (Oxford, 1976)
—— & Martin, F. X. *The Course of Irish History* (Cork, 1967)
O'Brien, Barry (ed.). *Autobiography of Wolfe Tone*, edited by his son (Dublin, 1893)
O'Faolain, Sean. *The Great O'Neill* (London, 1942)
O'Flaherty, Liam. *Famine* (Dublin, 1979)
Orel, Harold. *Irish History and Culture* (Kansas, 1976)
Otway, Ruthven. *History of Medieval Ireland* (London, 1968)
Powell, T. G. E. *The Celts* (London, revised ed. 1980)

Ryan, Rev. John. *Irish Monasticism* (Dublin, 1931)

Wall, Maureen. *The Penal Laws 1691–1760* (Dundalk, 1961)

Williams, Prof. Desmond, & Edwards, Dudley. *The Great Famine* (Dublin, 1957)

Wilson, Philip. *The Beginnings of Modern Ireland* (Dublin, 1912)

Woodham Smith, Cecil. *The Great Hunger* (London, 1962)

ACKNOWLEDGEMENTS

I should like to express my deep thanks to Father Giblon, OFM, of the Franciscan House, Killiney, Co. Dublin and to Sean J. White, Dean of the School of Irish Studies, Dublin, both of whom have devoted a very great deal of time and trouble to helping me with this book and to correcting errors in it. Neither, of course, is responsible for the opinions, which are my own, nor for any faults in the text that may remain.

My gratitude to Mrs Robene Quigly grows with each book of mine that she types, and this was not the easiest.

My wife, Marjorie, managed admirably to conceal the boredom she must, on occasion, have felt at my endless references to Irish matters. I cannot find suitable words of thanks, but I can express an admiration amounting at times to astonishment at her tolerance.

Dublin, 1982

INDEX

abbots: appointments, 50; hereditary, 78, 96, 99; power, 111
absentee landlords, 116, 215; Great Famine, 286; Statute of Absentees, 116
Act of Conformity, 186
Act of Settlement, 195
Act of Union, 162, 261, 269; effect on trade, 250
administration: Cromwellian, 195-6; in eighteenth c., 250; medieval, 117; Norman, 116; 'plantation', 154, 166; Stuart, 184, 187, 189, *see also* Strafford; 'surrender and regrant', 154, 166; Tudor, 139, 165
agriculture: Celtic, 41, 61, 97; eighteenth c., 212-13, 251; Great Famine, 282, 283, 286, 287; nineteenth c., 272; Stuart, 185-6; Tudor, 141, 142, 167
aisling, see poetry
Anglo-Irish War, 312
Anglo-Irish writing, 12, 290, 303
architecture, 201-2, 219, 242-7; medieval, 105; pre-Christian, 199; town planning, 245; *see also* monasteries, stonework
Ard Ri, see chieftains
Armagh, and Patrician Church, 63, 82-3
armies: Grattan's, 219, 255; Strafford's, 189, disbanded by William III, 206; private, 139, twentieth c., 306
art: abstract, 60; Celtic (La Tène), 33, 59, decline, 93; Christian, 30, illuminated mss., 81, 93, 198; eighteenth c., 242; symbolic, 60, 197; Viking, 93
asceticism, 55, 77-8; monastic life, 53-4, 74
Aughrim, Battle of, 205
Augustinians, 98, 111

Badh, 48
'bag men', 26, 27
ballads, 41
Banishment Act, 249
bards, 39, 41, 227
Beckett, Samuel, 238-9
beggars: eighteenth c., 222-3; nineteenth c., 270, 283; *see also* poor
Beltain, 41, 48
Berkeley, Bishop, 8, 47, 140, 240
betaghs, 142
bigamy, 34, 103, 160, 165
bishoprics: under Henry II, 110; Patrician, 75; reorganised, 103
bishops, functions of, 54, 74, 76; *see also* episcopal rule
Black-and-Tans, 311; *see also* policing
Black Death, 97, 105, 113
Blind Rafferty, 41, 44n
Bonaparte, 1797 invasion, 266
Book of Armagh, 51
Book of Durrow, 81, 89
Book of Kells, 81, 89
boycott movement, 298; political, 311
Boyne, Battle of the, 204, 205
Brehon law, 59, 103, 107, 145, 153
Brendan, St., 85
Brian Boru, 92, 107, 112

Brigid, St., 47, 48, 50n, 72, 120, 170
British Renunciation Act (1783), 255
Burke, Edmund, 8, 240
Butlers, the, 117; and Geraldines, 179; 'loyal Irish', 144, 160, 176; Stuart patronage, 202
Butt, Isaac, 273

Calvin, 159
campaniles, 93-4, 200
Camperdown, Battle of, 260
'Captain Moonlight', 293
Carmelites, 98, 111
Carolan, Turlogh, 227-8; see also bards
Cashel, 59, 68, 103, 104, 110
castle building, 110, 199; Dublin, 104
cathedral and church building, 64, 65n; Dublin, 201
Catholic Association, see O'Connell
Catholic Committee, 270, 271
Celts: administration, 32-3; agriculture, 61; armies (fianna), 42; art, 59-60; chieftains (ri), 34; conquest of Britain, 45, 46; conquest of Gaul, 45; conquest of Ireland, 23, 24, 46; ethnic origin, 45; magic, 46-7; migration, 45; names, 49; ollamh, 39; post-nomadic, 34; proto-religion, 47-9; Romans, 45; settlements, 61; social organisation (tuatha), 26, 33, 34, 74, 75, 79; trade, 61; Vikings, 91, 96; warfare, 43; warriors, 41
Charlemagne, 87, 94
Charles I, see Strafford
Charles II, 202
chieftains (ri), 34; Kings of Ireland (Ard Ri), 163; succession, 38
Christianity: in art, 197; asceticism, 55; bishops' role, 54; Canterbury, 62; celibacy of clergy, 77, 78, 161; early administration, 53; Eastern vs. Western, 53; under Henry II, 109-10; heresies, 53-4, 82; in Ireland, 78; medieval, 99;

decline, 143; monasticism, 55; morality, 78; papal power, 100-2; schism, 76, 99; sale of benefices, 161; Vikings, 99; see also Patrick, Reformation, Roman Catholics
Cistercians, 103; decline, 111
Citizens' Army, see Larkin
civil war: English, 189, 194; Irish, 312
Clan na Gael and U.S. funding, 292
class structure, 153, 171, 255, 276
Clontarf, Battle of, 91, 92, 96
coinage, restricted use, 60, 153, 159, 172, 215, 283, 285
Collins, Michael, 311-12
Columban, St., 73
Columcille, St., 72, 73, 79
combarba, 99
conacre system, 220, 251; see also land tenure
Confederation of Kilkenny, 193
Connaught, 58, 169; Tudor conquest, 175, 179; see also Geraldines
Connolly, James, 308; Citizens' Army, 310; Easter Rising, 310
Constitution (1937), 315
Corn Laws, 284, 285
Cosgrave, W. T., 312
Council of Trent, 159
Counter-reformation, 134, 136, 158
coyne and livery, 143, 144
crannogs, see lake dwellings
crime: agrarian, 220, 221, 252-3, 273, 294; nineteenth c., 270; sectarian, 257; and temperance, 274; Tudor, 161; see also secret societies
Cromwell, Oliver, 190; massacre of Catholics, 195
'Croppies', see Society of United Irishmen
Cuchulain, 40, 48

Dáil Eireann, 312
Danaans, the, 27-9; Book of Invasions, 29
Davitt, Michael, 294, 299, 300
Derry, 183; sold, 184; see also Londonderry

de Valera, Eamon, 10, 307, 309; Easter Rising, 311; Fianna Fáil, 314; Head of State, 311; parliamentary oath, 314; U.S. fundraising, 311; World War II neutrality, 314

Diamond, Battle of the, 258

diet: eighteenth c., 251; medieval, 105; nineteenth c., 270, 275; seventeenth c., 220; Tudor, 171, 185; *see also* agriculture, poor, potato

divorce, 34

Dominicans, 98, 111

Donation of Constantine, 53; conquest of Ireland, 101; forgery, 101-2; and Holy See, 102

Druids: Anglesey base, 58; Christian conversion, 64-5, 71, 75, 79; in Christian practice, 64, 71-2; law, 34; literacy, 49, 50; role, 43-4, 49; training, 49; Viking revival, 96; in war, 42, 43

Dublin, 104, 112; eighteenth c., 228, 242; English power base, 136; medieval, 104, 201; sixteenth c., 201; Tudor, 157; twentieth c., 315; *see also* the Pale

Dublin dockers' strike, 308

Dublin Metropolitan Police, 293

Dungannon Convention, 219

Duns Scotus, 140

Dutch mercenaries, *see* Boyne

Earc, St., 63

Easter Rising, 310; *see also* Connolly

economy, 294, 312; taxation, 139, 143-5, 164, 186, 250; *see also* trade

Elizabeth I, 149, 154, 163-4, 169, 176, 177

Emancipation Act (1829), 264

emigration, 251, 253; Great Famine, 274, 283, 286

Emmet, Robert, 265

Encumbered Estates Act (1849), 283, 286, 294

Enda Cennsalech, 63

episcopal rule, 68, 78

eviction, 251; and Encumbered

Estates Act, 294; *see also* conacre system, land tenure

'faction fights', 172

fairs, 172

Fenians, 280; 1867 uprising, 292; the *Irish People*, 292

feudalism, 85, 99, 106, 110-11; breakdown, 116, 167

Fiacre, St., 64, 78

fianna (warriors), 39, 42

Field, John, 228

file (pl. *filidh*) (poets), 39, 119

Finnbar, St., 75

fir bolg, see 'bag men'

Fitzgeralds, the, 'loyal Irish', 144

FitzGilbert, Richard (Strongbow), 95, 107

FitzMaurice (FitzGerald), 178, 179

FitzOther, Walter, 95

Flood, Henry, 217, 254

Formorians, 25-6

fosterage, 38, 165

Franciscans, 98

French Revolution, influence in Ireland, 258-9

Gaelic Athletic Association, 309

galloglasses, 42, 94, 112, 139-40

George III, opposition to emancipation, 261

George V, 312

Geraldines, the, 95, 176; established in Ireland, 132

Germanus, St., 57

Gladstone, W. E.: disestablishment of Church of Ireland, 298-9; Home Rule, 300; Land Act, 298; Land Purchase Act, 297

gold work, Celtic, 59

'gombeen men', 175, 252, 262n

Grattan, Henry, 217, 223, 254, 255, 264; Emancipation Bill, 265

Grattan's parliament, 219; English veto, 256; franchise, 219, 223-4, 253; powers, 255, 256

Grattan's revolution, 217, 218; *see also* Dungannon Convention

Great Famine (1845-6), 274, 282-8;

government and *laissez faire*, 283, 285, 286; mortality, 285; Relief Commission, 285; *see also* emigration, potato

Gregory VII, 100, 101

'grey merchants', 172

Griffith, Arthur, 308, 311

'hedge schools', 213, 223, 251

Henry II, 107-9

Henry VII, 124-7

Henry VIII, 128-9, 132-4; conquest of Ireland, 149; declared King of Ireland, 162

hermits, 74, 75

Historical Society and 'Young Ireland', 280

Home Rule, 275, 293, 299; and Liberal Party, 300, 306; deferred by World War, 306

hostings (sept warfare), 37

Huguenots in Ireland, 216

illiteracy, prevalence of: medieval, 106; nineteenth c., 276; Tudor, 151

industry, 250; discriminatory laws, 250, 270; in Free State, 315; in Ulster, 270

Innocent III, 102

Invincibles, the, 280; Phoenix Park murders, 301

Iona, 73, 79, 83; Viking raids, 89

Ireland, Church of: absentee clergy, 161; bishoprics, 105, 109; disestablished, 273, 298; in eighteenth c., 213; established, 103; Henry VIII, 134; parishes, 110; Reformation, 160; sale of benefices, 161; tithes, 269-70

Irish Act of Conformity, 178

Irish Free State, 41, 312

Irish language, 276; effect of Famine, 290

Irish National Volunteers, 306, 308-9; Easter Rising, 310

Irish Parliamentary Party, 306; and Parnell, 297, 302

Irish Republican Army (I.R.A.), 280; banned in Free State, 315

Irish Republican Brotherhood, 280, 292, 306, 310

Irish Socialist Republican Party, 308

Irish Special Branch, 293; *see also* policing

Irish T.G.W.U. (1909), 308

James I, 180, 182-3

James II, 204, 205

Jansenism, *see* Maynooth

jewellery, Celtic, 59, 80, 198

John I, 115

kerns ('idlemen'), 98, 114, 139

Kilkenny, Confederation, 193

Kilkenny, Statutes of, 117, 153

'Kilmainham treaty', 298, 299

Knox, John, 182

lake dwellings, 61

Lament for Art O'Leary, 230-7

Land Acts (1881, 1891), 287, 294

Land of Cockaigne, The, 120

Land League (1879), 294, 298

Land Purchase Act (1891), 297, 298

land tenure, 152, 220; Encumbered Estates Act, 294; poverty, 282; Roman Catholic, 248, 273; shires and hundreds, 152; subdivision, 212, 223; *see also* conacre system, eviction

land tribute, 97, 98

Land War (1879–82), 298, 299

language, 33; and concept of nation, 10, 11; Irish, 276, decline, 290

Larkin, James, 308-9

La Tène, 33, 59

legends, 24, 25; Book of Invasions, 29; Formorians, 26; *tuatha de Danaan*, 27

Leinster, 58, 96, 107, 109; Tudor conquest, 169, 170

Lindisfarne, 85; Viking raids, 86

literature, Anglo-Irish, 238-40

Londonderry, 257

Louis XIV, 204, 205

Luther, 154; *see also* Reformation

MacMurrough, Dermot, 107
MacNeill, E., 308, 310
Magee case, 271
magic, Celtic: calendar, 47; in poetry, 40, 46-7
Malachy, St., and reorganisation of Church, 103
marriage, 34; of clergy, 76, 77; patterns in nineteenth c., 291
Mary Tudor, 148, 158-9, 162-3
Mathew, Father Theobald and abstinence, 274
Maynooth, St. Patrick's College, 249, 265, 276, 289
Mellifont Abbey, 103-4, 110, 111
mercantilism, 185; rise under Tudors, 131, 160
middle classes: rise of, 216, 253; Roman Catholic, 250, 270
missionaries (*episcopi regionarii/ gentium*), 76-7, 79, 99
monasteries, 55-6, 73; endowments, 80, 99; funding of priests, 110; looted, 80, 81; post-Patrician, 99, 107; sacked, 121; stone-built, 103-4, 110, 111, 199; wooden, 199
monasticism: established, 71, 73; vs. episcopal rule, 78-9; organisation, 50; Reformation, 157; training for, 103

nationalism: concept of, 7-9; and culture, 238; and language, 276, 279; and republicanism, 255, 261, 274, 307-8; and sport, 309; Tudor, 160; *cf.* patriotism
'New English', 184; antipathy to Established Church, 193
Non-conformists, 183; Methodism, 213; in North, 187, 193; Penal Laws, 207
Normans: administration, 116; assimilation in Ireland, 117; feudalism, 110-11; intermarriage with Celts, 111; society, 116-17; Statutes of Kilkenny, 117; taxa-tion, 116; withdrawal from Ireland, 119

'Oakboys', 257; *see also* sectarianism
O'Brien, Murtagh, 103
O'Briens, the, 38, 160
O'Byrnes, the, 97
O'Connell, Daniel, 10, 38, 217; ancestral lands and wealth, 266; Catholic Association, 272; duel, 271-2; education and training, 267-8; Emancipation Bill, 265; Magee case, 271; 'Monster Meetings', 269, 274; parliamentary candidate (1828), 272-3; religion, 268-9
O'Connell, Eibhlin Dubh, 229
O'Connors, the, 97-8; vs. Strongbow, 107-8
O'Donovans, the, 34
Ogham inscriptions, 49
O'Kennedys, the, 38
'Old English', 193
O'Neill, Hugh, 179-80
O'Neills, the, 34, 37, 98, 159, 160; Elizabethan wars, 176; titular High Kings, 179; vs. Vikings, 92
O'Riarda, Sean, 228
O'Rourke, Dervorgilla, 103, 107
O'Shea divorce, 299, 302, 306
oral history, 39, 49
Orange Lodges, 280
Orange Order, 257
Orangemen, 205; Home Rule, 306; population, 293
Ossian, 237

P-Celts, 33, 45, 46, 94, 112
paganism, 96, 99, 111, 119-20, 122
Pale, the: diminution, 119; English power base, 128, 136, 165; established, 113
parliaments: Irish, 117; Poynings' Law, 127
Parnell, Charles Stewart, 38, 273, 292; career, 297-302
Patrick, St., 13; birthplace, 51; Bishop of Ireland, 58; church building, 63, 64; organisation of

church, 64, 71; in France, 52; in Ireland, 52, 57, 58, 62, 71, 79; kidnapped, 51-2; monasticism, 56, 58; religious centres, 63

patriotism, 216, 309-10; *cf.* nationalism

Patriot Party, 254

Pearse, Padraic, 306

Peep o'Day boys, 257

Penal Laws, 206, 207-8, 224, 248; abolition, 208, 249, 255

Phoenix Park murders, 301

Picts, 58; Christian conversion, 79

'plantation', 154; Cromwell, 193; James I, 180, 183; Tudor, 166

policing, 293, 311

population: Cromwell and decline, 195; eighteenth c., 219, 220, 223, 245; Famine, 274, 282; growth, 252; medieval, 113, 158n; priests' influence, 289; sixteenth c., 170; Viking, 99; *see also* emigration

poor, condition of, 200-1, 251, 270, 283; *see also* beggars, diet, emigration

poorhouses, 285

Poor Law (1838), 282

potato: blight, 270, regional, 282; crop failure (1821-2), 272; eighteenth c., 221; Great Famine, 274; introduced, 186, 196n

poetry, 39-40; lyric, 118-19; Tudor, 140, 208-9, 227, 228-38

Poynings, Edward, 165

Poynings' Law, 127-8; repealed (1781), 255

Poynings' parliament, 117, 127

Presbyterianism, 182, 183; Ulster, 280; *see also* Scots–Irish

priesthood, 77, 112; education (*see* 'hedge schools') and leadership of people, 289; eighteenth c., 213; Penal Laws, 207, 249; Restoration, 203

primogeniture, *see* feudalism, land tenure, succession

property: concept of, 39; confiscations, 196, 202-3; distribution, 207, 220, 248

Protestant Ascendancy, 207, 216; patronage of arts, 238

Protestant massacres (1641), 193

provinces, *see* Connaught, Leinster, Munster, Ulster

Q-Celts, 33, 45, 46

racial composition of Irish, 135

racism, English, 9-10, 117

rapparees, 213, 255; *see also* crime

recusancy, 187; fines for, 189

Redmond, John, 306-7

Reformation, 133, 149, 150, 158, 159, 162

Relief Acts (1778, 1782), 255; Hobart's (1793), 258, 259

Religious Wars, 203

revolution: concept of, 218, 253-4; Chartism, 284; in Europe, 281-2; I.R.B., 292, 310; Wolfe Tone, 258

Ribbonmen, 220

Richard II, 117, 118

road building, 203; to finance relief work, 285

roads, 61, 104; medieval, 112; Tudor, 142, 167

Roman Catholics: confiscation of property, 196; Cromwell's massacres, 195; education, 250; status in eighteenth c., 213; emancipation, 264, 271; Emancipation Bill, 273; land tenure, 248; 'Old English', 193; Penal Laws, 207, 248-50; percentage of population, 203, 220, 248; restrictions, 250

Roman empire, 53-4, 58; barbarian invasions, 66-8, 85

Royal Irish Constabulary, 293

sagas, 39; in bibles, 79; Norse, 85; sources, 40

St. Ruth, Gen., 205

Samhain, 47

Sarsfield, Patrick, 205-6, 216

Schomberg, Gen., 204

Scots–Irish, 97, 135; and Protestant work ethos, 182; Ulster, 182, 256
secret societies, 220, 221, 292
sectarianism, 264, 293; Catholic ghettos, 280; 1798 uprising, 261; Ulster, 256-7
septs: administration, 171; inter-tribal wars, 122, 167; mergers, 97, 167; servile, 39; social organisation, 26-9, 34
silverwork, 59
Simnel, Lambert, 125-6
Sinn Féin, 308; 1918 Election, 311
slavery, Celtic, 34, 38
smuggling, 216, 223
Society of United Irishmen, 258-9; persecution, 260; 1798 uprising, 260
'Steelboys', 257
stone circles, 19-20, 47, 197
stonework, 80, 119, 197; cromlechs, 197; dolmens, 197; gravestones, 81; High Crosses, 81, 93, 197-8; Round Towers, 93-4, 201; Sheela-na-gigs, 198
Strafford, Thomas Wentworth, 184, 186-9
Strongbow, 107, 108-9
succession, 38, 92, 152, 165, 201, 248-9, 251
superstition, 72-3
'surrender and regrant', 154, 155; failure of, 166-7
Swift, Dean, 7, 216, 238

Tara, 37, 59, 104
temperance, 274
Test Act (1780), 255
Thomas, 'Silken', 146-7; see also Geraldines
tinkers, 222
tithes, 228, 250; opposition, 261, 269-70
Tithes War, 273
tombs: Dowth, 14; Knowth, 14; New Grange, 14, 15-19
Tone, Wolfe, 258-9, 262; 1789 uprising, 260
torcs, 59

tories, 213, 255
trade: Celtic, 61; in Famine, 286; ports, 215; restrictions, 212, repealed (1779), 255; Tudor, 141-2, 172; Stuart, 185; 203; with U.S., 215
transportation, 195
Treaty of Limerick, see William III
Trinity College, Dublin, 203, 223, 241; Historical Society, 280; visitation of Lord Clare, 265
tuatha, 26, 97; administration, 127; breakdown, 96, 107; decay, 143
tuatha de Danaan, 27

Ulster, 58, 175; Elizabethan conquest, 180, 182; massacre of Protestants, 193; 'plantation', 183; sectarian murders, 264; William III, 205; U.K. province, 312; see also O'Neills, Orange Order
'Ulster custom', 220, 251, 256; see also emigration, eviction, land tenure
Unionists, 280; and Home Rule, 301
United Irishman, 308

Vikings, 68, 85; assimilation in Ireland, 90-1; documents, 88; in France, 94-5; raids, 66, 81, 86; settlements, 86, 88, 90; ships, 85, 86, 89; social organisation, 87; thing (parliament), 88
Volunteers, the, see Henry Grattan

wages, 252; see also poor
Warbeck, Perkin, 126
warfare: Celtic, 41, tactics 42-3, taxation for 42; inter-tribal, 91, 92, 107, 115, 167, 171; medieval technology, 108, 109
warriors; mercenaries, see galloglasses; status, 42
Wars of the Roses, 125-6; factions in Ireland, 127, 144
Welsh, 135; mercenaries, 107-9
'White Boys', 220, 253

'Wild Geese', 195, 207, 216, 217, 253
William the Conqueror, 95
William III, 204
World War I, 305-6; conscription, 311; Irish volunteers, 307

World War II: Irish neutrality, 314, 315; Irish volunteers, 315

Young, Arthur, 61, 251
'Young Ireland', 216, 268, 276, 279-82